Global Economic Prospects

A World Bank Group Flagship Report

JUNE 2024

Global Economic Prospects

1818 H Street NW, Washington, DC 20433
Telephone: 202-473-1000; Internet: www.worldbank.org

1 2 3 4 27 26 25 24

ISSN: 1014-8906
ISBN (paper): 978-1-4648-2058-8
ISBN (electronic): 978-1-4648-2059-5
DOI: 10.1596/978-1-4648-2058-8

Cover design: Bill Pragluski (Critical Stages)

Library of Congress Control Number: 2024910800.

The cutoff date for the data used in the report was June 4, 2024.

Summary of Contents

Contents

Figures

Figures

Tables

Tables

Acknowledgments

This World Bank Flagship Report is a product of the Prospects Group in the Development Economics (DEC) Vice Presidency. The project was managed by M. Ayhan Kose and Carlos Arteta, under the general guidance of Indermit Gill.

The report was prepared by a team that included Amat Adarov, Marie Albert, Francisco Arroyo Marioli, John Baffes, Mirco Balatti, Samuel Hill, Philip Kenworthy, Jeetendra Khadan, Joseph Mawejje, Valerie Mercer-Blackman, Alen Mulabdic, Nikita Perevalov, Dominik Peschel, Peter Selcuk, Shijie Shi, Naotaka Sugawara, Takuma Tanaka, Garima Vasishtha, and Collette Wheeler.

Research assistance was provided by Guillermo Caballero, Mattia Coppo, Franco Diaz Laura, Jiayue Fan, Yi Ji, Maria Hazel Macadangdang, Rafaela Martinho Henriques, Vasiliki Papagianni, Lorëz Qehaja, Kaltrina Temaj, Urja Singh Thapa, Matias Urzua, and Juncheng Zhou. Modeling and data work was provided by Shijie Shi.

Online products were produced by Graeme Littler, with assistance from the Open Knowledge Repository. Joe Rebello managed communications and media outreach with a team that included Nandita Roy, Kristen Milhollin, and Mariana Lozzi Teixeira, and with extensive support from the World Bank's media and digital communications teams. Graeme Littler provided editorial support, with contributions from Adriana Maximiliano and Michael Harrup.

The print publication was produced by Adriana Maximiliano, in collaboration with Maria Hazel Macadangdang.

Regional projections and write-ups were produced in coordination with country teams, country directors, and the offices of the regional chief economists.

Many reviewers provided extensive advice and comments. The analysis also benefited from comments and suggestions by staff members from World Bank country teams and other World Bank Vice Presidencies as well as Executive Directors in their discussion of the report on June 4, 2024. However, both forecasts and analysis are those of the World Bank staff and should not be attributed to Executive Directors or their national authorities. The Prospects Group gratefully acknowledges financial support from the Policy and Human Resources Development (PHRD) Fund provided by the Government of Japan, which helped underpin the analytical work in chapter 3.

Foreword

The good news is that global growth is holding steady, having slowed for three consecutive years. Inflation has been cut to a three-year low. Financial conditions have brightened. The world economy, in short, appears to be in final approach for a "soft landing."

Yet, more than four years after the upheavals of the COVID-19 pandemic and subsequent global shocks, it's clear the world—and developing economies, in particular—has yet to rediscover a reliable path to prosperity. Global growth is stabilizing at a rate insufficient for progress on key development goals—2.7 percent a year on average through 2026, well below the 3.1 percent average in the decade before COVID-19.

By the end of this year, one in four developing economies will be poorer than it was on the eve of the pandemic. By 2026, countries that are home to more than 80 percent of the world's population would still be growing more slowly, on average, than they were in the decade before COVID-19. Without better policies, it would take a stroke of luck for that outlook to improve: global interest rates are expected to average 4 percent through 2026, double the average of the previous two decades.

Progress toward prosperity occurs when governments put in place policies that foster productivity, entrepreneurship, and innovation—and when they do so in a setting of closer international cooperation. That was the model that flourished after the fall of the Berlin Wall. By encouraging the flow of goods, capital, and ideas across borders, it ushered in an extraordinary era of global prosperity: a span of roughly 25 years when the incomes of the poorest nations, on average, were catching up with those of the wealthiest, and when the world came within striking distance of ending extreme poverty.

This edition of *Global Economic Prospects* offers a sobering assessment of the extent to which that model of international cooperation has been fracturing—and what it will take to retool it for the needs of this decade and the next. Trade-policy uncertainty has reached this century's highest level if you consider years involving major elections—when countries that collectively account for at least 30 percent of GDP went to the polls. Trade measures designed to restrain cross-border commercial flows are proliferating at a historic pace. From 2013 through 2023, investment growth in developing economies more than halved, on average, from the pace of the 2000s.

Against this backdrop, nearly half of developing economies will see their per capita income gap relative to advanced economies widen over the first half of the 2020s—the highest share since the 1990s. Per capita income growth in developing economies is expected to average just 3 percent through 2026, well below the average of 3.8 percent in the decade before COVID-19. Many developing economies are expected to see no relative catch-up with advanced economies in the near term.

There are, of course, notable bright spots in the global economy. The U.S. economy, in particular, has shown impressive resilience. Growth has remained buoyant in the teeth of the fiercest monetary policy tightening in four decades. U.S. dynamism, in fact, is one reason the global economy enjoys some upside potential over the next two years.

India and Indonesia are two additional examples of robust performance. India's economy has been buoyed by strong domestic demand, with a surge in investment, and robust services activity. It is projected to grow an average of 6.7 percent per fiscal year from 2024 through 2026—making South Asia the world's fastest-growing region. Indonesia is expected to benefit from a growing middle class and generally prudent economic policies, expanding by an average of 5.1 percent over the next two years.

The performance of these and a few other economies makes it clear that high growth can be sustained—even in difficult conditions. Countries can enhance long-term growth by enacting policies that build human capital, boost productivity, improve the efficiency of public spending, and encourage more women to enter the labor force.

This edition of *Global Economic Prospects* features two analytical chapters of topical importance to policymakers. The first outlines how public investment can boost economic growth and facilitate private investment. In developing economies, public investment accounts for just a quarter of total investment, on average, but it can be a powerful policy lever. Scaling up public investment by 1 percent of GDP can increase the level of GDP by more than 1½ percent over the medium term. The impact on private investment is also significant—it grows by as much as 2 percent over five years. These benefits are greatest when countries meet two criteria: they enjoy the fiscal space to increase public spending, and they have a track record of efficient public investment.

The second analytical chapter explores the tragic predicament of developing economies that are small states—those with a population of around 1.5 million or less. These economies are home to just 17 million people but are often at the frontline of climate challenges. They face chronic fiscal difficulties. Two-fifths of them are at high risk of debt distress or already in it. They face climate-related natural disasters at a frequency eight times the average of other developing economies.

Comprehensive reforms can alleviate these challenges. First, small states should improve their ability to mobilize revenue from domestic sources, which constitute a more stable base than other alternatives. Second, they should improve spending efficiency—especially in health, education, and infrastructure. They should establish fiscal frameworks capable of managing frequent natural disasters and other shocks. These steps are all essential, together with coordinated global policies and financial support, to help them stay on a sustainable fiscal path.

Policymakers have cause to celebrate today: a global recession has been avoided despite the steepest rise in global interest rates since the 1980s. But they would be wise to keep their eye on the ball: growth rates remain too slow for progress. Without stronger international cooperation and a concerted push for policies that advance shared prosperity, the world could become stuck in the slow lane.

Indermit Gill
Senior Vice President and Chief Economist
The World Bank Group

Executive Summary

Global Outlook. *Global growth is projected to stabilize at 2.6 percent this year, holding steady for the first time in three years* despite flaring geopolitical tensions and high interest rates. It is then expected to edge up to 2.7 percent in 2025-26 amid modest growth in trade and investment. Global inflation is projected to moderate—but at a slower clip than previously assumed, averaging 3.5 percent this year. Given continued inflationary pressures, central banks in both advanced economies and emerging market and developing economies (EMDEs) will likely remain cautious in easing monetary policy. As such, average benchmark policy interest rates over the next few years are expected to remain about double the 2000-19 average.

Despite an improvement in near-term growth prospects, the outlook remains subdued by historical standards in advanced economies and EMDEs alike. Global growth over the forecast horizon is expected to be nearly half a percentage point below its 2010-19 average pace. In 2024-25, growth is set to underperform its 2010s average in nearly 60 percent of economies, representing more than 80 percent of global population and world output. EMDE growth is forecast to moderate from 4.2 percent in 2023 to 4 percent in both 2024 and 2025. Prospects remain especially lackluster in many vulnerable economies—over half of economies facing fragile- and conflict-affected situations will still be poorer by the end of this year than on the eve of the pandemic.

Global risks remain tilted to the downside despite the possibility of some upside surprises. Escalating geopolitical tensions could lead to volatile commodity prices, while further trade fragmentation risks additional disruptions to trade networks. Already, trade policy uncertainty has reached exceptionally high levels compared to other years that have featured major elections around the world since 2000. The persistence of inflation could lead to delays in monetary easing. A higher-for-longer path for interest rates would dampen global activity. Some major economies could grow more slowly than currently anticipated due to a range of domestic challenges. Additional natural disasters related to climate change could also hinder activity. On the upside, global inflation could moderate more quickly than assumed in the baseline, enabling faster monetary policy easing. In addition, growth in the United States could be stronger than expected.

Against this backdrop, decisive global and national policy efforts are needed to meet pressing challenges. At the global level, priorities include safeguarding trade, supporting green and digital transitions, delivering debt relief, and improving food security. At the national level, persistent inflation risks underscore the need for EMDE monetary policies to remain focused on price stability. High debt and elevated debt-servicing costs will require policy makers to seek ways to sustainably boost investment while ensuring fiscal sustainability. To meet development goals and bolster long-term growth, structural policies are needed to raise productivity growth, improve the efficiency of public investment, build human capital, and close gender gaps in the labor market.

Regional Prospects. *Growth is projected to soften in most EMDE regions in 2024.* In East Asia and Pacific, the expected slowdown this year mainly reflects moderating growth in China. Growth in Europe and Central Asia, Latin America and the Caribbean, and South Asia is also set to decelerate amid a slowdown in their largest economies. In contrast, growth is projected to pick up this year in the Middle East and North Africa and Sub-Saharan Africa, albeit less robustly than previously forecast.

Harnessing the Benefits of Public Investment. *Public investment can be a powerful policy lever in EMDEs to help ignite growth, including by catalyzing private investment.* However, public investment in these economies has experienced a significant slowdown in the past decade. In

EMDEs with ample fiscal space and a record of efficient government spending, scaling up of public investment by one percent of GDP can increase output by up to 1.6 percent over the medium term. Public investment also crowds in private investment and boosts productivity, promoting long-run growth in these economies.

To maximize the impact of public investment, EMDEs should undertake wide-ranging policy reforms to improve public investment efficiency—by, among other things, strengthening governance and fiscal administration—and create fiscal space through revenue and expenditure measures. The global community can play an important role in facilitating these reforms—particularly in lower-income developing countries—through financial support and technical assistance.

Fiscal Challenges in Small States: Weathering Storms, Rebuilding Resilience. *The COVID-19 pandemic and the global shocks that followed have worsened fiscal and debt positions in small states.* This has intensified their already substantial fiscal challenges—especially the need to manage more frequent climate change-related natural disasters. Two-fifths of the 35 EMDE small states are at high risk of debt distress or already in it, roughly twice the share for other EMDEs. Fiscal deficits in small states have widened since the pandemic, reflecting increased government spending to support households and firms, as well as weaker revenues.

Comprehensive fiscal reforms are essential to address the fiscal challenges confronting small states. First, small states' revenues, which are highly volatile, should be drawn from a more stable and secure tax base. Second, spending efficiency needs to be improved. These changes should be complemented by reforms to fiscal frameworks, including better utilization of fiscal rules and sovereign wealth funds. Finally, the global community can bolster funding for small states to invest in climate change resilience and adaptation, and other priority areas, including technical assistance in fiscal policy and debt management.

Abbreviations

CEMAC	Central African Economic and Monetary Union
CFA	African Financial Community
CPI	consumer price index
EAP	East Asia and Pacific
ECA	Europe and Central Asia
EM7	Emerging Market Seven (Brazil, China, India, Indonesia, Mexico, the Russian Federation, and Türkiye)
EMDE	emerging market and developing economy
EU	European Union
FCS	fragile and conflict-affected situations
FY	fiscal year
GCC	Gulf Cooperation Council
GDP	gross domestic product
GEP	*Global Economic Prospects*
GNFS	goods and nonfactor services
GPR	geopolitical risk index
HDI	human development index
IDA	International Development Association
ILO	International Labour Organization
IMF	International Monetary Fund
LAC	Latin America and the Caribbean
LIC	low-income country
MNA/MENA	Middle East and North Africa
OECD	Organisation for Economic Co-operation and Development
OPEC	Organization of the Petroleum Exporting Countries
OPEC+	OPEC and Azerbaijan, Bahrain, Brunei Darussalam, Kazakhstan, Malaysia, Mexico, Oman, the Russian Federation, South Sudan, and Sudan
SOEs	state-owned enterprises
PMI	purchasing managers' index
PPI	private participation in infrastructure
PPP	purchasing power parity
PPP	public-private partnership
RHS	right-hand scale
RRF	European Union's Recovery and Resilience Facility
SAR	South Asia
SDGs	Sustainable Development Goals
SSA	Sub-Saharan Africa
UN	United Nations
UNHCR	United Nations High Commissioner for Refugees
VAR	vector autoregression
VATs	value-added taxes
WAEMU	West African Economic and Monetary Union

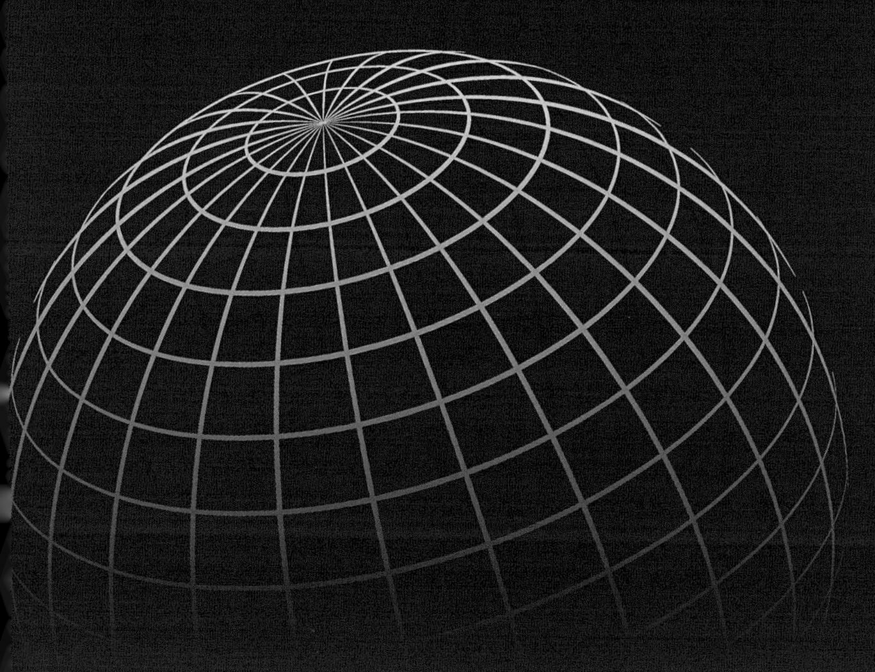

CHAPTER 1

GLOBAL OUTLOOK

The global economy is stabilizing, following several years of negative shocks. Global growth is projected to hold steady at 2.6 percent this year, despite flaring geopolitical tensions and high interest rates, before edging up to 2.7 percent in 2025-26 alongside modest expansions of trade and investment. Global inflation is expected to moderate at a slower clip than previously assumed, averaging 3.5 percent this year. Central banks in both advanced economies and emerging market and developing economies (EMDEs) are likely to remain cautious in easing policy. As such, markedly higher interest rates than prior to the pandemic are set to sustain for an extended period. Despite some improvement, the outlook remains subdued. Global growth over the forecast horizon is expected to be nearly half a percentage point below its 2010-19 average, with a slower pace of expansion in economies comprising over 80 percent of the global population. EMDE growth is projected to moderate from 4.2 percent in 2023 to 4 percent in 2024. Amid heightened conflict and violence, prospects remain especially lackluster in many vulnerable economies—over half of fragile and conflict-affected economies will still be poorer in 2024 than on the eve of the pandemic. Risks have become more balanced but remain tilted to the downside. Escalating geopolitical tensions could lead to volatile commodity prices. In a context of elevated trade policy uncertainty, further trade fragmentation risks additional disruptions to trade networks. More persistent inflation could lead to higher-for-longer interest rates. Other risks include weaker-than-anticipated activity in key economies and disasters related to climate change. Against this backdrop, policy makers face daunting challenges. Global efforts are needed to safeguard trade, support green and digital transitions, deliver debt relief, and improve food security. Still-pronounced inflation risks underscore the need for EMDE monetary policies to remain focused on price stability. High debt and elevated debt-servicing costs will require EMDE policy makers to balance sizable investment needs with fiscal sustainability. To meet development goals, policies are needed to raise productivity growth, improve the efficiency of public investment, build human capital, and close gender gaps in the labor market.

Summary

The global economy is stabilizing, following several years of overlapping negative shocks. Despite elevated financing costs and heightened geopolitical tensions, global activity firmed in early 2024. Global growth is envisaged to reach a slightly faster pace this year than previously expected, due mainly to the continued solid expansion of the U.S. economy. However, the extent of expected declines in global interest rates has moderated amid lingering inflation pressures in key economies. By historical standards, the global outlook remains subdued: both advanced economies and emerging market and developing economies (EMDEs) are set to grow at a slower pace over 2024-26 than in the decade preceding the pandemic (figure 1.1.A).

Domestic demand is projected to improve in many EMDEs this year, in line with a moderate cyclical recovery from the effects of high inflation, tight financial conditions, and anemic industrial activity. Aggregate EMDE growth is nonetheless poised to decelerate slightly mainly because of idiosyncratic factors in some large economies. Moreover, significant challenges persist in vulnerable economies—including in low-income countries (LICs) and those facing elevated levels of conflict and violence—where growth prospects have deteriorated markedly since January.

Global trade growth is recovering, supported by a pickup in goods trade. Services-trade growth is expected to provide less of a tailwind this year, given that tourism has nearly recovered to pre-pandemic levels. However, the trade outlook remains lackluster compared to recent decades, partly reflecting a proliferation of trade-restrictive measures and elevated trade policy uncertainty.

Aggregate commodity prices have increased since late last year. Amid fluctuations, average oil prices are expected to be slightly higher in 2024 than in 2023, underpinned by a tight demand-supply balance in a context of continued geopolitical tensions. Nonetheless, average energy prices are projected to be marginally lower this year than

Note: This chapter was prepared by Carlos Arteta, Phil Kenworthy, Nikita Perevalov, Peter Selcuk, Garima Vasishtha, and Collette Wheeler, with contributions from John Baffes, Mirco Balatti, Samuel Hill, Alen Mulabdic, Dominik Peschel, Shijie Shi, Naotaka Sugawara, and Takuma Tanaka.

TABLE 1.1 Real GDP[1]

(Percent change from previous year unless indicated otherwise)

	2021	2022	2023e	2024f	2025f	2026f	Percentage point differences from January 2024 projections 2024f	2025f
World	**6.3**	**3.0**	**2.6**	**2.6**	**2.7**	**2.7**	**0.2**	**0.0**
Advanced economies	**5.5**	**2.6**	**1.5**	**1.5**	**1.7**	**1.8**	**0.3**	**0.1**
United States	5.8	1.9	2.5	2.5	1.8	1.8	0.9	0.1
Euro area	5.9	3.4	0.5	0.7	1.4	1.3	0.0	-0.2
Japan	2.6	1.0	1.9	0.7	1.0	0.9	-0.2	0.2
Emerging market and developing economies	**7.3**	**3.7**	**4.2**	**4.0**	**4.0**	**3.9**	**0.1**	**0.0**
East Asia and Pacific	7.6	3.4	5.1	4.8	4.2	4.1	0.3	-0.2
China	8.4	3.0	5.2	4.8	4.1	4.0	0.3	-0.2
Indonesia	3.7	5.3	5.0	5.0	5.1	5.1	0.1	0.2
Thailand	1.6	2.5	1.9	2.4	2.8	2.9	-0.8	-0.3
Europe and Central Asia	7.2	1.6	3.2	3.0	2.9	2.8	0.6	0.2
Russian Federation	5.9	-1.2	3.6	2.9	1.4	1.1	1.6	0.5
Türkiye	11.4	5.5	4.5	3.0	3.6	4.3	-0.1	-0.3
Poland	6.9	5.6	0.2	3.0	3.4	3.2	0.4	0.0
Latin America and the Caribbean	7.2	3.9	2.2	1.8	2.7	2.6	-0.5	0.2
Brazil	4.8	3.0	2.9	2.0	2.2	2.0	0.5	0.0
Mexico	6.0	3.7	3.2	2.3	2.1	2.0	-0.3	0.0
Argentina	10.7	5.0	-1.6	-3.5	5.0	4.5	-6.2	1.8
Middle East and North Africa	6.2	5.9	1.5	2.8	4.2	3.6	-0.7	0.7
Saudi Arabia	4.3	8.7	-0.9	2.5	5.9	3.2	-1.6	1.7
Iran, Islamic Rep. [2]	4.7	3.8	5.0	3.2	2.7	2.4	-0.5	-0.5
Egypt, Arab Rep. [2]	3.3	6.6	3.8	2.8	4.2	4.6	-0.7	0.3
South Asia	8.6	5.8	6.6	6.2	6.2	6.2	0.6	0.3
India [2]	9.7	7.0	8.2	6.6	6.7	6.8	0.2	0.2
Bangladesh [2]	6.9	7.1	5.8	5.6	5.7	5.9	0.0	-0.1
Pakistan [2]	5.8	6.2	-0.2	1.8	2.3	2.7	0.1	-0.1
Sub-Saharan Africa	4.4	3.8	3.0	3.5	3.9	4.0	-0.3	-0.2
Nigeria	3.6	3.3	2.9	3.3	3.5	3.7	0.0	-0.2
South Africa	4.7	1.9	0.6	1.2	1.3	1.5	-0.1	-0.2
Angola	1.2	3.0	0.9	2.9	2.6	2.4	0.1	-0.5
Memorandum items:								
Real GDP[1]								
High-income countries	5.5	2.8	1.5	1.6	1.9	1.9	0.3	0.1
Middle-income countries	7.5	3.5	4.5	4.1	4.0	4.0	0.1	0.0
Low-income countries	4.1	5.0	3.8	5.0	5.3	5.5	-0.5	-0.3
EMDEs excluding China	6.5	4.3	3.4	3.5	4.0	3.9	0.0	0.2
Commodity-exporting EMDEs	5.8	3.4	2.6	2.8	3.4	3.2	-0.1	0.3
Commodity-importing EMDEs	8.0	3.9	4.9	4.7	4.3	4.3	0.3	-0.1
Commodity-importing EMDEs excluding China	7.3	5.3	4.5	4.4	4.6	4.7	0.2	0.1
EM7	7.8	3.3	5.1	4.5	4.0	4.0	0.4	-0.1
World (PPP weights) [3]	6.6	3.3	3.1	3.1	3.2	3.2	0.2	0.1
World trade volume [4]	**11.2**	**5.6**	**0.1**	**2.5**	**3.4**	**3.4**	**0.2**	**0.3**
							Level differences from January 2024 projections	
Commodity prices [5]								
WBG commodity price index	100.9	142.5	108.0	106.0	102.1	101.5	1.1	-0.1
Energy index	95.4	152.6	106.9	104.0	100.0	99.0	0.6	0.0
Oil (US$ per barrel)	70.4	99.8	82.6	84.0	79.0	78.1	3.0	1.0
Non-energy index	112.1	122.1	110.2	110.1	106.4	106.6	2.4	-0.2

Source: World Bank.

Note: e = estimate (actual data for commodity prices); f = forecast. EM7 = Brazil, China, India, Indonesia, Mexico, the Russian Federation, and Türkiye. WBG = World Bank Group. World Bank forecasts are frequently updated based on new information. Consequently, projections presented here may differ from those contained in other World Bank documents, even if basic assessments of countries' prospects do not differ at any given date. For the definition of EMDEs, developing countries, commodity exporters, and commodity importers, please refer to table 1.2. The World Bank is currently not publishing economic output, income, or growth data for Turkmenistan and República Bolivariana de Venezuela owing to lack of reliable data of adequate quality. Turkmenistan and República Bolivariana de Venezuela are excluded from cross-country macroeconomic aggregates.

1. Headline aggregate growth rates are calculated using GDP weights at average 2010-19 prices and market exchange rates.

2. GDP growth rates are on a fiscal year (FY) basis. Aggregates that include these countries are calculated using data compiled on a calendar year basis. For India and the Islamic Republic of Iran, the column for 2022 refers to FY2022/23. For Bangladesh, the Arab Republic of Egypt, and Pakistan, the column for 2022 refers to FY2021/22. Pakistan's growth rates are based on GDP at factor cost.

3. World growth rates are calculated using average 2010-19 purchasing power parity (PPP) weights, which attribute a greater share of global GDP to emerging market and developing economies (EMDEs) than market exchange rates.

4. World trade volume of goods and nonfactor services.

5. Indexes are expressed in nominal U.S. dollars (2010 = 100). Oil refers to the Brent crude oil benchmark. For weights and composition of indexes, see https://worldbank.org/commodities.

last—reflecting notable declines in prices for natural gas and coal—while remaining well above pre-pandemic levels. Metals prices are expected to be little changed over the forecast horizon, as demand related to metals-intensive clean energy investments and a broader pickup in global industrial activity attenuate the impact on commodity demand of declining real estate activity in China. Well-supplied markets for grains and other agricultural commodities should see edible food crop prices decline modestly.

Inflation continues to wane globally, making progress toward central bank targets in advanced economies and EMDEs, but at a slower pace than previously expected. Core inflation has remained stubbornly high in many economies, supported by rapid growth of services prices. Over the remainder of 2024, continued tight monetary policy stances and slowing wage increases should help reduce inflation further. By the end of 2026, global inflation is expected to settle at an average rate of 2.8 percent, broadly consistent with central bank targets (figure 1.1.B).

The anticipated extent of monetary easing in advanced economies this year has diminished substantially since late 2023—by more than a percentage point in the case of the United States. Expected policy rate paths diverge across major economies, as the European Central Bank proceeds with policy easing while the U.S. Federal Reserve keeps rates on hold for longer. Indeed, aside from short-term fluctuations, market expectations for the path of U.S. interest rates have repeatedly moved higher since 2022 (figure 1.1.C). Despite this market reassessment, global financial conditions have eased this year, reflecting solid risk appetite following last year's progress on disinflation and diminished concerns about the possibility of a sharp slowdown in global growth. In particular, global equity markets have made sizable gains.

EMDE financial conditions similarly became more accommodative early this year, aided by declining domestic policy rates, improving global sentiment, and expected easing of advanced-economy monetary conditions. EMDE conditions turned somewhat less accommodative in the

FIGURE 1.1 Global prospects

The global economy is stabilizing but the outlook remains subdued—both advanced economies and EMDEs are projected to grow at a slower pace over 2024-26 than in the pre-pandemic decade. Recent upward pressures on global core inflation are anticipated to gradually ease, such that headline inflation converges to levels broadly consistent with central bank targets by 2026. Market expectations for the path of U.S. policy rates have been repeatedly revised higher. Amid elevated borrowing costs, about two-fifths of EMDEs are acutely vulnerable to debt stress. In 2024-25, growth is expected to underperform its 2010-19 average in countries comprising more than 80 percent of global output and population. The multiple shocks of recent years have impeded per capita income catch-up, with almost half of EMDEs losing ground relative to advanced economies over 2020-24.

A. Contributions to global growth

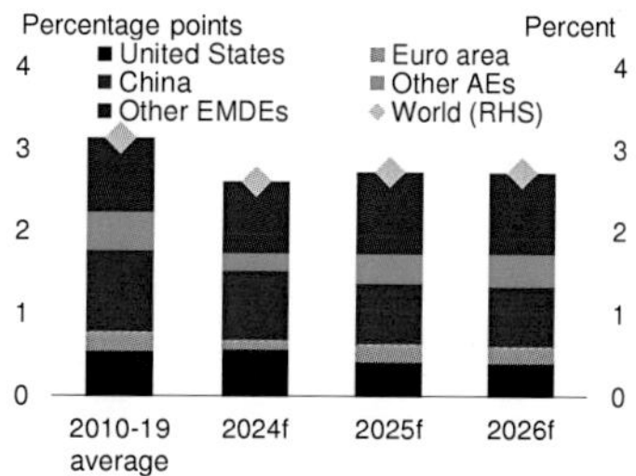

B. Global consumer price inflation

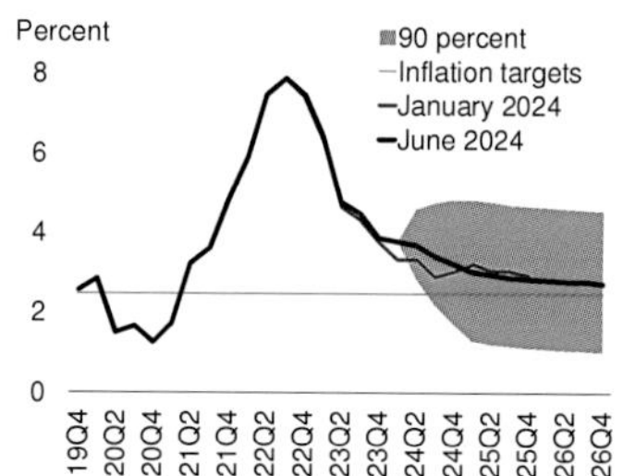

C. Market expectations of U.S. policy rates

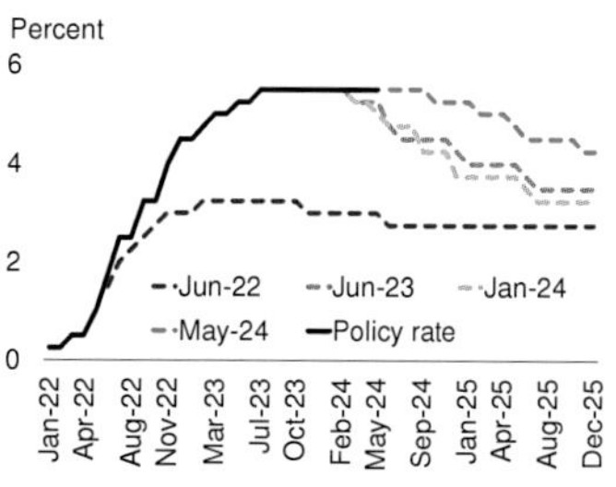

D. Share of EMDEs vulnerable to debt-related stress

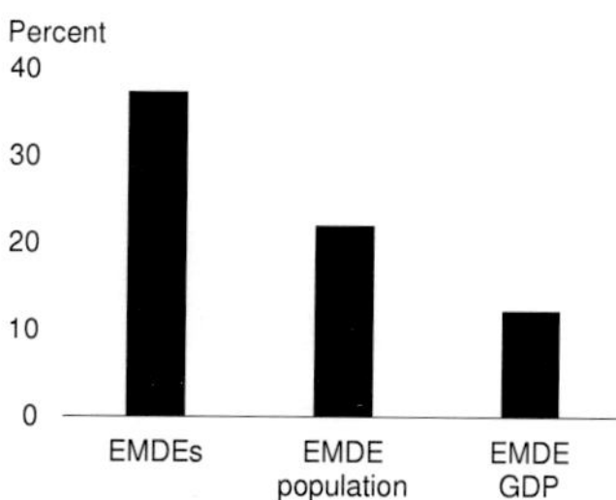

E. Lower average GDP growth in 2024-25 compared to 2010-19

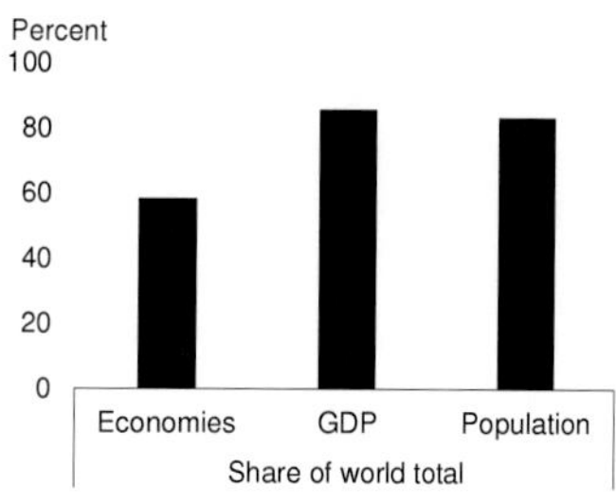

F. Share of EMDEs with GDP per capita growth lower than in advanced economies

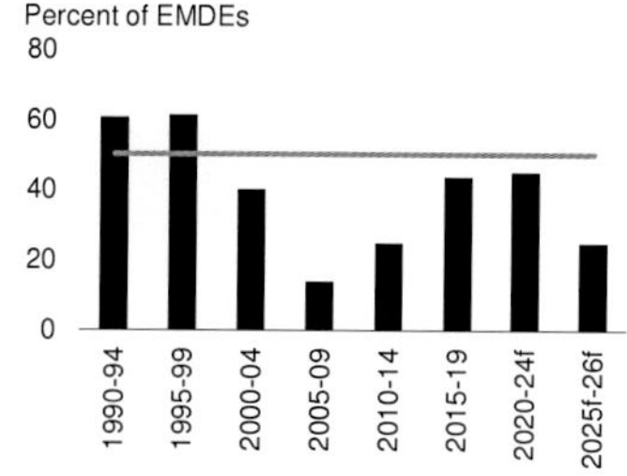

Sources: Bloomberg; Consensus Economics; Fitch Ratings; International Monetary Fund; Moody's Analytics; Oxford Economics; S&P 500 Index; UN World Population Prospects; World Bank.

Note: f = forecast; AEs = advanced economies; EMDEs = emerging market and developing economies. GDP aggregates are calculated using real U.S. dollar GDP weights at average 2010-19 prices and market exchange rates.

B. Model-based GDP-weighted projections of consumer price inflation using Oxford Economics' Global Economic Model. Sample includes 65 economies, including 31 EMDEs, and excludes Argentina and República Bolivariana de Venezuela. Confidence bands are derived from Consensus Economics forecast errors using the pre-pandemic sample. Horizontal line shows the average of most recent country-specific inflation targets, where available, or the 2015-19 average.

C. Solid blue line is the upper bound of the target range for the U.S. federal funds rate. Dotted lines are vintages of market-based policy rate expectations, derived from derivatives markets.

D. Sample includes those with weak credit ratings and those judged by the International Monetary Fund and the World Bank to be in or at high risk of debt distress.

E. "Economies" refers to the share of countries, "GDP" refers to the share of world GDP, and "population" is the share of the world population.

F. Horizontal line indicates the 50 percent threshold.

second quarter, as a strengthening of the U.S. dollar—prompted by geopolitical tensions and firm inflation data in the United States—coincided with a bout of capital outflows. Although market perceptions of sovereign credit risk have generally eased this year, EMDE borrowing costs continue to be high, and marked divergences persist. Indeed, credit ratings and debt sustainability analyses indicate that about 40 percent of EMDEs remain acutely vulnerable to debt-related stress (figure 1.1.D).

Following two years of sharp fiscal consolidation at the global level, fiscal policy became generally supportive of growth in 2023, especially in advanced economies. Going forward, fiscal consolidation is projected to resume, exerting a material drag on near-term growth in advanced economies and a modest headwind in EMDEs. This reflects government efforts to rebuild fiscal space, which has been eroded by the run-up in debt since the onset of the pandemic and the sharp increases in borrowing costs.

Against this backdrop, global growth is expected to remain subdued at 2.6 percent in 2024—unchanged from the previous year—reflecting tepid investment growth amid broadly restrictive monetary policies, and moderating consumption growth, in part because of receding savings buffers and diminishing fiscal support. Growth is projected to edge up to an average of 2.7 percent in 2025-26, as trade growth strengthens and broad but measured monetary policy easing supports activity in both advanced economies and EMDEs.

Across the forecast horizon, global growth remains lackluster by recent historical standards, at about 0.4 percentage point below the 2010-19 average. In 2024-25, growth is set to underperform its average pace in the 2010s in nearly 60 percent of economies, representing more than 80 percent of global output and population (figure 1.1.E). The subdued outlook—despite the anticipated moderation of various cyclical headwinds—underscores a secular deceleration of potential growth in many large economies. Relative to pre-pandemic norms, growth has weakened notably in countries that experienced high rates of inflation, much of which emanated from shocks to supply chains and commodity prices. Yet this trend is set to continue in the coming years, suggesting potentially enduring supply-side weakness.

Growth in EMDEs is forecast to hover around 4 percent a year over 2024-26. Growth in China is expected to slow this year and ease further in 2025 and 2026, with cyclical headwinds weighing on growth in the near term, along with a continuing structural slowdown. Excluding China, EMDE growth is projected to edge up to 3.5 percent this year and then firm to an average of 3.9 percent in 2025-26. In many EMDEs, this pickup reflects improving domestic demand, supported by receding inflation and easing financial conditions, and a cyclical rebound in trade, reflecting firming demand from some advanced economies. Across EMDE regions, the outlook is expected to diverge somewhat, with growth forecast to be weaker than the 2010-19 average in East Asia and Pacific, Europe and Central Asia, and South Asia, but broadly returning to pre-pandemic averages in most other regions over 2025-26.

Growth in LICs is forecast to improve over the forecast horizon from a subdued 3.8 percent in 2023 to 5 percent this year. This reflects increasing activity among several commodity-exporting economies—mainly metal exporters—as well as expected improvement among fragile economies. However, forecasts have been downgraded significantly for several countries amid elevated uncertainty and ongoing conflicts. Moreover, despite the projected pickup, the recovery from the 2020 global recession will remain weak: growth in many LICs and economies in fragile and conflict-affected situations (FCS) is expected to underperform pre-pandemic growth rates by at least half a percentage point. Many LICs are poorer now than they were in 2019, and will continue to contend with acute economic challenges, including slow progress in poverty reduction, depleted fiscal space, and elevated susceptibility to debt distress.

GDP per capita in EMDEs is forecast to grow at about 3 percent on average over 2024-26, well below the average in 2010-19. Excluding China, EMDE per capita GDP growth is forecast to be lower still, averaging 2.5 percent over 2024-26. Some large EMDEs, such as India, are expected to see continued solid per capita growth. Yet the trend of the 2020s so far is one of uneven and limited progress. Nearly half of EMDEs are set to lose ground relative to advanced economies when viewed over the 2020-24 period (figure 1.1.F). Although this trend is expected to improve somewhat over 2025-26 in EMDEs as a whole, per capita growth is set to remain stagnant in many LICs and FCS.

Risks to the outlook have become somewhat more balanced since January, with the global economy thus far proving resilient to high financing costs. However, the balance of risks remains tilted to the downside amid elevated uncertainty (figure 1.2.A). Heightened geopolitical tensions could sharply depress sentiment, disrupt trade and commodity markets, push up inflation, and hurt economic activity; in particular, a conflict-related disruption to global oil supply could push oil prices markedly higher and undermine the disinflation process. Elevated trade policy uncertainty—already at an unusually high level relative to previous years with major elections since 2000—and proliferating trade restrictions could weigh on trade prospects and economic activity (figure 1.2.B). Further trade fragmentation could have adverse global repercussions via declining economic confidence, increasing trade distortions, and related financial market reactions.

Advanced-economy interest rates are at levels last seen before the 2008-09 global financial crisis, and, in light of persistently above-target inflation and tight labor markets, they are likely to remain high for some time. Over the next couple of years, policy interest rates in advanced economies are expected to be more than double their 2000-19 average (figure 1.2.C). Although the global economy has withstood high interest rates better than was anticipated, interest rate-sensitive components of activity will continue to be restrained. Moreover, if further delays in the disinflation process emerge, policy rate cuts may be postponed. A higher resulting path for interest rates, relative to the baseline, could give rise to markedly tighter financial conditions and significantly weaker global growth (figure 1.2.D).

FIGURE 1.2 Global risks and policy challenges

Risks to the outlook are somewhat more balanced but remain skewed to the downside. Pronounced trade policy uncertainty—already at its highest level compared with other years of major elections since 2000—could portend further trade restrictions and weigh on global trade. Advanced-economy interest rates are expected to remain well above 2000-19 average levels and could turn out higher still if inflationary pressures persist, substantially slowing global growth. Conflict-related oil supply disruptions could raise oil prices, dampen economic activity, and undermine the disinflation process. EMDE fiscal policy makers confront exacting trade-offs, given elevated borrowing costs and large financing needs. Improving public investment efficiency in EMDEs is crucial, especially given constrained fiscal space.

A. Probability distribution around global growth forecast

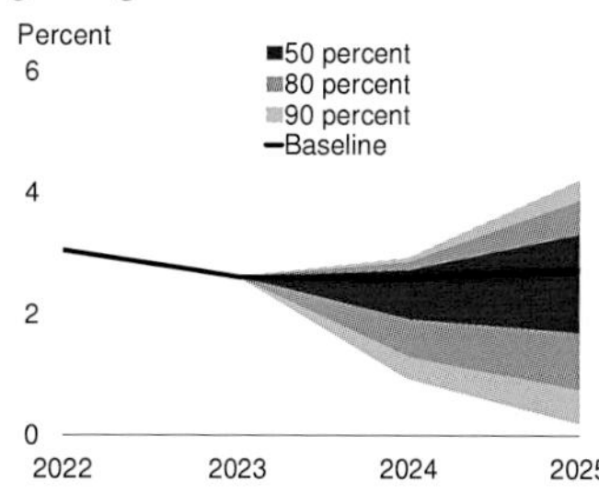

B. Global trade policy uncertainty in years with major elections

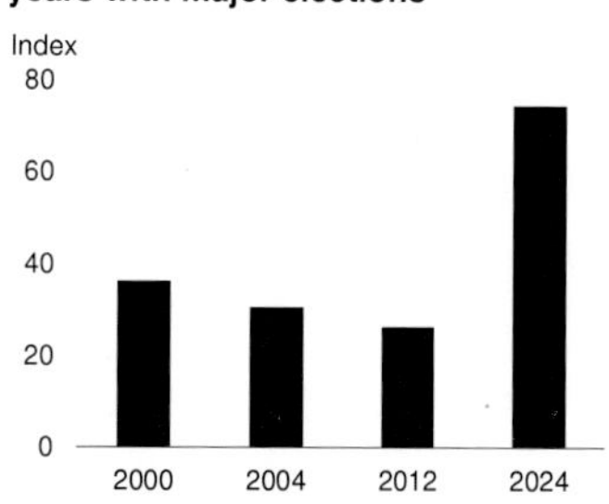

C. Monetary policy interest rates in advanced economies

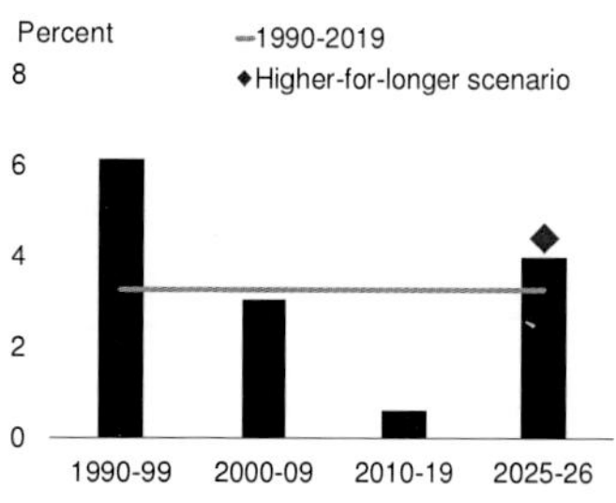

D. Change in global growth in alternative scenarios

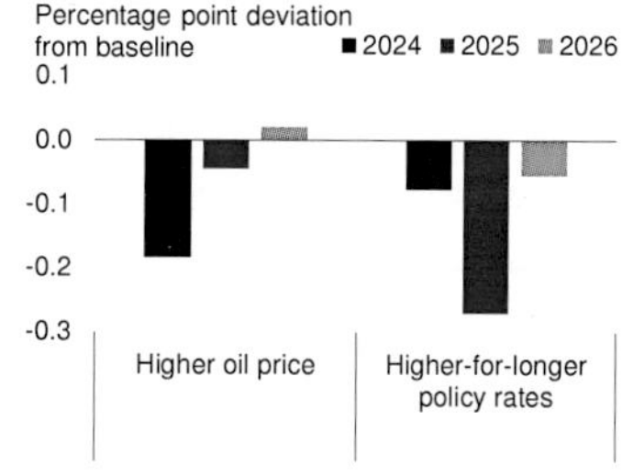

E. Gross public financing needs

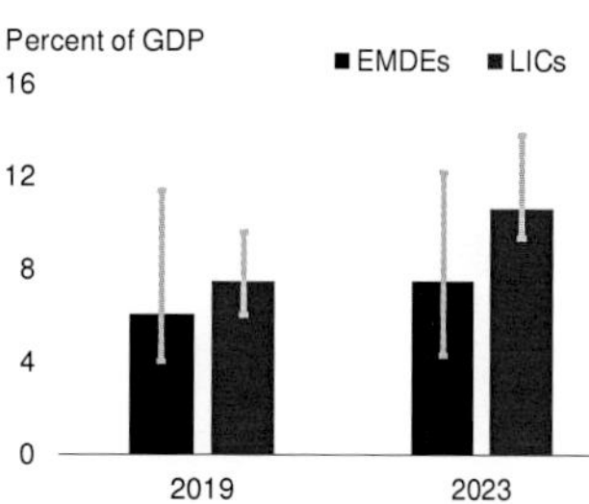

F. Public infrastructure investment efficiency

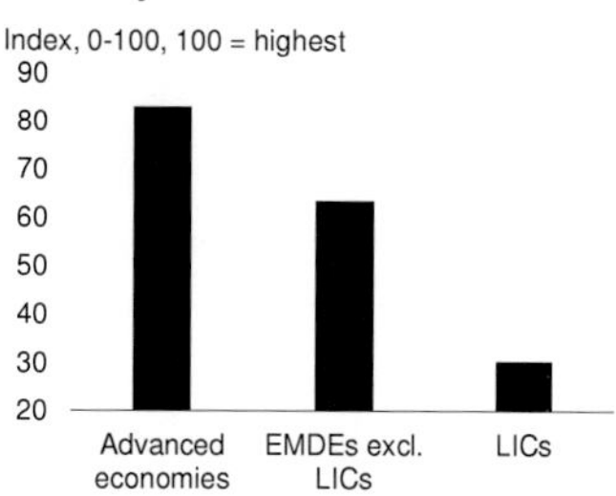

Sources: Bloomberg; Caldara et al. (2020); Consensus Economics; Federal Reserve Bank of St. Louis; Haver Analytics; IMF (2021); Ohnsorge, Stocker, and Some (2016); Oxford Economics; IMF-WEO (database); World Bank.

Note: EMDEs = emerging market and developing economies; LICs = low-income countries.

A. Probabilities use the range and skewness implied by oil and equity price derivatives, and term spread forecasts. Values for 2024 and 2025 use 6-month- and 18-month-ahead forecast distributions. Last observation is May 30, 2024, and May 2024 for Consensus Economics forecasts.

B. Panel shows the average trade policy uncertainty index in the first five months of each year in which elections were held in countries cumulatively representing more than 30 percent of global GDP. Last observation is May 2024.

C. Average annual policy rates. Aggregates are calculated as GDP-weighted averages of the policy rates and policy rate expectations for the United States, the euro area (using aggregated national policy rates as a proxy over the 1990-99 period), and the United Kingdom. Policy rate expectations are based on futures curves observed on May 31, 2024.

D. Scenarios are produced using Oxford Economics' Global Economic Model.

E. Sample includes 98 EMDEs and 10 LICs. Data are medians. Whiskers show interquartile range.

F. Bars show group medians of the IMF (2021) public infrastructure efficiency index. Sample includes 27 advanced economies and 93 EMDEs, of which 15 are LICs.

Weaker-than-expected growth in China—triggered, for instance, by a more prolonged and deeper property sector downturn—could have notable negative spillovers, particularly for EMDE commodity exporters. Severe climate-change-related natural disasters could result in considerable losses in lives, livelihoods, and output. Such events could also cause spikes in food prices, stalling or even reversing the decline in global inflation and exacerbating food insecurity. These downside risks, should they materialize, would likely hit the poorest and most vulnerable EMDEs hardest.

On the upside, global disinflation could proceed at a faster pace than currently envisioned, aided by stronger productivity growth. This could be driven by the rapid adoption of new technologies, enabling advanced economies to extend recent gains and EMDEs to recoup post-pandemic productivity losses. Other possible triggers for lower inflation might include improvements in supply chains and greater declines in commodity prices than currently projected. Faster global disinflation would allow central banks to lower policy rates more than assumed. Global activity would likely strengthen as a result of both stronger productivity and lower policy rates, reflecting easier financial conditions, higher real incomes, and improved sentiment. In addition, EMDEs could benefit from firming capital inflows. Another upside risk is that U.S. growth could be higher than expected on account of continued strong labor supply dynamics, underpinned by rising labor force participation and elevated absorption of working-age migrants.

Policy makers face a range of daunting challenges. Coordinated improvements in debt relief will be necessary to free up resources for growth-enhancing investments, particularly in some of the most vulnerable EMDEs, given elevated financing needs (figure 1.2.E). Enhanced international cooperation is needed to tackle the threat of climate change, the fragmentation of trade networks, and mounting food insecurity and conflict. Global cooperation is also essential to leverage the benefits of new technologies such as artificial intelligence (AI), including by tapping AI solutions to address global challenges.

By late last year, most EMDE central banks were holding policy rates steady or lowering them, as inflation declined. However, in many EMDEs, bringing inflation durably to target will require a moderation of persistent service-sector price pressures. In this context, EMDE central banks can help anchor inflation expectations by communicating a steadfast focus on price stability and willingness to pause easing if necessary. Given reduced expectations for policy rate cuts by major advanced-economy central banks, continued monetary easing in EMDEs may further narrow interest rate differentials relative to advanced economies, potentially leading to increased financial market volatility. As such, confined interventions to manage capital flows and currency volatility could become appropriate in limited circumstances. In addition, close supervision of bank credit quality and capital levels, complemented by macroprudential policies, can help strengthen the resilience of EMDE financial sectors.

Fiscal space remains narrow in many EMDEs amid weak revenues and elevated debt-servicing costs. Decisive measures will be needed to boost fiscal resources for public investment. These could include reforms to mobilize domestic revenues, the harnessing of digital technologies to simplify tax payments and records management, and reform of costly and inefficient subsidies. Furthermore, even with increased public resources, improved spending efficiency will be needed to meet a wide range of development challenges. In particular, it is critical to improve infrastructure investment efficiency, where EMDEs significantly lag advanced economies (figure 1.2.F). In the case of small states, elevated exposure to external shocks poses a formidable fiscal challenge, underscoring the need to balance additional investments in human capital and climate-resilient infrastructure with the maintenance of adequate fiscal buffers.

To raise productivity growth, advance prosperity, and address persistent longer-term challenges, policies should aim to increase the scale and efficacy of public investment programs, enhance human capital, address climate change, and confront persistent food insecurity. Additionally, targeted policies are needed to better leverage women's economic potential and reduce gender discrimination, as well as to address high youth unemployment rates in many EMDEs.

Global context

The near-term global economic landscape has improved, but notable challenges remain. Trade growth, which came to a halt last year, is showing signs of recovery amid a pickup in goods trade. Commodity prices have come off their 2022 peaks and supply-chain pressures have waned, helping to moderate global inflation. Yet the pace of disinflation has slowed since last year, particularly with respect to core prices. Monetary policy easing, as a result, is expected to proceed at a cautious pace as policy makers remain focused on ensuring price stability. Financial conditions in EMDEs have become less restrictive, in part because robust risk appetite has counterbalanced higher benchmark borrowing costs. However, about 40 percent of EMDEs remain vulnerable to debt-related stress.

Global trade

Global trade in goods and services was nearly flat in 2023—the weakest performance outside of global recessions in the past 50 years. Amid a sharp slowdown in global industrial production, the volume of goods trade contracted for most of 2023 and fell by 1.9 percent for the year as a whole (figure 1.3.A). The evolution of goods trade diverged across regions, with volumes declining in advanced economies, especially in Europe, and stagnating in EMDEs as expansions in China and Europe and Central Asia (ECA) offset contractions in Latin America and the Caribbean (LAC), Sub-Saharan Africa (SSA), and Middle East and North Africa (MNA).

The value of global services trade grew about 9 percent in 2023, driven primarily by a recovery in tourism flows—exports of travel services surged by about 38 percent (WTO 2024). However, the pace of expansion in tourism was substantially below that in 2022, with recent data indicating tourism activity in line with pre-pandemic levels, suggesting a near-full recovery in most regions. Stabilization in services trade is reflected in the steadying of the global services PMI for new export orders, which has remained closer to neutral thresholds compared to last year (figure 1.3.B).

FIGURE 1.3 Global trade

Global trade in goods and services was nearly flat in 2023 amid goods trade contractions for most of the year. Leading indicators suggest that services trade has stabilized. Global trade in goods and services is projected to expand by 2.5 percent in 2024 and 3.4 percent in 2025 but remain well below the average rates of the two decades preceding the pandemic. In all, global trade growth in 2020-24 is set to register the slowest half decade of growth since the 1990s.

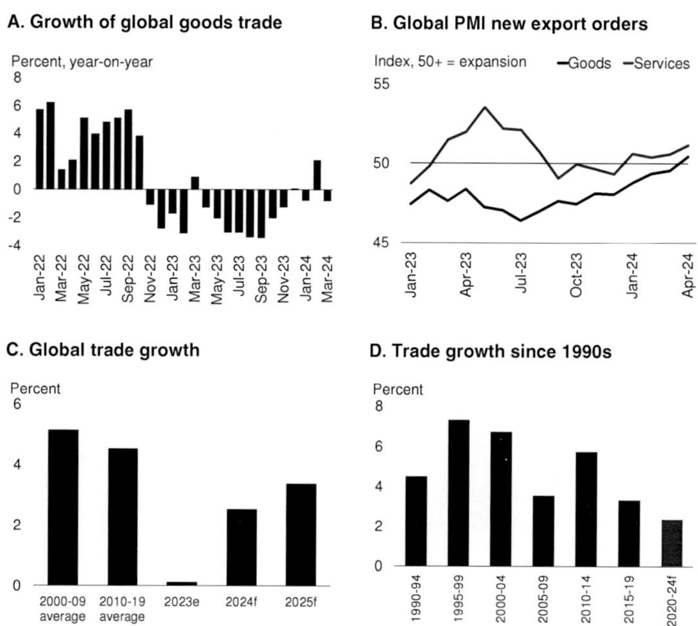

Sources: CPB Netherlands Bureau of Economic Analysis; Haver Analytics; World Bank.

Note: e = estimate; f = forecast; PMI = purchasing managers' index. Trade in goods and services is measured as the average of export and import volumes.

A. Panel shows goods trade volumes. Last observation is March 2024.

B. Panel shows manufacturing and services subcomponents of the global purchasing managers' index (PMI) new export orders series. PMI readings above (below) 50 indicate expansion (contraction). Last observation is April 2024.

D. Panel shows five-year averages of growth in global trade in goods and services.

The number of new trade-restricting measures is still well above pre-pandemic levels—although down from the historical high reached in 2023—exerting a further drag on global trade. Recent attacks on commercial vessels in the Red Sea, coupled with climate-related shipping disruptions in the Panama Canal, have affected maritime transit and freight rates along these critical routes (Bogetic et al. 2024). These disruptions, however, have not yet led to a substantial increase in global supply chain pressures or lengthened global supplier delivery times. Adverse effects have been limited to a few regions and specific industries so far.

Global trade growth is projected to pick up to 2.5 percent this year, a significant improvement from last year but well below the average rates observed in the two decades preceding the pandemic (figure 1.3.C). The forecast entails a pickup in goods trade growth after a sluggish start to the year, supported by a rebound in global goods demand as inventory restocking resumes in the United States and the euro area, and as demand from China stabilizes. Meanwhile, services trade growth is expected to stabilize near its pre-pandemic pace. In 2025, trade growth is expected to firm to 3.4 percent, in tandem with a pickup in growth in the euro area and EMDEs excluding China, and remain steady in 2026.

Despite the expected growth in trade this year, by the end of 2024 global trade is set to register the slowest half-decade of growth since the 1990s, mirroring subdued global GDP growth (figure 1.3.D). In the near term, the responsiveness of global trade to global output is likely to remain lower than before the pandemic, reflecting muted investment growth and the recent proliferation of trade restrictions worldwide.

The trade outlook is subject to various downside risks, including weaker-than-anticipated global demand, escalating geopolitical tensions, and further disruptions in maritime transport. Moreover, with elections taking place in many countries this year, heightened trade policy-related uncertainty and the potential for more inward-looking policies could weigh on trade prospects and economic activity.

Commodity markets

After a sharp decline between mid-2022 and mid-2023, commodity price swings were less pronounced in the second half of last year. In 2024, aggregate commodity prices have generally risen against a backdrop of tight supply conditions and signs of firmer industrial activity (figure 1.4.A). Average commodity prices are nonetheless forecast to recede slightly over the forecast period, mainly reflecting improving supply conditions, while remaining well above pre-pandemic levels (figure 1.4.B).

Oil prices have fluctuated this year, trending substantially higher in April in the context of escalating tensions in the Middle East, but subsequently pulling back (figure 1.4.C). Against a backdrop of continued geopolitical risks, the average price of Brent oil is forecast to be slightly higher this year than last, at $84/bbl, before receding to $79/bbl in 2025 amid the partial unwind of OPEC+ supply cuts and expanding non-OPEC+ production. The near-term oil price forecast is notably uncertain, however, given the potential for price spikes resulting from conflict-related supply disruptions.

Natural gas prices fell nearly 28 percent in the first quarter of 2024, relative to the previous quarter, amid robust production, mild winter weather, and elevated inventories. After reaching a nearly 30-year low in March, the price of U.S. natural gas surged in May, in part due to increased liquefied natural gas (LNG) exports. U.S. natural gas prices are expected to stabilize in the near term, before increasing further in 2025 as gas liquefaction capacity expands, allowing more supplies to be diverted to other markets (figure 1.4.D). European natural gas prices rebounded in the second quarter of 2024, reflecting persistent supply risks related to ongoing conflicts. Despite the anticipated growth of U.S. LNG exports, average European gas prices are envisaged to rise by 11 percent in 2025, as industrial activity picks up, supporting demand.

Most metal prices were relatively stable during the first quarter of this year. However, among precious metals, gold prices reached record highs, fueled by geopolitical concerns and central bank purchases. In the second quarter, copper prices rose to a record nominal high on supply concerns, while benchmark aluminum prices spiked after the introduction of new sanctions on the Russian Federation. Metals prices, excluding those of precious metals, are projected to remain little changed, on average, in 2024-25, staying well above pre-pandemic levels. Weaker metals demand associated with lower real estate investment in China is likely to be substantially counterbalanced by firming global industrial demand and metals-intensive clean energy investments (figure 1.4.E).

Agricultural commodity prices were close to unchanged, in aggregate, in the first quarter. Average prices are set to soften somewhat in 2024-25. Food prices are forecast to dip by 6 percent in 2024 and 4 percent in 2025, mainly reflecting ample supplies for grains as well as oils and meals (figure 1.4.F). Volatile weather and increasing trade restrictions or disruptions could nonetheless push prices higher. Despite declining consumer food price inflation, acute food insecurity is estimated to have further worsened last year and doubled globally since 2019. Surging hunger is linked to a combination of still-elevated consumer food prices and proliferating violence and instability in vulnerable areas, notably in parts of the Middle East and Sub-Saharan Africa.

Global inflation

Global inflation has continued to decline, yet it remains above target in most advanced economies and in about one-fourth of inflation-targeting EMDEs. The initial phase of disinflation after the pandemic was underpinned by falling energy prices as well as waning supply chain pressures. Recently, the pace of consumer price disinflation has slowed, reflecting a partial rebound in energy prices, along with a notable slowdown in the rate of decline in core inflation (figure 1.5.A).

In advanced economies, disinflation in consumer goods prices appears to have bottomed out, while inflation in consumer services remains elevated (figure 1.5.B). In the United States, resilient economic activity, alongside rapid increases in the cost of shelter, has given rise to persistently high services and, more broadly, core inflation over the past few months. To some extent, the strength of U.S. productivity growth has mitigated these trends, likely lessening the inflationary effects of rising wages. In contrast, subdued productivity in the euro area has driven economy-wide labor costs higher, underpinning elevated core and services inflation, despite anemic euro area demand.

FIGURE 1.4 Commodity markets

Aggregate commodity prices have generally increased in 2024 after declining, on average, last year. Over the forecast period, commodity prices are projected to decline slightly but remain well above 2015-19 levels. Oil prices have remained volatile this year amid a confluence of heightened geopolitical tensions and OPEC+ production cuts. U.S. natural gas liquefaction capacity is set to advance next year, enabling more gas supplies to be diverted to other markets. Robust growth of clean energy investment is expected to continue supporting base metals prices. Food prices are projected to soften in the next two years, aided by growing supplies of grains and edible crops.

A. Commodity prices

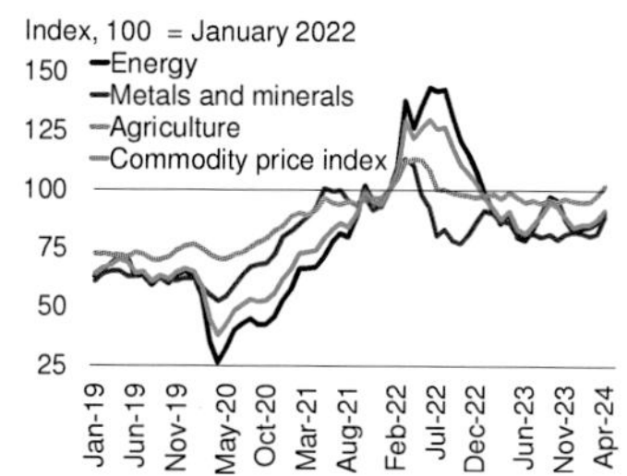

B. Commodity price projections

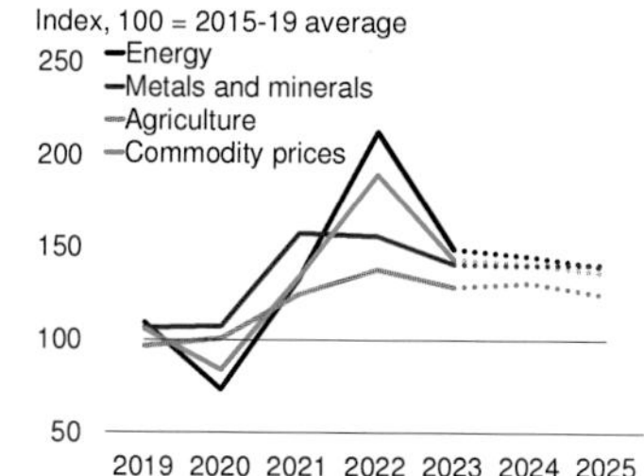

C. Oil prices and key events

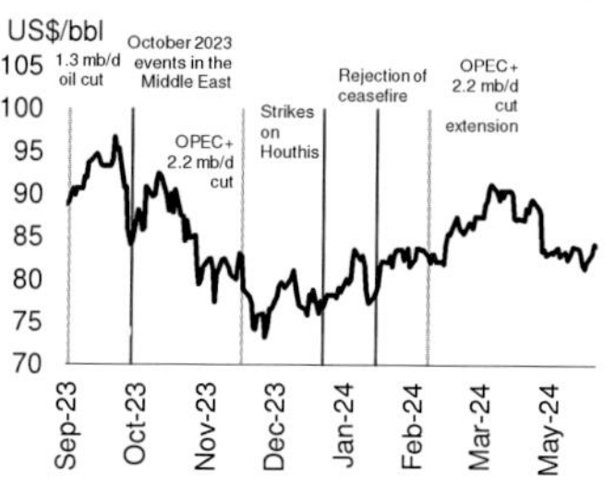

D. Additional U.S. natural gas liquefaction capacity

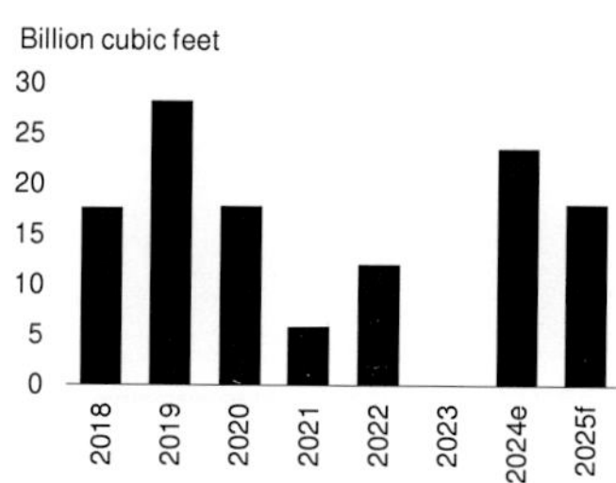

E. Global clean energy investment

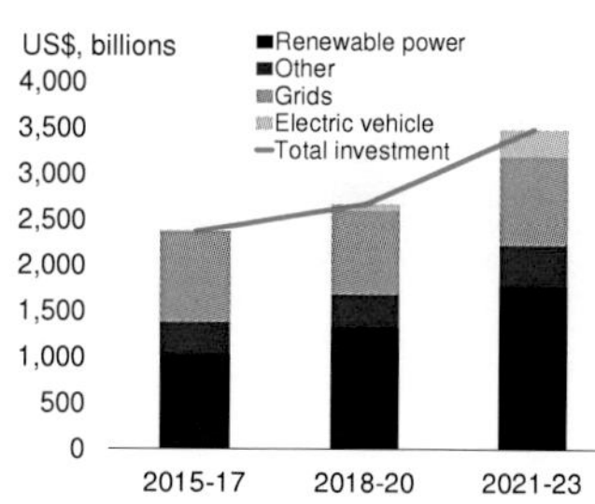

F. Food commodity price forecasts

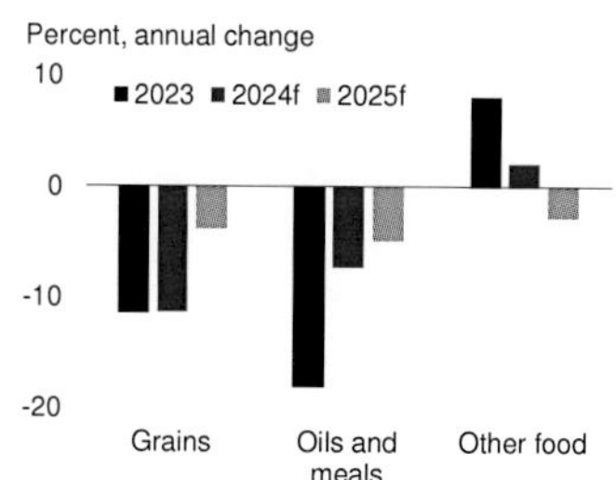

Sources: Bloomberg; IEA (2023); U.S. Energy Information Administration (EIA); World Bank.

Note: bbl = barrels; OPEC+ = Organization of the Petroleum Exporting Countries and Azerbaijan, Bahrain, Brunei Darussalam, Kazakhstan, Malaysia, Mexico, Oman, the Russian Federation, South Sudan, and Sudan.

A. Monthly data in U.S. dollar terms. Last observation is April 2024.

B. Commodity prices line refers to the World Bank commodity price index, excluding precious metals. Dashed lines indicate forecasts.

C. Daily Brent prices. Last observation is May 29, 2024. Yellow lines show the 1.3 and 2.2 million barrels per day (mb/d) cuts. Red lines indicate geopolitical events, including the October 2023 events in the Middle East, the strikes on Houthis by the United Kingdom and United States, and the rejection of the ceasefire in Gaza.

D. 2024 and 2025 are EIA estimates based on up-to-date project information. Last update is 2024Q1.

E. Total global investment in each three-year period. 2023 values are estimated. "Other" refers to end-use renewable energy, electrification in building, transport, and industrial sectors, and battery storage.

F. 2024 and 2025 values are forecasts.

FIGURE 1.5 Global inflation

The pace of decline in core inflation has slowed this year. In major advanced economies, disinflation in consumer goods prices appears to have bottomed out, while inflation in consumer services prices remains elevated. High core inflation in EMDEs was driven by services, including shelter. Global inflation is expected to gradually decelerate toward average inflation targets by 2026, amid softening core inflation.

A. Core inflation, three-month annualized

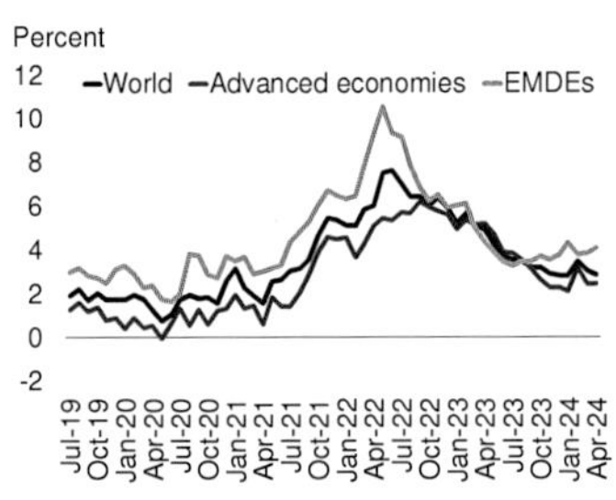

B. Goods and services inflation

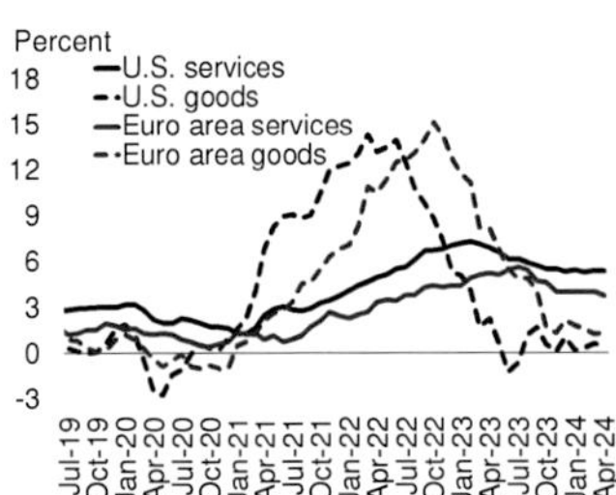

C. Inflation by component, three-month annualized

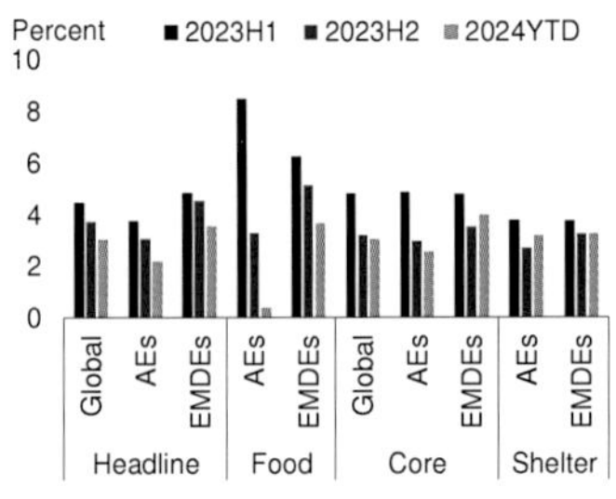

D. Global consumer price inflation

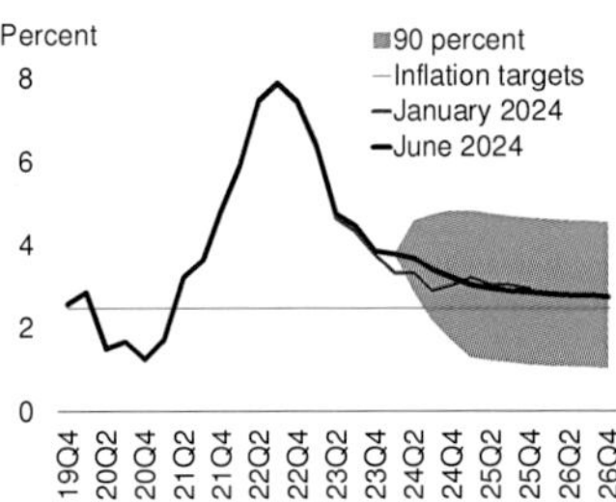

Sources: Eurostat; Federal Reserve Bank of St. Louis; Haver Analytics; Oxford Economics; World Bank.

Note: AEs = advanced economies; EMDEs = emerging market and developing economies; YTD = year to date.

A. Panel shows median consumer price inflation excluding food and energy, measured in three-month annualized percent changes. Sample includes up to 32 advanced economies and 46 EMDEs. Last observation is April 2024.

B. Panel shows year-on-year consumer price inflation in the goods and services categories. U.S. goods inflation is a weighted average of consumer durable and nondurable price inflation rates, U.S. services excludes energy services. Last observation is April 2024.

C. Median three-month annualized inflation rates by component; averages computed over months in the first and second halves of 2023, and year-to-date in 2024. Sample includes up to 36 advanced economies and 100 EMDEs. Last observation is April 2024.

D. Model-based GDP-weighted projections of consumer price inflation using Oxford Economics' Global Economic Model. Sample include 65 economies, including 31 EMDEs, and excludes Argentina and República Bolivariana de Venezuela. Confidence bands are derived from Consensus Economics forecast errors using the pre-pandemic sample. The green line shows the average of most recent country-specific inflation targets. The 2015-2019 average is used when the target is not available.

In EMDEs, headline inflation has generally continued to recede on a 12-month basis. Across most EMDEs in East Asia and Pacific (EAP) and LAC, headline inflation broadly continued to trend near or below pre-pandemic averages through late 2023 and early 2024, despite reaccelerating in some countries. However, progress has been slow and uneven in other regions, with elevated core price increases contributing to high headline inflation rates. As in advanced economies, persistently high core inflation in EMDEs has been driven by services prices, including for shelter (figure 1.5.C).

Greater-than-anticipated inflationary pressures earlier this year have led to an upward revision to the projection for near-term global inflation (figure 1.5.D). Nevertheless, aside from a small group of countries where very high inflation reflects idiosyncratic domestic challenges, global inflation is expected to decline to 3.5 percent in 2024, before easing further, to 2.9 percent in 2025 and 2.8 percent in 2026, broadly consistent with average country inflation targets. The slowdown is expected to be driven by softening core inflation, as services demand moderates and wage growth slows, in addition to a modest decline in commodity prices. Surveys of inflation expectations similarly imply gradual global disinflation over the next two years.

Global financial developments

Global financial conditions have eased, on balance, since last year, primarily reflecting declines in risk premia amid still-elevated interest rates. Central banks across major advanced economies are expected to gradually lower policy rates this year, but the level of real interest rates is set to remain a headwind to economic activity—albeit a diminishing one—for some time. Policy rate projections derived from financial markets have been volatile since U.S. policy tightening started in 2022, with expectations repeatedly revised higher over time (figure 1.6.A). Meanwhile, most advanced-economy central banks continue to emphasize that the pace of easing will be cautious, reflecting persistent inflationary pressures—and, in the case of the United States, robust economic activity. As such, government bond yields are well above pre-pandemic levels and are likely to remain so, absent large negative shocks to growth.

Risk appetite picked up globally early in the year—particularly in advanced economies—signaling optimism that continued steady disinflation might accompany resilient growth. With volatility subdued, advanced economy equity valuations reached elevated levels, especially in the United States, where confidence regarding potential productivity gains from AI played a key role (figure 1.6.B). Sentiment briefly wilted in April, amid firm U.S. inflation data and escalating geopolitical tensions, but rebounded thereafter. Although the cost of credit remains high, perceptions of corporate credit risk appear muted—except for asset classes, such as office real estate, that have been adversely affected by structural post-pandemic shifts in activity. Corporate credit spreads remain well below 2010-19 average levels in both the United States and the euro area (figure 1.6.C). Banks in these jurisdictions continue to report tightening of standards for lending to firms, but by markedly narrowing majorities.

EMDE financial conditions also eased in the first quarter of 2024, reflecting expectations of easing advanced-economy monetary conditions, improving global investor sentiment, and ongoing policy rate cuts in many large EMDEs (figure 1.6.D). Conditions turned less accommodative early in the second quarter, as safe haven flows and declining expectations of U.S. rate cuts stoked a notable strengthening of the U.S. dollar and a bout of debt and equity portfolio outflows. Sovereign spreads have nonetheless trended to below 2010-19 levels in the majority of middle-income EMDEs, signaling investor confidence that financial stress risks are broadly contained. In contrast, spreads remain elevated among EMDEs with weak credit ratings, even if they have declined substantially this year (figure 1.6.E).

Indeed, despite some easing of global conditions, financial stress concerns remain acute in about 40 percent of EMDEs—comprising those with weak credit ratings, and those where debt sustainability analyses indicate a high risk of, or existing, debt distress (figure 1.6.F). Among weakly rated countries that had market access in the 2010s, a combination of political instability, the pandemic and other external shocks, and financial crises in the 2020s has rendered non-concessional debt prohibitively expensive. Among unrated countries—many of them low-income countries—debt burdens have grown increasingly severe owing to a decade of debt build-up in the 2010s, coupled with anemic post-pandemic recoveries and rising debt-service costs (World Bank 2023a).

FIGURE 1.6 Global financial developments

Financial market expectations for the path of U.S. policy rates have been repeatedly revised higher. The tightening of global financial conditions through higher interest rates has been dampened, however, by narrowing risk premia, reflected in buoyant equity valuations and tight corporate credit spreads. On net, EMDE central banks have been easing policy since the second half of 2023. EMDE sovereign risk spreads have declined, but they remain elevated among economies with weak credit ratings. In all, nearly 40 percent of EMDEs—home to about one-fifth of the EMDE population—face an elevated likelihood of debt-related stress.

A. Market expectations of U.S. policy rates

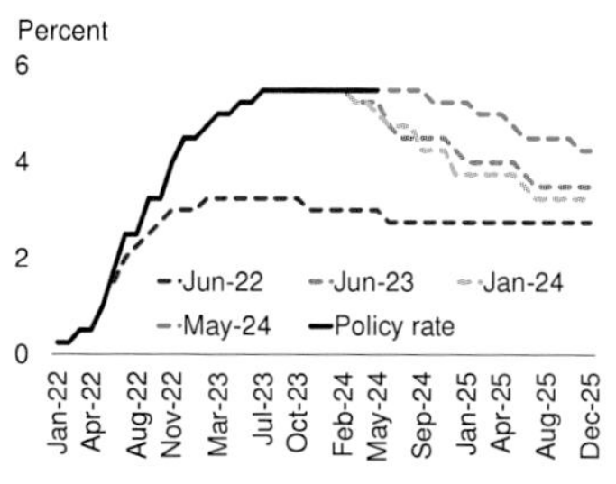

B. Equity market valuation by percentile, 1998-2024

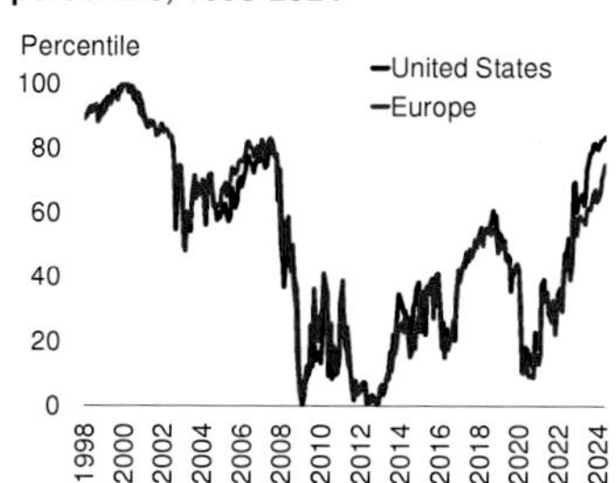

C. Non-investment-grade corporate credit spreads

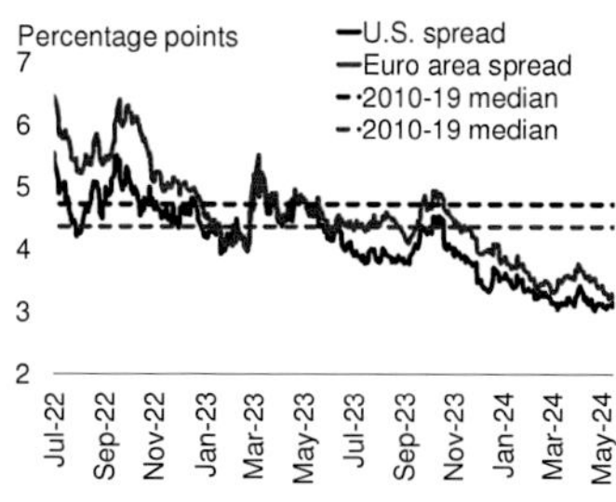

D. EMDE monetary policy rate changes

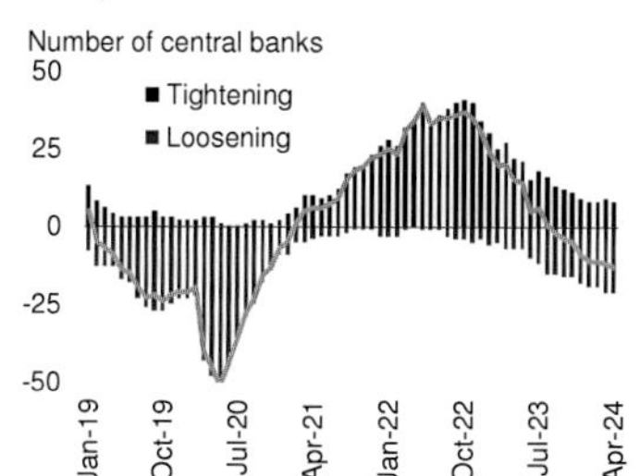

E. EMDE sovereign spreads by credit rating

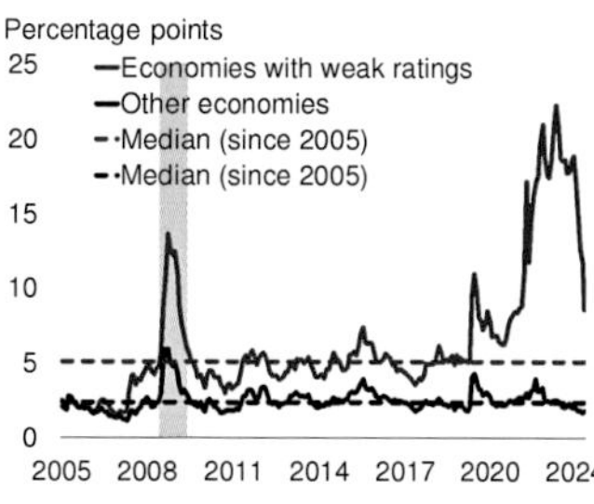

F. Share of EMDEs vulnerable to debt-related stress

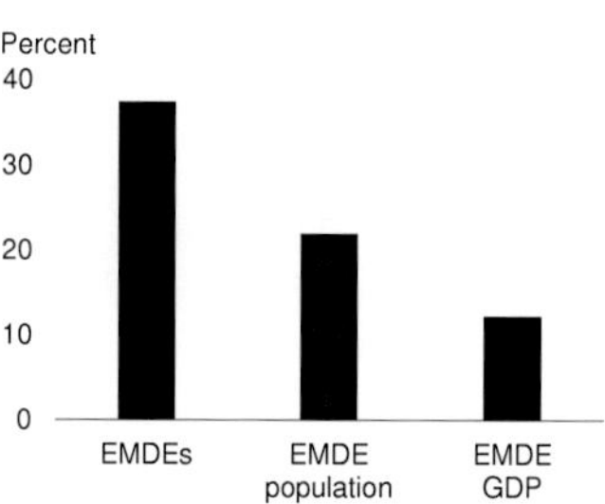

Sources: Barclays; Bloomberg; Federal Reserve Bank of St Louis; Fitch Ratings; Haver Analytics; Ice Data Indices; International Monetary Fund; J.P. Morgan; Moody's Analytics; MSCI (database); S&P 500 Index; UN World Population Prospects; World Bank.

Note: EMDEs = emerging market and developing economies.

A. Solid blue line represents the upper bound of the target range for the U.S. federal funds rate. Dotted lines represent vintages of market-based expectations for the upper bound of the policy rate range.

B. Lines depict the percentile rank of equity index valuations. Underlying valuation is based on the excess earnings yield, where lower (higher) excess yield implies higher (lower) valuation. Excess earnings yield is the cyclically adjusted earnings yield (inverse CAPE ratio) minus the 10-year inflation-protected U.S. Treasury yield. Last observation is April 2024.

C. Corporate credit spreads derived from indexes of option-adjusted high-yield corporate bonds. Last observation is May 29, 2024.

D. Bars indicate number of central banks raising (lowering) policy rates in the preceding three months. Yellow line indicates net number of central banks. Sample includes 58 EMDEs and excludes economies with strict currency pegs. Last observation is April 2024.

E. Median spreads for up to 22 weakly rated EMDEs and up to 49 other EMDEs. Weak ratings are defined as Caa+/CCC+ and below for long-term foreign currency debt. Shaded areas represent September 2008-August 2009 and January-December 2020.

F. Sample of vulnerable EMDEs includes those with weak credit ratings, and those judged by the International Monetary Fund and the World Bank to be in or at high risk of debt distress.

Major economies: Recent developments and outlook

Advanced economies

Growth in advanced economies slowed to 1.5 percent in 2023, with notable divergences. Growth in the United States strengthened to 2.5 percent last year, owing primarily to robust consumption, government spending, and significantly reduced imports of goods and services. Consumption was supported by continued spending out of savings accumulated during the pandemic and a healthy expansion of household balance sheets as equity prices gained rapidly last year. A substantial widening of the U.S. budget deficit in 2023 (fiscal year), to over 6 percent of GDP at the federal level, also played a role in boosting growth (CBO 2024a). In contrast, euro area growth slowed sharply last year, driven by weak consumption growth, reflecting the impact of high energy prices on household budgets.

Aggregate growth in advanced economies is projected to remain at 1.5 percent in 2024, with activity in key economies continuing to diverge. Weak activity in the euro area and Japan, in large part as a result of continued feeble domestic demand, will be accompanied by resilient growth in the United States. Next year, amid a projected slowdown in the United States, coupled with firming growth in the euro area, the contrast in growth performance across major economies is likely to become less stark.

The near-term outlook for monetary policy differs among advanced economies. The easing of monetary policy in the United States is expected to begin later than previously assumed—given resilient activity and above-target inflation. This lags the recent policy rate cut in the euro area, where the impacts of past supply shocks on inflation continue to fade. Meanwhile, fiscal policy is envisaged to tighten substantially in 2024 relative to 2023 for many advanced economies, exerting a drag on growth.

In the **United States**, growth is forecast to average 2.5 percent this year, and moderate to a below-trend rate of 1.8 percent in 2025. Relative to previous projections, growth in 2024 has been revised up by 0.9 percentage point, as data releases earlier this year surprised to the upside, particularly on the consumer spending side. The slowdown in 2025 is expected to be driven primarily by the cumulative effects of past monetary tightening and a contractionary fiscal stance. Elevated real borrowing rates are set to restrain household spending on durable goods and residential investment. In line with the recent softening in high-frequency indicators, broader consumer spending is expected to slow due to moderating growth in household income as labor market tightness recedes and savings diminish.

The boost to consumption growth from household wealth gains is likely to moderate owing to slowing increases in real estate net worth, which has historically had substantial effects on consumer spending (Carroll, Otsuka, and Slacalek 2011). Increases in house prices tapered off toward the end of 2023 and are expected to remain well below the strong pace seen over the past few years. As wealth gains slow, household income growth is also expected to ease sequentially throughout 2024, with the labor market continuing to soften and U.S. job openings declining (figure 1.7.A). Rising labor supply is expected to contribute to labor market rebalancing, including from continued robust net migration (figure 1.7.B). On the fiscal side, with a relatively stable or slightly lower deficit expected over the next few years, fiscal policy is not expected to be a significant driver of growth.

In 2026, growth is expected to remain at 1.8 percent, as a further slowdown in fiscal spending offsets a modest pickup in consumer spending and business investment. By the end of 2026, borrowing rates are expected to have declined substantially as inflation returns close to target.

In the **euro area**, growth slowed sharply in 2023, reflecting tight credit conditions, feeble exports, and elevated energy prices. Trade volumes declined in 2023 for the first time outside of an annual euro area contraction, in large part reflecting a loss of export competitiveness amid elevated energy prices. Growth appears to have bottomed out, however, though with key differences across sectors and member countries. Services activity suggests incipient improvement in early 2024, but this has been offset by weaker-than-expected industrial activity, especially in the manufacturing sector in Germany. Growth is forecast to firm only slightly in 2024, to 0.7 percent, supported by an ongoing recovery in real incomes but dampened by still-subdued investment and export growth. Consumer spending is expected to edge higher in 2024, as inflation declines and wages continue to rise, albeit at a more moderate pace (figure 1.7.C).

Growth is forecast to pick up in 2025, to 1.4 percent, as the recovery in export and investment growth gathers pace, with the latter benefiting from lower policy rates and the absorption of EU funds. In 2026, economic activity is projected to expand at a relatively stable pace of 1.3 percent, slightly above potential growth estimates as reforms under the European Union's NextGenerationEU plan start to bear fruit. In some large euro area members, national fiscal policy is expected to exert a drag on activity in the near term.

In **Japan**, growth is expected to decelerate to 0.7 percent in 2024, due to a feeble expansion in consumption and slowing exports amid normalizing auto production and stabilizing tourism demand. Output is projected to grow at an average rate of 1 percent in 2025 and 0.9 percent in 2026, on slight improvements in consumer spending and capital investment. The Bank of Japan discontinued major unconventional policy measures—yield curve control, negative interest rates, and some asset purchases—in March 2024, and raised the range for the short-term policy rate to 0-0.1 percent, while also signaling possible further monetary action if inflation risks rise, including in the context of rapid depreciation of the yen.

FIGURE 1.7 Major economies: Recent developments and outlook

U.S. labor market tightness has been receding, with the level of job openings declining since its mid-2022 peak. Rising labor supply, including that from robust net migration, is expected to continue to support the rebalancing in the U.S. labor market. Euro area consumer spending is expected to edge higher in 2024, partly on the back of continued wage growth. In China, overall investment growth remained tepid in early 2024, with solid infrastructure and manufacturing investment set against continued declines in real estate investment.

A. U.S. nonfarm payrolls and job openings

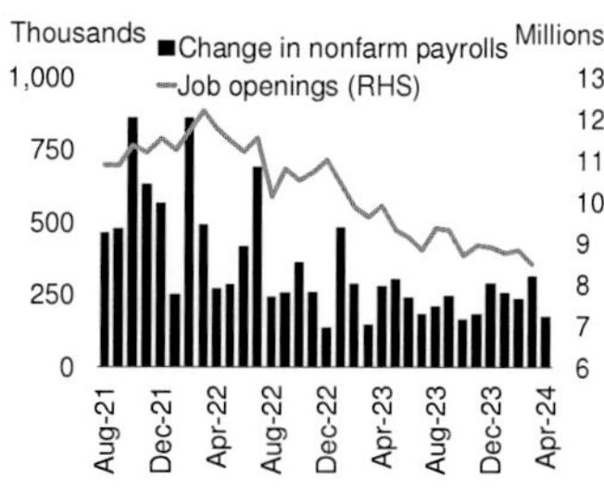

B. Population increase

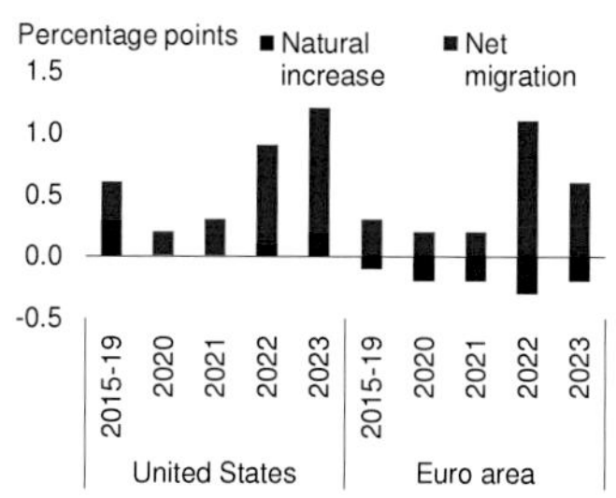

C. Wage growth

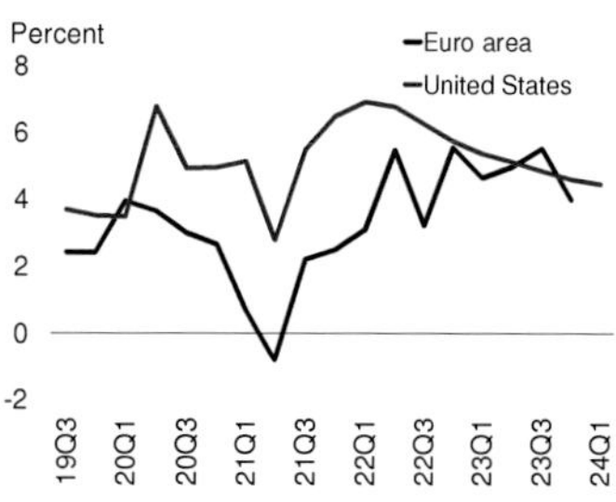

D. Fixed-asset investment growth in China

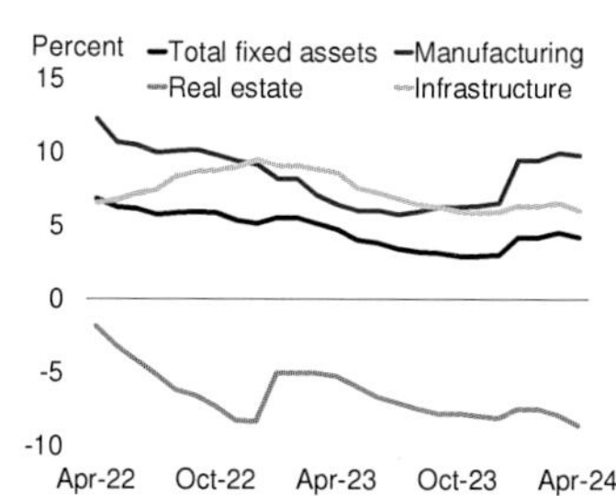

Sources: Congressional Budget Office (2024b); Eurostat; Federal Reserve Bank of St. Louis; Haver Analytics; National Bureau of Statistics of China; Organisation for Economic Co-operation and Development; World Bank.

A. Panel shows the level of total nonfarm job openings in millions, and the change in nonfarm payrolls in thousands. Last observation is April 2024 for unemployment and March 2024 for job openings.

B. Blue bars show the contribution to the annual change in population (in percentage points) from the natural increase (the difference between the number of births and deaths); red bars show the contribution from net migration, which is the difference between immigration and emigration. Statistics for the euro area for 2023 are based on Eurostat's baseline projections.

C. Solid lines show year-on-year growth in wages: nonsupervisory average hourly wages in the United States and private sector earnings in the euro area.

D. Year-on-year growth of year-to-date total fixed assets, manufacturing, real estate, and infrastructure investment. Last observation is April 2024.

China

Growth in China edged up in early 2024, supported by a positive contribution from net exports that offset softening domestic demand. Following weakness last year, exports and imports have both strengthened. Meanwhile, overall investment growth has remained tepid, with solid infrastructure and manufacturing investment set against declining real estate investment as the property sector downturn—now in its third year—continues (figure 1.7.D). Property prices and sales have fallen further, and property developers have experienced renewed financing pressures. Amid weak consumer confidence, domestic consumption has also remained subdued, with retail sales growth below pre-pandemic averages. Headline consumer prices have increased modestly this year, after declining late last year on the back of falling food prices, and core inflation has remained well below the target of about 3 percent. Producer prices have continued to decline, reflecting weak demand.

To bolster demand, additional spending measures have been announced—including for infrastructure projects—building on a raft of policies implemented late last year. In tandem, the People's Bank of China cut interest rates and the reserve requirement ratio. As property-related bank lending declined, the government established a scheme to facilitate liquidity provision to real estate developers to support the completion of viable property projects, as well as to help promote confidence. Further measures were also introduced aimed at boosting property demand, including removing the residential mortgage rate floor and lowering down payment requirements for borrowers.

With activity anticipated to soften in the second half of this year, growth is projected to slow to 4.8 percent in 2024, from 5.2 percent in 2023, as an expected uptick in goods exports and industrial activity supported by the global trade recovery is offset by weaker consumption. Compared with January projections, growth has been revised up 0.3 percentage point, reflecting stronger-than-expected activity in early 2024, particularly exports. Investment is envisaged to remain subdued. While government spending will continue to prop up infrastructure investment, local government financing pressures will constrain fiscal support. The property sector is assumed to stabilize only toward the end of the year. Although inflation is set to pick up this year as the drag from falling food prices fades, it is anticipated to remain well below target amid slowing consumption and weak demand pressures. Producer price pressures are also set to remain weak in the context of subdued activity and softening prices for commodities, particularly energy and metals.

Growth is projected to decline further in 2025 to 4.1 percent—0.2 percentage point lower than projected in January owing primarily to a weaker outlook for investment—and 4 percent in 2026, as slowing productivity growth and investment as well as mounting public and private debt weigh on activity. With the population falling for the second consecutive year in 2023, and amid a low and declining fertility rate, demographic headwinds are expected to intensify, dragging potential growth lower.

Emerging market and developing economies

EMDE growth is projected to edge down from 4.2 percent in 2023 to 4 percent in 2024 and then remain broadly stable over the forecast horizon. Decelerating activity in China is projected to be offset by firming growth in other EMDEs due to improvements in domestic demand and a recovery in trade. However, aggregate EMDE output is projected to remain on a path notably below its pre-pandemic trajectory, indicating sizable long-term scarring from the crises of the past four years. After a sharp slowdown last year, growth in LICs is projected to pick up over the forecast horizon, although to an appreciably lesser degree than previously expected.

Recent developments

After softening in the second half of 2023, activity in EMDEs generally stabilized in early 2024, with indicators of domestic demand, including retail sales and consumer confidence, firming somewhat (figures 1.8.A and 1.8.B). In early 2024, headline manufacturing and services sector PMIs broadly moved up, with a still greater improvement in headline manufacturing PMIs for EMDEs excluding China (figure 1.8.C). Economic conditions have nonetheless continued to diverge, with ongoing weakness among vulnerable EMDEs. Growth in countries with stronger credit ratings has so far outpaced growth in weaker-rated countries, including many grappling with high debt and financing costs, and in those facing acute challenges, such as elevated levels of domestic conflict and violence.

EMDE goods trade growth has shown signs of improvement, with the manufacturing component of new export orders PMIs returning to expansionary territory in early 2024, for the first time since mid-2023 (figure 1.8.D). In contrast, services exports decelerated in most EMDEs, reflecting an increasingly mature tourism recovery following the pandemic. However, countries that lifted pandemic-related restrictions later, mostly in East Asia and Pacific (EAP), continue to see a rebound in tourist flows.

FIGURE 1.8 Recent developments in emerging market and developing economies

Activity in EMDEs generally stabilized in early 2024, with consumer confidence and retail sales firming somewhat. Measures of headline manufacturing and services activity firmed across EMDEs, and leading indicators of new export orders pushed into expansionary territory, in line with an anticipated rebound in global trade.

A. Consumer confidence

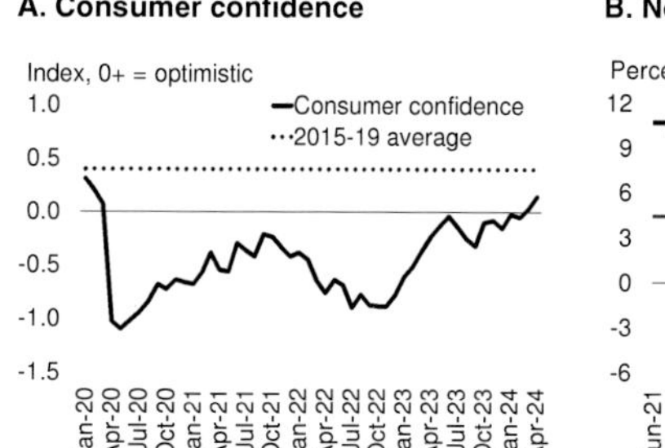

B. Nominal retail sales growth

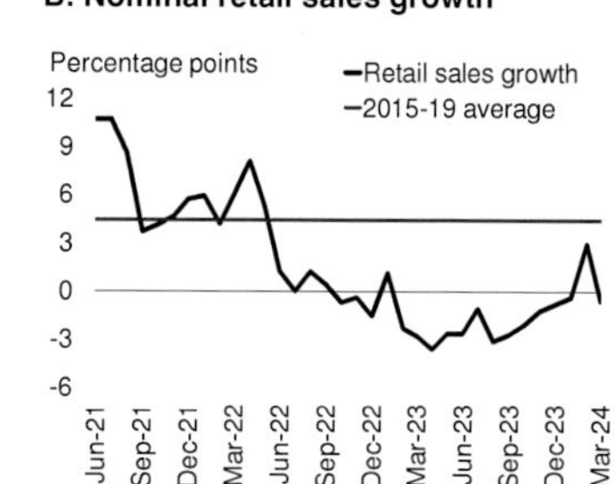

C. Headline PMIs: Manufacturing and services

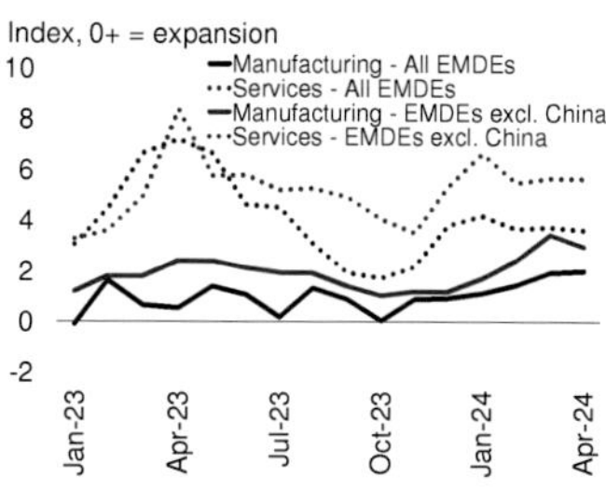

D. New export orders PMIs: Manufacturing

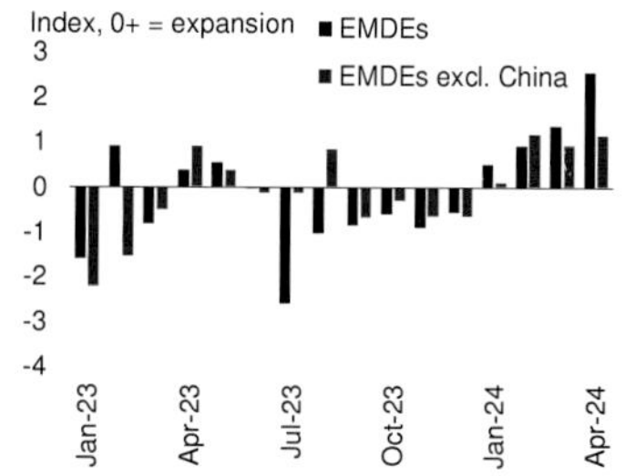

Sources: Haver Analytics; World Bank.

Note: EMDEs = emerging market and developing economies; PMI = purchasing managers' index.

A. Panel shows the standardized deviation of average consumer confidence from the 2015-19 average. Sample includes up to 12 EMDEs. Last observation is April 2024

B. Panel shows the percentage-point deviation of nominal monthly retail sales growth from pre-pandemic averages. Sample includes 15 EMDEs. Last observation is March 2024.

C. Panel shows the weighted average of a sample that includes 21 EMDEs. Readings above (below) zero indicate expansion (contraction). Monthly readings are centered on 50, the expansionary threshold. Last observation is April 2024.

D. Panel shows the weighted average of a sample that includes 21 EMDEs. Readings above (below) zero indicate expansion (contraction). Monthly readings are centered on 50, the expansionary threshold. Last observation is April 2024.

Activity in commodity exporters has continued to face headwinds in early 2024, amid sluggish global industrial production. In oil exporters, this has been somewhat offset by robust foreign direct investment (FDI) in the extractives sector. Still, activity, fiscal revenue, and export earnings in oil exporters have been dampened by subdued global demand—giving rise to OPEC+ oil production cuts—as well as by infrastructure constraints related to aging oil fields in some cases.

Activity in commodity importers excluding China has been robust. This mostly reflects resilience in some large economies, notably India, owing to continued strength in domestic demand. Growth has been more muted in other commodity importers so far this year. After goods export volumes contracted in 2023, the rebound seen in early 2024 has been somewhat limited, especially in economies with large export-oriented manufacturing sectors, partly owing to lukewarm external demand from major trading partners. Furthermore, elevated prices for food and energy remain a constraint on disposable incomes, dampening consumption growth.

Growth in LICs decelerated by 1.2 percentage points to 3.8 percent in 2023 from a year earlier, mainly reflecting violent conflict in some countries. Pervasive violence and political instability exacerbated challenging economic and humanitarian situations, particularly in the Sahel region of Africa and its adjacent countries. At the same time, activity in some major LICs continued to expand at a solid pace—such as in the Democratic Republic of Congo, on account of strong mining activity, and in Ethiopia, reflecting good harvests and steady services sector growth. Consumer price inflation in LICs has, on average, continued to decline in early 2024, providing some respite for consumption growth. Notably, food price inflation has slowed in many LICs. Food insecurity nonetheless remains elevated, with an estimated 127 million people in LICs suffering from food crisis or worse conditions in 2024 (FSIN and GNAFC 2024).

EMDE outlook

Aggregate growth in EMDEs is forecast to edge down from 4.2 percent in 2023 to 4 percent in 2024 and remain broadly stable over 2025-26, near estimates of EMDE potential growth for the 2020s. However, these aggregates mask notable differences in regional trends, with the expected pace of growth falling short of the 2010-19 average in EAP, ECA, and South Asia (SAR), but

FIGURE 1.9 Outlook in emerging market and developing economies

While domestic demand growth is expected to moderate in some large EMDEs due to idiosyncratic factors, it is projected to pick up in many other economies. In many EMDEs, trade growth is also expected to firm over the forecast horizon but would still fall short of pre-pandemic averages in some cases. Relatively supportive commodity prices are anticipated to lift growth among commodity exporters. Despite a cyclical upswing in growth in EMDEs excluding China over 2025-26, output is expected to remain noticeably below its pre-pandemic trend, suggesting significant economic scarring.

A. Domestic and external demand, by country group

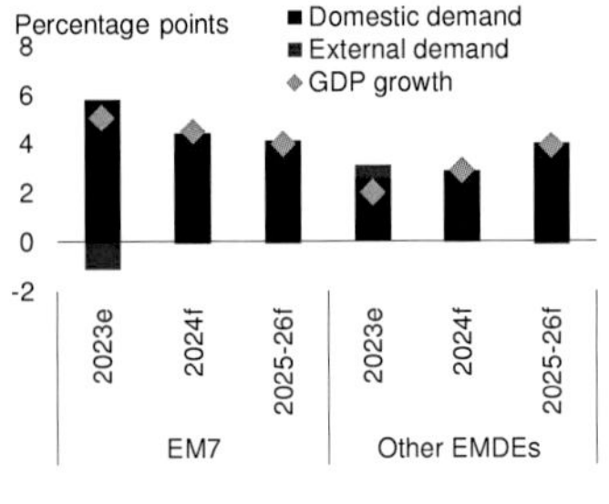

B. Trade growth, by country group

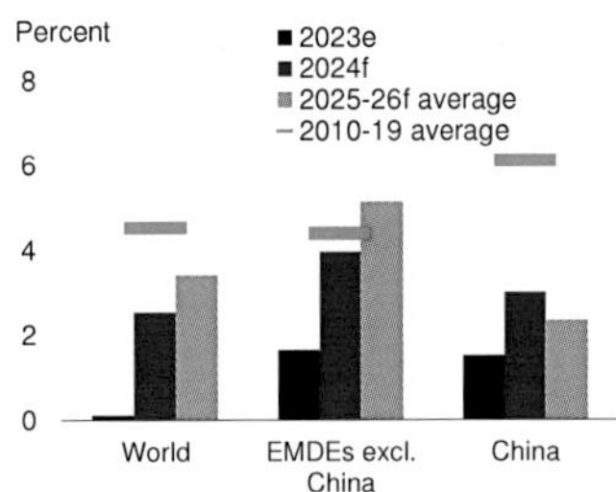

C. Growth and commodity prices in commodity exporters, deviation from 2010-19 averages

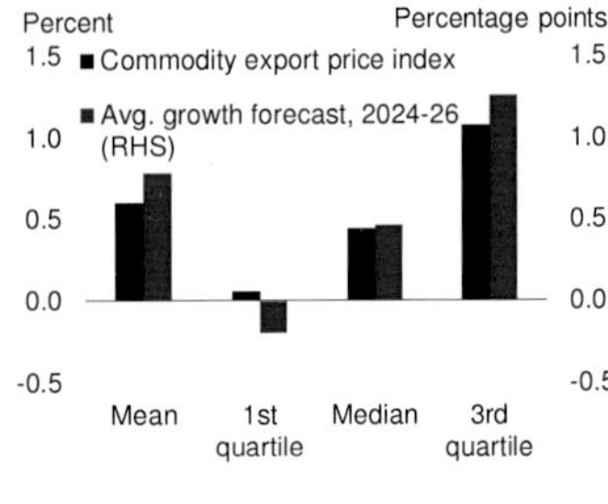

D. Output in EMDEs excluding China

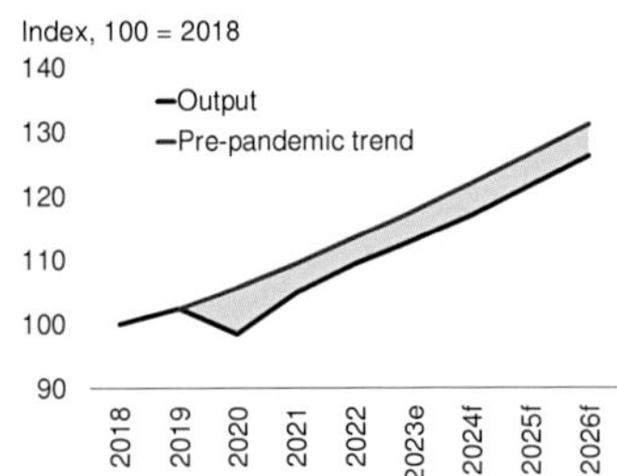

Sources: International Monetary Fund; World Bank.

Note: e = estimate; f = forecast; EMDEs = emerging market and developing economies; EM7 = Brazil, China, India, Indonesia, Mexico, the Russian Federation, and Türkiye. GDP aggregates calculated using real U.S. dollar GDP weights at average 2010-19 prices and market exchange rates.

A. Projected contribution to growth of domestic demand and net exports, and GDP growth for EM7 and Other EMDEs (EMDEs excluding the EM7). The discrepancy between GDP and sum of domestic demand and external demand (net exports) is explained by inventories and statistical residuals.

B. Forecast total trade growth 2024-26 compared to the 2010-19 average for selected country groups. Trade is measured as the average of import and export volumes.

C. Red bars show the deviation of projected GDP growth (averaged over 2024-26) in commodity exporters from their 2010-19 averages. Blue bars show the deviation of country-specific 2023 commodity export price indexes from their 2010-19 averages for these countries.

D. Panel shows the level of GDP for EMDEs excluding China compared to their pre-pandemic trends through 2026 (2018 = 100). For 2023 and beyond, the January 2020 baseline is extended using projected growth for 2022.

returning close to pre-pandemic averages in other regions over 2025-26, partly owing to still-supportive commodity prices (box 1.1). Excluding China, EMDE growth is projected to inch up to a still subdued pace of 3.5 percent this year, before firming to about 3.9 percent in 2025-26, reflecting a cyclical upswing as monetary policy becomes less restrictive and demand from advanced economies gathers pace.

In 2024, the contribution to growth from domestic demand in EMDEs is expected to soften relative to 2023, before firming over 2025-26. The weaker contribution from domestic demand this year, however, largely reflects idiosyncratic developments in some of the seven largest EMDEs (EM7), following strong performance in 2023 (chapter 2).[1] In most of these economies, consumption growth is anticipated to decelerate in 2024, as the boost from idiosyncratic factors fades, and then stabilize over 2025-26. In contrast, in other EMDEs, domestic demand is expected to gather pace over the forecast horizon (figure 1.9.A). Among these economies, private consumption is envisaged to rebound in 2024 and further strengthen over 2025-26, with declining inflation and interest rates supporting real household incomes and consumer confidence. The rebound in consumption is expected to be broad-based across most regions.

The profile of investment is projected to broadly mirror that of private consumption, with varying trends between the largest EMDEs and others. For the EM7 as a whole, investment growth is expected to decelerate this year, from 2023, and then proceed at a moderate rate over 2025-26. Notably, investment in China is anticipated to remain tepid, although this is envisaged to have a somewhat limited impact on other EMDEs, as declining commodity demand for real estate in China is counterbalanced by commodity-intensive infrastructure investments. Outside the largest economies, EMDE investment is expected to rebound in 2024, and accelerate further in 2025-26, in line with declining interest rates, improving business confidence, and firming manufacturing activity.

Across EMDEs, trade growth is expected to pick up in 2024, but nonetheless remain below pre-pandemic averages, particularly for some large economies, including China. Trade growth is then projected to strengthen further in many EMDEs in 2025-26, in line with increasing external

[1] The EM7 comprises Brazil, China, India, Indonesia, Mexico, Russia, and Türkiye. These economies are grouped together for analytical purposes on account of their large share of global output.

BOX 1.1 Regional perspectives: Outlook and risks

Although the economic outlook differs among emerging market and developing economy regions, it remains challenging for all, with growth projected to soften in most of them in 2024. The slowdown this year in East Asia and Pacific (EAP) mainly reflects moderating growth in China. Growth in Europe and Central Asia (ECA), Latin America and the Caribbean (LAC), and South Asia (SAR) is also set to decelerate as activity in their largest economies slows down. Growth is expected to pick up this year in the Middle East and North Africa (MNA) and Sub-Saharan Africa (SSA), albeit less robustly than previously forecast. In 2025, growth is projected to weaken further in EAP and ECA, and firm or remain stable in other regions. While somewhat more balanced than in January, risks to the outlook remain tilted to the downside for all regions, owing to the possibilities of intensified conflict and geopolitical tensions and further trade fragmentation. Tighter-than-expected global financial conditions and unexpected fiscal consolidations could also weigh on growth. Weaker-than-expected growth in China and natural disasters—including those associated with climate change—pose additional downside risks. On the upside, global inflation could moderate more quickly than assumed, enabling faster monetary policy easing, and growth in the United States could be stronger than expected.

Introduction

Emerging market and developing economy (EMDE) regions mostly face moderating growth prospects this year. Although inflation has generally declined from recent peaks and monetary policy has been easing in all EMDE regions, reductions in central bank policy rates have generally been limited, partly reflecting continued tight monetary policies in major advanced economies. Meanwhile, fiscal policy space has narrowed in all regions amid elevated public debt and increased debt-servicing costs. A pickup in global trade, which came to a standstill last year, is expected to support demand and economic activity in all EMDE regions; however, global trade growth is projected to remain below pre-pandemic averages. Despite the increase in oil prices earlier this year, overall, commodity prices are envisaged to ease slightly, providing a modest tailwind to growth in commodity-importing regions.

Next year, activity is anticipated to accelerate in some regions. However, growth will remain below pre-pandemic averages in East Asia and Pacific (EAP), Europe and Central Asia (ECA), and South Asia (SAR). While some easing in global financial conditions has made risks to the baseline growth projections more balanced since January, they remain tilted to the downside. With the outbreak of conflict in the Middle East and Russia's invasion of Ukraine, further intensification of armed conflicts and escalation of geopolitical tensions present a major downside risk to all EMDE regions.

Note: This box was prepared by Samuel Hill.

In this context, this box considers two questions:

- What are the cross-regional differences in the outlook for growth?
- What are the key risks to the outlook for EMDE regions?

Outlook

Although the economic outlook differs among the EMDE regions, it remains challenging for all. In 2024, growth is projected to slow in most regions, as economic activity in the largest economies—and key growth engines—in each region decelerates (figure B1.1.1.A). In EAP, slower growth primarily reflects weakening activity in China, where consumption growth is expected to slow amid subdued confidence. Meanwhile, in SAR, growth is set to ease in India as rapid investment growth cools. In ECA, growth in both the Russian Federation and Türkiye is expected to slow, in part reflecting the lagged effects of monetary policy tightening on consumption. In Latin America and the Caribbean (LAC), amid structural challenges, growth will ease across the largest economies in part reflecting tight macroeconomic policies.

Growth in Sub-Saharan Africa (SSA) is projected to accelerate this year, supported by a pick up in domestic demand, following a lackluster 2023. However, ongoing political instability and conflicts are expected to continue hindering economic activity in the region. In the Middle East and North Africa (MNA), the pickup in growth this year is mainly due to strengthening oil production and exports among oil-exporting economies, which will offset protracted weakness elsewhere. Despite an anticipated deceleration this year, SAR—the region with the highest potential

BOX 1.1 Regional perspectives: Outlook and risks (*continued*)

FIGURE B1.1.1 Regional outlooks

Growth is projected to slow in most EMDE regions this year, reflecting factors such as the adverse consequences of conflict and the drag from tight macroeconomic policies. Projected growth in 2024 has been revised downward in LAC, owing to tighter-than-expected macroeconomic policies, and in MNA, due to oil production cuts. In contrast, growth has been revised upward in EAP, reflecting surprisingly strong activity in China in early 2024, and in ECA and SAR, partly due to unexpectedly resilient domestic demand. Although official interest rates seem to have peaked across EMDE regions, substantial cuts have not yet been made.

A. Output growth

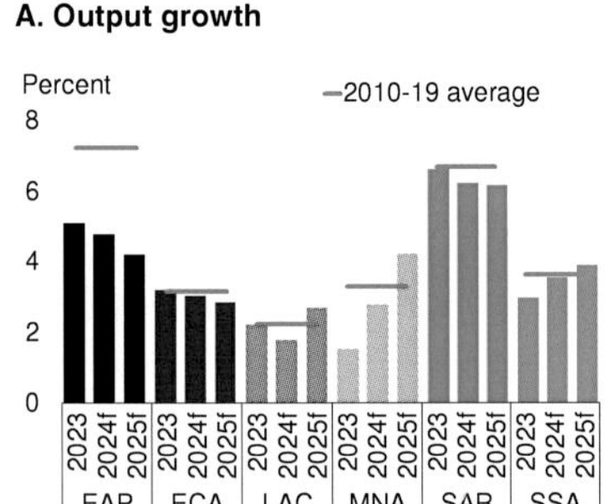

B. Growth forecast revisions

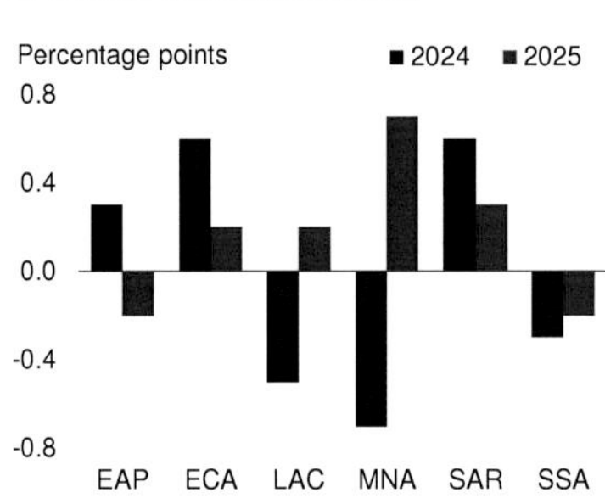

C. Official interest rates

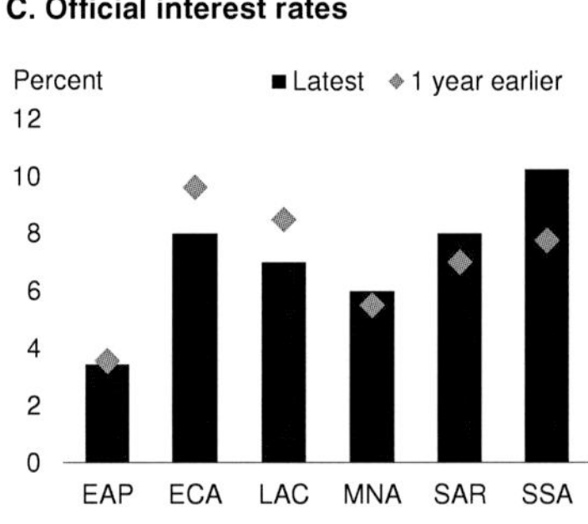

Sources: Haver Analytics; World Bank.

Note: f = forecast; EAP = East Asia and Pacific; ECA = Europe and Central Asia; EMDEs = emerging market and developing economies; LAC = Latin America and the Caribbean; MNA = Middle East and North Africa; SAR = South Asia; SSA = Sub-Saharan Africa.

A. Aggregate growth rates are calculated using GDP weights at average 2000-19 prices and market exchange rates. "2010-19" refers to the period averages of regional growth rates. Data for 2024 and 2025 are World Bank forecasts.

B. Revisions reflect differences in forecasts presented in the January 2024 edition of the *Global Economic Prospects* report. Data for 2024 and 2025 are World Bank forecasts.

C. Bars show the regional median of official policy interest rates. Diamonds show the regional median 12 months earlier. Sample includes 73 EMDEs (10 in EAP, 18 in ECA, 15 in LAC, 10 in MNA, 5 in SAR, and 15 in SSA). Last observation is April 2024.

growth rate—is projected to remain the fastest-growing region over the forecast horizon (Kose and Ohnsorge 2023).

Growth projections for 2024 have been revised down substantially since January in LAC, reflecting in part a sharp fiscal consolidation in Argentina, as authorities are seeking to address the country's significant economic challenges, and in MNA, owing to adverse effects of the conflict in the Middle East and an extension of oil production cuts (figure B1.1.1.B). Projected growth this year has also been downgraded for SSA, largely reflecting the adverse effects of a recent increase in political instability and conflict. In contrast, projected growth this year for EAP has been revised up, owing to surprisingly strong recent activity in China. Projected growth this year has also been revised up for ECA, largely due to a more-supportive-than-expected fiscal policy stance in some countries, and for SAR, reflecting surprisingly resilient activity around the turn of the year.

Following a substantial decline last year, headline inflation in most EMDE regions continued to moderate toward central bank targets in early 2024 in year-on-year terms, albeit at a slower pace. However, in some large economies in EAP and SSA, inflation ticked up. Core inflation also remained elevated in most regions. Inflation is generally expected to decline across EMDE regions this year as demand pressures ease and commodity prices soften slightly. However, inflation will remain elevated in some countries, particularly in SAR and SSA, reflecting a combination of adverse food supply shocks—partly due to drought—and currency depreciations.

All EMDE regions are anticipated to see some benefits from this year's projected pickup in global trade, including a rebound in goods trade. With the global tourism recovery largely complete, the tailwinds from stronger services exports have faded in most regions. However, particularly in EAP—where the tourism recovery has lagged because of a slow revival in tourism from some countries, notably China—increasing inbound tourism will provide some support to growth. An anticipated softening in overall commodity prices will weigh on exports and activity in key commodity-exporting regions, notably ECA, LAC, MNA, and SSA.

BOX 1.1 Regional perspectives: Outlook and risks (*continued*)

FIGURE B1.1.2 Regional risks

Risks to the baseline projections remain tilted to the downside for all EMDE regions. These include intensified armed conflict, particularly in ECA and MNA, and an escalation in geopolitical tensions that could prompt further trade policy restrictions and thwart the projected pickup in global trade. Slower-than-expected growth in China could also weaken demand, particularly for metal exports. Moreover, tighter global financial conditions than anticipated could add to borrowing costs—particularly in regions with high levels of external debt—and add to fiscal pressures, which would further weaken demand and growth.

A. Conflict

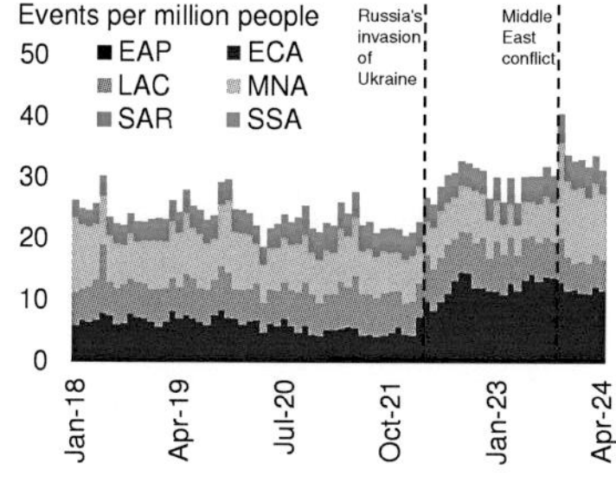

B. Export growth in 2023

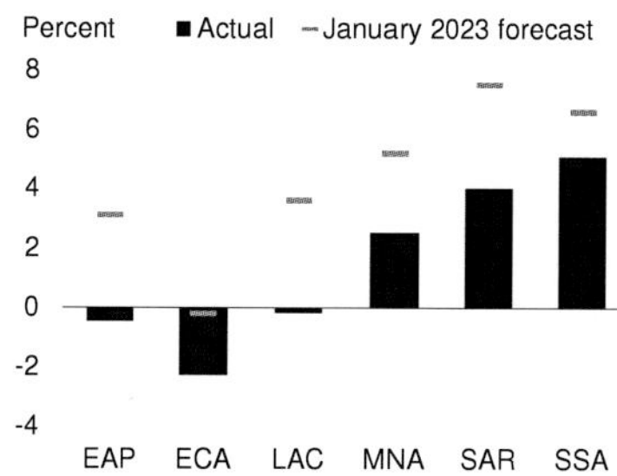

C. Correlation between regional GDP growth and world trade growth

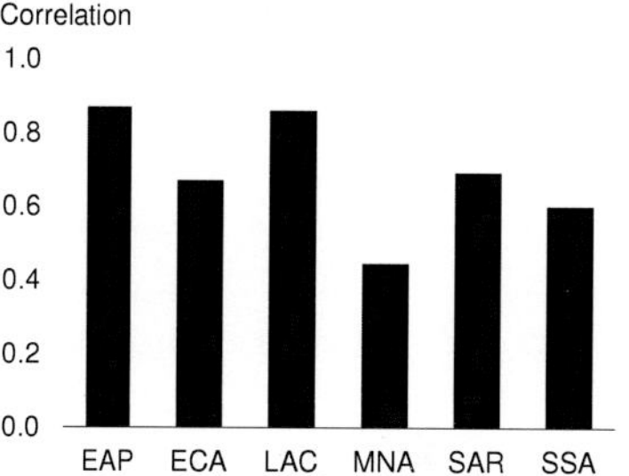

D. Share of metals in exports

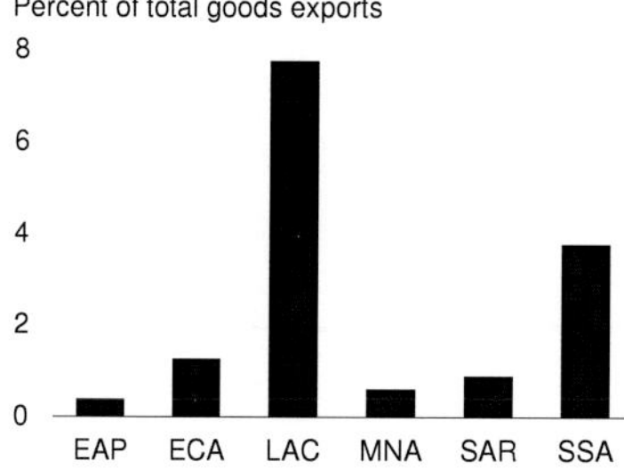

E. External debt

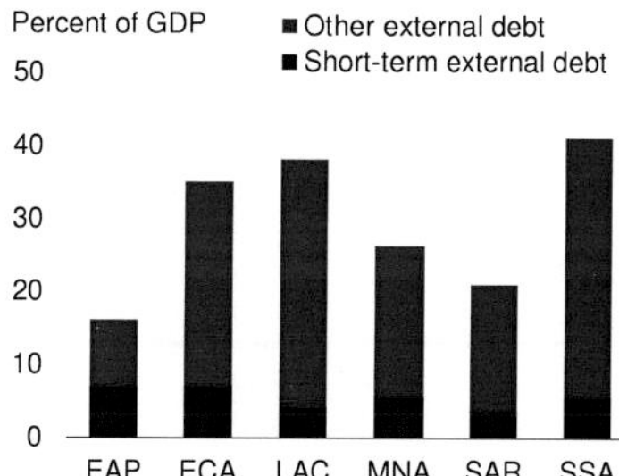

F. Public debt-servicing costs

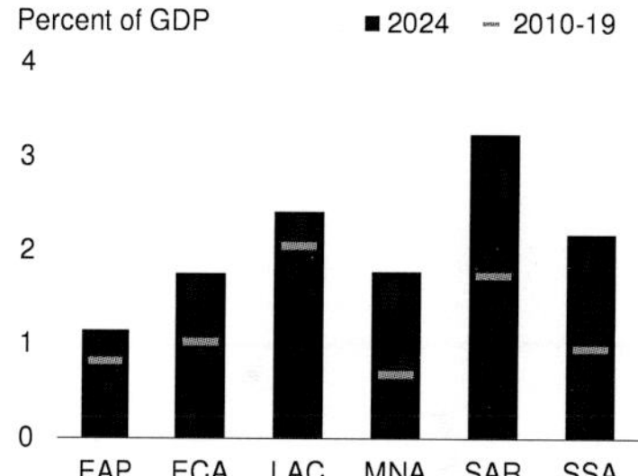

Sources: ACLED (database); International Debt Statistics (database); International Monetary Fund; UN Comtrade (database); World Bank.

Note: EAP = East Asia and Pacific; ECA = Europe and Central Asia; LAC = Latin America and the Caribbean; MNA = Middle East and North Africa; SAR = South Asia; SSA = Sub-Saharan Africa.

A. Stacked bars show the number of reported conflict events per million people in each of the six EMDE regions. Conflict events include battles, explosions, violence against civilians, riots, and protests. The date of Russia's invasion of Ukraine is February 24, 2022. The date of the Middle East conflict is October 7, 2023. Last observation is April 2024.

B. "January 2023 forecast" refers to the forecast for exports of goods and services in 2023, presented in the January 2023 edition of the *Global Economic Prospects* report.

C. Pairwise correlation of annual real GDP growth in each region and real world trade growth between 2010 and 2019.

D. Aggregates are GDP-weighted averages of exports of metals as a percent of total goods export, between 2018 and 2022.

E. GDP-weighted average of gross debt held by nonresidents as a share of GDP. Short-term external debt is external debt maturing in less than one year. Last observation is 2022.

F. Aggregates are the regional median of the difference between general government net lending/borrowing and general government primary net lending/borrowing as a percent of GDP. Lines show the regional median of the simple country average between 2010 and 2019. Data for 2024 are IMF forecasts.

In most regions, activity will be supported by solid consumption growth, bolstered by moderating inflation that will help lift real incomes. Investment is also projected to strengthen in some regions, supported by monetary policy easing. In SAR, robust investment growth also reflects strong public investment in India, which is anticipated to crowd-in private investment. However, investment growth this year is expected to cool in ECA, following exceptionally strong growth last year, and to remain subdued in EAP, weighed down by weakness in China's property sector.

Monetary policy easing is anticipated to support demand, particularly in ECA and LAC—where in many cases official interest rates began to be cut last year, ahead of other regions—and to a lesser extent in EAP (figure B1.1.1.C). However, across all regions, central banks remain wary of a resurgence in inflation

BOX 1.1 Regional perspectives: Outlook and risks (*continued*)

and are expected to remain cautious in easing monetary policy. Continuing tight monetary policies in key advanced economies, notably the euro area and the United States, also restrict their room for maneuver. Although the stance of fiscal policy will remain broadly accommodative in MNA and neutral in EAP and ECA, to varying degrees, fiscal consolidation amid elevated debt levels will drag on activity in LAC, SAR, and SSA.

Next year, growth is projected to pick up in some regions, as the global trade recovery strengthens further and monetary policy easing provides more support for demand, including investment. However, growth is projected to edge down further in EAP, as mounting structural headwinds slow activity in China, and in ECA. In 2026, growth is anticipated to edge up in SSA, but mostly soften in other EMDE regions. Taken together, the forecasts imply limited catch-up toward advanced-economy per-capita GDP levels over the forecast horizon—particularly in ECA, LAC, and MNA. In SSA, the poorest region, GDP per capita is expected to fall further behind, hobbled by the interrelated challenges of pervasive conflict, climate change, and widespread food insecurity (Bedasa and Deksisa 2024).

Risks

Although risks to the outlook have become somewhat more balanced for all EMDE regions since January, they remain tilted to the downside. An escalation of conflict or geopolitical tensions, or further trade fragmentation could have widespread adverse repercussions. To varying degress, weaker-than-expected growth in China could drag on growth in all regions, as could unexpectedly tighter global financial conditions. More frequent and severe climate-change-related natural disasters pose a further downside risk. In contrast, a faster decline in global inflation, enabling a more rapid global monetary easing, and faster-than-expected growth in the United States, present upside risks to EMDE regions.

Against the backdrop of conflict in the Middle East and Russia's invasion of Ukraine, intensification of armed conflict or an escalation in geopolitical tensions present notable downside risks to all EMDE regions (figure B1.1.2.A). Regions in which conflicts are concentrated—ECA MNA, and SSA—are most vulnerable to adverse direct impacts on activity, including disruptions to commercial activity and damage to physical capital (World Bank 2024a). However, the repercussions of intensified conflict could affect all regions. Worsening conflict could disrupt global oil supply, leading to higher energy prices and inflation, and weaker growth, particularly in regions dependent on imported energy, notably EAP and SAR (World Bank 2024b). As underscored by disruptions to agricultural production in Ukraine and its exports, conflict can also damage global food security (World Bank 2024c). Escalating conflict could also dent global business and consumer sentiment, and increase risk aversion, weighing on demand and growth.

Further increases in protectionism—following the recent proliferation of trade restrictions and industrial policy measures—present an important downside risk to growth in all regions. Restrictive trade policies, including both those targetting and those instigated by EMDEs, add to production costs and disrupt supply chains. The large number of elections taking place around the world this year—including in ECA and SSA, as well as in advanced economies—heightens the possibility of further protectionist measures. These could sow additional uncertainty and weigh on the anticipated global trade recovery this year. Export growth in every EMDE region fell short of expectations last year and could again surprise on the downside, with adverse implications for broader activity (figure B1.1.2.B). Regions whose economies are more integrated into global value chains and where growth is more synchronized with global trade, notably EAP and LAC, are especially vulnerable to protectionist measures (figure B1.1.2.C).

Weaker-than-expected growth in China would also reduce demand and growth globally, including across EMDE regions. Heightened policy uncertainty in China could weigh on investment, while protracted weak consumer sentiment could prolong the downturn in its resource-intensive property sector. The consequences would be particularly severe for regions more reliant on exports to China, particularly of metals, including LAC and SSA (figure B1.1.2.D). EAP economies with extensive trade linkages to China are also vulnerable (Copestake et al. 2023).

An unexpected tightening of global financial conditions could weigh on investment and growth in all regions.

BOX 1.1 Regional perspectives: Outlook and risks (*continued*)

This could be triggered by a range of factors, including a step-up in geopolitical tensions that may cause investor risk appetite to wane. Financial conditions could also tighten if disinflation in major advanced economies is slower than expected, resulting in higher-for-longer monetary policy rates. Higher global borrowing costs would weigh on investment and increase the risk of financial stress, particularly in regions with large stocks of external debt with shorter maturities—notably ECA, LAC, MNA, and SSA (figure B1.1.2.E). Against a backdrop of mounting public debt—notably in SAR and some MNA oil-importing countries, and to a lesser extent LAC—higher borrowing costs would also add to fiscal pressures. Debt-servicing costs have increased in all regions since the pandemic, and there is upward pressure on other spending, including outlays necessary to meet the Sustainable Development Goals—especially in SSA (figure B1.1.2.F; Aggarwal et al. 2024). Particularly where governments already face fiscal pressures, notably in some countries in LAC, MNA, SAR, and SSA, and to a lesser extent EAP and ECA, higher borrowing costs could force a sudden pivot to fiscal consolidation, significantly reducing demand.

Severe natural disasters, including those related to climate change, could weaken growth in all EMDE regions. Disruptive weather associated with El Niño and La Niña conditions could reduce agricultural production, particularly in EAP, LAC, SAR, and SSA. This would put upward pressure on food prices and inflation, sapping consumption. Small states, particularly in EAP and LAC, are especially vulnerable to more frequent destructive storms that can impose large human and economic costs, and severely weaken fiscal positions.

Conversely, the fact that global inflation declined substantially last year suggests the possibility that further progress with disinflation could be faster than expected, presenting an upside risk to the baseline projections for all regions. Lower inflation would enable easier than assumed monetary policy in major advanced economies, helping lift global sentiment and reduce borrowing costs, boosting demand in all regions. In addition, growth in the United States may exceed expectations, supported by higher labor force participation or immigration, presenting further upside potential to growth in EMDE regions. Economies in EAP and LAC with high export exposure to the United States—especially manufacturing- and tourism-dependent economies—stand to gain the most. Commodity-exporting regions, notably MNA, could also benefit from higher commodity prices resulting from stronger U.S. consumer and business demand.

demand and accelerating manufacturing activity (figure 1.9.B). Over the forecast horizon, net exports are anticipated to generate only a small drag on growth, as the pick-up in import growth is partially offset by improving exports alongside the recovery in global trade. The trade recovery should also support employment and investment in EMDEs.

Fiscal policy is envisaged to exert a modest drag on growth in most EMDEs over the forecast horizon. Fiscal consolidation is anticipated to proceed at a steady pace in EMDEs excluding China over 2024-26, reflecting governments' efforts to phase out support measures. However, growing net interest costs are expected to partially offset efforts to reduce expenditures.

Growth in commodity exporters is projected to edge up in 2024 to 2.8 percent, then strengthen to 3.3 percent on average over 2025-26. In 2024, OPEC+ production cuts will weigh on growth in some energy exporters, particularly in MNA. Thereafter, persistently elevated export prices should encourage expanded commodity production and support investment growth (figure 1.9.C). In commodity importers excluding China, growth is projected to ease slightly to 4.4 percent and then gather pace to an average of 4.7 percent in 2025-26. This acceleration should be sustained by robust consumption and investment growth in some large EMDEs, particularly India. In 2025-26, commodity importers excluding China are set to grow faster than China for two consecutive years for the first time in decades.

Growth is envisaged to remain weak in EMDEs with low credit ratings, which account for roughly one-fourth of rated economies. These countries continue to experience outsized negative effects from elevated global interest rates, which have exposed underlying vulnerabilities. For many of these economies, capital market access remains highly constrained amid domestic financial volatility, dampening consumer and business confidence and limiting the scope for governments to support activity.

Growth prospects have continued to deteriorate in many of the most vulnerable economies, contrasting with EMDEs in aggregate (Chrimes et al. 2024). Growth forecasts for 2024 have been downgraded in more than 75 percent of LICs and about two-thirds of FCS since January, compared to just under two-fifths of other EMDEs. The weakening outlooks of many vulnerable countries reflect significant domestic strains, including limited access to financing, highly constrained fiscal space amid elevated debt levels, and increases in conflict and violence.

The recovery of EMDEs from the shocks over the past four years is set to remain limited and uneven. The level of EMDE output is anticipated to remain below its pre-pandemic trajectory, indicating notable economic scarring; this is true even after excluding China, which is facing a structural slowdown (figure 1.9.D). Meanwhile, trade—a key driver of long-term EMDE growth—is set to be exacerbated by ongoing geopolitical tensions, trade fragmentation, and persistent trade policy uncertainty.

LICs outlook

Growth in LICs is projected to recover from a subdued 3.8 percent in 2023 to 5 percent this year and increase further to an average of 5.4 percent over 2025-26 (box 1.2). The pickup over the forecast horizon is underpinned by a moderate recovery in commodity-exporting LICs, where commodity prices remain broadly supportive of expanded production, as well as some stabilization in fragile and conflict-afflicted LICs.

Although growth is anticipated to strengthen in LICs, it will remain insufficient to raise output back to pre-pandemic trends. Moreover, the recovery is projected to be notably slower over the next two years than envisioned in January. This downward revision to growth mainly reflects slower improvements than anticipated in some fragile economies—particularly in the Sahel region of Africa following a surge in conflict last year. The revisions are among the largest for Niger and Sudan, where domestic strife has continued to hamper activity. Even so, the lifting of sanctions on Niger is expected to buoy activity there this year, with growth moderating thereafter. In Sudan, output is now projected to contract at a much sharper pace than anticipated in January amid ongoing violent conflict, which has paralyzed production, damaged infrastructure, and displaced a large portion of the population.

Beyond these specific cases, many LICs will continue to face daunting challenges, with projected growth insufficient to enable significant progress in reducing poverty. Elevated levels of violence and extreme weather events continue to displace people, disrupt food supplies, and exacerbate poverty. In addition, most LICs face difficult policy trade-offs as policy space, including to support the poor, has narrowed considerably. This situation is aggravated by elevated debt-service costs and slow progress in debt restructuring. Access to new external financing remains highly constrained, especially among the half of LICs already judged to be in, or at high risk of, debt distress.

Per capita income growth

The multiple shocks of the past four years have impeded income catch-up and poverty reduction in EMDEs. EMDE GDP per capita growth is projected to fall from 3.2 percent in 2023 to 3 percent in 2024 and remain near that pace over 2025-26—well below the 2010-19 average of 3.8 percent. Although about half of EMDEs are expected to see per capita GDP growth pick up this year and next, this follows a lengthy period of stagnation in living standards owing to an initial feeble recovery from the 2020 global recession and the sharp rise in the cost of living. Indeed, one in four EMDEs is expected to remain poorer in 2024 than on the eve of the pandemic. This includes

BOX 1.2 Recent developments and outlook for low-income countries

After slowing to 3.8 percent in 2023, growth in low-income countries (LICs) is projected to recover to 5 percent in 2024 and improve further to an average of 5.4 percent in 2025-26. Nevertheless, these figures represent substantial downward revisions from January projections, primarily due to an ongoing high level of conflict across LICs and a consequent delay in improvements in some heavily conflict-affected LICs. Gross domestic product (GDP) per capita growth in 2024-25 is projected to be less than half the rate of GDP growth. This means that improvements in average living standards are expected to be limited and the number of people struggling with extreme poverty and food insecurity will remain high. Public debt burdens and their servicing costs have risen, while access to financing has become more challenging for many LICs. Economic activity has also been disrupted by extreme weather events in some LICs. Against this backdrop, risks to the LICs outlook remain tilted to the downside. They include intensifying insecurity and violent conflict, weaker growth in China, increased debt distress, and more frequent or more intense extreme weather events.

Introduction

Growth in LICs is expected to rise from a subdued 3.8 percent in 2023 to 5 percent in 2024. Last year's tepid growth mainly reflected increased political instability and violent conflict in some LICs—especially Niger and Sudan—and sluggish performances in some metal-exporting LICs that faced feeble external demand and lower global metals prices. Projected growth in 2024 has been downgraded by 0.5 percentage point since January, with downward revisions for about three-quarters of LICs. An exception is Ethiopia—the largest LIC economy—where peacebuilding continues to yield dividends, and steady growth of 7 percent a year is projected over 2024-26.

Many LICs continue to struggle with persistent vulnerabilities and fragility, especially in the Sahel region of Africa, where the incidence of violent events has increased sharply in the past year (figure B1.2.1.A). Elevated violence and extreme weather events have continued to displace people, disrupt food supplies, and exacerbate poverty (figure B1.2.1.B). Many LICs face difficult policy trade-offs. The policy space to support the poor has narrowed or been depleted in many countries, while high financing needs and limited access to new funding continue to endanger debt sustainability.

Multiple downside risks cloud growth prospects among LICs, including an escalation of the conflict in the Middle East, further increases in local political instability and violent conflict, a sharper-than-expected economic slowdown in China, and more severe or more frequent adverse weather events. Also, higher global interest rates than assumed in the baseline could increase financial pressures, particularly on highly indebted countries.

With the prospect of only limited and uneven gains in per capita incomes, the number of people in these countries struggling with extreme poverty and food insecurity will remain high.

Against this backdrop, this box addresses the following questions:

- What have been the main recent economic developments in LICs?
- What is the baseline outlook for LICs?
- What are the risks to the outlook?

Recent developments

Growth in LICs slowed by 1.2 percentage points to 3.8 percent in 2023. Decelerations were most pronounced in Niger and Sudan. In Niger, a coup in mid-2023 led to international sanctions, and growth in the year slowed to 2 percent from 11.5 percent in 2022. Activity in Sudan declined even faster, with output contracting 12 percent, as a resumption of conflict damaged the country's industrial base. In other parts of the Sahel and nearby countries, pervasive violence and political instability exacerbated already-challenging economic and humanitarian situations—including in Burkina Faso, Mali, Somalia, and South Sudan.

At the same time, activity in major LICs, particularly in the Democratic Republic of Congo and Ethiopia, continued to expand at a solid pace. Strong mining

Note: This box was prepared by Dominik Peschel.

BOX 1.2 Recent developments and outlook for low-income countries (*continued*)

FIGURE B1.2.1 LICs: Recent developments

The incidence of violent events has risen in LICs, especially in the Sahel region of Africa, resulting in an increased number of displaced people. Moderating food price inflation has helped consumer price inflation in LICs decline from its highs in late 2022.

A. Violent events

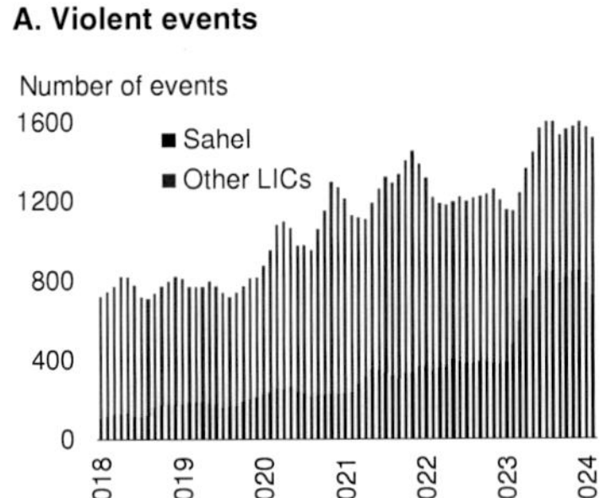

B. Displacement of people

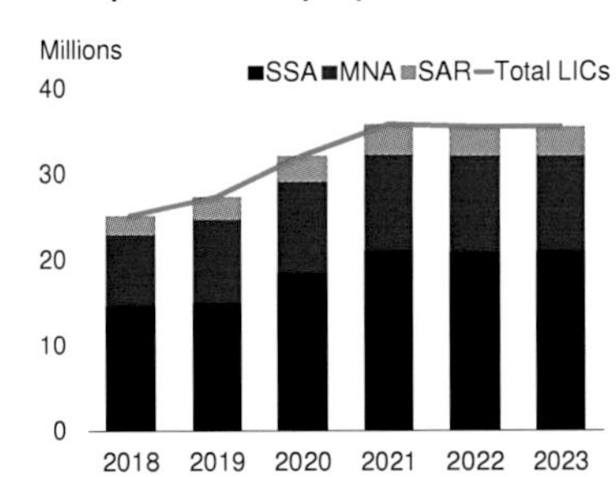

C. Consumer price inflation

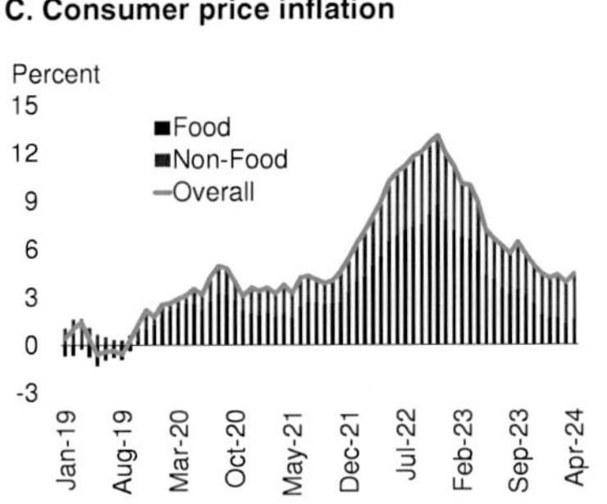

Sources: ACLED (database); Haver Analytics; United Nations High Commissioner for Refugees (UNHCR) Refugee Population Statistics Database; World Bank.
Note: LICs = low-income countries.
A. Three-months moving average; violent events include battles, explosions, violence against civilians, and riots. Sample only comprises SSA LICs. Last observation is April 2024.
B. MNA = Middle East and North Africa, SAR = South Asia, SSA = Sub-Saharan Africa. Statistic covers internally displaced persons (IDPs) due to conflict to whom UNHCR extends protection and/or assistance. The IDP population also includes people in an IDP-like situation. Sample includes 15 countries, of which at least 12 are in Sub-Saharan Africa.
C. Change in prices from 12 months earlier. Unweighted averages for the sample of 7 LICs.

activity supported growth in the Democratic Republic of Congo, while activity in Ethiopia was underpinned by good harvests and steady services sector growth. Upward revisions for these two economies also contributed to overall GDP growth in LICs last year being 0.3 percentage point higher than estimated in January, despite several downward revisions in the remainder of the group.

Output in agricultural-commodity exporters grew by 3.3 percent in 2023, markedly faster than in their industrial-commodity-exporting counterparts, where output expanded by only 0.9 percent on average, reflecting lower global metal prices as well as violent conflict in some of these countries. However, the growth performance of industrial-commodity-exporting economies varied widely in 2023. Whereas economic performance in Niger and Sudan deteriorated sharply, Chad grew strongly, reflecting higher oil production. Growth was also robust in Mozambique, primarily driven by the start of offshore liquified natural gas production, and in Uganda, supported by an oil-related construction boom. In early 2024, El Niño-related droughts weighed on agricultural output in some agricultural-commodity exporters (Madagascar, Malawi; OCHA 2024).

Consumer price inflation in LICs has, on average, continued to decline in early 2024, with food price inflation slowing in many countries as global food price pressures waned (figure B1.2.1.C). Still, food price inflation remains high in some LICs (Burundi, Ethiopia, The Gambia, Malawi, Sierra Leone; World Bank 2024d). Food insecurity remains elevated in LICs, with an estimated 127 million people in LICs suffering from food crisis conditions, or worse, in 2024 (FSIN and GNAFC 2024).

Outlook

Growth in LICs is projected to recover to 5 percent this year and to further improve to 5.3 percent in 2025 and 5.5 percent in 2026 (table B1.2.1). The forecast assumes that violence will recede in some LICs, no debt crises emerge, and inflation continues to moderate.

Nevertheless, the growth outlook for LICs has been revised down since January by 0.5 percentage point in 2024 and by 0.3 percentage point in 2025 (figure B1.2.2.A). Projections for growth in 2024 have been revised down for about three-quarters of LICs. The downgrades are mainly driven by slower-than-expected improvements in some LICs facing fragile and conflict-

BOX 1.2 Recent developments and outlook for low-income countries (*continued*)

FIGURE B1.2.2 LICs: Outlook and risks

The growth forecast for LICs has been revised downward. In per capita terms, growth is expected to be subdued overall, but to diverge markedly between most fragile and conflict-affected LICs, where it is expected to remain below its pre-pandemic level, and other LICs, where it is expected to be stronger. Increased interest payments, especially in the latter group of LICs, necessitate reductions in primary fiscal deficits to maintain government debt sustainability.

A. Growth forecast revisions for LICs since January 2024

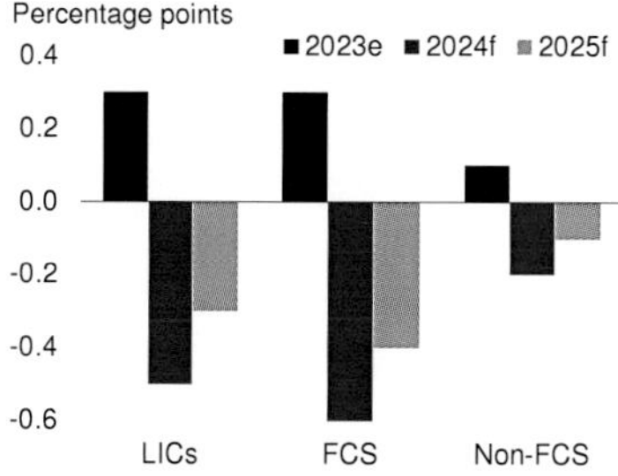

B. GDP per capita in LICs

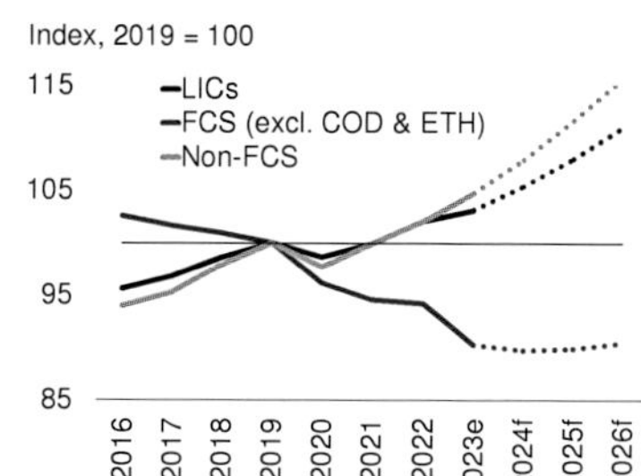

C. Fiscal balance in LICs

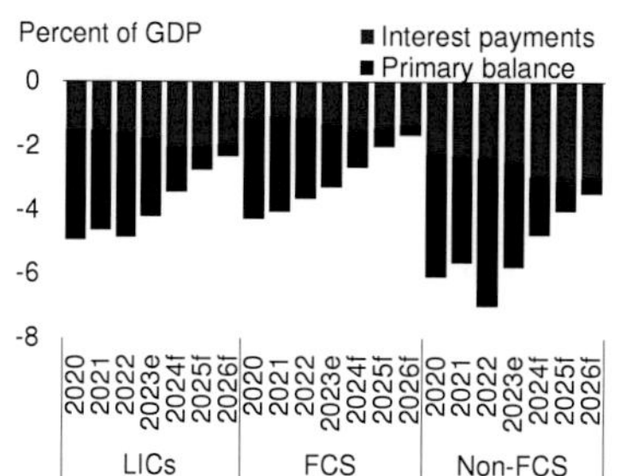

Sources: International Monetary Fund; World Bank.

Note: e = estimate; f = forecast; excl. = excluding; COD = Congo, Dem. Rep.; ETH = Ethiopia; FCS = fragile and conflict-affected situations; GDP = gross domestic product; LICs = low-income countries.

A. Revisions relative to forecast published in the January 2024 edition of the *Global Economic Prospects* report. Sample comprises 21 LICs.

C. Simple averages of country groupings. Sample includes 22 low-income countries.

affected situations (FCS)—countries with high levels of institutional and social fragility and those affected by violent conflict. The largest downward revisions are for Niger and Sudan, both FCS LICs. Conversely, the growth forecast for Ethiopia has been upgraded, mainly owing to a bumper harvest.

Growth in FCS LICs is forecast to increase from 3.3 percent in 2023 to 4.8 percent in 2024 and 5.3 percent in 2025—mainly on account of strong growth in the two largest economies in this group, Ethiopia and the Democratic Republic of Congo. Growth in other FCS LICs is projected to average only 2.6 percent in 2024-25, although this marks a notable improvement from the 1.5 percent output contraction in 2023. Assuming that no new shock disrupts economic stability, strong growth of 7 percent is expected to persist in Ethiopia in 2024-25, supported by increased investment and a recovery in government consumption. Growth in the Democratic Republic of Congo is expected to remain robust at about 6 percent annually in 2024-25, mainly thanks to mining sector activity.

Growth in non-FCS LICs is forecast to rise from 5.2 percent in 2023 to 5.6 percent in 2024 and to 6 percent in 2025. In Rwanda, steady growth averaging 7.7 percent a year is projected for 2024-25—with strong growth in construction and manufacturing projected to continue, while agricultural production is forecast to rebound following two years of weak performance. In Madagascar, growth is expected to be boosted by structural reforms relating to the mining sector, digital technology, and improvements in the investment climate. Growth in Uganda is projected to strengthen further, reflecting continued investments in the oil sector. Furthermore, growth in Madagascar, Rwanda, and Uganda is also expected to benefit from increased global tourism.

Per capita growth in LICs is expected to pick up from 1 percent in 2023 to 2.2 percent in 2024 and 2.5 percent in 2025—far from sufficient to enable effective poverty alleviation (figure B1.2.2.B). Furthermore, there is a sharp divergence between non-FCS LICs, where growth in per capita GDP is forecast to average 3.2 percent in 2024-25, and FCS LICs (excluding the Democratic Republic of Congo and Ethiopia), where average per capita GDP is expected to be largely stagnant, remaining markedly below pre-pandemic levels. Nearly one-third of LICs are forecast to still have lower per capita incomes in 2026 than in 2019.

Over the forecast horizon, projected growth in per capita GDP across LICs is on average only about 1

BOX 1.2 Recent developments and outlook for low-income countries (*continued*)

TABLE B1.2.1 Low-income country forecasts[a]

(Real GDP growth at market prices in percent, unless indicated otherwise)

	2021	2022	2023e	2024f	2025f	2026f	Percentage point differences from January 2024 projections: 2024f	2025f
Low-Income Countries, GDP[b]	4.1	**5.0**	**3.8**	**5.0**	**5.3**	**5.5**	**-0.5**	**-0.3**
GDP per capita (U.S. dollars)	1.3	2.2	1.0	2.2	2.5	2.7	-0.5	-0.3
Afghanistan[c]	-20.7	-6.2	..	..	..	..	..	..
Burkina Faso	6.9	1.8	3.2	3.7	3.8	4.2	-1.1	-1.3
Burundi	3.1	1.8	2.7	3.8	4.4	4.8	-0.4	-0.1
Central African Republic	1.0	0.5	0.9	1.3	1.7	1.9	-0.3	-1.4
Chad	-1.2	2.8	4.1	2.7	3.3	2.9	-0.1	0.6
Congo, Dem. Rep.	6.2	8.9	7.8	6.0	5.9	5.7	-0.5	-0.3
Eritrea	2.9	2.5	2.6	2.8	3.0	3.3	-0.4	-0.3
Ethiopia[d]	6.3	6.4	7.2	7.0	7.0	7.0	0.6	0.0
Gambia, The	5.3	4.9	5.3	5.5	5.8	5.4	0.2	0.3
Guinea-Bissau	6.4	4.2	4.2	4.7	4.8	4.9	-0.9	0.3
Liberia	5.0	4.8	4.7	5.3	6.2	6.3	-0.1	0.0
Madagascar	5.7	3.8	3.8	4.5	4.6	4.7	-0.3	-0.1
Malawi	2.8	0.9	1.5	2.0	3.9	4.1	-0.8	0.6
Mali	3.1	3.5	3.5	3.1	3.5	4.5	-0.9	-1.5
Mozambique	2.3	4.2	5.0	5.0	5.0	4.4	0.0	0.0
Niger	1.4	11.5	2.0	9.1	6.2	5.1	-3.7	-1.2
Rwanda	10.9	8.2	8.2	7.6	7.8	7.5	0.1	0.0
Sierra Leone	4.1	3.5	3.1	3.5	4.0	4.3	-0.2	-0.3
Somalia[e]	3.3	2.4	3.1	3.7	3.9	4.0	0.2	0.1
South Sudan[d]	-5.1	-2.3	-1.3	2.0	3.8	4.0	-0.3	1.4
Sudan	-1.9	-1.0	-12.0	-3.5	-0.7	1.2	-2.9	-0.9
Syrian Arab Republic[c]	1.3	-0.1	-1.2	-1.5	..	..	..	..
Togo	6.0	5.8	5.4	5.1	5.4	5.6	-0.1	-0.4
Uganda[d]	3.4	4.7	5.2	6.0	6.2	6.6	0.0	-0.4
Yemen, Rep.[c]	-1.0	1.5	-2.0	-1.0	1.5	..	-3.0	..

Source: World Bank.

Note: e = estimate; f = forecast. World Bank forecasts are frequently updated based on new information and changing (global) circumstances. Consequently, projections presented here may differ from those contained in other Bank documents, even if basic assessments of countries' prospects do not significantly differ at any given moment in time.

a. The Democratic People's Republic of Korea is not projected due to data limitations.

b. Aggregate growth rates are calculated using GDP weights at average 2010-19 prices and market exchange rates.

c. Forecasts for Afghanistan (beyond 2022), the Syrian Arab Republic (beyond 2024), and the Republic of Yemen (beyond 2025) are excluded because of a high degree of uncertainty.

d. GDP growth rates are on a fiscal year basis. For example, the column for 2022 refers to FY2021/22.

e. Percentage point differences are relative to the World Bank's October 2023 forecast. The January 2024 *Global Economic Prospects* did not include forecasts for Somalia.

percentage point higher than in advanced economies. Markedly higher GDP growth is needed in LICs to enable significant progress in poverty reduction and to accelerate economic development and catch-up in per capita incomes.

LIC governments often lack fiscal space to provide effective support for their populations' welfare. With public debt remaining high in many LICs, increases in debt-service costs in the past two years have absorbed government spending that otherwise could have been available for such productive uses as investment in healthcare, education, and infrastructure (figure B1.2.2.C). Public debt in LICs has increased by about 12 percentage points of GDP between 2019 and 2023 (Chrimes et al. 2024). In late 2023, more than half of

BOX 1.2 Recent developments and outlook for low-income countries (*continued*)

LICs were already in, or at high risk of, debt distress. Without debt relief agreements, several more LICs face an increasing likelihood of debt distress.

Risks

Risks to the baseline growth forecast remain tilted to the downside, particularly for countries grappling with fragility and those more susceptible to conflicts or adverse weather events. An escalation of conflict in the Middle East could cause a renewed pickup in inflation across LICs. In addition to causing higher fuel prices, a conflict-induced and sustained oil price spike could also raise food prices and exacerbate food insecurity across LICs by increasing costs of production—many fertilizers are byproducts of the oil and gas industry—and transportation.

Many LICs suffer from fragility stemming from persistent poverty, as well as festering violence and conflict, especially in East Africa and the Sahel (notably Burkina Faso, Democratic Republic of Congo, Ethiopia, Mali, Somalia, South Sudan, Sudan). While there has been progress with peacemaking efforts in the Democratic Republic of Congo and Ethiopia, violence in several LICs has increased, especially in the Sahel region, where political instability has risen, with several coups d'état in recent years. A further escalation of violence and conflict would not only push growth below the baseline, but also further increase the number of displaced people and extend humanitarian crises in these countries, many of which already suffer from high food insecurity.

If global interest rates remain elevated for longer than assumed, restrictive financing conditions will lead to higher debt-service costs, which in turn increase the likelihood of debt crises in some LICs. This, coupled with limited access to external financing at favorable interest rates, could markedly increase the risk of government debt distress, especially if coordination problems among a diverse group of creditors intensify (Bolhuis et al. 2024). In recent years, issues regarding debt restructuring in LICs have intensified, in spite of efforts to coordinate with an increasingly diverse set of creditors; the share of LICs' external debt to non-Paris Club creditors has increased markedly over time (Chrimes et al. 2024).

Slower-than-expected growth in China could adversely affect LICs, in particular metal exporters. A more persistent or deeper-than-expected property sector downturn in China would weigh directly on real estate investment and have knock-on effects on revenue collection that could further reduce fiscal space and constrain public infrastructure investment. A broad-based investment slowdown in China would markedly reduce global demand for and prices of minerals and metals.

Economic growth and poverty reduction in LICs could also decelerate if the effects of climate change become more severe. Extreme weather events have already had catastrophic consequences in several LICs. In particular, global warming has disproportionately hit the Sahel region (World Bank 2023b). The current El Niño weather pattern could bring further devastation and increase the incidence of vector-borne and waterborne diseases owing to increased rainfall and flooding in parts of Africa, especially East Africa (Burundi, Rwanda, Somalia, Uganda). At the same time, severe droughts in parts of Southern Africa could put renewed upward pressure on food prices in affected LICs (Madagascar, Malawi, Mozambique).

more than half of FCS economies. Over 2020-24, per capita income differentials relative to advanced economies are set to widen in nearly half of EMDEs—the highest share since the 1990s (figure 1.10.A). Although some improvement is expected in EMDEs over 2025-26, the share of LICs and FCS with weaker per capita income growth relative to advanced economies is projected to remain elevated.

The broader picture is of limited and highly unequal progress in the catch-up to advanced-economy GDP per capita levels. Given subdued per capita income growth, the catch-up process is anticipated to stall in EMDEs excluding China and India, with FCS falling further behind (figure 1.10.B). In EMDEs excluding China and India, the aggregate level of per capita income relative to advanced economies is expected to be lower in

FIGURE 1.10 Per capita income growth

Per capita income growth remains subdued and continues to lag advanced economies in about half of EMDEs, with income catch-up having stalled or reversed among many LICs and fragile and conflict-affected economies. Per capita GDP in EMDEs, excluding China and India, has stagnated relative to advanced economies and remains lower than in 2019. After rising sharply during the pandemic, extreme poverty rates remain elevated, especially in vulnerable EMDEs.

A. Share of EMDEs with GDP per capita growth lower than in advanced economies

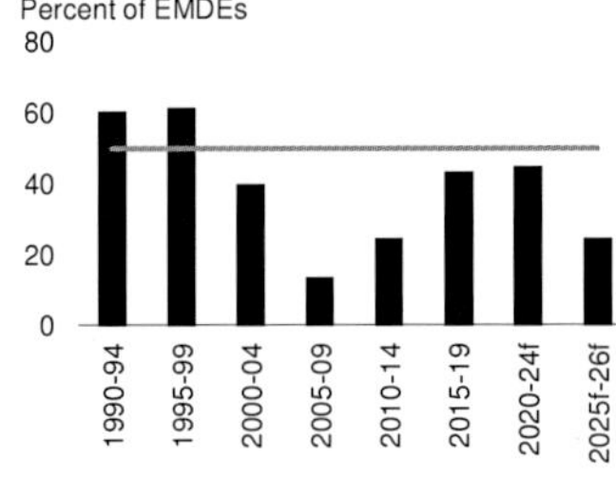

B. Differential in per capita GDP growth rates in EMDEs relative to advanced economies

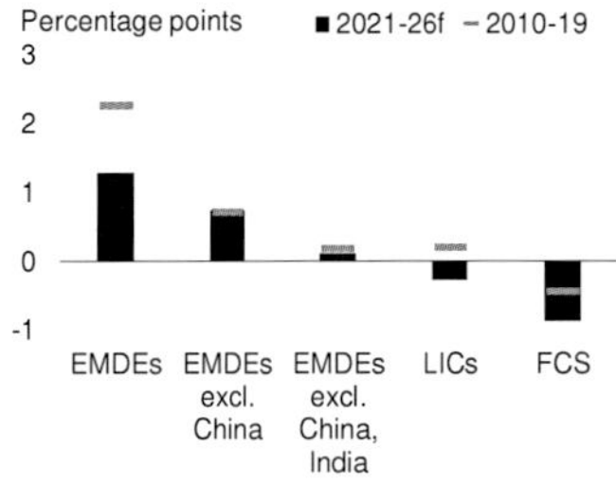

C. Per capita income in EMDEs as a share of average advanced-economy levels

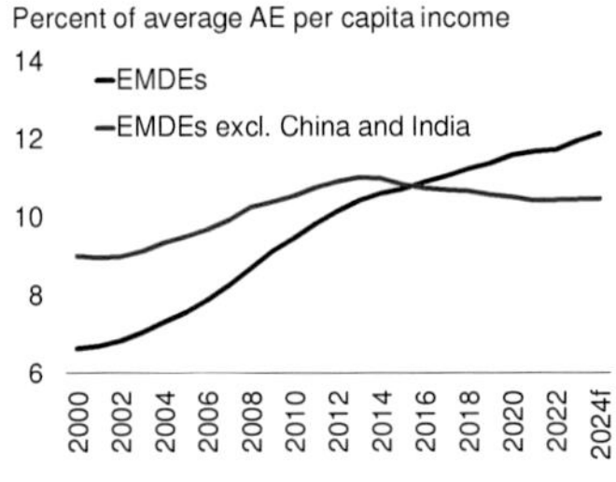

D. Extreme poverty rates in EMDEs

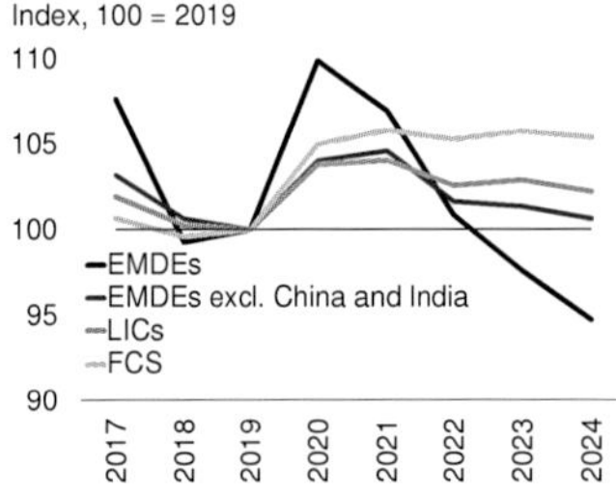

Sources: Mahler and Lakner (2022); UN World Population Prospects; World Bank Poverty and Inequality Platform; World Bank.

Note: f = forecast; AE = advanced-economy; EMDEs = emerging market and developing economies; FCS = fragile and conflict-affected situations; LICs = low-income countries. GDP per capita aggregates are calculated as aggregated GDP divided by the aggregate population. GDP aggregates are calculated using real U.S. dollar GDP weights at average 2010-19 prices and market exchange rates.

A. Orange horizontal line indicates the 50 percent threshold.

B. Bars and dashes calculated as annual average per capita growth for each country group, minus annual average per capita growth in advanced economies. The year 2020 is excluded on account of extreme volatility related to the pandemic.

D. Sample includes up to 154 EMDEs, 26 LICs, and 39 FCS. Poverty data from Mahler and Lakner (2022) and the World Bank Poverty and Inequality Platform.

2024 than in 2019, extending the stagnation that started in the 2010s (figure 1.10.C).

Weakness in per capita growth in the decade so far has been most pronounced among EMDEs where poverty levels were already elevated. In LICs, the anticipated firming in per capita growth in 2025-26 is insufficient to offset income losses relative to advanced economies since the pandemic. Fragile EMDEs, where the pervasive economic and social damages of conflict are most pronounced, have slipped even further behind.

The pandemic unwound three years of progress on poverty reduction in EMDEs, while the subsequent global shocks have taken a further toll. Consequently, poverty rates stand above 2019 levels in many EMDEs, especially in vulnerable economies (figure 1.10.D). Accordingly, the ambition to reduce global poverty to 3 percent of the world's population by 2030 increasingly appears out of reach. With many EMDEs already growing close to estimated potential growth rates, concerted efforts to further structural reforms and raise long-term growth will likely be needed to substantially accelerate poverty reduction. Progress in recent years on poverty reduction has primarily reflected robust growth in SAR and EAP, while extreme poverty is increasingly concentrated in SSA, as well as several fragile and conflict-affected states elsewhere.

Global outlook and risks

Summary of global outlook

Global growth is projected to remain subdued at 2.6 percent in 2024—half a percentage point below the 2010-19 average (figure 1.11.A). This reflects the lagged effects of monetary tightening, resumed fiscal consolidation, and moderate consumption growth in the context of receding savings buffers and diminishing labor market tightness. Investment growth is expected to remain subdued this year, constrained by elevated real interest rates and policy uncertainty amid elevated geopolitical tensions. After global trade growth ground to a halt last year, the initial rebound is forecast to be modest.

A slight upgrade to the global growth forecast in 2024 reflects continued robust expansion in the United States and somewhat stronger-than-expected economic activity in China. This contrasts with an unchanged projection of muted growth in the euro area and a tepid expansion of 3.5 percent in EMDEs excluding China.

In 2025 and 2026, global growth is forecast to edge up slightly to average 2.7 percent, as inflation gradually subsides, policy rates decline, and trade growth firms. Global investment growth is projected to pick up as monetary easing gains traction. On the other hand, fiscal policy is envisaged to exert a slight drag on global growth as many governments seek to repair pandemic-era fiscal deteriorations.

Growth in EMDEs is projected to hover around 4 percent in 2025-26—close to their aggregate potential growth estimate—but the forecasts entail considerable divergence. Growth in China is expected to slow notably. In contrast, growth is envisaged to gather momentum in EMDEs excluding China, aided by less restrictive financing conditions and improving consumption growth. Even so, the lingering effects of recent large shocks—including the pandemic, the invasion of Ukraine, and the sharp rise in global interest rates to combat inflation—are evident in continued sizable output losses relative to the pre-pandemic trajectory, particularly in some of the most vulnerable countries.

Elevated global inflation in recent years has weighed on growth both by curbing real incomes and by prompting the sharp and simultaneous tightening of monetary policies. In both advanced economies and EMDEs, growth in 2023 under-performed pre-pandemic trends by a wider margin in countries experiencing larger increases in post-pandemic inflation (figure 1.11.B). This divergence is not expected to reverse over the forecast horizon, reflecting tighter monetary policies and adverse supply developments in economies where inflation has proved to be more stubborn.

FIGURE 1.11 Global outlook

Global growth is projected to remain subdued in 2024—half a percentage point below the 2010-19 average. Growth is envisaged to pick up slightly in 2025-26, supported by modest firming of investment and trade growth. Growth is projected to be weaker than pre-pandemic trends in economies that experienced larger increases in inflation.

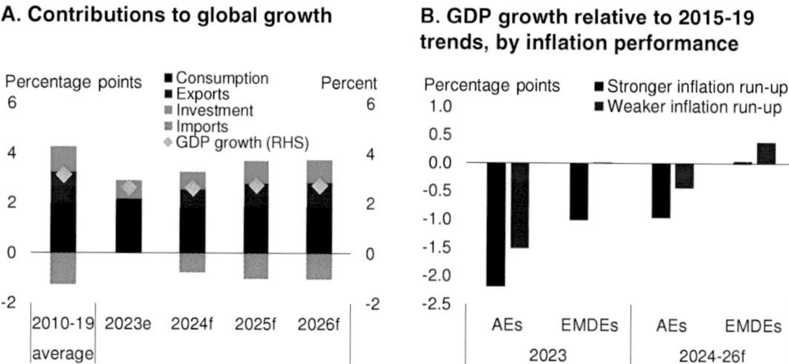

Sources: Haver Analytics; World Bank.

Note: e = estimate; f = forecast; AEs = advanced economies; EMDEs = emerging market and developing economies.

A. Country sample with data availability for components is different from the sample of countries reporting GDP level data. As such, GDP growth number derived from components differs from numbers presented in table 1.1. Components do not always equal headline growth on account of statistical discrepancies.

B. Panel shows the median country deviations from pre-pandemic growth averages (2015-19). Stronger (weaker) inflation run-up means above (below) median difference between post-pandemic inflation peak and pre-pandemic average.

Risks to the outlook

Risks to the outlook have become somewhat more balanced, given the continued resilience of the global economy to high financing costs. However, risks to the global outlook continue to be tilted to the downside amid heightened uncertainty.

Worsening conflicts or escalating geopolitical tensions could have adverse impacts on global growth through commodity markets, trade, and financial linkages. Further trade fragmentation amid resurgent inward-looking industrial policies carries the risk of additional disruptions to trade networks, supply chains, and economic activity. Stubbornly elevated core inflation in advanced economies could forestall anticipated monetary easing, tightening financial conditions, including in EMDEs, and weighing on global growth. Weaker-than-expected growth in China could have negative global spillovers through commodity markets and trade channels. Climate change looms ever larger, with more frequent and extreme weather events presenting risks to both near and long-term growth.

On the upside, further positive supply-side developments—such as a boost to productivity due to increased technology adoption and supply chain improvements—may result in stronger growth and continued disinflation. This could enhance confidence that inflation will durably return to targets, prompting central banks in some advanced economies and EMDEs to ease monetary policy more than currently assumed, further boosting global growth in the latter years of the forecast. In addition, U.S. growth could be higher than currently expected, reflecting continued strong labor supply dynamics, under-pinned by rising labor force participation and absorption of working-age migrants.

FIGURE 1.12 Risks from conflicts, trade fragmentation, and higher-for-longer policy rates

Conflict-related disruptions to oil supply from the Middle East could result in sizable oil price increases—in a more severe scenario, this could stall progress on global disinflation this year. Globally, trade policy uncertainty has risen to levels higher than those in other years with major elections since 2000. Among new trade-distorting policies, the use of subsidies has risen sharply since the pandemic. Advanced-economy interest rates are expected to remain well above 2000-19 average levels. Persistent core inflation in these economies could see interest rates remain higher for longer, substantially lowering global growth in 2025.

A. Brent oil prices under conflict-related oil supply disruption scenarios

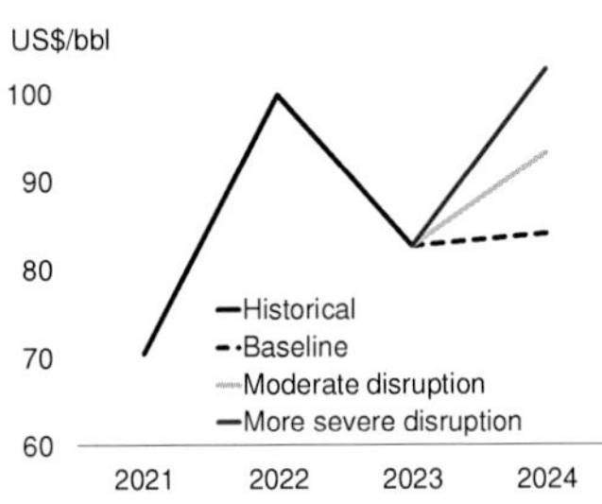

B. Global inflation under conflict-related oil supply disruption scenarios

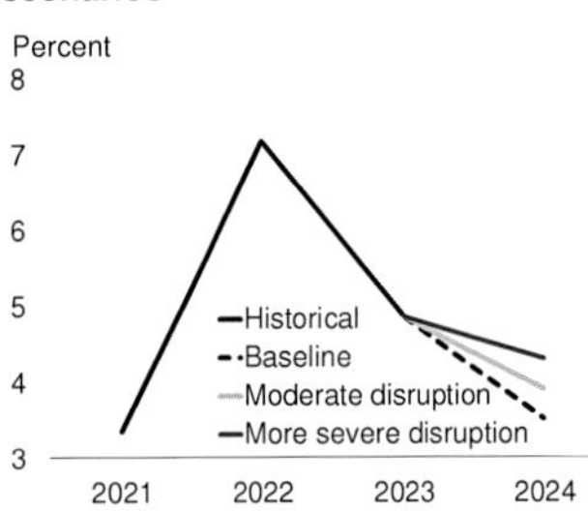

C. Global trade policy uncertainty in years with major elections

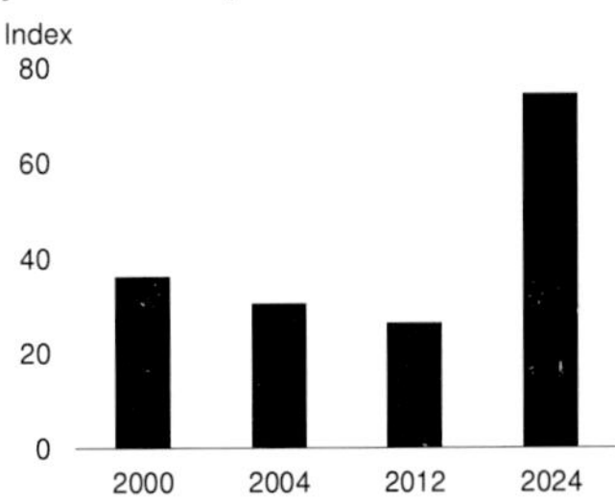

D. Trade-distorting policy measures affecting goods trade

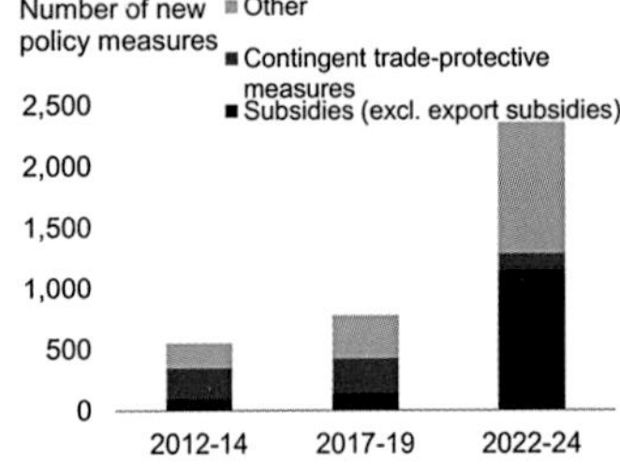

E. Monetary policy interest rates in advanced economies

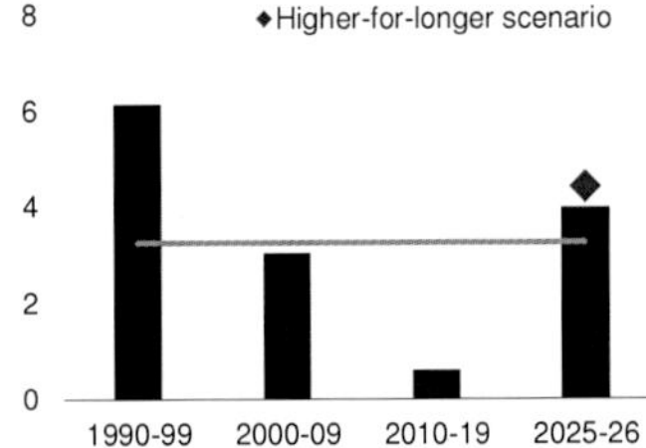

F. Change in global growth in alternative scenarios

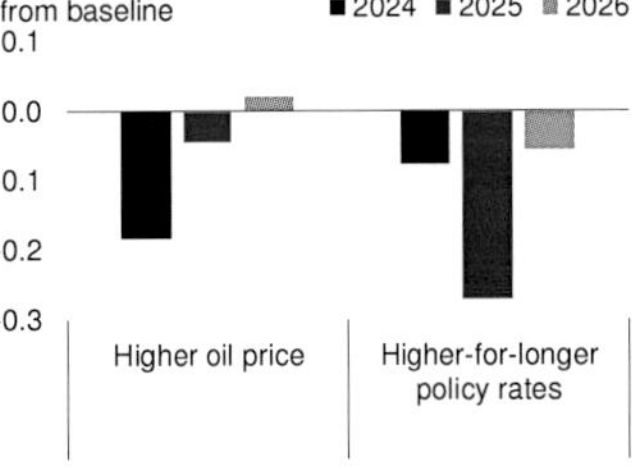

Sources: Bloomberg; Caldara et al. (2020); Federal Reserve Bank of St. Louis; GTA (database); Haver Analytics; Oxford Economics; World Bank.

A.B. The blue dashed lines indicate baseline forecasts for the price of Brent oil (panel A) and global consumer price inflation weighted by GDP (panel B), expressed as annual averages. Orange and red lines depict outcomes under moderate and more severe conflict-related disruptions to oil supply, occurring in mid-2024.

B.F. Model-based GDP-weighted projections using Oxford Economics' Global Economic Model.

C. Panel shows the average trade policy uncertainty index in the first five months of each year in which elections were held in countries cumulatively representing more than 30 percent of global GDP. Last observation is May 2024.

D. Panel shows implemented interventions that discriminate against foreign commercial interests. Contingent trade-protective measures include trade defense instruments such as safeguard investigations and anti-circumvention, antidumping, and countervailing measures. Subsidies cover state loans, financial grants, loan guarantees, production subsidies, and other forms of state support, excluding export subsidies. Adjusted data (for reporting lags) as of May 30, 2024.

E. Average annual policy rates. Aggregates are calculated as GDP-weighted averages of the policy rates and policy rate expectations for the United States, the euro area (using aggregated national policy rates as a proxy over the 1990-99 period) and the United Kingdom. Policy rate expectations are based on futures curves observed on May 31, 2024. Diamond shows the expected policy rate under the higher-for-longer policy rates scenario.

Downside risks

Proliferation of armed conflicts and broader geopolitical risks

Risks related to armed conflict have increased sharply given the ongoing conflict in the Middle East, attacks on vessels in the Red Sea, a marked deterioration in security conditions in parts of Sub-Saharan Africa, and Russia's ongoing invasion of Ukraine. More generally, the incidence of armed conflicts—in various forms and manifestations—has increased in recent years. Armed conflicts can result in loss of human life, destruction of physical and human capital, political instability, and heightened uncertainty, in turn stifling investment and economic activity. In addition, conflicts can pose fiscal challenges to the extent they are associated with higher military expenditures, lower revenues, and higher public debt. Human capital losses due to diminished educational and health provision in conflict-affected areas can compound these economic damages over the longer term.

More immediately, if the conflict in the Middle East intensifies, substantial disruptions to oil supply and large commodity price spikes could follow, potentially undermining efforts to bring inflation back to targets globally. The extent and duration of oil price impacts would depend on the nature of the initial shock, as well as the speed and size of other oil producers' responses to higher prices. Indicatively:

- *A moderate conflict-driven supply disruption* in mid-2024 could initially lower oil supply from the region by about 1 million barrels per day (mb/d). Given an already-tight demand-supply balance in oil markets, oil prices could rise significantly, pushing the average Brent price this year to \$92/bbl, about 10 percent above the baseline (figure 1.12.A). In such circumstances, progress on disinflation could slow notably, with average global consumer price inflation (weighted by GDP) in 2024 being 0.4 percentage point higher than the baseline forecast.[2]

[2] The alternative scenarios in this and subsequent sections are produced using the Oxford Economics Global Economic Model, a semi-structural macroeconomic projection model that includes 188 individual country blocks in its extended version, available at quarterly or annual frequencies (Oxford Economics 2019).

- *A more severe conflict-related supply disruption*, involving exports from one or more regional oil producers being substantially encumbered, could initially reduce global oil supply by 3 mb/d. With other oil exporters likely to quickly ramp up production in response, the global reduction in supply could ease to about 1 mb/d by late 2024. Under supply constraints of this magnitude, the average Brent oil price this year could be about 20 percent higher than the baseline, surpassing $100/bbl. In this instance, disinflation could stall globally, with global inflation pushed 0.8 percentage point above the 2024 baseline forecast (figure 1.12.B).

Furthermore, uncertainty around the evolution of Russia's invasion of Ukraine poses continued risks to commodity markets—including for oil products and grains—and regional security. The confluence of multiple armed conflicts and their knock-on effects threatens to exacerbate uncertainty about the geopolitical environment, forestalling investment, dampening both consumer and business sentiment, and increasing financial volatility. Negative economic effects would be most acute in the countries engaged in and adjacent to conflicts. However, other EMDEs could also suffer adverse spillovers due, for example, to rising import prices, partly resulting from higher shipping costs and increased global risk aversion. The recent surge in the price of gold—an asset that often gains value during periods of conflict and instability—underscores that the geopolitical environment is impacting market perceptions of risk. Moreover, some of the challenges posed by conflicts could be compounded in the longer term by wider geopolitical tensions, which could result in commodity, finance, trade, and labor markets becoming increasingly segmented into regional blocs. Historically, periods of heightened geopolitical risks have been associated with large adverse effects on global economic activity (Caldara and Iacoviello 2022).

Further trade fragmentation and trade policy uncertainty

A further proliferation of trade restrictions presents a substantial downside risk to global growth prospects. Restrictions divert trade away from the lowest-cost supplier, resulting in disruptions to global supply chains. Historically, global supply chains have facilitated technological diffusion, enabling rapid economic convergence and poverty reduction (World Bank 2020). Following Russia's invasion of Ukraine, trade and FDI flows between countries in geopolitically distant blocs have already declined considerably compared to flows between more closely aligned countries (Blanga-Gubbay and Rubínová 2023; Gopinath et al. 2024). Moreover, policies aimed at reducing dependence on specific suppliers do not necessarily achieve diversification, as these policies could lead to stronger indirect linkages as trade is diverted via other countries, resulting in more complex and less efficient supply chains (Freund et al. 2023). Reconfiguring supply chains is costly and can result in welfare losses as firms devote resources to search for alternative suppliers (Grossman, Helpman, and Redding 2024).

Heightened trade policy uncertainty and a further weakening of the multilateral trading system—both of which may follow from escalating trade-restrictive measures—could have adverse effects on growth. In the near term, increased trade policy uncertainty could slow business investment in both advanced economies and EMDEs (Caldara et al. 2019, 2020). In the longer term, less efficient supply chains could decrease returns on capital, posing headwinds for productivity growth. Over time, multinationals may elect to near-shore by outsourcing some manufacturing processes to nearby countries—even if such decisions would otherwise not be optimal—because of declining expectations that trade tensions will be resolved (Alessandria et al. 2024). While such developments may reflect strategic considerations, there is a risk they also embed norms that erode benefits from globalization—such as the depth and efficiency of global markets—and slow the dissemination of beneficial technologies. A less open global economy would likely be most disadvantageous to the poorest countries, given their limited market power and the historical role of international trade in raising living standards.

Growing public support for more inward-looking policies and an increasingly divided political landscape pose additional risks in the context of the large number of elections scheduled for this year—countries holding parliamentary or general elections in 2024 account for about 60 percent of global GDP. Indeed, trade policy uncertainty has reached an unusually high level relative to previous years of major elections around the world since 2000 (figure 1.12.C). Election outcomes could lean toward greater protectionism, such as increased tariffs and subsidies, which could hinder trade and FDI. This would accelerate already-emerging trends. For instance, the number of trade-distorting policies has already tripled compared to the pre-pandemic period. Among these policies, the use of subsidies has surpassed contingent trade-protective measures as governments have become more interventionist in pursuing industrial policy objectives (figure 1.12.D). These policies can lead to global inefficiencies through increased fragmentation of production processes and idle capacity, as well as by encouraging the entry of inefficient firms (Barwick, Kalouptsidi and Zahur 2024; Bown 2023). More generally, FDI flows to EMDEs could be dampened by a deterioration in institutional quality stemming from post-election policy changes, or by related political and social unrest.

Higher-for-longer interest rates and weaker risk appetite

Given that global inflation is projected to steadily moderate over the forecast horizon, central banks are assumed to gradually ease monetary policies in the remainder of 2024 and 2025 to prevent real interest rates from becoming unduly restrictive. Even so, advanced economy policy rates in 2025-26 are expected to remain markedly elevated compared to recent decades, at more than double the 2000-19 average (figure 1.12.E). Moreover, if inflationary pressures endure for longer than envisaged, policy rate cuts may be fewer or postponed, leaving monetary conditions tighter than in baseline forecasts.

More persistent inflation and higher-for-longer monetary policy rates in the United States and other advanced economies would weigh on global growth via several channels. Along with elevated borrowing costs, a higher path of advanced-economy inflation, if unmatched by nominal wage growth, would reduce real incomes and consumer spending. Many EMDE central banks could also postpone or slow monetary easing, in part to forestall inflation risks that might otherwise follow from currency depreciation, given shifting interest rate differentials. The pass-through from depreciation to inflation tends to be particularly pronounced when inflation expectations are less anchored, growing in a non-linear fashion with larger currency moves (Ha, Stocker, and Yilmazkuday 2020). With short-term interest rates turning out higher than anticipated, bond yields would likely also rise in advanced economies and EMDEs, exerting an additional drag on activity. Reduced risk appetite, which could accompany an inflation-driven shift in rate expectations, would tighten financial conditions further.

Growth implications of stubborn inflation and higher-for-longer monetary policy rates are quantified using a global macroeconomic model. In this scenario, elevated core inflation is assumed to keep headline inflation in major advanced economies above target levels through mid-2025, with policy interest rates in the United States and the euro area remaining at current levels until that time. This results in a path for advanced economy interest rates about 40 basis points higher than the baseline, on average, in 2025-26. Many EMDE central banks are also assumed to pursue more restrictive monetary policies than in the baseline, partly because of inflation pressures arising from potential currency deprecations.

Under this scenario, global growth slows due to a combination of tighter financial conditions and weaker real income gains than in the baseline, with the impact peaking in 2025. In addition, weaker external demand reduces export growth in EMDEs. Overall, global growth in 2025 is 0.3 percentage point below the baseline, with average growth in advanced economies and EMDEs 0.3 percentage point and 0.2 percentage point lower, respectively (figure 1.12.F).

The aforementioned scenario is predicated on a moderate decline in risk appetite. Larger increases in risk premia could result in more adverse outcomes. EMDEs at elevated risk of debt-related stress could see sharp currency depreciations and destabilizing capital outflows, triggering new crises or derailing nascent recoveries (Arteta, Kamin, and Ruch 2022). Other extant financial vulnerabilities—including office-related lending in advanced economies and high exposure to domestic sovereign debt in some EMDE banking sectors—could also be exacerbated. Such developments could amplify the drag on global growth via additional channels. For example, office loan defaults could slow advanced-economy credit growth, while EMDE fiscal authorities might pursue sharper fiscal consolidations to buttress stability.

Weaker-than-expected growth in China

The outlook for China is subject to various risks, the materialization of which could have a range of global spillovers. On the upside, greater-than-assumed policy support, such as higher government spending, could boost demand. On the downside, however, a more persistent or deeper-than-expected property sector downturn would directly weigh on investment and have broader knock-on effects. It would reduce household wealth and sap consumer confidence and spending. It would also undermine revenue collection, further reducing fiscal space and hindering fiscal support, particularly at the local government level.

Another downside risk relates to the possibility of prolonged weakness in business sentiment and private investment in a range of sectors, partly owing to elevated domestic or international policy uncertainty, including about the domestic regulatory environment (figure 1.13.A). Moreover, potential growth in China, already on a notable downward trend, could decline faster than expected, resulting in slower actual growth. Industrial policy, including government support for preferred manufacturing sectors, could have the unintended effect of exacerbating inefficient capital allocation and encouraging supply-demand imbalances.

Weaker growth in China could have adverse international spillovers via global trade and commodity markets. It would weigh on the anticipated global trade recovery, dampening activity in trade-intensive economies. Commodity-exporting EMDEs, notably energy and metal exporters, would be particularly affected, given China's share in global commodity demand and in an environment of softening commodity prices. Protracted weak consumer confidence could cause households in China to curtail discretionary spending, including on overseas travel, thereby dampening tourism-related activity, particularly in EAP economies where China is an important source of demand.

Although China's integration into global financial markets remains limited, a sharper slowdown

FIGURE 1.13 Other risks to the outlook

In China, elevated policy uncertainty could weigh on sentiment and investment. Economic losses from natural disasters in EMDEs have risen in recent years and are persistently larger as a share of GDP than in advanced economies. On the upside, global productivity could turn out better than expected, particularly if productivity growth rises above its pre-pandemic average in EMDEs, helping to offset some of the pandemic scarring affecting the level of labor productivity. U.S. growth has proven remarkably resilient, in part as a result of an expanding labor force.

A. Economic policy uncertainty in China

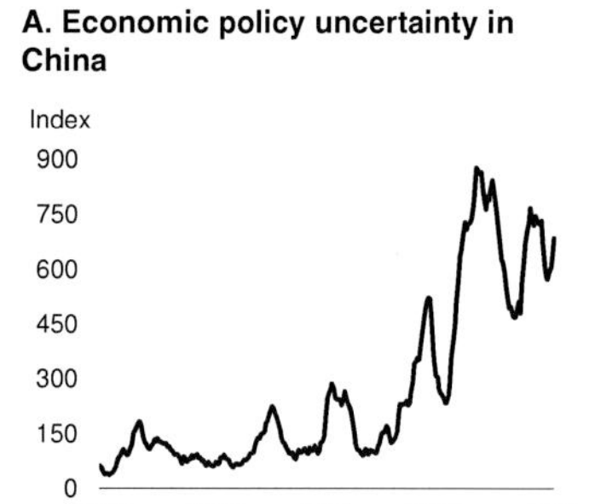

B. Cost of natural disasters

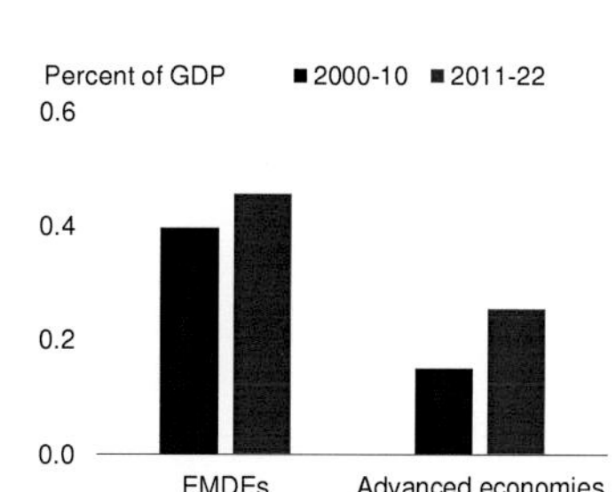

C. Growth in output per worker

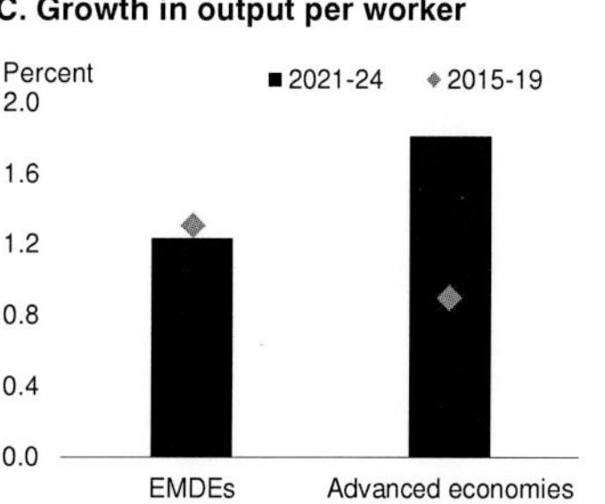

D. U.S. labor force participation rate

Sources: Baker et al. (2013); EM-DAT (database); Federal Reserve Bank of St Louis; International Labour Organization; World Bank.

Note: EMDEs = emerging market and developing economies.

A. Panel shows six-month moving average of Economic Policy Uncertainty index, based on the *South China Morning Post*. Last observation is November 2023.

B. Panel shows period averages of total costs of natural disasters as percent of GDP.

C. Median growth in annual output per worker from International Labour Organization (ILO) model estimates. Sample includes 189 countries, covering 2015-24.

D. Panel shows difference in percentage points in the three-month moving average of labor force participation rates since December 2019 for age groups 55 and above, 25-54, and all ages. Last observation is April 2024.

could create adverse financial spillovers, including by sapping global risk appetite (Gutierrez, Turen, and Vicondoa 2024). Against a backdrop of high and rising private and public sector debt, slower growth in China and concerns over mounting financial risks could prompt authorities to rein in credit growth and markedly pivot to fiscal consolidation. Such a shift in the policy stance could dampen global sentiment in anticipation of weakening global demand, resulting in a decline in investor risk appetite and equity prices. The ensuing tightening in global financial conditions would have disproportionately adverse effects on less creditworthy economies reliant on external financing.

More frequent natural disasters with worsening impacts

The frequency and severity of natural disasters have risen over time and are projected to increase further with climate change, posing a risk to global growth. Natural disasters have devastating impacts on output, lives, and livelihoods, with the effects falling disproportionately on the poor. Economic losses from natural disasters in EMDEs have risen considerably over time, averaging about 0.5 percent of GDP per year over 2011-22, about twice the impact in advanced economies (figure 1.13.B). Of all the deaths over 1970-2019 from weather, climate, and water hazards, 82 percent occurred in low- and lower-middle-income countries (WMO 2021).

Weather patterns, such as the ongoing El Niño and La Niña, risk harming agricultural output and result in price pressures in the near term. These weather patterns may become more extreme and increase in frequency under more acute greenhouse gas emission scenarios, inflicting damages over the long term. For instance, past experience suggests that El Niño combined with global climate change could reduce rice yields in Southeast Asia, pushing millions of people into food insecurity, as it did between 2014 and 2016 (FEWS NET 2023). More frequent and widespread crop failures resulting from climate change and associated natural disasters can cause food price spikes and exacerbate poverty and food insecurity. Under an adverse scenario, over 130 million people could be pushed into extreme poverty by 2030, most of them in low- and lower-middle-income countries (Hallegatte and Rozenberg 2017; Jafino et al. 2020). Additionally, reduced yields would adversely affect incomes across EMDEs where agriculture is a significant share of output.

Headwinds to growth deriving from weather events may be amplified by a lack of fiscal space to respond to them or through their impact on public sector balance sheets (Milivojevic 2023). Extreme weather events could also worsen the spread of disease, aggravate the hardships faced by those without access to adequate housing, and adversely affect the stability of banking sectors.

Upside risks

Lower global inflation and faster monetary easing

Global consumer price inflation has declined substantially since its mid-2022 peak, reflecting falling commodity prices, normalizing supply chains, and expanding labor supply. As much of the run-up in inflation was due to pandemic-related supply disruptions and higher energy prices, rapid disinflation occurred despite resilient output growth in many advanced economies and EMDEs. While the baseline outlook embeds continued disinflation, the pace is expected to slow, reflecting persistent service price pressures that will likely keep policy rates elevated, relative to the pre-pandemic period, throughout the forecast horizon. However, inflation could recede more rapidly compared to the baseline assumptions.

Several factors could support faster disinflation. Productivity could turn out to be better than expected globally, particularly if productivity growth rises above its pre-pandemic average in EMDEs, helping to offset some of the pandemic scarring affecting the level of labor productivity (figure 1.13.C). This could be driven by the consolidation of post-pandemic working practices and a calibrated and equitable integration of new technologies that unlock productivity gains. In addition, goods inflation could decline further due to moderating commodity prices or further improvements in global supply chains, leading to lower imported price inflation. With respect to energy prices, substantial spare oil capacity among OPEC+ producers raises the possibility of a downdraft in oil prices if increases in oil supply—driven either by OPEC+ decisions or production growth elsewhere—are greater than markets anticipate. As well as directly lowering headline inflation via energy disinflation, lower oil prices would feed through (with a lag) to many core prices, such as those for travel services and freighted goods.

If global inflation concerns were to abate faster than currently expected, central banks in advanced economies and EMDEs could ease monetary policy more than anticipated, reducing borrowing costs and supporting improved credit growth. Lower borrowing rates and inflation would also boost global consumer confidence, pushing up consumer spending and facilitating a stronger recovery in global trade. The resulting higher demand would provide additional impetus for increased investment in productive capacity. Finally, along with lower domestic policy rates, EMDEs would likely benefit from stronger global risk appetite, with foreign investment flows rekindled by lower yields in advanced economies, further easing access to finance for firms and governments in EMDEs.

Stronger growth in the United States

The United States has been a bright spot in the global economy, with growth proving more resilient than expected, despite the sharpest monetary policy tightening in decades. Meanwhile, as was the case globally, U.S. inflation continued to retreat, partly on account of waning energy and food prices, as well as some moderation in core inflation. The growth outlook this year has been revised up significantly following repeated upside surprises to activity, supported by the expansion of the supply side of the economy, particularly with respect to gains in productivity and the size of the workforce (figure 1.13.D).

It is possible that growth in the United States could continue to surpass expectations this year and the next, especially if elevated growth in labor supply and productivity turns out to be persistent. Continued expansion in the prime-age labor force due to elevated real wages, as well as strong increases in the working-age population due to immigration, could prove more enduring than projected. Such an expansion of the working-age population could boost consumer spending, while businesses could also be encouraged to increase capital investment in line with higher staffing levels, raising overall growth. An increase in labor supply would help bring labor markets into better balance, enabling higher employment and reducing labor market tightness, which would help to ease wage growth. If this greater employment occurred in more productive sectors, economy-wide productivity might sustain solid growth. Slowing wage growth and continued increases in productivity would support the ongoing disinflation process. Thus, in such a scenario, stronger growth would be accompanied by continued disinflation, requiring little change to the Federal Reserve's policy rate path.

Policy challenges

The tepid growth outlook and multiple downside risks on the horizon underscore the importance of forceful policy responses to address persistent and substantial challenges. Global policy efforts are needed to support the green and digital transitions, safeguard international trade, and ensure food and energy security. Addressing many of these issues is likely to require increased investment in the provision of public goods in an environment of rising debt and high debt-servicing costs. Still-elevated inflation underscores the need for monetary policy makers to continue to focus on price stability. To meet development goals and bolster long-term growth prospects, reforms at the national level are needed to enhance the efficiency of public investment, boost human capital, and strengthen resilience and inclusion.

Key global challenges

Elevated debt

Many EMDEs are contending with high debt in an environment of weak growth, steep borrowing costs, and a multitude of downside risks (figure 1.14.A). These challenges are particularly acute for

FIGURE 1.14 Global policy challenges

High levels of debt across many EMDEs, notably LICs, highlight the need for global policy action to prevent costly debt crises. LICs are especially exposed to climate change risks and have the largest investment needs to achieve a resilient and low-carbon pathway. Despite improvements over the past two decades, EMDEs continue to lag advanced economies in access to key infrastructure. The adoption of trade agreements has slowed in the 2020s to less than half the rate of the 2000s.

A. Government debt

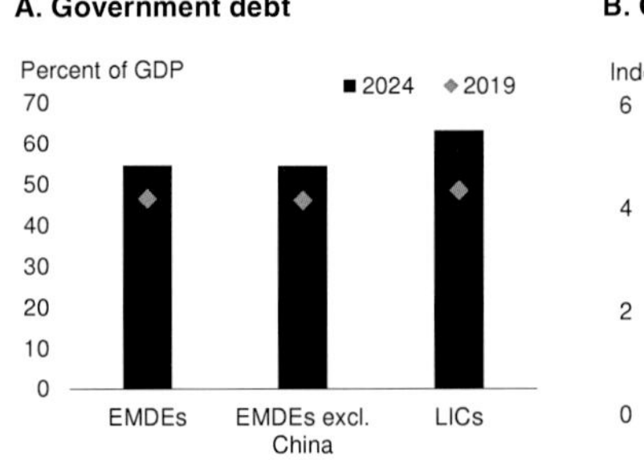

B. Climate change exposure risk

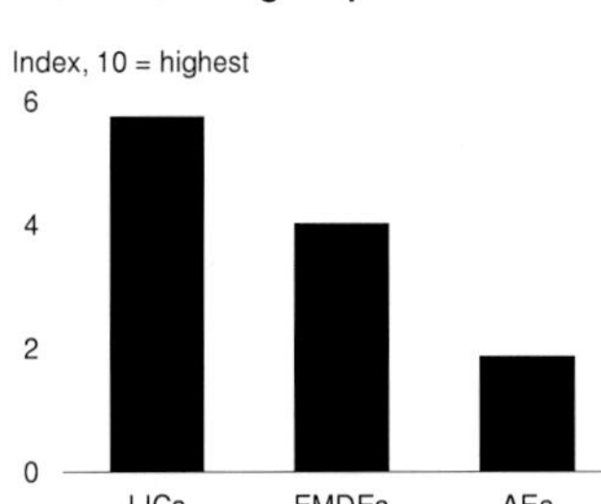

C. Access to infrastructure

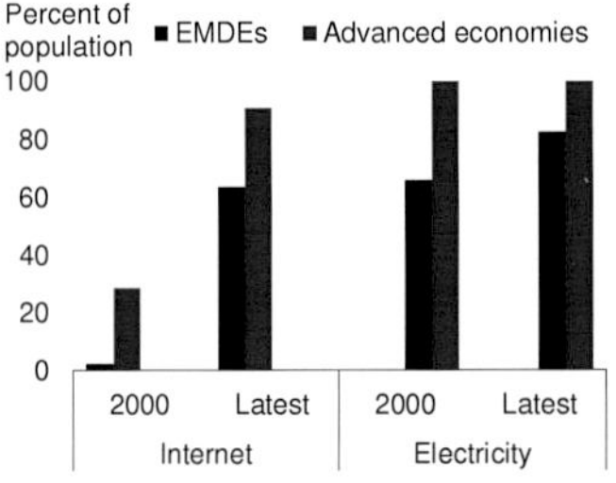

D. New trade agreements

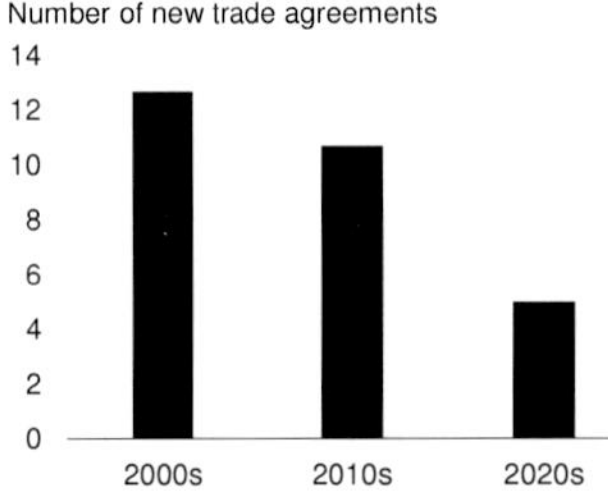

Sources: INFORM (database); Kose and Mulabdic (2024); WDI (database); IMF-WEO (database); World Bank; World Trade Organization.

Note: AEs = advanced economies; EMDEs = emerging market and developing economies; LICs = low-income countries.

A. Bars show the median for each country group.

B. Bars show average INFORM Climate Change Risk Index for each country group. The index provides quantified estimates of the impacts of climate change on the future risk of humanitarian crises and disasters, with 0 being no risk and 10 being the highest risk. Data are for 2022.

C. Panel shows simple averages. Data as of 2021. Electricity: unbalanced sample of 153 EMDEs and 37 advanced economies. Internet: 139 EMDEs and 37 advanced economies.

D. Panel shows average number of new trade agreements yearly as of February 1, 2024. Sample excludes agreements signed by the United Kingdom.

the poorest countries, where many sources of financing are drying up or have become cost-prohibitive. EMDEs with weak credit ratings—many of which are middle-income—face interest rates more than 10 percentage points above the global benchmark rate, leaving them effectively locked out of commercial markets and highly vulnerable to debt crises. Decisive action by the international community is needed to address developing risks to avoid the economic costs of debt crises. Debt restructuring and relief processes, particularly the G20 Common Framework, have so far delivered little relief and need to be upgraded to reflect the rapidly evolving sovereign landscape. These efforts can be complemented with domestic reforms to build the fiscal space necessary to boost growth and resilience, strengthen governance frameworks, and enhance debt transparency, which can in turn help prevent debt-related vulnerabilities from escalating further.

Climate change

Decarbonizing the global economy will require sizable investments and financing, yet policies worldwide remain inadequate to meet global climate goals. Reaching net zero by 2050 will require cutting greenhouse gas emissions by between one-fourth and one-half by 2030 relative to 2019; however, current global commitments are estimated to reduce emissions by only about 10 percent by the end of this decade. In EMDEs, the amount of investment spending needed to tackle development goals and reduce emissions by 73 percent by 2050 ranges from about 1 to 10 percent of GDP per year over the remainder of this decade—with notably higher needs in LICs, in part owing to their wider existing gaps in development and infrastructure spending and their exposure to climate change risks (figure 1.14.B; Neunuebel 2023; World Bank 2022a). The cost of achieving these goals will increase further if progress is delayed (World Bank 2022b).

In EMDEs, mobilizing public resources, including through subsidy reforms and carbon pricing, can help finance the needed public investments and social transfers to ensure a low-emission and equitable development pathway (World Bank 2023c). This can be complemented with measures to attract private investment, including policies that strengthen the regulatory environment and tackle corruption. Strong global cooperation is also needed to increase access to financing to address climate change, especially for vulnerable countries facing significant budgetary constraints (Chrimes et al. 2024).

Trade policies can be integrated more closely with climate initiatives to expedite the transition to renewable energy and to make progress on achieving global climate goals. Reducing restrictions on trade in green energy technologies is crucial for facilitating investment in energy transitions and the implementation of climate action plans, particularly in EMDEs with limited access to finance and technologies domestically (Park 2024). Measures such as environmental provisions in trade and investment agreements can support the transfer of greener technologies and facilitate broader technology spillovers to EMDEs.

Climate change is a growing threat to food security, with the impacts of rising temperatures and extreme weather events becoming increasingly evident in reduced crop yields and disruptions to food supply chains (IFPRI 2022). For wheat, rice, and maize in tropical and temperate regions, climate change, without adaptation measures, is projected to impair crop production at local temperature increases of 2 degrees Celsius (Aggarwal et al. 2024). To increase the resilience of the agriculture sector and ensure food security, countries can implement new technologies, such as irrigation systems to improve water use efficiency; increase access to insurance and risk finance; enhance early warning systems; and advance climate risk and adaptation knowledge (World Bank 2023c). Measures to help address food insecurity include avoiding export restrictions, strengthening agricultural food systems, and targeting social protection and cash transfers to poor and vulnerable households. Governments can also promote additional investments in research and development to boost agricultural productivity. Given heightened geopolitical tensions, collective global action is also needed to safeguard energy security by avoiding restrictions on trade in materials critical for the energy transition.

Digital transition

Although digital adoption is accelerating globally, the digital divide continues to widen (World Bank 2023d). About one-third of the global population, or 2.6 billion people, remained offline in 2023, with the vast majority living in EMDEs. Despite improvements over the past two decades, in 2021, about 18 percent of the population in EMDEs lacked electricity while only about 63 percent had access to the internet, compared with over 90 percent in advanced economies (figure 1.14.C). In addition to exacerbating development challenges, weak investment in digital infrastructure and research and development in EMDEs constrains the adoption of new technologies, such as AI.

Facilitating digital adoption and diffusion is critical to narrow the digital divide. Governments can play a role by catalyzing private investment in digital infrastructure. This can be achieved by rationalizing restrictions on foreign participation and ownership in internet service providers, promoting infrastructure sharing, ensuring competition, and monitoring the quality of internet services (ITU 2020; World Bank 2023d). Developing digital infrastructure can help raise investment growth and financial inclusion by enabling small firms and financial institutions to access financial markets and digital payments (UN 2022; World Bank 2022c). New digital technologies can help low- and middle-income countries address various development challenges. Still, some technologies, such as AI, are likely to be better leveraged by advanced economies given their more digitalized economies, highly skilled workforces, and institutional frameworks that can better adapt to the changing landscape. As advances in AI foster greater automation, the rationale for investing in and trading with low- and middle-income countries could become weaker, especially if their workforces lack the skills to take advantage of new roles created by AI. This may lead to a deterioration in their terms of trade, and eventually widening productivity and income gaps with advanced economies (World Bank 2023d).

To maximize the potential of AI and other new technologies, global coordination on international standards is needed to ensure their responsible development. A thorough assessment of the adequacy of existing legal frameworks in addressing emerging challenges—such as those related to data privacy and cybersecurity—is warranted. This can be complemented by national policies that balance innovation and regulation.

Trade fragmentation

Trade has been a key engine of global prosperity. The rapid expansion of global trade after 1990 enabled one billion people to escape extreme poverty and helped EMDEs narrow the income

FIGURE 1.15 EMDE monetary and financial policy challenges

The share of EMDEs with above-target inflation has declined, even though wage growth and core inflation remain elevated in some countries. Monetary easing in EMDEs has narrowed interest rate differentials between EMDEs and key advanced economies; this trend could lead to heightened financial and exchange rate volatility in some economies. Net capital inflows to EMDEs have been modestly positive recently; they could increase as central banks in advanced economies ease policy.

A. Share of EMDEs with above-target inflation

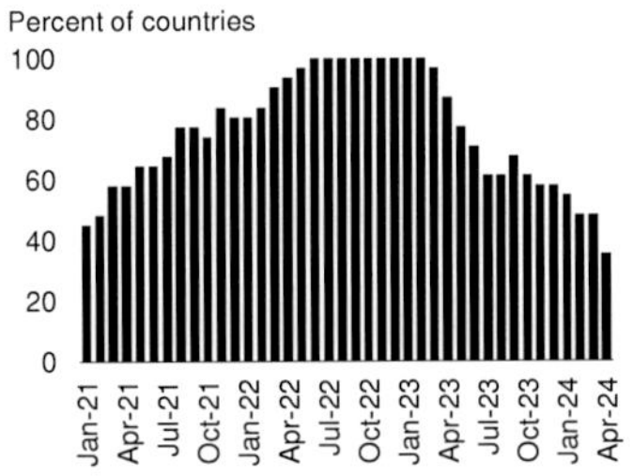

B. EMDE nominal wage growth and core inflation

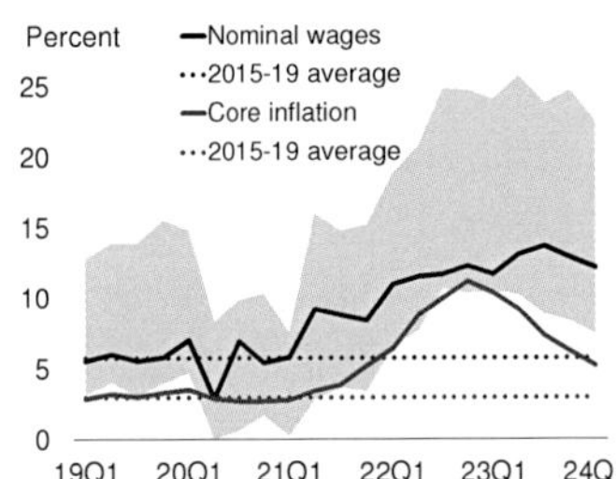

C. Interest rate differential between EMDEs excluding China, and the United States

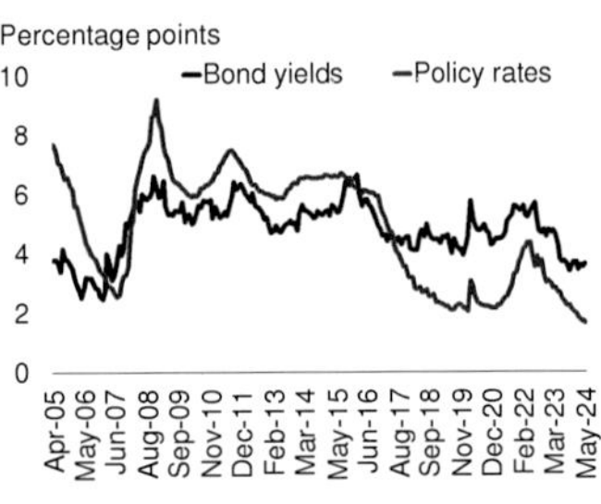

D. Capital flows to EMDEs

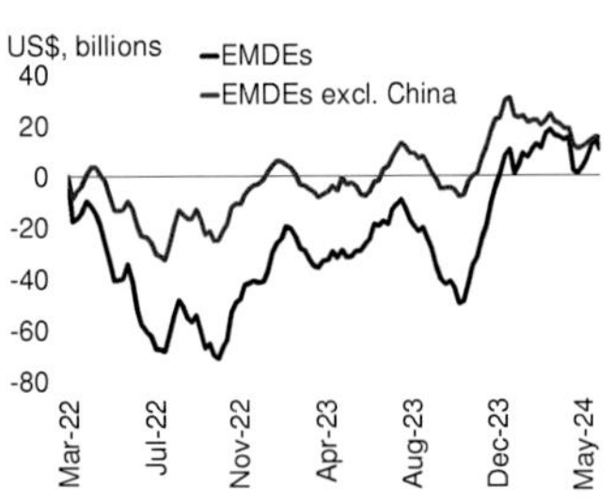

Sources: Bloomberg; Haver Analytics; IIF (database); World Bank.

Note: EMDEs = emerging market and developing economies.

A. Panel shows the share of EMDEs with inflation above target. Sample includes 31 EMDEs. Last observation is April 2024.

B. Nominal wage growth in the last quarter of available data compared to 2015-19 average and deviation of three-month moving average of core inflation from the 2015-19 average. Shaded area indicates the range of the first and third quartile of quarterly wages. Sample includes up to 20 EMDEs. Last observation is 2024Q1.

C. Red line indicates the differential between U.S. federal funds rate and a GDP-weighted average of policy rates for up to 18 EMDE central banks. Blue line indicates the differential between U.S. 10-year government bond yield and a GDP-weighted average of 10-year government bond yield for up to 14 EMDEs. Last observation is May 2024.

D. Net non-resident debt and equity flows to EMDEs since the U.S. Federal Reserve Bank started its hiking cycle in March 2022. Cumulative total using weekly data. Last observation is May 31, 2024. Sample includes 17 EMDEs for equity flows and 10 EMDEs for debt flows.

gap with high-income economies (Kose and Mulabdic 2024). Accordingly, the weakness in global trade in recent years and the subdued near-term outlook do not portend well for development and living standards. Critically, the proliferation of trade-restricting measures, disruptions to global value chains, and a further weakening of the multilateral trading system could lead to significant welfare losses globally, with particularly adverse impacts for EMDEs.

To reinvigorate trade growth and guard against trade fragmentation, it is key to restore the rules-based multilateral trade system, mitigate the adverse effects of geopolitical tensions on trade networks, foster a level playing field for international commerce, and reduce trade policy uncertainty. At the multilateral level, measures are needed to reinstate and reform the dispute settlement system, and enhance transparency, especially regarding distortions from industrial policy measures (IMF, OECD, World Bank, and WTO 2022). Countries could also resume efforts to expand trade agreements to bolster trade. In the 2020s so far, an average of just five agreements have been signed each year, less than half the rate of the 2000s (figure 1.14.D).

EMDE monetary and financial policy challenges

Many EMDE central banks began to cut policy rates last year amid declining inflation. With the broad trend in disinflation continuing this year, the share of EMDEs with above-target inflation has fallen below 50 percent for the first time since early 2021 (figure 1.15.A). Nevertheless, wage growth and service sector inflation are still elevated in some countries, and core inflation has remained persistently high (figure 1.15.B).

Bringing inflation durably to targets in these countries will require further easing of labor market tightness, as well as moderation in the growth of shelter and other services prices. Because of their persistence, reducing wage and services inflation sustainably toward pre-pandemic levels may be a lengthy process requiring carefully calibrated monetary policies (Amatyakul, Igan, and Lombardi 2024). If inflation were to surprise to the upside, it would be critical for central banks to signal their readiness to pause or reduce the pace of monetary easing, and even increase policy rates, if needed. This, together with continued emphasis on clear central bank communications, should help keep inflation expectations anchored and inflation trending toward targets, especially in the context of EMDEs (Ha, Kose, and Ohnsorge 2019).

In the near term, continued monetary easing in EMDEs could result in further narrowing of interest rate differentials relative to key advanced economies, as the expected pace of easing in the latter has diminished this year (figure 1.15.C). Such narrowing could trigger currency depreciations and endanger progress on disinflation, depending on the extent to which currency movements are transmitted to domestic prices. It could also exacerbate financial market volatility, particularly in economies with large external financing needs and elevated debt. Destabilizing capital outflows are less likely to occur, however, if EMDE monetary policy frameworks and commitments to price stability are seen as credible (Kalemli-Özcan and Unsal 2024). In addition, if limited in scope and duration, interventions to manage capital flow and currency volatility could be considered, should a sudden bout of outflows threaten to destabilize domestic financial systems.

To prepare for unforeseen shocks, close scrutiny of EMDE bank credit quality and capital levels is crucial. This can help ensure that banking sectors can weather potential losses without constricting credit in an unduly procyclical manner. More broadly, improved surveillance and supervision of banking sectors, along with strengthened fiscal frameworks, may reduce vulnerabilities and risks associated with the sovereign-bank nexus (Feyen and Igor 2019). Such financial sector reforms, along with broader structural and fiscal adjustments, can help improve investor perceptions and attract foreign capital, especially among EMDEs at elevated risk of debt-related stress.

In EMDEs with open capital accounts and strong financial market access, sound macroprudential policies can be important for the health and resilience of financial sectors. Measures of cumulative net portfolio flows to EMDEs have been close to neutral since the start of the U.S. monetary tightening cycle; however, if the inflationary persistence observed in early 2024 proves temporary, as currently expected, capital inflows could increase significantly as advanced-economy central banks ease policy (figure 1.15.D). Under such a scenario, EMDE central banks could enhance macroprudential buffers to help contain potential financial stability risks.

EMDE fiscal policy challenges

Fiscal policy in EMDEs is anticipated to modestly tighten over 2024-26, reflecting efforts to attenuate elevated debt stocks (figure 1.16.A). Rebuilding fiscal buffers will be important in containing debt-service burdens and regaining market confidence, helping reduce funding costs. That said, while fiscal adjustment can improve long-term growth prospects by fostering confidence and expanding fiscal space, the potentially adverse impacts on near-term growth and inequality need to be minimized through careful design and implementation—including by prioritizing critical spending on health, education, and social protection (Balasundharam et al. 2023). Facing high borrowing costs, EMDEs will need to mobilize resources to tackle development challenges without damaging the sustainability of their fiscal positions, including through strengthening public investment management. Countries can also implement measures to increase revenues, including through phasing out pandemic-era tax cuts and strengthening tax administration and enforcement.

The elevated cost of servicing debt could crowd out spending on other priorities, including public investment in physical and human capital, and social safety nets (figure 1.16.B; chapter 3). In EMDEs with limited fiscal space, redirecting spending to the highest priorities—including growth-enhancing investment and targeted support to the poor and the vulnerable—and improving spending efficiency are critical to help meet spending needs as fiscal policy is tightened. Such efforts can be supported by strong and effective fiscal institutions and management, backed by reforms to improve the transparency, accountability, and efficiency of fiscal policy.

Mobilizing revenues remains a key challenge in EMDEs. As tax collection, particularly of direct taxes such as income taxes, is often limited, EMDEs tend to be more reliant on other sources of revenues compared to advanced economies. These sources include rental income, interest, dividends, and sales of goods and services, which tend to be more volatile than tax revenues

FIGURE 1.16 EMDE fiscal policy challenges

Fiscal policy in EMDEs is anticipated to modestly tighten over 2024-26, with fiscal deficits narrowing to help address elevated debt stocks. A larger debt-service burden is associated with lower spending on public investment in EMDEs. Fiscal challenges are particularly acute in small states, where fiscal deficits are generally larger and the risk of debt distress is higher than in other EMDEs.

A. Cyclically adjusted primary balances in EMDEs

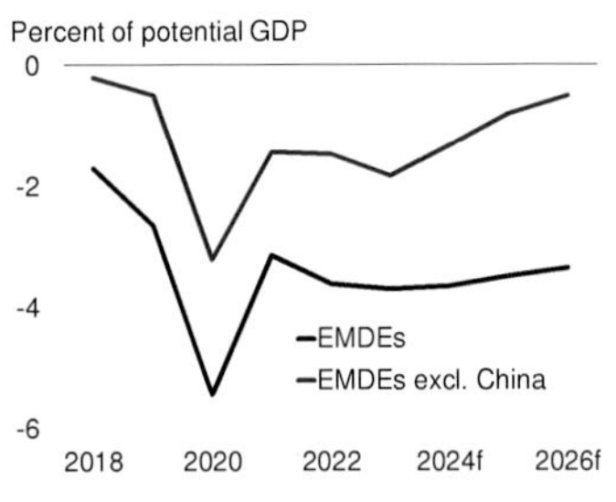

B. Public investment and interest payments in EMDEs in 2010s

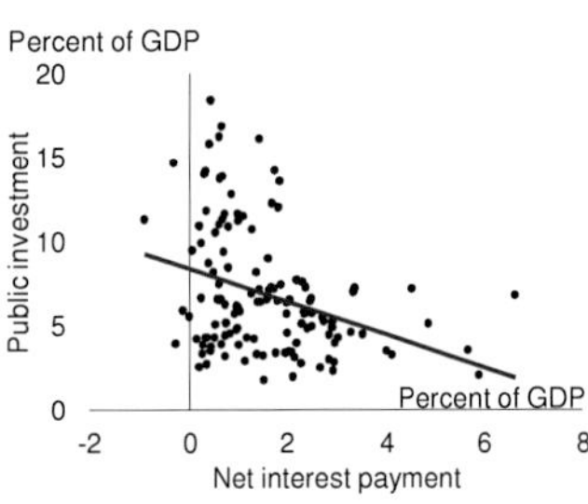

C. Primary fiscal balance in EMDEs

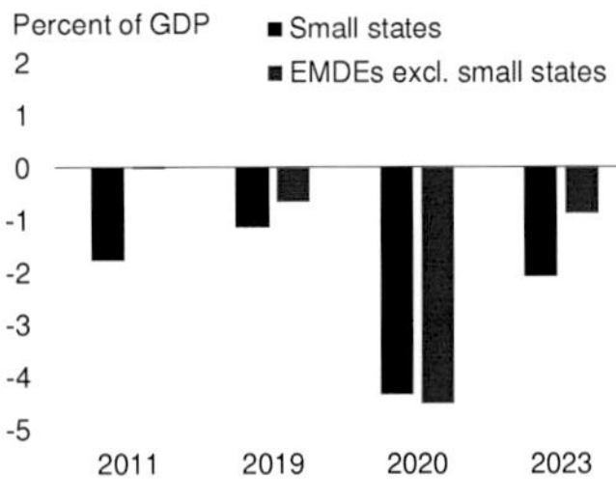

D. Risk of debt distress in EMDEs

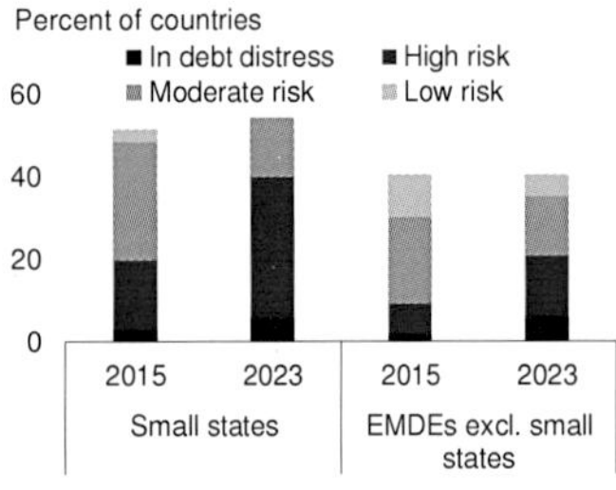

Sources: IMF (2015); Kose et al. (2022); IMF-WEO (database); World Bank; World Bank-IMF Debt Sustainability Framework.

Note: f = forecast; EMDEs = emerging market and developing economies.

A. Aggregates are computed as weighted averages using potential GDP as weights. Sample includes 46 EMDEs. Data for 2023 are estimates, while data for 2024-26 are forecasts.

B. Panel shows the relationship between public investment in percent of GDP in the 2010s and net interest payments, computed as differences between primary balances and fiscal balances. Correlation coefficient is -0.34 and is statistically significant at the 1 percent level, based on data for 130 EMDEs.

C. Panel shows the average primary fiscal balance for a sample of 32 small states and up to 109 EMDEs.

D. Share of small states and other EMDEs in overall debt distress or at risk of debt distress, based on the joint World Bank-IMF Debt Sustainability Framework for Low Income Countries (LIC-DSF) as of March 30, 2024.

(Mourre and Reut 2017). Government revenues are particularly weak in LICs—in 2024, they are set to be just under 14 percent of GDP, much lower than in other EMDEs and advanced economies. They also tend to be more volatile in LICs, which are often more dependent on commodities for export and fiscal revenues.

Strengthening tax collection by widening the tax base—including through eliminating costly tax exemptions, deductions, and other special preferences—and simplifying tax codes can improve domestic revenue mobilization and help generate lasting revenue gains for EMDEs. At the same time, limits in mobilizing domestic resources, especially in the short run, make funding from external sources particularly important for LICs (UNCTAD 2023). The receipt of official development assistance has increased since 2010, and external grants account for about 16 percent of government revenues in LICs.

The number of EMDEs with a heightened risk of debt distress or already in outright default remains elevated. The composition of debt also poses considerable challenges. In EMDEs with lower income levels and with less developed financial markets, the composition of government debt tends to be skewed toward riskier sources—including foreign-currency-denominated debt and non-resident holdings of debt—rendering countries more vulnerable to sudden shifts in global financing conditions. Additionally, the stock of short-term government debt has risen, increasing vulnerability to refinancing costs in a context of higher global interest rates.

Small states face unique fiscal challenges stemming from their exposure to large external shocks (chapter 4). The pandemic and subsequent global shocks have worsened fiscal and debt positions in small states (figure 1.16.C). More than one-third of small states are at high risk of debt distress or already in it, roughly twice the share in other EMDEs (figure 1.16.D).

Small states have an even more acute challenge in striking a balance between maintaining adequate fiscal buffers and increasing investments in human capital and climate-resilient infrastructure. As revenues are highly volatile and dependent on sometimes unreliable sources, a more stable and secure tax base is needed. Spending efficiency also needs to be improved, especially given that expenditure levels are already relatively high. These efforts should be complemented by reforms to fiscal frameworks, including better utilization of fiscal rules and sovereign wealth funds. With limited institutional capacity and opportunities to borrow privately, ongoing international support will also be important to help meet spending needs and strengthen policies.

EMDE structural policy challenges

EMDEs face pressing longer-term challenges, many of which have been aggravated by the overlapping shocks of the last four years. Comprehensive reform efforts are needed to boost investment to achieve sustained growth and development. Crucially, reversing the scarring effects of the pandemic on growth prospects will require investments in education and human capital. Bolstering food security is vital, particularly in light of increased hunger, growing trade-restrictive policies, and conflict. Widening gender gaps in labor force participation and elevated youth unemployment rates in EMDEs highlight the need for labor market reforms and social protection measures.

Accelerating public investment

Sustained investment is needed to deliver robust potential output growth, improve living standards, and make progress in achieving development and climate-related goals. Effective public investment could play an important role, including to catalyze broader investment. Nonetheless, for many EMDEs, fiscal space is limited, reflecting weak revenue collection, especially relative to advanced economies. To accelerate public investment in EMDEs, it is critical to expand fiscal buffers, including through reforms aimed at increasing domestic revenue mobilization and by enhanced support from the global community.

Mobilizing public resources could, in turn, help facilitate private investment through various channels. Public investment in infrastructure—notably, transport and communications infrastructure—can raise returns on private capital, thereby encouraging private sector investment. Public investment programs can also catalyze private investment directly by leveraging private capital in the implementation of investment projects—for instance, via public-private partnerships. Furthermore, public investment can help reduce uncertainty and risks associated with large private investment projects. Estimates show that an increase in public investment equivalent to one percent of GDP leads to a 2.2 percent increase in private investment over four years (figure 1.17.A; chapter 3). Policies to overcome common obstacles to private investment—such as poor business conditions, insufficient project pipelines, and underdeveloped domestic capital markets—are also essential.

It is also critical to improve public investment efficiency, notably in infrastructure, where more than one-third of spending by EMDEs is estimated to be wasted, leaving a large efficiency gap in EMDEs relative to advanced economies (figure 1.17.B; chapter 3). Spending efficiency could be improved, and waste reduced, by tackling corruption and poor governance, and by improv-

FIGURE 1.17 EMDE structural policy challenges

Public investment can have significant crowding-in effects on private investment in EMDEs. Infrastructure investment efficiency in EMDEs is considerably lower than in advanced economies. Learning losses from the pandemic have been more pronounced in regions where school closures were extensive. Food insecurity in EMDEs has surged since the pandemic.

A. Impact of higher public investment on private investment

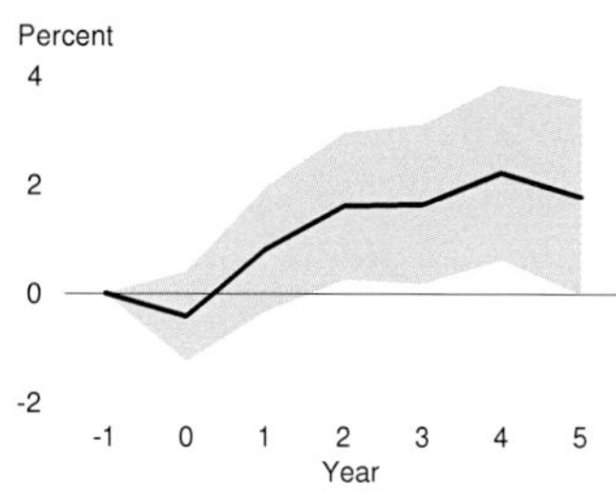

B. Public infrastructure investment efficiency

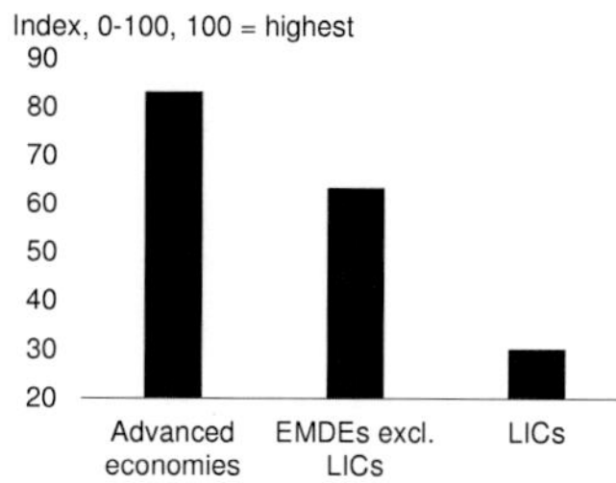

C. Learning losses

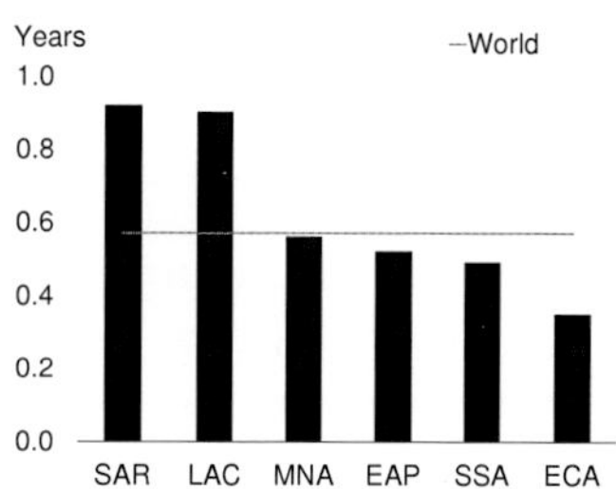

D. Food insecurity in EMDEs

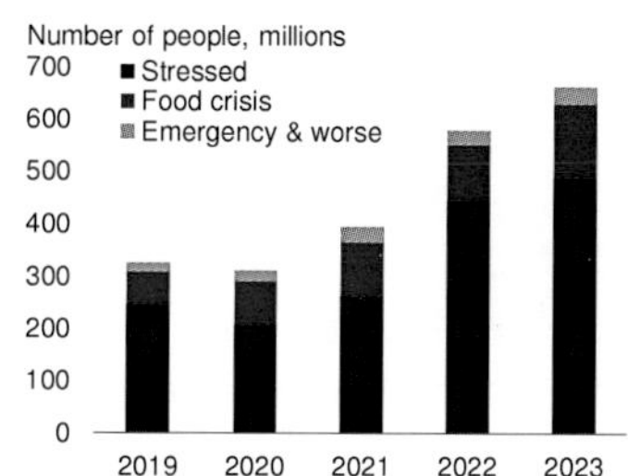

Sources: IMF (2021); GRFC (database); Schady et al. (2023); World Bank.

Note: EAP = East Asia and Pacific; ECA = Europe and Central Asia; EMDEs = emerging markets and developing economies; LAC = Latin America and the Caribbean; LICs = low-income countries; MNA = Middle East and North Africa; SAR = South Asia; SSA = Sub-Saharan Africa.

A. Response of real private investment (cumulative change in year *t* relative to year *t*-1, in percent) to a public investment shock equivalent to 1 percent of GDP; *t* = 0 is the year of the shock. Shaded areas denote 90-percent confidence bands, based on standard errors clustered at the country level. Sample includes 129 EMDEs.

B. Bars show group medians of the IMF (2021) public infrastructure efficiency index. Sample includes 27 advanced economies and 93 EMDEs, of which 15 are LICs.

C. Panel shows the average learning-adjusted years of schooling (LAYS) lost by World Bank region, weighted by population. Regional averages exclude high-income countries. For each country, lost LAYS are calculated for each level of schooling and then averaged across levels, weighted by the duration of each level, as shown in Schady et al. (2023). Horizontal line shows the global average.

D. Panel shows the number of people suffering food insecurity in phases 2 to 5, according to the acute food insecurity reference table from GRFC report. Sample includes data for up to 135 EMDEs.

ing investment project management frameworks. This could include an overarching investment planning framework comprising a transparent set of development and climate goals; multiyear budgeting; robust project management; enhanced monitoring and procurement processes; as well as improved risk management and mitigation. Finally, without enhanced global financial support and technical assistance, EMDEs with limited fiscal space, deep structural challenges, and vast infrastructure needs—especially LICs, FCS, and some small states—may not be able to finance and implement substantial, growth-enhancing public investment projects.

Lifting human capital

In many EMDEs, the negative effects of the COVID-19 pandemic on human capital have not been reversed and have exacerbated challenges that predate the pandemic. In particular, the pandemic brought about considerable disruption to schooling and learning and is likely to have a lasting and unequal impact on learning levels. Learning losses have been more pronounced in regions where school closures were extensive, notably in LAC and SAR (figure 1.17.C). Since 2019, the learning poverty rate—the share of children unable to read and understand a simple text by age 10—is estimated to have risen by 13 percentage points to 70 percent, on average, in low- and middle-income countries (World Bank et al. 2022). The long-term effect of these learning losses is likely to be substantial. This generation of students could lose an estimated 17 percent of GDP in future earnings as a result of lost schooling and learning, with losses likely to be greater for poor and other vulnerable students (Schady et al. 2023).

Despite these potential losses, most EMDEs have not implemented policy measures to support a recovery in learning. Such measures could include targeted instruction programs, particularly for vulnerable students, and enhanced training for teachers. New learning technologies can also be harnessed to improve teaching effectiveness and educational outcomes (World Bank 2019). Re-integrating of workers separated from the labor markets during the pandemic, including through upskilling and reskilling, is also needed. Nontraditional modes of education, such as short-cycle higher education programs, can play an important role in skills development and training workers in new fields (Ferreyra et al. 2021).

Confronting food insecurity

Food insecurity in EMDEs has surged since the pandemic, affecting about 660 million people in 2023 compared with about 325 million in 2019 (figure 1.17.D). Major drivers of food insecurity and malnutrition—conflict, extreme weather patterns, economic downturns, and inequality—have intensified in recent years, often occurring in combination. The rise of trade-restrictive measures has further accentuated food insecurity, particularly in EMDEs that rely heavily on food imports, exposing them to fluctuations in international food prices (Laborde, Lakatos, and Martin 2019). Beyond immediate concerns over food insecurity, rising food prices significantly impact poverty, welfare, and outcomes later in life (Gatti et al. 2023; Lederman and Porto 2016). To shore up food security, urgent action is needed to protect vulnerable households, along with measures to tackle the root causes of food insecurity. Governments need to support production by ensuring access to and availability of agricultural inputs, such as fertilizers, while facilitating increased trade in food and agricultural inputs. Policies are also needed to improve the resilience of food systems. These could include investing in more social protection programs that ensure both the climate resilience of food systems and affordability of healthy diets. Investing in agricultural technology can help improve climate-resilient food production and raise agricultural productivity.

Bolstering inclusion in the labor force

Progress in closing gender gaps in labor force participation in EMDEs lags considerably behind that in advanced economies (WEF 2023; World Bank 2024e). This reflects unequal access to services, discriminatory laws, inadequate childcare, and other barriers that prevent women from realizing their full economic potential. Reforms that aim to reduce the gender gap in the labor force can ignite new sources of economic growth, particularly given the secular decline in potential growth (Kose and Ohnsorge 2023). Such reforms include targeted social protection measures that provide adequate social safety nets, access to education, and support for childcare and job re-entry programs (Bussolo et al. 2022; World Bank 2022c).

Low labor force participation and high unemployment among youth populations is another major challenge in many EMDEs, particularly in LICs. Labor market outcomes for youth remain below pre-pandemic trends (ILO 2023). The share of people in LICs aged 15-24 years who were neither employed nor in education or training was 1 percentage point higher (at 27.7 percent) in 2022 than in 2019, while the youth unemployment rate was 1.1 percentage points higher (Elder and O'Higgins 2023). To boost the recovery in youth employment, governments could prioritize policies targeted to youth. Active labor market policies, youth employment programs, career guidance, and apprenticeships are vital for increasing employment opportunities (World Bank and ILO 2024). This is particularly important for more vulnerable sections of the youth population, such as migrants and refugees.

TABLE 1.2 Emerging market and developing economies[1]

Commodity exporters[2]		Commodity importers[3]	
Algeria*	Kyrgyz Republic	Afghanistan	Samoa
Angola*	Lao PDR	Albania	Serbia
Argentina	Liberia	Antigua and Barbuda	Somalia
Armenia	Libya*	Bahamas, The	Sri Lanka
Azerbaijan*	Madagascar	Bangladesh	St. Kitts and Nevis
Bahrain*	Malawi	Barbados	St. Lucia
Belize	Mali	Belarus	St. Vincent and the Grenadines
Benin	Mauritania	Bosnia and Herzegovina	Syrian Arab Republic
Bhutan*	Mongolia	Bulgaria	Thailand
Bolivia*	Mozambique	Cambodia	Tonga
Botswana	Myanmar*	China	Tunisia
Brazil	Namibia	Djibouti	Türkiye
Burkina Faso	Nicaragua	Dominica	Tuvalu
Burundi	Niger	Dominican Republic	Vanuatu
Cabo Verde	Nigeria*	Egypt, Arab Rep.	Viet Nam
Cameroon*	Oman*	El Salvador	
Central African Republic	Papua New Guinea	Eswatini	
Chad*	Paraguay	Georgia	
Chile	Peru	Grenada	
Colombia*	Qatar*	Haiti	
Comoros	Russian Federation*	Hungary	
Congo, Dem. Rep.	Rwanda	India	
Congo, Rep.*	São Tomé and Príncipe	Jamaica	
Costa Rica	Saudi Arabia*	Jordan	
Côte d'Ivoire	Senegal	Kiribati	
Ecuador*	Seychelles	Lebanon	
Equatorial Guinea*	Sierra Leone	Lesotho	
Eritrea	Solomon Islands	Malaysia	
Ethiopia	South Africa	Maldives	
Fiji	South Sudan*	Marshall Islands	
Gabon*	Sudan	Mauritius	
Gambia, The	Suriname	Mexico	
Ghana*	Tajikistan	Micronesia, Fed. Sts.	
Guatemala	Tanzania	Moldova	
Guinea	Timor-Leste*	Montenegro	
Guinea-Bissau	Togo	Morocco	
Guyana*	Uganda	Nauru	
Honduras	Ukraine	Nepal	
Indonesia*	United Arab Emirates*	North Macedonia	
Iran, Islamic Rep.*	Uruguay	Pakistan	
Iraq*	Uzbekistan	Palau	
Kazakhstan*	West Bank and Gaza	Panama	
Kenya	Yemen, Rep.*	Philippines	
Kosovo	Zambia	Poland	
Kuwait*	Zimbabwe	Romania	

* Energy exporters.

1. Emerging market and developing economies (EMDEs) include all those that are not classified as advanced economies and for which a forecast is published for this report. Dependent territories are excluded. Advanced economies include Australia; Austria; Belgium; Canada; Cyprus; Czechia; Denmark; Estonia; Finland; France; Germany; Greece; Hong Kong SAR, China; Iceland; Ireland; Israel; Italy; Japan; the Republic of Korea; Latvia; Lithuania; Luxembourg; Malta; the Netherlands; New Zealand; Norway; Portugal; Singapore; the Slovak Republic; Slovenia; Spain; Sweden; Switzerland; the United Kingdom; and the United States. Since Croatia became a member of the euro area on January 1, 2023, it has been removed from the list of EMDEs, and related growth aggregates, to avoid double counting.

2. An economy is defined as commodity exporter when, on average in 2017-19, either (1) total commodities exports accounted for 30 percent or more of total exports or (2) exports of any single commodity accounted for 20 percent or more of total exports. Economies for which these thresholds were met as a result of re-exports were excluded. When data were not available, judgment was used. This taxonomy results in the classification of some well-diversified economies as importers, even if they are exporters of certain commodities (for example, Mexico).

3. Commodity importers are EMDEs not classified as commodity exporters.

References

ACLED (The Armed Conflict Location & Event Data Project) database. Accessed on May 31, 2024. https://acleddata.com/data-export-tool

Aggarwal, R., M. P. Carapella, T. Mogues, and C. J. Pico-Mejia. 2024. "Accounting for Climate Risks in Costing the Sustainable Development Goals." IMF Working Paper 24/49, International Monetary Fund, Washington, DC.

Alessandria, A. G., Y. S. Khan, A. Khederlarian, J. K. Ruhl, and B. J. Steinberg. 2024. "Trade War and Peace: U.S.-China Trade and Tariff Risk from 2015–2050." NBER Working Paper 32150, National Bureau of Economic Research, Cambridge, MA.

Amatyakul, P., D. Igan, and M. J. Lombardi. 2024. "Sectoral Price Dynamics in the Last Mile of Post-Covid-19 Disinflation." BIS Quarterly Review, Bank for International Settlement, Basel, Switzerland.

Arteta, C., S. Kamin, and F. U. Ruch. 2022. "How Do Rising U.S. Interest Rates Affect Emerging and Developing Economies? It Depends." Policy Research Working Paper 10258, World Bank, Washington, DC.

Balasundharam, V., O. Basdevant, D. Benicio, A. Ceber, Y. Kim, L. Mazzone, H. Selim, and Y. Yang. 2023. "Fiscal Consolidation: Taking Stock of Success Factors, Impact, and Design." IMF Working Paper 23/63, International Monetary Fund, Washington, DC.

Barwick, J. P., M. Kalouptsidi, and B. N. Zahur. 2024. "Industrial Policy Implementation: Empirical Evidence from China's Shipbuilding Industry." *Review of Economic Studies* (in press).

Bedasa, Y., and K. Deksisa. 2024. "Food Insecurity in East Africa: An Integrated Strategy to Address Climate Change Impact and Violence Conflict." *Journal of Agriculture and Food Research* 15 (March): 100978.

Blanga-Gubbay, M., and S. Rubínová. 2023. "Is the Global Economy Fragmenting?" WTO Staff Working Paper ERSD-2023-10, Economic Research and Statistics Division, World Trade Organization, Geneva.

Bogetic, Z., L. Zhao, H. Krambeck, E. A. Chamorro, S. Sarva, J. Matossian, and Y. Zhao. 2024. "Dire Strait: The Far-Reaching Impact of the Red Sea Shipping Crisis." MENA FCV Economic Series Brief, World Bank.

Bolhuis, M., H. Mighri, H. Rawlings, I. Reyes, and Q. Zhang. 2024. "How Vulnerable Is Sub-Saharan Africa to Geoeconomic Fragmentation?" IMF Working Paper 24/83, International Monetary Fund, Washington, DC.

Bown, P. C. 2023. "Modern Industrial Policy and the WTO." Working Paper 23-15, Peterson Institute for International Economics, Washington, DC.

Bussolo, M., J. A. Ezebuihe, A. M. Munoz Boudet, S. Poupakis, T. Rahman, and N. Sarma. 2022. "Social Norms and Gender Equality: A Descriptive Analysis for South Asia." Policy Research Working Paper 10142, World Bank, Washington, DC.

Caldara, D., and M. Iacoviello. 2022. "Measuring Geopolitical Risk." *American Economic Review* 112 (4): 1194-225.

Caldara, D., M. Iacoviello, P. Molligo, A. Prestipino, and A. Raffo. 2019. "Does Trade Policy Uncertainty Affect Global Economic Activity?" FEDS Notes, Board of Governors of the Federal Reserve System, Washington, DC.

Caldara, D., M. Iacoviello, P. Molligo, A. Prestipino, and A. Raffo. 2020. "The Economic Effects of Trade Policy Uncertainty." *Journal of Monetary Economics* 109 (January): 38-59.

Carroll, D. C., M. Otsuka, and J. Slacalek. 2011. "How Large Are Housing and Financial Wealth Effects? A New Approach." *Journal of Money, Credit and Banking* 43 (1): 55-79.

CBO (Congressional Budget Office). 2024a. "The Long-Term Budget Outlook: 2024 to 2054." Nonpartisan Analysis for the U.S Congress, Washington, DC.

CBO (Congressional Budget Office). 2024b. "The Demographic Outlook: 2024 to 2054." Nonpartisan Analysis for the U.S Congress, Washington, DC.

Chrimes, T., B. Gootjes, M. A. Kose, and C. Wheeler. 2024. *The Great Reversal: Prospects, Risks, and Policies in International Development Association (IDA) Countries.* Washington, DC: World Bank.

Copestake, A., M. Firat, D. Furceri, and C. Redl. 2023. "China Spillovers: Aggregate and Firm-Level Evidence." IMF Working Paper 23/206, International Monetary Fund, Washington, DC.

Elder, S., and N. O'Higgins. 2023. "Has Youth Employment Recovered?" ILO Brief, Employment Policy Department, International Labour Organization, Geneva.

EM-DAT (The International Disaster Database) database. Centre for Research on the Epidemiology of

Disasters (CRED), UCLouvain, Brussels. Accessed on May 14, 2024. https://www.emdat.be/

Ferreyra, M., L. D. Díaz, S. Urzúa, and M. Bassi. 2021. *The Fast Track to New Skills: Short-Cycle Higher Education Programs in Latin America and the Caribbean*. Washington, DC: World Bank.

FEWS NET (Famine Early Warning Systems Network). 2023. "Strong El Niño Event Will Contribute to High Food Assistance Needs Through 2024." Global Food Security Alert, Washington, DC.

Feyen, E., and Z. Igor. 2019. "The Sovereign-Bank Nexus in EMDEs: What Is It, Is It Rising, and What Are the Policy Implications?" Policy Research Working Paper 8950, World Bank, Washington, DC.

Freund, C., A. Mattoo, A. Mulabdic, and M. Ruta. 2023. "Is US Trade Policy Reshaping Global Supply Chains?" Policy Research Working Paper 10593, World Bank, Washington, DC.

FSIN (Food Security Information Network) and GNAFC (Global Network Against Food Crises). 2024. Global Report on Food Crises 2024. Rome: FSIN.

Gatti, R., D. Lederman, M. A. Islam, R. F. Bennett, J. P. B Andree, H. Assem, R. Lotfi, and E. M. Mousa. 2023. "*Altered Destinies: The Long-Term Effects of Rising Prices and Food Insecurity in the Middle East and North Africa*." Middle East and North Africa Economic Update. Washington, DC: World Bank.

Gopinath, G., P. Gourinchas, F. A. Presbitero, and P. Topalova. 2024. "Changing Global Linkages: A New Cold War?" IMF Working Paper 24/76, International Monetary Fund, Washington, DC.

GRFC (Global Report on Food Crises) database. Food Security Information Network. Accessed on May 30, 2024. https://fsinplatform.org/our-data

Grossman, G. M., E. Helpman, and S. J. Redding. 2024. "When Tariffs Disrupt Global Supply Chains." *American Economic Review* 114 (4): 988-1029.

GTA (Global Trade Alert) database. Accessed on May 30, 2024. https://globaltradealert.org/data_extraction

Gutierrez, C., J. Turen, and A. Vicondoa. 2024. "Chinese Macroeconomic Surprises and the Global Financial Cycle." Doumento de Trabajo 577, Instituto de Economia, Pontificia Universidad Católica de Chile, Santiago, Chile.

Ha, J., M. A. Kose, and F. Ohnsorge, eds. 2019. *Inflation in Emerging and Developing Economies: Evolution, Drivers, and Policies*. Washington, DC: World Bank.

Ha, J., M. Stocker, and H. Yilmazkuday. 2020. "Inflation and Exchange Rate Pass-through." *Journal of International Money and Finance* 105 (July): 102187

Hallegatte, S., and J. Rozenberg. 2017. "Climate Change Through a Poverty Lens." *Nature Climate Change* 7: 250-56.

IEA (International Energy Agency). 2023. "*World Energy Investment 2023*." May. Paris: International Energy Agency.

IFPRI (International Food Policy Research Institute). 2022. *2022 Global Food Policy Report: Climate Change and Food Systems*. Washington, DC: International Food Policy Research Institute.

IIF (Institute of International Finance) database. Accessed on May 31, 2024. https://iif.com/Research/Download-Data

ILO (International Labour Organization). 2023. "World Employment and Social Outlook; Trends 2023." ILO Flagship Report. Geneva: International Labour Organization.

IMF (International Monetary Fund). 2015. "Making Public Investment More Efficient." IMF Staff Report, International Monetary Fund, Washington, DC.

IMF (International Monetary Fund). 2021. *Fiscal Monitor: A Fair Shot*. April. Washington, DC: International Monetary Fund.

IMF (International Monetary Fund), OECD (Organisation for Economic Co-operation and Development), World Bank, and WTO (World Trade Organization). 2022. *Subsidies, Trade, and International Cooperation*. Washington, DC: IMF, OECD, World Bank, and WTO.

IMF-WEO (International Monetary Fund) database. "World Economic Outlook: April 2024." Accessed on April 20, 2024. https://www.imf.org/en/Publications/WEO/weo-database/2024/April

INFORM (database). "INFORM Climate Change Brochure Data." DRMKC—INFORM, European Commission, Brussels. Available at https://drmkc.jrc.ec.europa.eu/inform-index/INFORM-Climate-Change/Results-and-data

ITU (International Telecommunication Union). 2020. *Connecting Humanity: Assessing Investment Needs of*

Connecting Humanity to the Internet by 2030. Geneva: International Telecommunication Union.

Jafino, B. A., B. Walsh, J. Rozenberg, and S. Hallegatte. 2020. "Revised Estimates of the Impact of Climate Change on Extreme Poverty by 2030." Policy Research Working Paper 9417, World Bank. Washington, DC.

Kalemli-Özcan, Ş., and F. Unsal. 2024. "Global Transmission of FED Hikes: The Role of Policy Credibility and Balance Sheets." NBER Working Paper 32329, National Bureau of Economic Research, Cambridge, MA.

Kose, M. A., S. Kurlat, F. Ohnsorge, and N. Sugawara. 2022. "A Cross-Country Database of Fiscal Space." *Journal of International Money and Finance* 128 (November): 102682.

Kose, M. A., and A. Mulabdic. 2024. "Global Trade Has Nearly Flatlined. Populism Is Taking a Toll on Growth." *Voices* (blog). February 22, 2024. https://blogs.worldbank.org/en/voices/global-trade-has-nearly-flatlined-populism-taking-toll-growth

Kose, M. A., and F. Ohnsorge, eds. 2023. *Falling Long-Term Growth Prospects: Trends, Expectations, and Policies*. Washington, DC: World Bank.

Laborde, D., C. Lakatos, and W. Martin. 2019. "Poverty Impacts of Food Price Shocks and Policies." In *Inflation in Emerging and Developing Economies: Evolution, Drivers, and Policies*, edited by J. Ha, M. A. Kose, and F. Ohnsorge, 371-99. Washington, DC: World Bank.

Lederman, D., and G. Porto. 2016. "The Price Is Not Always Right: On the Impacts of Commodity Prices on Households (and Countries)." Policy Research Working Paper 7583, World Bank, Washington, DC.

Mahler, D. G., and C. Lakner. 2022. "The Impact of COVID-19 on Global Inequality and Poverty." Policy Research Working Paper 10198, World Bank, Washington, DC.

Milivojevic, L. 2023. "Natural Disasters and Fiscal Drought." Policy Research Working Paper 10298, World Bank, Washington, DC.

Mourre, G., and A. Reut. 2017. "Non-Tax Revenue in the European Union: A Source of Fiscal Risk?" European Economy Discussion Paper 44, European Commission, Brussels.

MSCI (Powering Better Investment Decisions) database. Accessed on March 25, 2024. https://www.msci.com

Neunuebel, C. 2023. "What the World Bank's Country Climate and Development Reports Tell Us about the Debt-Climate Nexus in Low-income Countries." World Resources Institute, Washington, DC.

OCHA (United Nations Office for the Coordination of Humanitarian Affairs). 2024. "The Humanitarian Impact of El Niño in Southern Africa." Regional Interagency Standing Committee, United Nations Office for the Coordination of Humanitarian Affairs, New York.

Ohnsorge, F. L., M. Stocker, and M. Y. Some. 2016. "Quantifying Uncertainties in Global Growth Forecasts." Policy Research Working Paper 7770, World Bank, Washington, DC.

Oxford Economics. 2019. "Global Economic Model." July. Oxford Economics, Oxford, U.K.

Park, C. 2024. "Prolonged Trade Tensions Hamper Efforts to Reach Global Net Zero Goals." *Asian Development* (blog). February 9, 2024. https://blogs.adb.org/blog/prolonged-trade-tensions-hamper-efforts-reach-global-net-zero-goals

Schady, N., A. Holla, S. Sabarwal, J. Silva, and A. Y. Chang. 2023. *Collapse and Recovery: How the COVID-19 Pandemic Eroded Human Capital and What to Do about It*. Washington, DC: World Bank.

UNCTAD (United Nations Conference on Trade and Development). 2023. *Least Developed Countries Report 2023: Crisis-Resilient Development Finance*. Geneva: United Nations.

UNHCR (United Nations High Commissioner for Refugees) Refugee Population Statistics Database. Accessed on April 4, 2024. https://www.unhcr.org/refugee-statistics/download/?url=IAr67y

United Nations, Inter-Agency Task Force on Financing for Development. 2022. "*Financing for Sustainable Development Report 2022*." New York: United Nations.

WEF (World Economic Forum). 2023. "*Global Gender Gap Report 2023*." Insight Report. June. Cologny, Switzerland: World Economic Forum.

WMO (World Meteorological Organization). 2021. "WMO Atlas of Mortality and Economic Losses from Weather, Climate and Water Extremes (1970-2019)." World Meteorological Organization, Geneva.

World Bank—WDI (World Development Indicators) database. "World Development Indicators." Accessed on May 30, 2024. https://databank.worldbank.org/source/world-development-indicators

World Bank. 2019. *World Development Report 2019: The Changing Nature of Work.* Washington, DC: World Bank.

World Bank. 2020. *World Development Report 2020: Trading for Development in the Age of Global Value Chains.* Washington, DC: World Bank.

World Bank. 2022a. "Climate and Development: An Agenda for Action—Emerging Insights from World Bank Group 2021-22 Country Climate and Development Reports." World Bank, Washington, DC.

World Bank. 2022b. "Update on World Bank Group Efforts to Facilitate Private Capital Investments." World Bank, Washington, DC.

World Bank. 2022c. *South Asia Economic Focus: Reshaping Norms: A New Way Forward.* Spring. Washington, DC: World Bank.

World Bank. 2023a. *Global Economic Prospects.* June. Washington, DC: World Bank.

World Bank. 2023b. "Sahel Adaptive Social Protection Program (SASPP) Annual Report." World Bank, Washington, DC.

World Bank. 2023c. "The Development, Climate, and Nature Crisis: Solutions to End Poverty on a Livable Planet." Insights from World Bank Country Climate and Development Reports, World Bank, Washington, DC.

World Bank. 2023d. *Digital Progress and Trends Report 2023.* Washington, DC: World Bank.

World Bank. 2024a. "Gaza Strip Interim Damage Assessment Summary Note." Washington, DC: World Bank.

World Bank. 2024b. *Commodity Markets Outlook.* April. Washington, DC: World Bank.

World Bank. 2024c. "Food Security Update." March. World Bank, Washington, DC.

World Bank. 2024d. "Food Security Update." April. World Bank, Washington, DC.

World Bank. 2024e. *Global Economic Prospects.* January. Washington, DC: World Bank.

World Bank and ILO (International Labour Organization). 2024. "Active Labor Market Programs Improve Employment and Earnings of Young People." Brief. World Bank, Washington, DC; International Labour Organization, Geneva.

World Bank, UNESCO, UNICEF, Foreign, Commonwealth & Development Office, USAID, and Bill & Melinda Gates Foundation. 2022. "The State of Global Learning Poverty: 2022 Update." Conference Edition, World Bank, Washington, DC.

WTO (World Trade Organization). 2024. "Global Trade Outlook and Statistics." World Trade Organization, Geneva.

CHAPTER 2

REGIONAL OUTLOOKS

EAST ASIA and PACIFIC

Growth in the East Asia and Pacific (EAP) region is projected to slow from 5.1 percent in 2023 to 4.8 percent in 2024, mainly reflecting a deceleration of activity in China. In the region excluding China, growth is projected to increase to 4.6 percent this year, supported by a recovery in global trade. Over the next two years, growth in EAP is projected to continue moderating—to 4.2 percent in 2025 and 4.1 percent in 2026, as a further slowdown in China again offsets a modest pickup elsewhere in the region. While risks to the outlook are somewhat more balanced than in January, they remain tilted to the downside. Risks stem particularly from worsening conflicts and heightened geopolitical tensions at the global level, further trade policy fragmentation, and a sharper-than-projected slowdown in China, with adverse spillovers to the broader region. Tighter global financial conditions and climate-related natural disasters pose additional downside risks. In contrast, faster-than-expected U.S. growth could have positive spillovers to regional activity.

Recent developments

Economic growth in the East Asia and Pacific (EAP) region strengthened in early 2024. In China, growth edged up, as exports expanded robustly alongside firming industrial production (figure 2.1.1.A). Manufacturing investment was firm, reflecting solid demand for products like electric vehicles and batteries, as well as ongoing government support for priority sectors such as semiconductors (World Bank 2023a). Meanwhile, China's infrastructure investment was solid, benefiting from public spending. In contrast, real estate investment continued to decline amid the ongoing downturn in the property sector. Following debt defaults in 2022 and 2023, real estate developers experienced further financial strains from falling property prices and sales (figure 2.1.1.B). The authorities implemented additional measures to support the property sector, including facilitating liquidity provision to developers, and reducing down payment requirements for borrowers. Although consumer spending on some services was firm, overall, it was subdued amid weak confidence, following a strong expansion in 2023 supported by reopening after the pandemic (figures 2.1.1.C and 2.1.1.D).

Note: This section was prepared by Samuel Hill.

Elsewhere in EAP, growth strengthened in some economies in early 2024 as exports ticked up from a slump in 2023 caused by a global goods trade downturn (figures 2.1.2.A and 2.1.2.B). After contracting through much of last year, goods exports have since firmed across some major export-oriented economies. In tandem, manufacturing activity showed signs of improvement, with purchasing managers' indexes ticking up in most larger economies. In some tourism-dependent economies, service exports continued to benefit from the recovery in global tourism. Private consumption growth remained resilient across the region, aided by low inflation. However, investment was subdued, partly reflecting the delayed impact of monetary policy tightening and heightened global and domestic uncertainty.

After declining last year, headline consumer price inflation ticked up in early 2024 in some countries, partly because of increasing oil prices. However, both headline and core inflation mostly remained below or near targets in the largest regional economies, reflecting a combination of moderating food prices, subsidies, and spare capacity (figure 2.1.2.C). In China, headline consumer prices declined through much of the second half of last year, weighed down by falling food prices, including pork, owing to ample supplies. Although headline consumer prices

FIGURE 2.1.1 China: Recent developments

Growth in China picked up in early 2024, supported by an acceleration in exports that helped offset continued weakness in the real estate sector marked by falling property prices and sales. Following a robust performance in 2023 driven by the release of pent-up demand, consumption was subdued in early 2024, with retail sales expanding below the pre-pandemic average pace as consumer confidence remained weak.

A. China: GDP growth

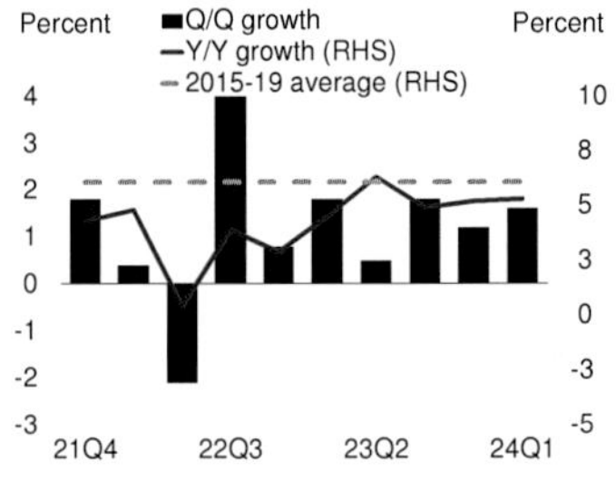

B. China: Property sales growth

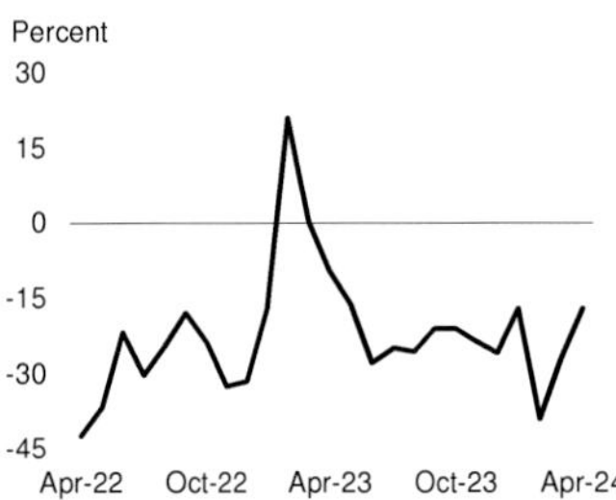

C. China: Retail sales growth

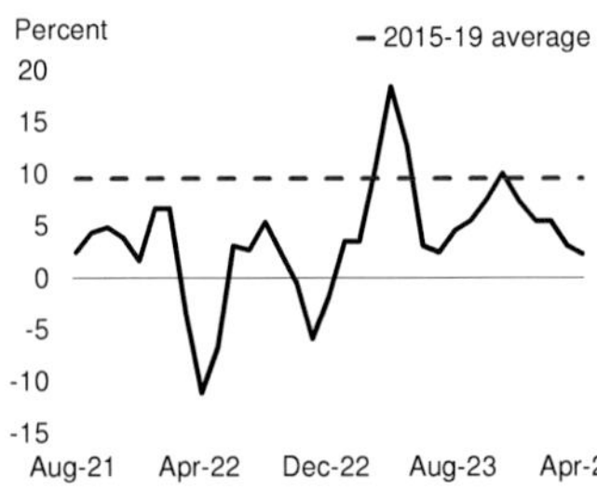

D. China: Consumer confidence

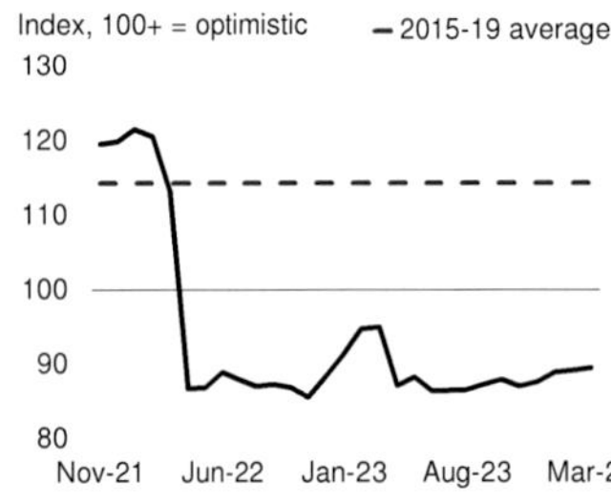

Sources: Haver Analytics; National Bureau of Statistics of China; World Bank.

A. Quarter-on-quarter (Q/Q) and year-on-year (Y/Y) real GDP growth. 2015-19 average denotes the period average of year-on-year growth. Last observation is 2024Q1.

B. Year-on-year growth of sales, by volume, of residential building floor space. Last observation is April 2024.

C. Year-on-year growth of nominal retail sales. Last observation is April 2024.

D. Consumer confidence on a scale of 0 to 200, where 200 indicates extreme optimism, 0 extreme pessimism, and 100 neutrality. Last observation is March 2024.

began increasing modestly in early 2024, core inflation remained well below both pre-pandemic averages and the official target of about 3 percent amid weak demand. In Thailand, after declining for several months due to falling food prices and subsidies that pushed down energy prices, headline consumer prices also recently edged up (World Bank 2023b).

Financial conditions in the region have eased slightly since last year. With inflation remaining below or near targets, central banks have mostly held interest rates steady or reduced them slightly, with Indonesia—where rates were hiked in April—a notable exception. In China, the five-year lending rate—the benchmark for mortgages—and the reserve requirement ratio were cut in early 2024, reducing borrowing costs, particularly for households. Downward pressure on exchange rates—partly the result of reduced net portfolio inflows—moderated across major EAP economies late last year, as global financial conditions eased. However, capital inflows have recently declined in China and elsewhere in the region, as markets priced in tighter monetary policies in major advanced economies (figure 2.1.2.D).

Outlook

Regional growth is projected to decline to 4.8 percent this year, as a slowdown in China offsets faster growth in several other large economies (figures 2.1.3.A and 2.1.3.B). Growth in EAP is then expected to continuing softening, to 4.2 percent in 2025 and 4.1 percent in 2026, as growth in China continues to slow, outweighing a slight pickup elsewhere in the region. Compared with January projections, growth in EAP is expected to be 0.3 percentage point higher in 2024 and 0.2 percentage point lower in 2025.

In China, growth is projected to slow to 4.8 percent in 2024, 0.3 percentage point higher than January forecasts, mainly reflecting stronger-than-expected activity in early 2024, particularly exports. Following a strong expansion in 2023, consumption is expected to slow markedly this year amid weak consumer confidence. Overall investment growth will remain tepid, supported by government spending—notably on infrastructure—but dampened by enduring property sector weakness. With both new property construction starts and bank lending for real estate declining in early 2024, real estate activity is envisaged to stabilize only toward the end of the year, supported by measures to prop up the sector, including lower borrowing costs and deposit requirements (figure 2.1.3.C). Growth is projected to soften further, to 4.1 percent in 2025—0.2 percentage point lower than forecast in January, owing primarily to a weaker outlook for investment—and 4.0 percent in 2026, as potential growth is weighed down by slowing productivity, softer investment, and mounting demographic headwinds.

In EAP excluding China, following below-average growth last year, activity is projected to pick up to 4.6 percent this year. Growth will be supported by an upswing in global goods trade that will benefit exports and industrial activity, offsetting the effects of softening growth in China. Accelerations of activity are expected to be strongest in some of the most export-orientated economies, including Thailand and Viet Nam. The global tourism recovery from the pandemic is nearing completion but continues in EAP where reopening was delayed in some countries, notably in China. This will help boost service exports in some economies, including Cambodia and Thailand. In 2025, growth is expected to edge up to 4.7 percent, and then to 4.8 percent in 2026, as global trade firms and growth rates across the region converge toward potential.

Over the forecast horizon, GDP growth in most EAP economies except China—including Indonesia, Malaysia, and the Philippines—will be anchored by solid growth of private consumption supported by low inflation, declining borrowing costs, and firm labor market conditions. However, both private and public investment are projected to remain subdued. Heightened uncertainty, related in some cases to recent political transitions and conflict, and including about global trade policies, is expected to dampen private investment. In tandem, rising public debt—which exceeds pre-pandemic levels in most countries in the region—and budget approval delays are anticipated to constrain public investment growth in some economies.

FIGURE 2.1.2 EAP excluding China: Recent developments

Activity in EAP excluding China showed signs of strengthening in early 2024. After some economies experienced below-average growth in 2023, partly reflecting a slump in global trade, exports in the region have firmed. Headline inflation generally remained near or below central bank targets, reflecting softening food price increases and ample spare capacity. While net portfolio capital inflows picked up across the region late last year, they have decreased more recently, partly reflecting tight monetary policy in advanced economies.

A. Growth in selected EAP economies

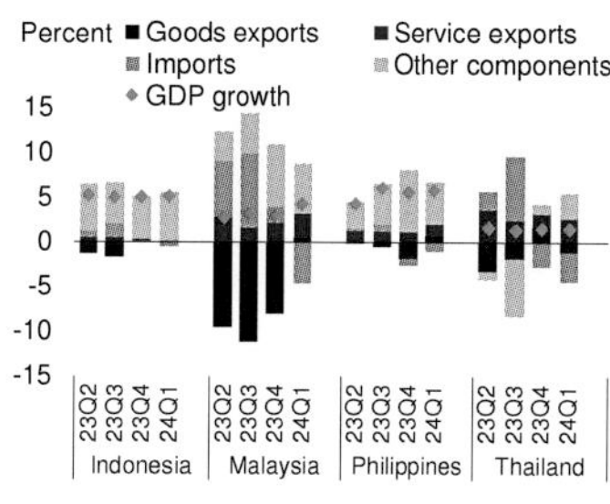

B. Growth of goods exports

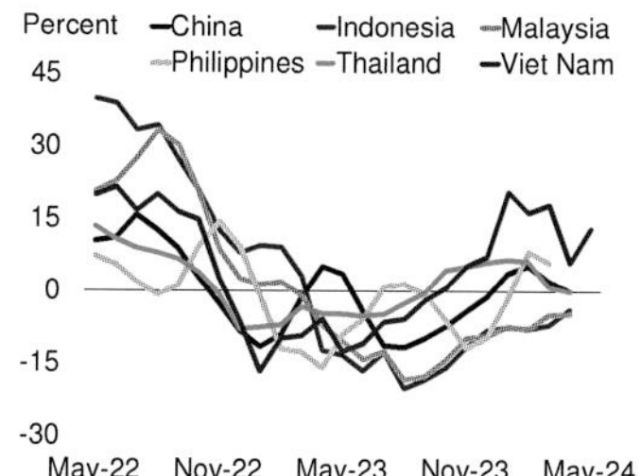

C. Consumer price inflation

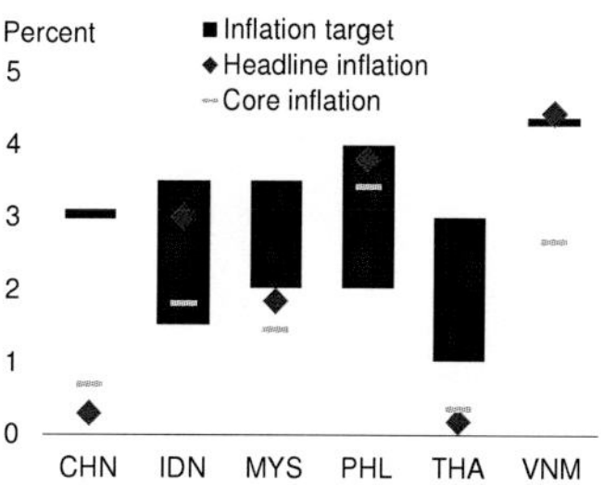

D. Net capital inflows

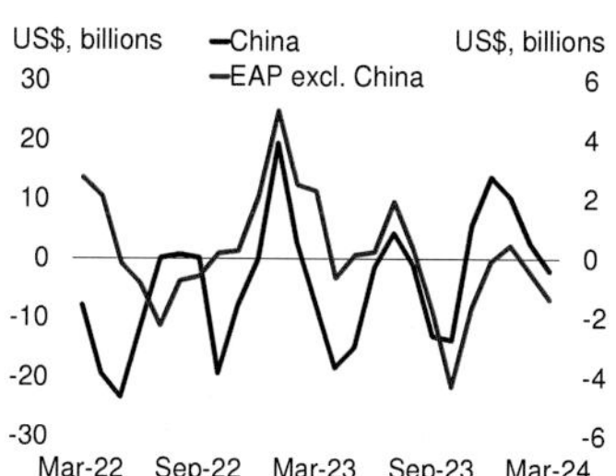

Sources: Haver Analytics; Institute of International Finance (database); World Bank.

Note: CHN = China; EAP = East Asia and Pacific; IDN = Indonesia; MYS = Malaysia; PHL = the Philippines; THA = Thailand; VNM = Viet Nam.

A. Year-on-year real GDP growth. Last observation is 2024Q1.

B. Value of goods exports in U.S. dollars. Three-month moving average of year-on-year change. Last observation is March 2024 for the Philippines. Last observation is April 2024 for China, Indonesia, Malaysia, and Thailand. Last observation is May 2024 for Viet Nam.

C. Year-on-year headline consumer price inflation and core consumer price inflation. Blue bars refer to the inflation target/range set by central banks. Last observation is April 2024 for China, Indonesia, Malaysia, the Philippines, and Thailand. Last observation is May 2024 for Viet Nam.

D. Three-month moving average of net portfolio (debt and equity) inflows. Last observation is March 2024.

Growth is projected to diverge among Pacific Island economies this year. Activity is set to accelerate in Papua New Guinea, due to an uptick in mining activity, and in Palau, as a delayed recovery in tourism gains traction. Elsewhere, however, growth will slow, including in Fiji and Samoa, as tailwinds from the pandemic recovery fade and growth moderates to around long-run averages (World Bank 2024a).

Inflation in major EAP economies this year is generally envisaged to edge down further or remain low, dampened by easing commodity prices, spare capacity, and, in some cases, subsidies. In China, inflation is anticipated to pick up slightly, as food prices normalize following declines last year, but remain well below target amid slowing consumption growth. In contrast, inflation will continue to be elevated in Mongolia, as a weather-related contraction in agricultural production squeezes food supply and puts upward pressure on prices. Inflation will also remain elevated in the Lao People's Democratic Republic and Myanmar, partly due to significant exchange rate depreciations. While easing, inflation is also set to remain elevated in some Pacific Island economies, reflecting various factors, including

FIGURE 2.1.3 EAP: Outlook

Growth in EAP is projected to slow to 4.8 percent this year, 4.2 percent in 2025, and 4.1 percent in 2026, mainly reflecting decelerating activity in China. A pickup in global goods trade is expected to support growth across the region, with tourism-dependent economies also set to benefit from a further recovery in tourism this year. In China, the property sector is anticipated to remain weak as lending to the sector contracts. Nevertheless, monetary policy easing will provide a modest boost to growth in China and elsewhere in the region as real policy rates decline.

A. China: Contributions to growth

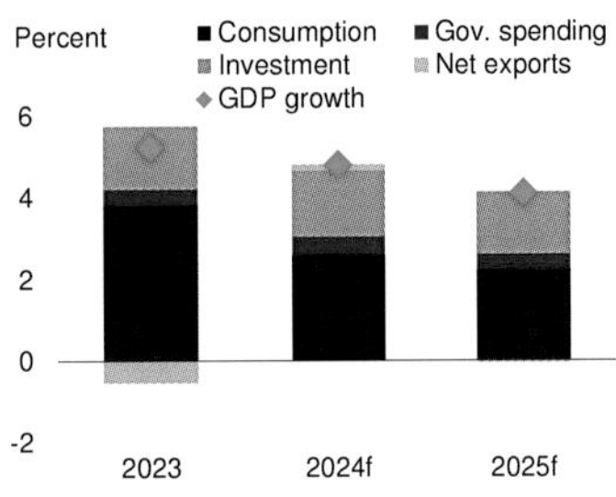

B. Growth in East Asia and Pacific Island economies

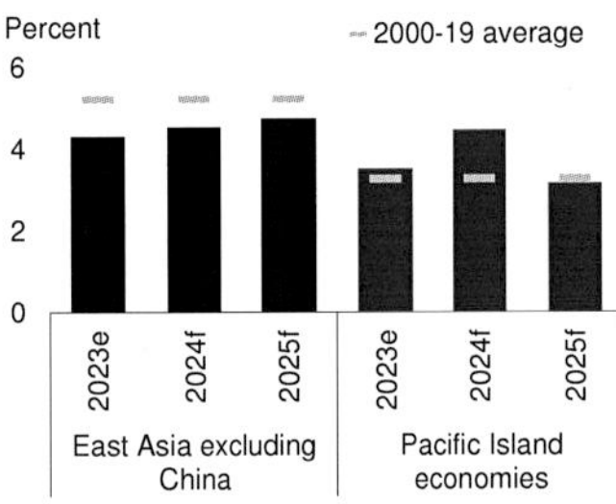

C. China: Bank lending growth

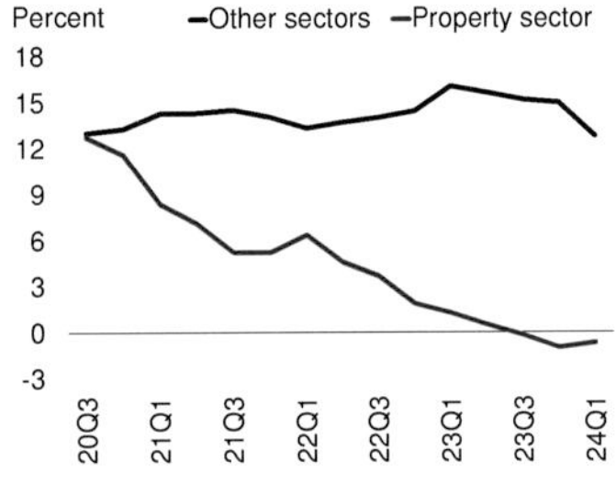

D. Real policy interest rates

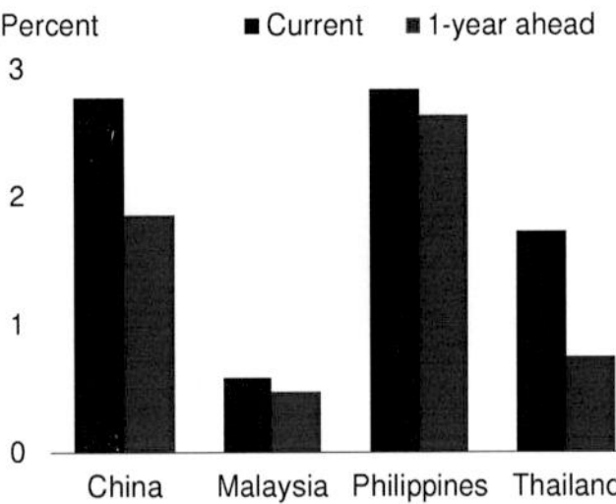

Sources: Bloomberg; Consensus Economics; Haver Analytics; World Bank.

Note: e = estimate; f = forecast; Gov. = government.

A. Annual real GDP growth and contributions of expenditure components. Projections for 2024 and 2025 are by the World Bank.

B. Annual real GDP growth. Projections for 2024 and 2025 are by the World Bank. Aggregate growth rates are calculated using average 2010-19 GDP weights and market exchange rates.

C. Year-on-year growth in loans to the property sector and loans to other sectors. Last observation is 2024Q1.

D. Current real rate is the current policy rate minus the Consensus Economics 2024 inflation forecast; "1-year ahead" is the 30-day rolling average of the one-year-ahead market-implied policy rate minus the Consensus Economics 2025 inflation forecast. Last observation is May 2024.

tight labor market conditions, supply bottlenecks, and increases in consumption tax rates.

Monetary policy is expected to ease this year and next in most economies, with declining real borrowing costs set to provide some modest support to domestic demand (figure 2.1.3.D). However, interest rate cuts are anticipated to be small due to central bank concerns about a resurgence in inflation. Still-tight monetary policies in major advanced economies will also reduce central banks' room to maneuver. With interest rates in some EAP economies, notably China and Thailand, already below those in the United States, further interest rate cuts could also reduce net capital inflows and put downward pressure on exchange rates.

Fiscal policy is anticipated to provide moderate support to activity in China, as additional borrowing by the central government, in particular, is used to fund higher spending. However, funding pressures will constrain spending increases by local governments. Elsewhere in the region, fiscal policy is likely to have a generally neutral influence on activity, with only modest changes in projected deficits in most countries, despite elevated debt levels.

Risks

Although risks to the regional outlook have become somewhat more balanced since January, they remain tilted to the downside. Downside risks include a proliferation of armed conflicts and heightened geopolitical tensions around the world, further trade policy fragmentation, and weaker-than-expected growth in China, with adverse spillovers to the broader region. Tighter-than-expected financial conditions and natural disasters, including more frequent climate-change-related extreme weather events—notably damaging tropical storms and floods—could also result in slower-than-projected growth (World Bank 2023c).

Against the backdrop of the conflict in the Middle East and Russia's invasion of Ukraine, an escalation in armed conflicts and geopolitical tensions could have various adverse effects on growth in the EAP region. A widening of the Middle East conflict could disrupt global oil supplies, leading to higher energy prices that could push up inflation, reduce household disposable incomes, and slow consumption growth (World Bank 2024b). Further disruptions to international shipping routes, including those through the Red Sea, would also increase transport costs for many EAP exporters. More generally, escalating armed conflict could heighten uncertainty and sap confidence, weighing on investment and consumption.

Following recent increases in global trade restriction measures, further trade policy fragmentation or moves toward protectionist measures that would weaken trade dynamism present a significant downside risk to the region. In May, the United States announced tariffs on an additional $18 billion of imports from China covering a variety of products including electric vehicles, batteries, and solar cells. This followed the imposition of a wide range of trade restriction measures by the two countries on each other in recent years. Trade or industrial policy measures intended to reduce dependence on imports from particular countries or to shorten global value chains could be particularly detrimental to many EAP economies, given their high degree of integration into complex manufacturing global value chains. In a context of mounting trade frictions between China and the United States, trade patterns in the region have already been affected. Some EAP economies' shares of U.S. imports are increasing and others, notably China's, are falling (figure 2.1.4.A; Freund et al. 2023).

In China, the outlook is subject to various risks, the materialization of which would have spillovers across the region, particularly in EAP economies with extensive trade linkages with China—including through regional or global value chains. On the upside, greater-than-assumed policy support in China, such as higher government spending, could boost demand. On the downside, however, the downturn in China's property sector, which has seen residential investment slump to its lowest share of output in almost two decades, could prove sharper or more persistent than assumed (figure 2.1.4.B). This would be an additional drag on investment, with other adverse knock-on effects on economic activity. Continued weakness in China's property prices would weigh on household wealth and confidence, while declining land sale revenue would further reduce the spending capacity of already fiscally constrained local governments. China import demand could weaken, particularly if household spending slows more than envisaged, weighing on exports in other economies. Weaker demand in China could also put downward pressure on global energy and

FIGURE 2.1.4 EAP: Risks

Against a backdrop of heightened geopolitical tensions, trade and output growth in EAP could be dampened by escalations in conflict and trade protectionism that further disrupt trade flows. Slower-than-expected growth in China would also adversely impact the broader region. China's property sector downturn could worsen, weighing on investment, consumption, and government revenue. Protracted weak sentiment and heightened policy uncertainty could also hinder investment, including from foreign firms. With public debt elevated across the region, tighter-than-expected global financial conditions could push up borrowing costs.

A. Changes in shares of U.S. imports

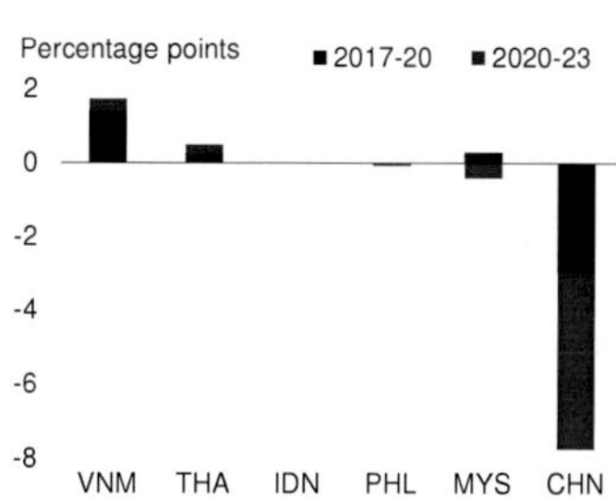

B. China: Real estate investment

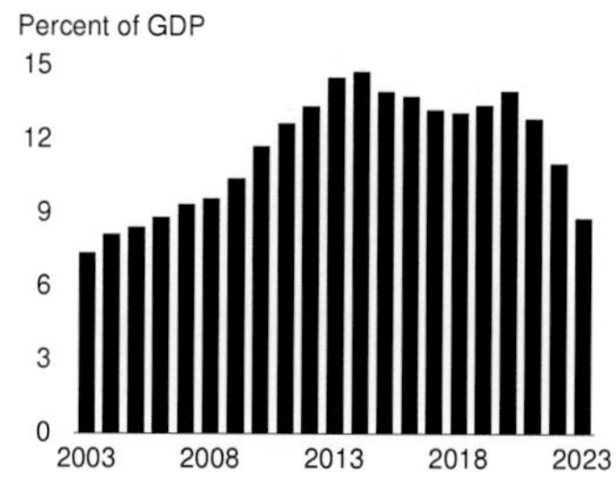

C. China: Inward foreign direct investment

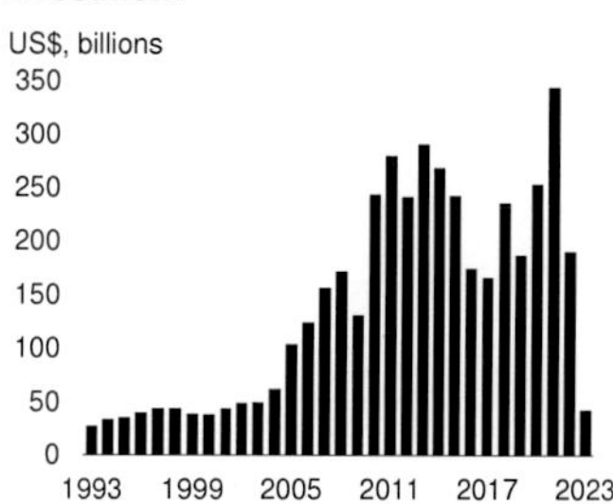

D. Government debt, 2023

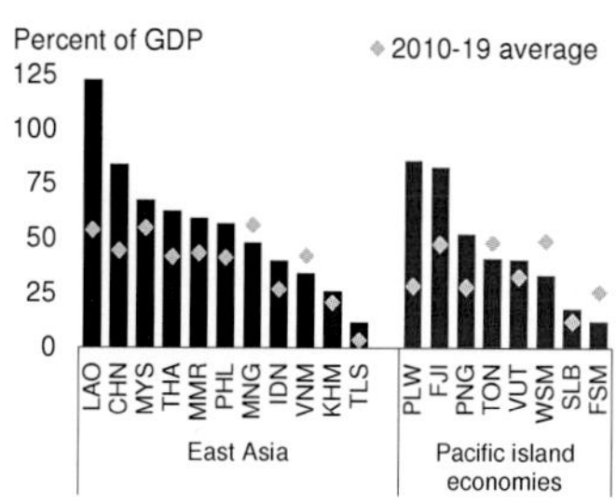

Sources: Haver Analytics; International Monetary Fund; U.S. Census Bureau; World Bank.

Note: CHN = China; EAP = East Asia and Pacific; FJI = Fiji; FSM = Federated States of Micronesia; IDN = Indonesia; LAO = Lao PDR; KHM = Cambodia; MMR = Myanmar; MNG = Mongolia; MYS = Malaysia; PHL = the Philippines; PLW = Palau; PNG = Papua New Guinea; SLB = Solomon Islands; THA = Thailand; TLS = Timor-Leste; TON = Tonga; VNM = Viet Nam; VUT = Vanuatu; WSM = Samoa.

A. Period change in shares of U.S. imports from respective trading partners.

B. Investment completed in real estate development as a share of GDP. Last observation is end-2023.

C. Net inward foreign direct investment. Last observation is 2023.

D. General government gross debt as a percent of GDP. Bars refer to the share in 2023. Diamonds show 2010-19 averages.

metals prices, with adverse consequences for EAP commodity exporters.

Prolonged weak business and consumer sentiment present a further downside risk in China. Policy uncertainty in China, including in relation to the regulatory environment, or heightened geopolitical tensions could result in foreign firms postponing or shelving investments, as underscored by the sharp fall in inflows of foreign direct investment last year (figure 2.1.4.C). Potential growth in China could also disappoint, resulting in weaker-than-expected actual growth. Industrial policy intended to support preferred sectors of production could have the unintended consequence of encouraging supply-demand imbalances and capital misallocation—which would weaken productivity growth.

Global financial conditions could become tighter than expected if the anticipated disinflation in major advanced economies fails to materialize or if geopolitical shocks trigger a sudden decline in investor risk appetite. Especially because of the elevated levels of debt in many economies in the region, higher borrowing costs would dampen private consumption and investment. Although fiscal deficits have generally narrowed since the pandemic, in most economies they remain above pre-pandemic levels. At the same time, public debt levels have ratcheted up and are poised to climb further due to persistent fiscal deficits, higher borrowing costs, and moderating growth (figure 2.1.4.D; World Bank 2024c). Consequently, the scope for fiscal policy to respond to adverse shocks has narrowed, while the risk has increased that sharp fiscal consolidations might be forced by adverse market conditions, reducing domestic demand and output growth.

In contrast, faster-than-expected growth in the United States—underpinned, for example, by expanding labor supply—would support stronger external demand in EAP, presenting an upside risk to the region's baseline forecast. Major manufacturing hubs across the region that rely on exports to the United States would benefit most, but stronger external demand could also boost commodity and tourism exports. A faster-than-expected decline in global inflation—for example, from stronger-than-expected productivity growth—presents a further upside risk. This would enable a more rapid easing of monetary policy in major advanced economies, supporting capital inflows to EAP economies, putting downward pressure on borrowing costs, and boosting activity.

TABLE 2.1.1 East Asia and Pacific forecast summary

(Real GDP growth at market prices in percent, unless indicated otherwise)

	2021	2022	2023e	2024f	2025f	2026f	Percentage point differences from January 2024 projections 2024f	2025f
EMDE EAP, GDP [1]	**7.6**	**3.4**	**5.1**	**4.8**	**4.2**	**4.1**	**0.3**	**-0.2**
GDP per capita (U.S. dollars)	7.2	3.2	4.8	4.5	3.9	3.9	0.2	-0.2
(Average including countries that report expenditure components in national accounts)[2]								
EMDE EAP, GDP [2]	7.7	3.4	5.1	4.8	4.2	4.1	0.3	-0.2
PPP GDP	7.3	3.6	5.1	4.8	4.3	4.2	0.2	-0.1
Private consumption	9.6	1.9	9.0	6.2	5.5	5.3	0.3	0.1
Public consumption	3.5	4.3	2.7	3.4	2.9	2.9	0.3	0.1
Fixed investment	3.2	3.5	3.7	4.0	3.9	3.9	-0.1	-0.2
Exports, GNFS [3]	17.1	1.5	-0.5	3.6	2.8	2.9	1.2	0.1
Imports, GNFS [3]	13.0	-0.6	1.0	3.4	3.4	3.6	0.4	0.5
Net exports, contribution to growth	1.1	0.5	-0.3	0.1	0.0	0.0	0.1	0.0
Memo items: GDP								
China	8.4	3.0	5.2	4.8	4.1	4.0	0.3	-0.2
East Asia and Pacific excluding China	2.9	5.8	4.3	4.6	4.7	4.8	-0.1	0.0
Indonesia	3.7	5.3	5.0	5.0	5.1	5.1	0.1	0.2
Thailand	1.6	2.5	1.9	2.4	2.8	2.9	-0.8	-0.3
Commodity exporters	2.6	5.2	4.8	4.8	4.8	4.8	0.0	0.0
Commodity importers excluding China	3.2	6.3	3.9	4.4	4.7	4.8	-0.2	0.0
Pacific Island Economies[4]	-1.4	6.1	3.5	4.5	3.2	3.0	-0.1	0.0

Source: World Bank.

Note: e = estimate; f = forecast; PPP = purchasing power parity; EMDE = emerging market and developing economy. World Bank forecasts are frequently updated based on new information and changing (global) circumstances. Consequently, projections presented here may differ from those contained in other Bank documents, even if basic assessments of countries' prospects do not differ at any given moment in time.

1. GDP and expenditure components are measured in average 2010-19 prices and market exchange rates. Excludes the Democratic People's Republic of Korea and dependent territories.

2. Subregion aggregate excludes the Democratic People's Republic of Korea, dependent territories, Fiji, Kiribati, the Marshall Islands, the Federated States of Micronesia, Myanmar, Palau, Papua New Guinea, Samoa, Timor-Leste, Tonga, Tuvalu, and Vanuatu, for which data limitations prevent the forecasting of GDP components.

3. Exports and imports of goods and nonfactor services (GNFS).

4. Includes Fiji, Kiribati, the Marshall Islands, the Federated States of Micronesia, Nauru, Palau, Papua New Guinea, Samoa, the Solomon Islands, Tonga, Tuvalu, and Vanuatu.

TABLE 2.1.2 East Asia and Pacific country forecasts[1]

(Real GDP growth at market prices in percent, unless indicated otherwise)

	2021	2022	2023e	2024f	2025f	2026f	Percentage point differences from January 2024 projections: 2024f	2025f
Cambodia	3.0	5.2	5.4	5.8	6.1	6.4	0.0	0.0
China	8.4	3.0	5.2	4.8	4.1	4.0	0.3	-0.2
Fiji	-4.9	20.0	8.0	3.5	3.3	3.3	-0.5	-0.4
Indonesia	3.7	5.3	5.0	5.0	5.1	5.1	0.1	0.2
Kiribati	8.5	3.9	4.2	5.6	2.0	2.1	3.2	-0.3
Lao PDR	2.5	2.7	3.7	4.0	4.1	4.1	-0.1	-0.2
Malaysia	3.3	8.7	3.7	4.3	4.4	4.3	0.0	0.2
Marshall Islands[2]	1.0	-0.6	3.0	3.0	2.0	1.5	0.0	0.0
Micronesia, Fed. Sts.[2]	3.0	-0.9	0.8	1.1	1.7	1.1	-1.7	0.4
Mongolia	1.6	5.0	7.1	4.8	6.6	6.3	-1.4	0.2
Myanmar[2,3]	-12.0	4.0	1.0	1.0	..	..	-1.0	..
Nauru[2]	7.2	2.8	0.6	1.4	1.2	1.0	0.0	0.0
Palau[2]	-13.4	-2.0	0.8	12.4	11.9	3.5	0.0	0.0
Papua New Guinea	-0.8	5.2	2.7	4.8	3.1	3.0	-0.2	0.0
Philippines	5.7	7.6	5.6	5.8	5.9	5.9	0.0	0.1
Samoa[2]	-7.1	-5.3	8.0	5.5	3.5	2.7	1.0	-0.1
Solomon Islands	-0.6	-4.1	1.9	2.8	3.1	3.0	0.1	0.0
Thailand	1.6	2.5	1.9	2.4	2.8	2.9	-0.8	-0.3
Timor-Leste	2.9	4.0	2.1	3.4	4.0	3.8	-0.1	-0.3
Tonga[2]	-2.7	-2.0	2.6	2.5	2.2	1.6	0.0	0.0
Tuvalu	1.8	0.7	3.9	3.5	2.4	2.2	0.0	0.0
Vanuatu	0.6	1.9	2.5	3.7	3.5	3.1	1.1	0.0
Viet Nam	2.6	8.0	5.0	5.5	6.0	6.5	0.0	0.0

Source: World Bank.

Note: e = estimate; f = forecast. World Bank forecasts are frequently updated based on new information and changing (global) circumstances. Consequently, projections presented here may differ from those contained in other Bank documents, even if basic assessments of countries' prospects do not significantly differ at any given moment in time.

1. Data are based on GDP measured in average 2010-19 prices and market exchange rates.

2. Values for Timor-Leste represent non-oil GDP. For the following countries, values correspond to the fiscal year: the Marshall Islands, the Federated States of Micronesia, and Palau (October 1–September 30); Myanmar (April 1–March 31); Nauru, Samoa, and Tonga (July 1–June 30).

3. Data for Myanmar beyond 2024 (which corresponds to the year ending March 2025) are excluded because of a high degree of uncertainty.

EUROPE and CENTRAL ASIA

Growth in Europe and Central Asia (ECA) is projected to soften to 3.0 percent this year and to 2.9 percent in 2025. The slowdown in 2024 largely reflects decelerations in the Russian Federation and Türkiye. Excluding these two economies and Ukraine, growth is projected to firm this year and next, as inflation eases, monetary policy rates are cut, and the growth of exports, particularly to the euro area, strengthens. Geopolitical developments remain the predominant downside risk to the growth outlook, especially those linked to Russia's invasion of Ukraine and conflict in the Middle East. Uncertainty about economic policies is also likely to remain elevated. Although the risks of higher-than-expected inflation have decreased, there could still be upward pressure on commodity prices or wages, along with potential new episodes of financial strains.

Recent developments

Growth in Europe and Central Asia strengthened to 3.2 percent in 2023, primarily reflecting a shift from contraction to expansion in the Russian Federation and Ukraine, and a more robust recovery in Central Asia. The regional picture was mixed: growth in Türkiye slowed and activity in Central Europe barely expanded, primarily reflecting stagnation in Poland due to falling real incomes, and amid spillovers from euro area weakness. High-frequency economic indicators, including manufacturing purchasing managers' indexes and retail sales, suggest a resilient activity in early 2024 in ECA's largest economies—Russia, Türkiye, and Poland (figure 2.2.1.A).

In Russia, growth picked up to 3.6 percent in 2023—a 1 percentage point upward revision from January's estimate. The upgrade largely reflects stronger-than-expected private demand, supported by subsidized mortgages, fiscal measures, and a tight labor market (figure 2.2.1.B). Increased military expenditures also boosted activity. After cuts in early 2024, oil production hovered around 9.2 mb/d in the second quarter, down by 0.4 mb/d from 2023 (IEA 2024).

Türkiye's growth slowed to a still-robust 4.5 percent in 2023. Economic activity has remained resilient into 2024, supported by a significant rise in the minimum wage—the fifth increase since 2022 –and despite monetary policy tightening. Policy interest rates have been hiked nine times since June 2023, from 8.5 to 50 percent, to contain inflation—which remains persistently high, at 75.4 percent year-on-year in May. Large wage increases, currency depreciation, and tax adjustments have contributed to inflation.

The region's median headline inflation fell to 3.7 percent and core inflation to 4.3 percent on a year-on-year basis in April 2024—about one-third of the levels prevailing a year earlier. Monetary policy has shifted toward easing in most countries, with the notable exception of Russia and Türkiye (figure 2.2.1.C). Real wages rose by 11.8 percent year-on-year in the first quarter of 2024, while the unemployment rate dropped to historic lows in the region (figure 2.2.1.D).

Outlook

Growth in ECA is projected to decelerate gradually to 3 percent in 2024, 2.9 percent in 2025, and 2.8 percent in 2026. The primary growth drivers in most countries are expected to be private consumption and investment—buoyed by the easing of monetary policies and decreasing inflation—and a recovery in exports, particularly

Note: This section was prepared by Marie Albert.

FIGURE 2.2.1 ECA: Recent developments

High-frequency indicators in the three largest ECA economies, that is the Russian Federation, Türkiye and Poland, suggest a resilient activity in early 2024. An increase in subsidized household mortgages contributed to Russia's economic resilience in 2023, although these mortgages declined in early 2024. Monetary policy interest rates have recently been reduced in several countries following declines in inflation. Labor market conditions have tightened, with unemployment falling and wage growth rising.

A. High-frequency indicators in the Russian Federation, Türkiye and Poland

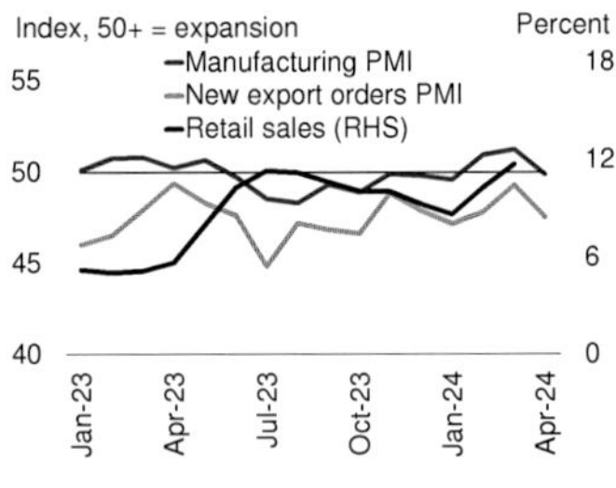

B. New household mortgages in the Russian Federation

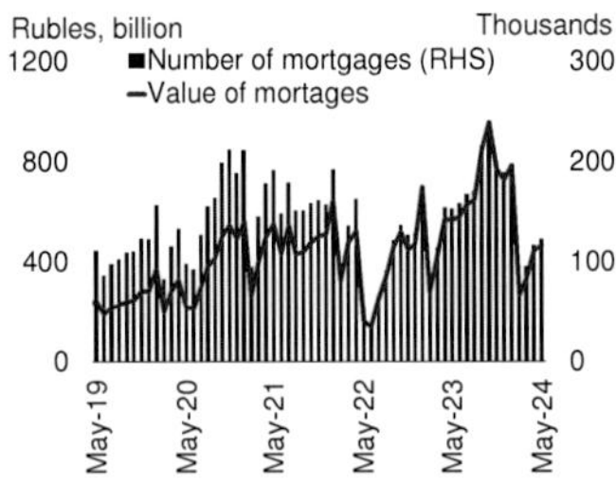

C. Inflation and monetary policy interest rates

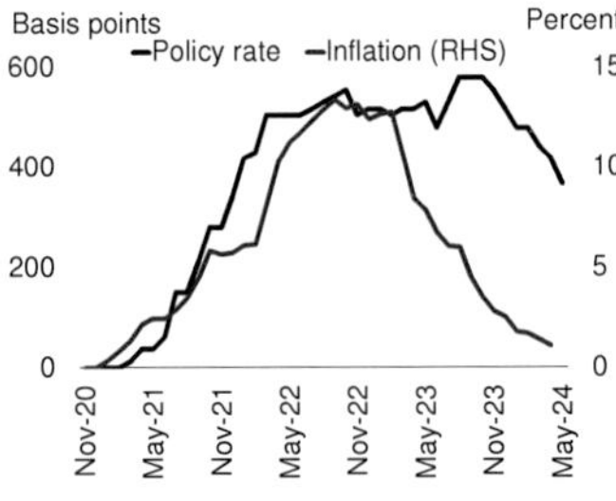

D. Labor market tightness

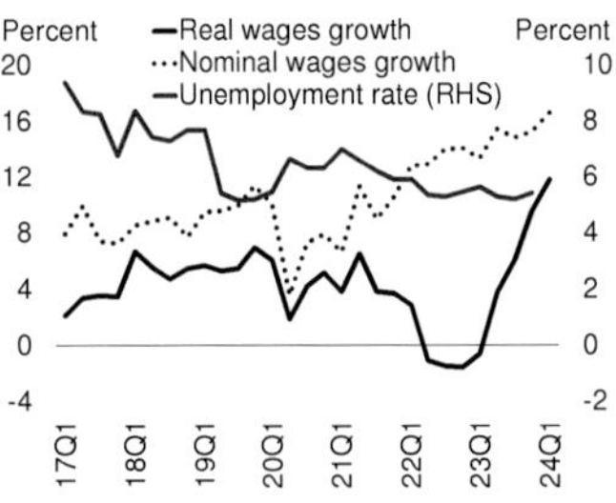

Sources: Central Bank of Russia; Haver Analytics; World Bank.

Note: PMI = purchasing managers' index.

A. Lines show average value for PMI manufacturing and new export orders, and three months rolling average for retail sales. Sample comprises Poland, the Russian Federation, and Türkiye. Last observation is April 2024.

B. Bars show monthly new number of household mortgages, while line shows monthly volume in rubles. Last observation is May 2024.

C. Lines show cumulative change in ECA median policy rate and median year-on year headline inflation rate since November 2020. Sample includes 23 countries. Last observation is May 2024.

D. Median values of year-on-year change in wages and unemployment rate for 16 countries. Last observation is 2024Q1.

as activity in the euro area firms. The slowdown this year is mainly attributed to decelerations in Russia and Türkiye. Nevertheless, the 0.6 percentage point upward revision for this year since January is mainly due to an upgrade for Russia, reflecting unexpectedly strong activity in late 2023 and early 2024 (figure 2.2.2.A). Elevated uncertainty regarding the evolution of the invasion of Ukraine continues to play an essential role in shaping the regional outlook. Excluding Russia, Türkiye, and Ukraine, growth in the region is expected to accelerate to 3.1 percent this year and 3.6 percent on average in 2025–26, with growth picking up in about half of ECA's economies.

Inflation is expected to continue moderating, paving the way for more substantial monetary policy easing. In April 2024, inflation was above official targets in about half of ECA countries, but market-based expectations are consistent with inflation close to targets in most cases by 2025. Despite the need for fiscal consolidation to ensure sustainability, prospects for significant fiscal adjustments in the region appear to be limited, amid many upcoming elections.

Growth in Russia is forecast to decelerate to 2.9 percent in 2024, 1.4 percent in 2025 and 1.1 percent in 2026, near its potential rate. While the carry-over from strong growth in late 2023 and the beginning of 2024 is expected to boost activity throughout 2024, the anticipated tightening of macroprudential measures and the scaling back of the provision of subsidized mortgages are set to temper private demand. Military production is projected to continue supporting activity. Amid ongoing trade diversion, Russia's trade linkages with China have grown as more Russian trade transactions are being conducted in the Chinese renminbi (figure 2.2.2.B).

Growth in Türkiye is projected to moderate to 3 percent in 2024 as the tightening of monetary policy feeds through to the economy and contributes to reducing macroeconomic vulnerabilities. However, activity is forecast to increase by 3.6 percent in 2025 and 4.3 percent in 2026, driven by stronger domestic demand and net exports. Inflation will remain above the central bank's target, easing only to 29 percent on average in 2025. The fiscal deficit is expected to remain elevated, partly reflecting the costs of assisting rehabilitation and reconstruction following the February 2023 earthquakes.

In Ukraine, growth is anticipated to rise from 3.2 percent in 2024 to an average of 5.8 percent a year in 2025–26, under the assumption that active hostilities continue throughout 2024 and subsequently moderate. The recovery will depend, first and foremost, on the evolution of Russia's invasion, and is expected to be supported by an increase in exports and reconstruction investments. Reconstruction costs are estimated at $486 billion over the next decade, approximately 2.8 times nominal GDP in 2023, and a significant increase from previous estimates (World Bank 2024d). More than 6.4 million people have fled the country. Loss of jobs, incomes and assets, as well as high inflation, have reversed 15 years of poverty reduction (UNHCR 2024; World Bank 2024e).

Output in Central Europe is envisaged to firm to 3 percent in 2024 and 3.5 percent in 2025 before easing to 3.3 percent in 2026. This mirrors the expected pickup in the euro area, and the support from the European Union's Recovery and Resilience Facility (RRF). Poland's growth is envisaged to be the main driver of the subregion's growth, with private demand boosted by disinflation and wage growth. After delays, the country has received its first payment from the RRF. The facility is expected to provide Poland with about €59.8 billion by the end of 2026.

Growth in the Western Balkans is forecast to rebound to 3.2 percent in 2024, to 3.5 in 2025 and 3.8 percent in 2026. Private demand is projected to be the main driver of growth, while the drag from weak net exports is expected to be less significant than in 2023, reflecting a pickup in exports alongside the euro area's recovery. The new European Union (EU) growth plan for the subregion will enhance economic integration and boost socio-economic convergence (World Bank 2024f).

In South Caucasus, growth is projected to stabilize at about 3.5 percent annually over 2024–26. Azerbaijan is expected to pick up supported by some recovery in hydrocarbon exports, which were notably low in 2023. This rebound is expected to be counterbalanced by the easing of growth in Armenia and Georgia from exceptionally high levels in recent years. Trade diversion, resulting from the invasion in Ukraine, is expected to continue.

Growth in Central Asia is forecast to weaken to 4.1 percent in 2024, before picking up to 4.9 percent in 2025 and softening again to 4.2 percent in 2026. The normalization of financial, trade and

FIGURE 2.2.2 ECA: Outlook

Growth in the region is projected to weaken over the next three years. After 2024, while growth is expected to strengthen in Türkiye, it is projected to weaken in the Russian Federation. Trade diversion, notably the deepening of Russia's trade ties with China, is expected to continue. Investment is expected to accelerate slightly, with opportunities for productivity enhancements bolstered by the region's advantageous position in artificial intelligence compared to other EMDEs.

A. Contributions to ECA GDP growth

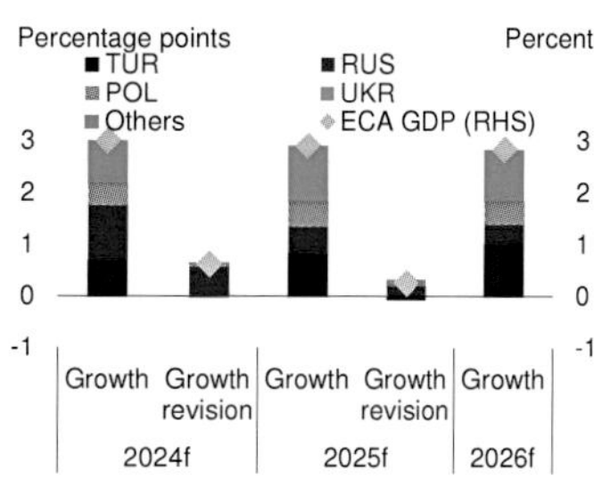

B. Russian Federation: Composition of trade

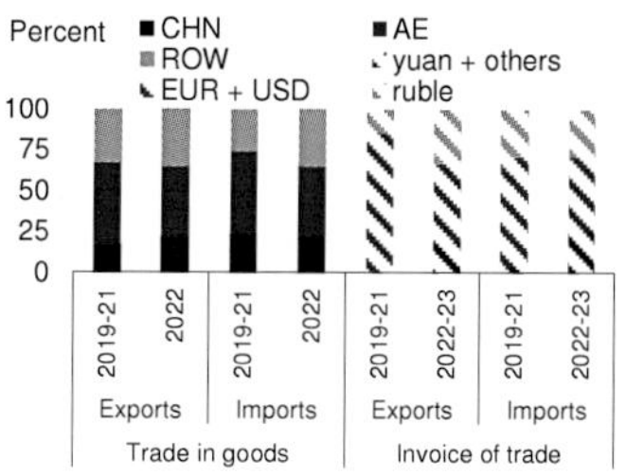

C. Investment and productivity

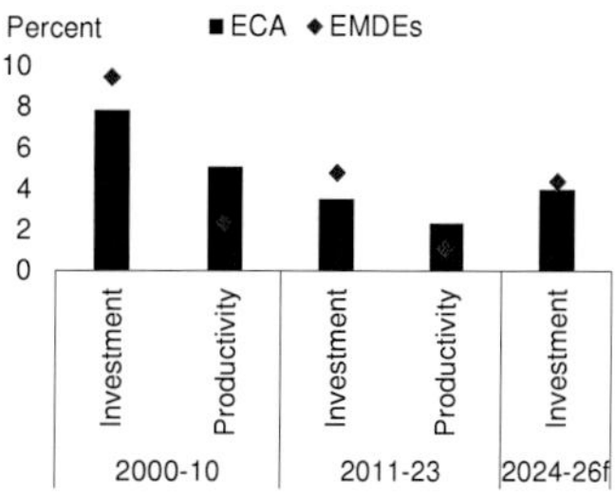

D. Artificial intelligence readiness

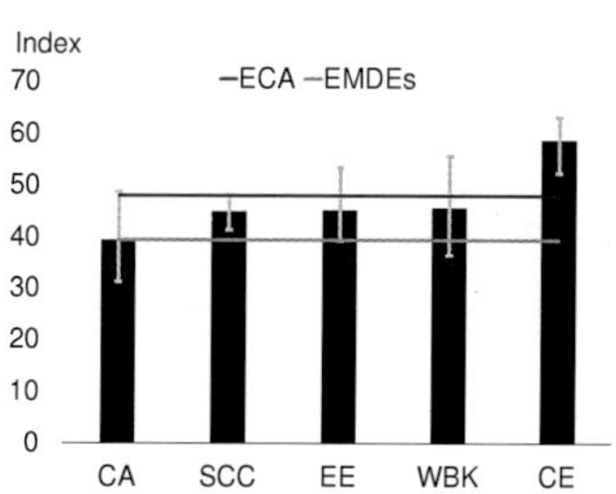

Sources: Central Bank of Russia; Haver Analytics; International Labor Organization; Oxford Insights; WITS (database); World Bank.

Note: f = forecast; AE = advanced economies; CA = Central Asia; CE = Central Europe; CHN = China; ECA = Europe and Central Asia; EE = Eastern Europe; EMDEs = emerging market and developing economies; EUR = euro; POL = Poland; ROW = rest of the world; RUS = Russian Federation; SCC = South Caucasus; TUR = Türkiye; UKR = Ukraine; USD = U.S. dollar; WBK = Western Balkans.

A. Bars show contributions of various economies to ECA GDP growth and to ECA GDP growth revision compared with the January 2024 *Global Economic Prospects* report. Diamonds show ECA GDP growth and ECA GDP growth revision.

B. Bars show the Russian Federation's trade in goods by partner country and the breakdown of currency used for transactions in both goods and services, reflecting the main currencies associated with the category of "unfriendly" countries, as designated by Russia. As Russia hasn't released bilateral trade data since 2022, bilateral imports (exports) of Russia's trading partners are used to mirror exports (imports).

C. Bars and diamonds show average annual growth rates of investment and productivity (output per worker, measured in GDP constant 2017 international dollars at purchasing power parity) for ECA and EMDEs, respectively.

D. Bars show the average score of each subregion on Oxford Economics' 2023 Government AI Readiness Index. Red and orange lines show the average for ECA and EMDEs, respectively. Score ranges from 0 to 100, with a higher score pointing to better readiness. Whiskers show minimum-maximum values for the countries in the subregions.

tourism linkages with Russia following the invasion is projected to contribute to the slowdown. In particular, remittance inflows from Russia are expected to continue to decline, albeit from elevated levels. The subregion growth profile closely aligns with Kazakhstan's economic trajectory, influenced by the postponement to 2025 of the expansion of the Tengiz oil field—a

FIGURE 2.2.3 ECA: Risks

Risks to the outlook remain tilted to the downside. Elevated geopolitical tensions persist following the Russia's invasion of Ukraine. Various elections across the region this year underscore the possibility of heightened uncertainties regarding economic policies. Rising trade restrictions would further hamper declining trade growth. Vulnerability to climate change and readiness to address the associated challenges vary significantly across countries.

A. Geopolitical risk

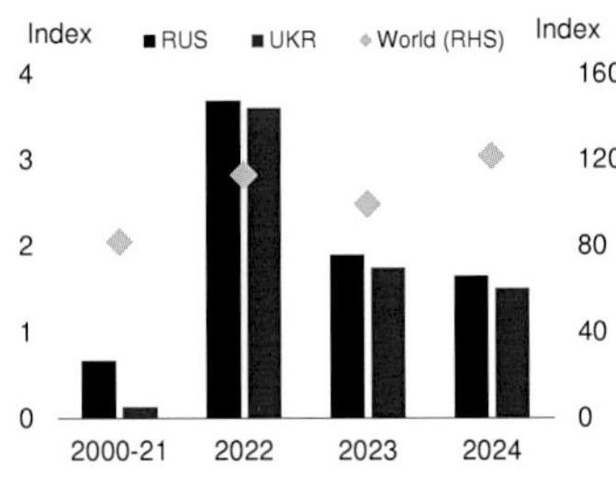

B. Elections in ECA countries

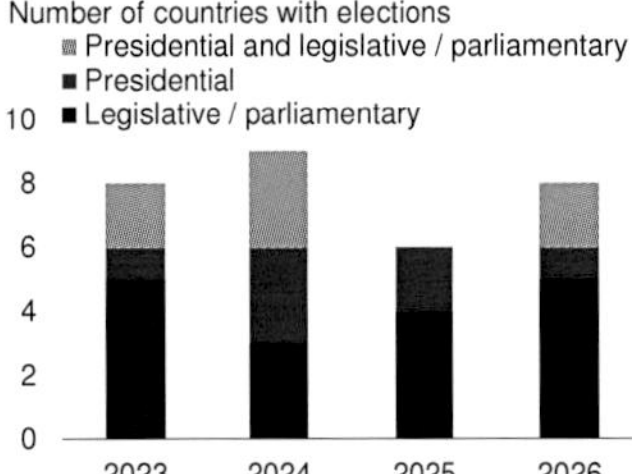

C. Exports growth

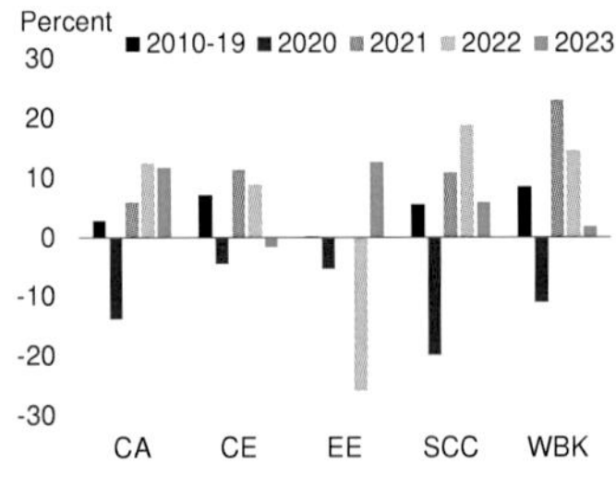

D. Climate readiness and vulnerability

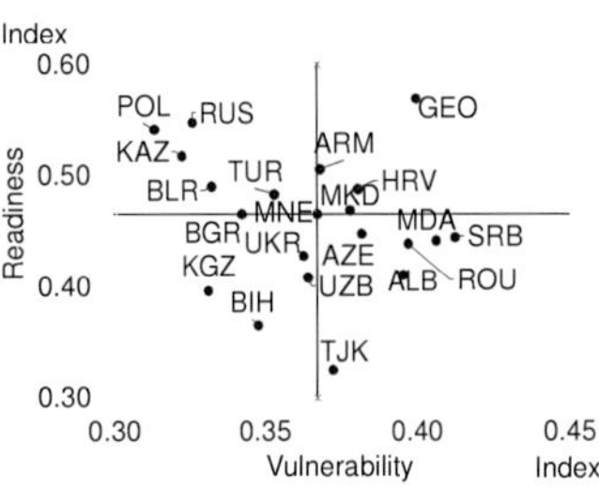

Sources: Caldara and Iacoviello (2022); Haver Analytics; Notre Dame Global Adaptation Initiative; WDI (database); World Bank.

Note: ALB = Albania; ARM = Armenia; AZE = Azerbaijan; BGR = Bulgaria; BIH = Bosnia and Herzegovina; BLR = Belarus; CA = Central Asia; CE = Central Europe; ECA = Europe and Central Asia; EE = Eastern Europe; GEO = Georgia; HRV = Croatia; KAZ = Kazakhstan; KGZ = Kyrgyz Republic; MDA = Moldova; MNE = Montenegro; MKD = North Macedonia; POL = Poland; ROU = Romania; RUS = Russian Federation; SCC = South Caucasus; SRB = Serbia; TJK = Tajikistan; TUR = Türkiye; UKR = Ukraine; UZB = Uzbekistan; WBK = Western Balkans.

A. Columns show the average value of country's geopolitical risk index (GPR) for each period. Diamonds show the average of the GPR world historical index. Last observation is May 2024.

B. Bars show total number of countries with elections for each year.

C. Bars show the annual growth rates of exports of goods and services (constant 2015 U.S. dollars) for each subregion. Dark blue bars show the average annual growth rates for the period 2010-2019.

D. Scatter plot shows the climate vulnerability and readiness components of the University of Notre Dame Global Adaptation Initiative (ND-GAIN) index for 2021. Vertical and horizontal lines are the median values of vulnerability and readiness components for ECA.

project expected to increase oil production by approximately 8 percent.

Between 2011 and 2023, both investment and labor productivity in ECA grew more slowly than during 2000–10 (World Bank 2024g). In the forecast period, however, investment growth in ECA is expected to firm somewhat, particularly in the EU countries of the region and Ukraine (figure 2.2.2.C). Artificial intelligence (AI) is envisaged to increasingly influence investment strategies. ECA countries in the EU stand to benefit from the EU's RRF investments in green and digital transitions. Most Central European countries already have developed an AI strategy and exhibit high scores on the Artificial Readiness Index. Central Asia's readiness more closely aligns with the average for emerging market and developing economies (EMDEs), but the subregion's countries are working to develop a unified strategy toward AI adoption which will boost their investment in this area (figure 2.2.2.D; Oxford Insights 2023).

Risks

Risks to the outlook are tilted to the downside. Geopolitical tensions, particularly stemming from Russia's invasion of Ukraine, pose significant risks. Additionally, an escalation of trade restrictions, and frequent or extreme weather events, would also weigh on growth prospects. Although inflation has declined, higher or more persistent inflation is possible. In contrast, lower-than-expected inflation also represents a potential upside.

Geopolitical tensions remain a major risk for the region. Geopolitical risk indexes in Russia and Ukraine remain substantially higher than before the invasion in 2022 (figure 2.2.3.A). Considerable uncertainty remains about whether the invasion, which has entered its third year, will deepen or widen. Intensifying tensions and conflicts could worsen already-heavy human and economic losses. The potential continued effects of the invasion, coupled with the conflict in the Middle East and their possible escalation, cloud prospects for ECA. Political uncertainty in the region is also heightened. Nine countries have presidential or legislative elections, or both, in 2024, underscoring the possibility of uncertainty about future economic policies (figure 2.2.3.B).

An escalation of trade restrictions could further hamper trade activity and weigh on growth. Exports have been decelerating in recent years across several subregions (figure 2.2.3.C). The region is highly open to trade, with the total value of exports and imports combined making up 109 percent of its GDP in 2022. This high level of trade activity leaves it vulnerable to increasing trade barriers. The number of restrictive trade measures on goods from the region has increased, largely as a result of sanctions as a response to Russia's invasion of Ukraine. Export restrictions on critical raw materials have increased, especially since 2019 (EBRD 2023). In addition, a slower-than-expected recovery in China could adversely impact commodity exporters in the region.

Despite recent moderation, inflation could be fueled by an escalation of conflict in the Middle East, which could increase energy prices and potentially feed back into core inflation, which remains sticky (World Bank 2024b). This could trigger further monetary policy tightening, limiting the growth recovery and hurting business confidence and investment. If wages were to grow more robustly than expected, especially in Central Europe where core inflation significantly outpaces headline inflation, that could also add to inflationary pressures. On the other hand, a faster-than-expected decline in inflation, potentially driven by an easing of labor market pressures, represents a potential upside.

Climate-related risks have increased, amid rising conflicts and uncertainties in the energy markets. The region has experienced a rise in extreme weather events. The summer of 2023 registered record-breaking temperatures, wildfires, and floods. Central Asia is especially at risk from climate change, exhibiting both heightened vulnerability and limited preparedness (figure 2.2.3.D). The overall region is less vulnerable to climate change and better equipped for climate adaptation than other EMDE regions. Nevertheless, ECA is among the world's largest carbon emitters per capita (World Bank 2024h). Transitioning to renewable energy and reducing reliance on fossil fuels, essential for meeting the Net Zero Energy goal for 2060, is projected to require an investment of close to 4 percent of the region's GDP between 2023 and 2060 (World Bank 2024i).

TABLE 2.2.1 Europe and Central Asia forecast summary

(Real GDP growth at market prices in percent, unless indicated otherwise)

	2021	2022	2023e	2024f	2025f	2026f	Percentage point differences from January 2024 projections: 2024f	2025f
EMDE ECA, GDP [1]	**7.2**	**1.6**	**3.2**	**3.0**	**2.9**	**2.8**	**0.6**	**0.2**
GDP per capita (U.S. dollars)	7.2	1.7	3.2	2.9	2.7	2.7	0.6	0.1
EMDE ECA excluding Russian Federation, Türkiye, and Ukraine, GDP	6.4	4.5	1.8	3.1	3.7	3.4	0.0	0.1
EMDE ECA excluding Russian Federation and Ukraine, GDP	8.3	4.9	2.9	3.1	3.6	3.8	0.0	-0.1
EMDE ECA excluding Türkiye, GDP	6.0	0.5	2.8	3.0	2.6	2.3	0.8	0.2
(Average including countries that report expenditure components in national accounts) [2]								
EMDE ECA, GDP [2]	7.4	1.4	3.1	3.0	2.7	2.7	0.7	0.2
PPP GDP	7.3	0.7	3.2	3.0	2.8	2.7	0.7	0.2
Private consumption	10.8	4.8	6.4	2.7	2.9	3.0	0.6	0.3
Public consumption	3.0	3.5	3.9	3.4	2.8	2.3	1.4	1.2
Fixed investment	6.4	2.8	9.6	3.7	4.1	4.2	-0.2	-0.3
Exports, GNFS [3]	10.3	0.0	-1.6	2.7	4.6	4.4	-0.5	0.5
Imports, GNFS [3]	12.4	2.2	5.6	4.1	5.4	5.1	0.6	0.2
Net exports, contribution to growth	-0.3	-0.8	-2.5	-0.5	-0.3	-0.3	-0.5	0.0
Memo items: GDP								
Commodity exporters [4]	5.7	-1.8	3.9	3.1	2.2	1.8	1.2	0.5
Commodity exporters excl. Russian Federation and Ukraine	5.5	4.5	4.9	3.9	4.5	4.0	-0.4	0.1
Commodity importers [5]	8.8	4.9	2.6	3.0	3.5	3.8	0.1	-0.1
Central Europe [6]	6.7	5.0	0.5	3.0	3.5	3.3	0.2	0.0
Western Balkans [7]	7.9	3.4	2.5	3.2	3.5	3.8	0.2	0.0
Eastern Europe [8]	3.6	-20.0	4.5	2.4	4.2	3.4	0.0	0.0
South Caucasus [9]	6.7	7.3	3.8	3.5	3.5	3.4	0.2	0.2
Central Asia [10]	5.3	4.2	5.5	4.1	4.9	4.2	-0.6	0.1
Russian Federation	5.9	-1.2	3.6	2.9	1.4	1.1	1.6	0.5
Türkiye	11.4	5.5	4.5	3.0	3.6	4.3	-0.1	-0.3
Poland	6.9	5.6	0.2	3.0	3.4	3.2	0.4	0.0

Source: World Bank.

Note: e = estimate; f = forecast; PPP = purchasing power parity; EMDE = emerging market and developing economy. World Bank forecasts are frequently updated based on new information and changing (global) circumstances. Consequently, projections presented here may differ from those contained in other Bank documents, even if basic assessments of countries' prospects do not differ at any given moment in time. The World Bank is currently not publishing economic output, income, or growth data for Turkmenistan owing to a lack of reliable data of adequate quality. Turkmenistan is excluded from cross-country macroeconomic aggregates. Since Croatia became a member of the euro area on January 1, 2023, it has been added to the euro area aggregate and removed from the ECA aggregate in all tables to avoid double counting.

1. GDP and expenditure components are measured in average 2010-19 prices and market exchange rates, thus aggregates presented here may differ from other World Bank documents.
2. Aggregates presented here exclude Azerbaijan, Bosnia and Herzegovina, Kazakhstan, Kosovo, the Kyrgyz Republic, Montenegro, Serbia, Tajikistan, Turkmenistan, and Uzbekistan, for which data limitations prevent the forecasting of GDP components.
3. Exports and imports of goods and nonfactor services (GNFS).
4. Includes Armenia, Azerbaijan, Kazakhstan, the Kyrgyz Republic, Kosovo, the Russian Federation, Tajikistan, Ukraine, and Uzbekistan.
5. Includes Albania, Belarus, Bosnia and Herzegovina, Bulgaria, Georgia, Hungary, Moldova, Montenegro, North Macedonia, Poland, Romania, Serbia, and Türkiye.
6. Includes Bulgaria, Hungary, Poland, and Romania.
7. Includes Albania, Bosnia and Herzegovina, Kosovo, Montenegro, North Macedonia, and Serbia.
8. Includes Belarus, Moldova, and Ukraine.
9. Includes Armenia, Azerbaijan, and Georgia.
10. Includes Kazakhstan, the Kyrgyz Republic, Tajikistan, and Uzbekistan.

TABLE 2.2.2 Europe and Central Asia country forecasts [1]

(Real GDP growth at market prices in percent, unless indicated otherwise)

	2021	2022	2023e	2024f	2025f	2026f	Percentage point differences from January 2024 projections: 2024f	2025f
Albania	8.9	4.9	3.3	3.3	3.4	3.5	0.1	0.2
Armenia	5.8	12.6	8.7	5.5	4.9	4.5	0.8	0.4
Azerbaijan	5.6	4.6	1.1	2.3	2.4	2.4	-0.1	-0.1
Belarus	2.4	-4.7	3.9	1.2	0.7	0.5	0.4	-0.1
Bosnia and Herzegovina[2]	7.4	4.2	1.7	2.6	3.3	4.0	-0.2	-0.1
Bulgaria	7.7	3.9	1.8	2.1	3.1	2.7	-0.3	-0.2
Croatia	13.0	7.0	3.1	3.0	2.8	2.7	0.3	-0.2
Georgia	10.6	11.0	7.5	5.2	5.0	5.0	0.4	0.5
Kazakhstan	4.3	3.2	5.1	3.4	4.7	3.6	-0.9	0.2
Kosovo	10.7	4.3	3.3	3.7	3.9	3.9	-0.2	-0.1
Kyrgyz Republic	5.5	9.0	6.2	4.5	4.2	4.0	0.5	0.2
Moldova	13.9	-4.6	0.7	2.2	3.9	4.5	-2.0	-0.2
Montenegro	13.0	6.4	6.0	3.4	2.8	3.0	0.2	-0.3
North Macedonia	4.5	2.2	1.0	2.5	2.9	3.0	0.0	0.0
Poland	6.9	5.6	0.2	3.0	3.4	3.2	0.4	0.0
Romania	5.7	4.1	2.1	3.3	3.8	3.8	0.0	0.0
Russian Federation	5.9	-1.2	3.6	2.9	1.4	1.1	1.6	0.5
Serbia	7.7	2.5	2.5	3.5	3.8	4.0	0.5	0.0
Tajikistan	9.4	8.0	8.3	6.5	4.5	4.5	1.0	0.0
Türkiye	11.4	5.5	4.5	3.0	3.6	4.3	-0.1	-0.3
Ukraine	3.4	-28.8	5.3	3.2	6.5	5.1	0.0	0.0
Uzbekistan	7.4	5.7	6.0	5.3	5.5	5.7	-0.2	0.0

Source: World Bank.

Note: e = estimate; f = forecast. World Bank forecasts are frequently updated based on new information and changing (global) circumstances. Consequently, projections presented here may differ from those contained in other Bank documents, even if basic assessments of countries' prospects do not significantly differ at any given moment in time. The World Bank is currently not publishing economic output, income, or growth data for Turkmenistan owing to a lack of reliable data of adequate quality. Turkmenistan is excluded from cross-country macroeconomic aggregates.

1. Data are based on GDP measured in average 2010-19 prices and market exchange rates, unless indicated otherwise.

2. GDP growth rate at constant prices is based on production approach.

LATIN AMERICA and THE CARIBBEAN

Growth in Latin America and the Caribbean (LAC) is forecast to decelerate from 2.2 percent in 2023 to 1.8 in 2024 (after the peak in interest rates in 2023) before picking up to 2.7 percent in 2025. The forecast for 2024 has been revised downward since January, mainly because of a marked downgrade for Argentina, which is now expected to contract this year before resuming growth next year. Risks to the forecast are tilted to the downside. Tighter-than-assumed global financial conditions, as well as elevated local debt levels, could weigh on private demand and require accelerated fiscal consolidation in the region. A further growth slowdown in China could hurt LAC's exports, particularly from South America. Extreme weather events related to climate change pose another downside risk. On the upside, stronger-than-expected activity in the United States could enhance regional growth, particularly in Central America and the Caribbean.

Recent developments

Growth weakened across the LAC region in the last quarter of 2023 as the effects of previous monetary hikes followed through (figure 2.3.1.A). Although recent indicators suggest activity has firmed in early 2024, the improvement has not been broad-based across the region. Activity indicators showed partial rebounds in some countries during the first quarter of the year, whereas regional trade remains weak. Business confidence has remained positive in Brazil and Mexico, and has improved in Colombia, and recovered in Argentina after deteriorating strongly in the first months of the year. Purchasing managers' indexes have indicated improving activity in Brazil and Mexico but have fallen to weak levels in Colombia (figures 2.3.1.B and 2.3.1.C). Monthly economic activity indicators in Chile and Peru have also been positive. In Argentina, recent data have indicated continuing output declines, except in agriculture.

Headline and core inflation have continued to fall across the region, although at a slowing pace (figure 2.3.1.D). The exception among major LAC countries is Argentina, which experienced a significant increase in monthly inflation at the start of 2024 and is now showing signs of easing in both inflation and inflation expectations. Food inflation in the region has recently rebounded, but at much lower rates than in 2022. All major central banks have reduced their policy interest rates from the elevated levels they reached in the fight against inflation in 2023H2, though they remain at high levels. Over the past 12 months, Brazil and Chile have cut rates the most, while Colombia and Peru have reduced rates to a lesser degree. Mexico's central bank initiated rate cuts later than its regional peers and has reduced its policy rate more cautiously, by 0.25 percentage point.

Outlook

Growth in LAC is projected to weaken further, to 1.8 percent in 2024 due to elevated real interest rates in 2023 and weak trade growth in 2024. Growth is expected to pick up to 2.7 percent in 2025 as interest rates normalize alongside lower inflation. Growth for 2024 has been revised down by 0.5 percentage point since January, mainly because of reduced regional exports and a marked deterioration in the near-term outlook for Argentina, where fiscal and monetary policy steps needed to address chronic imbalances are expected to cause a temporary contraction.

Note: This section was prepared by Francisco Arroyo Marioli.

FIGURE 2.3.1 LAC: Recent developments

Growth across the region decelerated significantly in late 2023, with some rebounds in the first quarter of 2024. In Brazil and Mexico, business confidence has been positive, and purchasing managers' indexes have recently improved. In Argentina, business confidence has bounced back after deteriorating markedly. Although inflation in many LAC economies has fallen significantly since early 2022, core inflation has proven more stubborn than expected in recent months.

A. Output growth

Percent ■2023Q4 ■2024Q1

2
1
0
-1
-2
-3

ARG BRA CHL COL MEX PER

B. Business confidence indicators

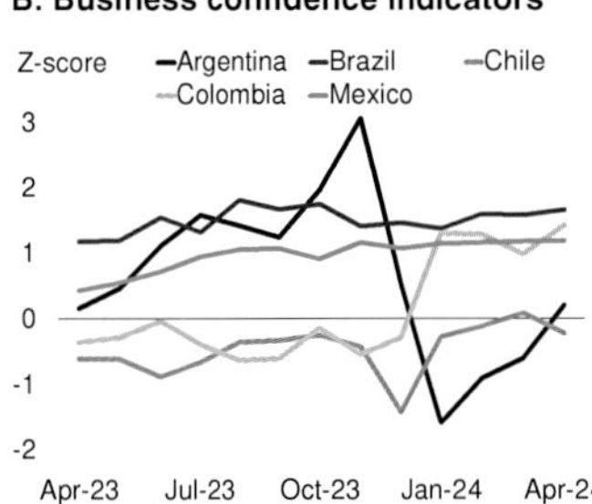

C. Purchasing managers' indexes

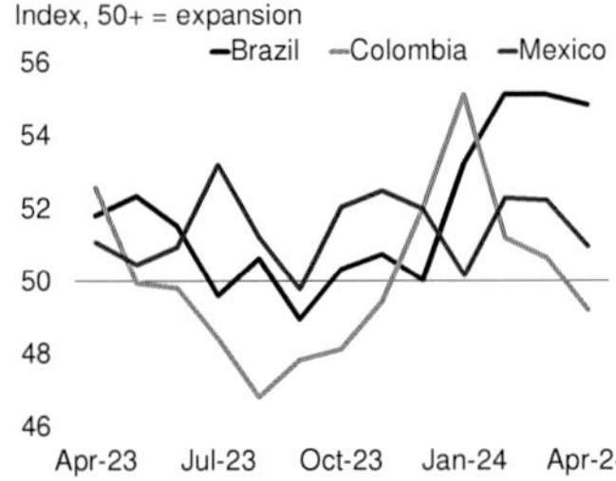

D. Consumer price inflation

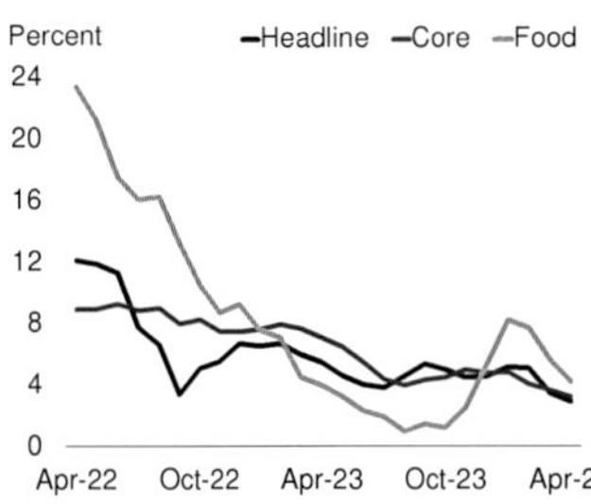

Sources: Haver Analytics; World Bank.

Note: ARG = Argentina; BRA = Brazil; CHL = Chile; COL = Colombia; LAC = Latin America and the Caribbean; MEX = Mexico; PER = Peru.

A. Bars show quarter-on-quarter growth in 2023Q4 and 2024Q1. 2024Q1 for Argentina is estimated using monthly economic activity. Last observation is March 2024.

B. Figure shows the z-score for business confidence in Chile and consumer confidence in Brazil, Colombia, and Mexico. Last observation is April 2024.

C. A purchasing managers' index (PMI) of 50 or higher (lower) indicates expansion (contraction). Composite PMI for Brazil and manufacturing PMI for Colombia and Mexico. Last observation is April 2024.

D. Seasonally adjusted annual rate of consumer price inflation. Aggregate is 3-month moving weighted average for Brazil, Chile, Colombia, Mexico, and Peru. Last observation is April 2024.

In many LAC countries, the adverse effects of past monetary tightening on activity have started to wane as inflation has declined and central banks have initiated rate cuts. With inflation in most countries expected to fall within central bank target ranges this year, reductions in policy rates are expected to continue (figures 2.3.2.A and 2.3.2.B). Argentina is the exception, with inflation remaining above 200 percent year-over-year, reflecting significant recent currency depreciation and upward adjustments in regulated prices.

Commodity prices are expected to remain broadly supportive for LAC commodity exporters, with prices for LAC's metal exports projected to remain mostly stable this year. In contrast, agriculture products and energy prices are forecast to experience a moderate decline. The subdued growth projected for China suggests soft growth in demand for most key commodity exports from LAC with the exception of oil, such as copper, iron, and soybeans.

Brazil's growth is expected to moderate to 2 percent in 2024 and 2.2 percent in 2025. The projection for 2024 reflects both a carry-over from the slowdown in the second half of last year and a weaker agricultural harvest this year. As inflation continues to moderate in line with the central bank's target, further policy rate cuts are expected, which will support private consumption and investment in 2025. Meanwhile, after being broadly supportive last year, fiscal policy is expected to exert a moderate drag on growth in 2024 and 2025 as the government resumes efforts to improve fiscal sustainability.

Growth in Mexico is forecast to slow to 2.3 percent in 2024 and 2.1 percent in 2025. This moderation is attributed to an anticipated easing in domestic demand after years of growing above its potential pace, indicating reduced economic slack and tight monetary policy. Monetary policy has remained tight despite the recent interest rate cut as declining inflation remains above the central bank's target, which will likely continue to restrain growth in the near term. Nevertheless, with inflation and interest rates envisaged to fall later this year, investment and consumption are expected to pick up in 2025. Fiscal policy is projected to expand in 2024 and consolidate in 2025 as several public investment and social programs take place this year and reach completion in the next.

Argentina's economy is projected to contract markedly, by 3.5 percent in 2024, before rebounding by 5.0 percent in 2025. The authorities are seeking to address the country's significant economic challenges with a new policy approach based partly on fiscal consolidation and the realignment of relative prices, including the exchange rate. Inflation is expected to remain elevated this year, albeit decreasing at a rapid pace.

Economic activity is expected to firm in 2025 as macroeconomic imbalances are addressed, further market distortions are removed, and inflation falls under control.

Colombia's growth is forecast to rise up to 1.3 percent in 2024 and 3.2 percent in 2025, closer to the economy's potential growth rate. After a weak growth performance in 2023, private consumption and exports are projected to recover, with the central bank expected to continue reducing policy rates as inflation declines. Investment growth is also envisaged to support economic activity as policy uncertainty abates. Fiscal support will remain limited as the government seeks to meet its budgetary targets.

Growth in Chile is forecast to rise to 2.6 percent in 2024 and 2.2 percent in 2025, as private consumption recovers from its 2023 weakness. The central bank has cut interest rates aggressively as annual core and headline inflation have fallen close to its 3 percent target, which should also allow investment to recover in 2024 and 2025. Strong external demand for green energy-related commodities, such as copper and lithium, is expected to boost the country's overall exports.

Growth in Peru is projected to rebound to 2.9 percent in 2024, then ease to 2.6 percent in 2025. Inflation is expected to continue declining as weather-related increases in food prices dissipate. This would allow further policy rate cuts, supporting private consumption in 2024 and 2025. Investment, however, is expected to recover only slowly from its fall in 2023, as political uncertainty weighs on business confidence. Although the price of copper is projected to moderate in 2024, increased mining production will support export growth.

Growth in the Caribbean economies will accelerate to 7.1 percent in 2024 and remain robust at 5.7 percent in 2025. Even excluding Guyana, which continues to experience a resource-based boom after the discovery of oil in 2015, the subregion's growth is expected to pick up to 3.9 in 2024 and 4 percent in 2025. But prospects continue to diverge in the subregion. The Dominican Republic is forecast to grow by an average of 5.1 percent in 2024-25, amid structural reforms to attract foreign direct investment. Growth in Jamaica, however, is expected to weaken to 2 percent in 2024 and 1.6 in 2025 because of subdued private consumption growth. Economic contraction in Haiti is envisaged to continue this year because of chronic violence and political instability. Tourism in the subregion has recovered close to pre-pandemic levels and should continue to support economic growth, though more moderately than in 2023 (figure 2.3.2.C; Maloney et al. 2023). Remittances into the

FIGURE 2.3.2 LAC: Outlook

After several quarters of tight monetary policy, one-year-ahead inflation expectations for economies in the region have mostly converged to within central bank target ranges. With further policy rate cuts expected, real interest rates are projected to fall. Tourism has mostly recovered to pre-pandemic levels, limiting prospects for this sector to drive further regional growth. Remittances have increased significantly—except in the Caribbean, where they have leveled off since 2021.

A. Inflation: expectations and official targets

Percent ■ Latest ■ GEP January 2024 ◆ Inflation target Percent
6 4 2 0 | 200 160 120 80 40 0
ARG (RHS) BRA CHL COL MEX PER

B. Market-implied real policy interest rates

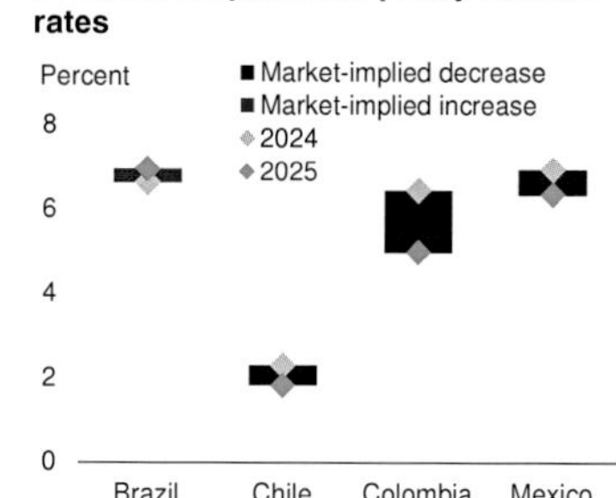

C. Tourist arrivals

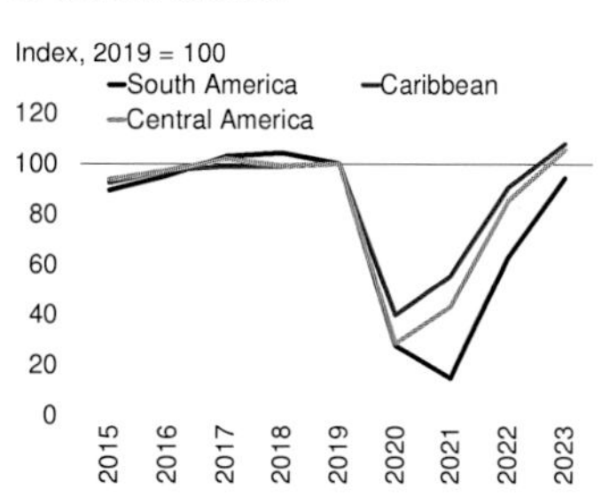

D. Remittances inflows

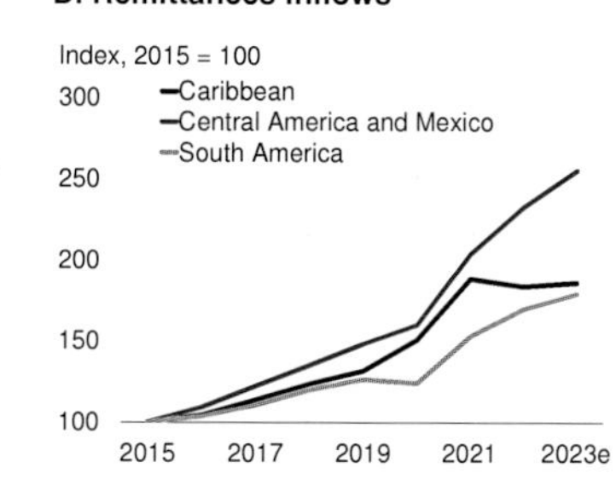

Sources: Bloomberg; Consensus Economics; Haver Analytics; International Monetary Fund; KNOMAD (database); UN Tourism; World Bank.

Note: ARG = Argentina; BRA = Brazil; CHL = Chile; COL = Colombia; LAC = Latin America and the Caribbean; MEX = Mexico; PER = Peru.

A. Bars show one-year-ahead inflation expectations reported in the January 2024 *Global Economic Prospects* report and the latest one-year-ahead inflation expectation calculated based on Consensus Economics in May 2024. Inflation targets are those set by the respective central banks.

B. Red diamonds denote the policy rate minus the 2024 inflation expectation from Consensus Economics. Orange diamonds denote the 30-day rolling average of one-year-ahead market implied policy rate, minus 2025 inflation expectation from Consensus Economics. Bars show the expected change in real interest rates from 2024 to 2025. Last observation is May 31, 2024.

C. International tourist arrivals. Last observation is 2023.

D. Remittance inflows are measured as the sum of personal transfers and compensation of employees from the International Monetary Fund's *Balance of Payments Statistics Yearbook*. 2023 is estimated.

FIGURE 2.3.3 LAC: Risks

Fiscal deficits in LAC are expected to narrow in 2025, though they will remain elevated compared to the previous decade. Both high debt and deficits pose a risk to fiscal sustainability. Moreover, if China's growth softens more than expected, prices of key LAC commodity exports could weaken materially. LAC has been experiencing frequent extreme weather events, which are driving up costs—an issue likely to worsen due to climate change.

A. Fiscal balances

B. Government debt

C. Commodity exports to China

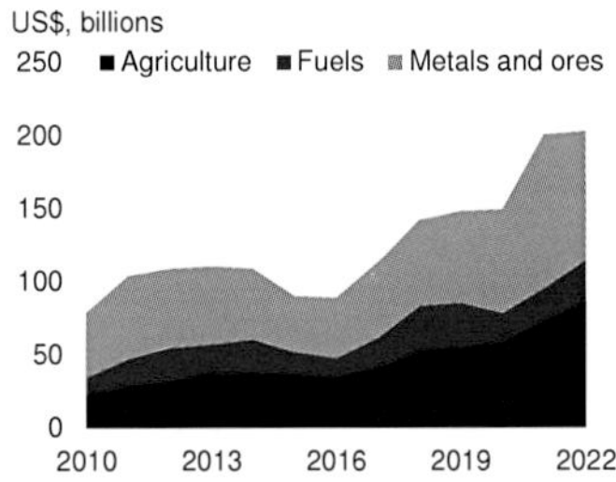

D. Vulnerability to climate change

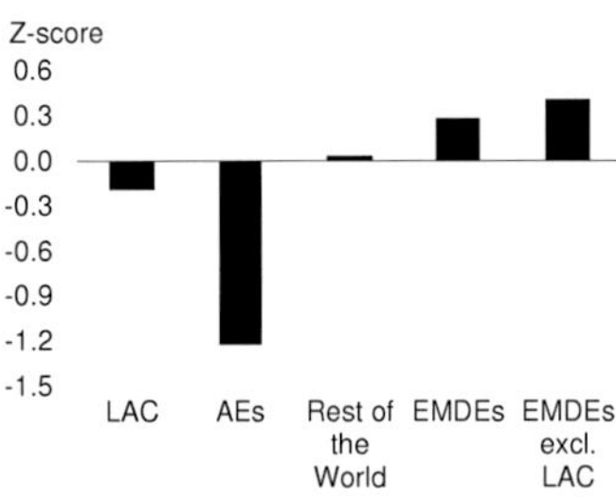

Sources: International Monetary Fund; National Centers for Environment Information; UN Comtrade (database); World Bank.

Note: f = forecast; AEs = advanced economies; ARG = Argentina; BRA = Brazil; CHL = Chile; COL = Colombia; EMDEs = emerging market and developing economies; LAC = Latin America and the Caribbean; MEX = Mexico; PER = Peru.

A. Period averages of general government net lending/borrowing during 2010-19.

B. General government gross debt as a percent of GDP. Period averages of general government gross debt during 2010-19.

C. Last observation is 2022.

D. Vulnerability measures exposure, sensitivity and capacity to adapt to the negative effects of climate change. Notre Dame Global Adaptation Initiative measures overall vulnerability by considering six life-supporting sectors – food, water, health, ecosystem service, human habitat, and infrastructure. Z-score is calculated by normalizing the simple average of the respective group by the entire sample average which consists of 192 countries. Last observation is 2021.

Caribbean are expected to continue increasing, albeit at a slower pace (World Bank 2023d).

Growth in Central America is forecast to weaken further, to 3.2 percent in 2024, before picking up to 3.5 percent in 2025, helped by faster growth in remittances (figure 2.3.2.D). Growth in Costa Rica is expected to moderate to 3.9 percent in 2024 and 3.7 percent in 2025, while growth in Panama, underpinned by services exports, is projected to slow to 2.5 percent this year, partly reflecting the closure of the Cobre Panama mine and the recent drought-related reduction in shipping through the Panama Canal, then strengthen to 3.5 percent in 2025. Inflation across the subregion varies as well. El Salvador and Panama, dollarized economies, and Costa Rica, have inflation rates close to those in the United States. Inflation in other countries, such as Guatemala, Honduras, and Nicaragua, has declined to more moderate rates.

Estimated potential economic growth in LAC during 2011–21 was notably lower than in the preceding decade, and projected potential growth in the 2020s shows a further deceleration, reflecting declines in the growth rates of both total factor productivity and the labor force (Kose and Ohnsorge 2023). This deceleration is, in part, attributable to the enduring adverse effects of the pandemic, particularly on human capital formation, as well as lack of competition and increasing violence (World Bank, 2024j).

Risks

Risks are tilted to the downside for the region. Large fiscal deficits raise concerns about financial stability. Stubborn core inflation could demand tighter-than-expected monetary policy stances. Additional weakness in China's real estate sector could weigh on LAC exports. Climate change continues to pose downside risks, including stronger El Niño effects and natural disasters. On the upside, positive supply-side developments in advanced economies would result in a faster decline in core inflation.

Fiscal positions have become more precarious due to higher levels of debt, increasing interest rates, and the prospects of slower growth (figures 2.3.3.A and 2.3.3.B). While fiscal deficits in most LAC economies have narrowed since the pandemic, they remain substantial. If markets were to perceive these fiscal positions as unsustainable, risk appetite for LAC government bonds could decline materially, forcing more abrupt fiscal consolidations than assumed in the baseline.

Inflation has fallen over the last year, though at a decelerating pace, with core inflation proving somewhat stickier than expected. Continuing persistence of core or headline inflation above targets could force central banks to halt interest rate cuts. Because markets expect policy rates to fall, this would reduce growth relative to the baseline.

As a key trading partner for the region, developments in China have significant implications for Latin America (figure 2.3.3.C). Although the real estate sector in China remains weak and subject to risks, other sectors, such as infrastructure investment, have performed better. If the downside risks in China were to materialize the overall demand in China would fall, particularly for commodities. This would depress the prices of key industrial commodities, particularly metals, adding a further downside risk to growth in some Latin American economies, principally Chile and Peru.

The effects of climate change could pose risks to sectors that are sensitive to extreme weather events, such as agriculture, fishing, and energy. Climate change can create stronger El Niño-Southern Oscillation effects, such as heavier rains in southern Latin America and droughts in the northern part of South America (figure 2.3.3.D; Cai et al. 2015; Wang et al. 2019). This could hurt the region's growth and add to its inflation (Jafino et al. 2020). Additionally, natural disasters, such as floods, could burden countries in the region, particularly those with poor infrastructure.

On the upside, positive supply-side developments could result in lower-than-expected inflation in advanced economies. This would lead to faster-than-expected cuts in global interest rates, allowing faster growth in the region through higher exports, and remittances. This scenario might also support higher commodity prices (Arteta, Kamin, and Ruch 2022), benefiting some LAC economies. Moreover, if this were accompanied by stronger growth in the United States, Central America and the Caribbean could experience additional growth spillovers via trade and remittances.

TABLE 2.3.1 Latin America and the Caribbean forecast summary

(Real GDP growth at market prices in percent, unless indicated otherwise)

	2021	2022	2023e	2024f	2025f	2026f	Percentage point differences from January 2024 projections: 2024f	2025f
EMDE LAC, GDP [1]	**7.2**	**3.9**	**2.2**	**1.8**	**2.7**	**2.6**	**-0.5**	**0.2**
GDP per capita (U.S. dollars)	6.4	3.2	1.5	1.1	2.0	1.9	-0.4	0.2
(Average including countries that report expenditure components in national accounts)[2]								
EMDE LAC, GDP [2]	7.2	3.8	2.1	1.7	2.6	2.5	-0.4	0.1
PPP GDP	7.4	3.9	2.1	1.7	2.7	2.5	-0.5	0.2
Private consumption	7.6	5.4	2.5	1.7	2.4	2.3	-0.1	-0.1
Public consumption	4.4	2.0	1.9	-0.3	1.4	1.4	-1.5	0.4
Fixed investment	16.1	4.7	2.4	0.7	4.1	3.7	-1.7	0.5
Exports, GNFS [3]	7.8	7.7	-0.2	4.0	3.7	4.0	-0.5	-0.3
Imports, GNFS [3]	18.3	7.7	0.7	2.5	3.8	4.0	-0.6	0.0
Net exports, contribution to growth	-2.3	-0.1	-0.2	0.3	-0.1	-0.1	0.0	-0.1
Memo items: GDP								
South America [4]	7.3	3.7	1.6	1.3	2.7	2.5	-0.5	0.3
Central America [5]	10.6	5.6	4.7	3.2	3.5	3.6	-0.5	-0.3
Caribbean [6]	9.7	8.4	4.8	7.1	5.7	6.0	-0.5	0.3
Caribbean excluding Guyana	9.2	5.2	2.3	3.9	4.0	3.9	-0.2	0.1
Brazil	4.8	3.0	2.9	2.0	2.2	2.0	0.5	0.0
Mexico	6.0	3.7	3.2	2.3	2.1	2.0	-0.3	0.0
Argentina	10.7	5.0	-1.6	-3.5	5.0	4.5	-6.2	1.8

Source: World Bank.

Note: e = estimate; f = forecast; PPP = purchasing power parity; EMDE = emerging market and developing economy. World Bank forecasts are frequently updated based on new information and changing (global) circumstances. Consequently, projections presented here may differ from those contained in other Bank documents, even if basic assessments of countries' prospects do not differ at any given moment in time. The World Bank is currently not publishing economic output, income, or growth data for República Bolivariana de Venezuela owing to a lack of reliable data of adequate quality. República Bolivariana de Venezuela is excluded from cross-country macroeconomic aggregates.

1. GDP and expenditure components are measured in average 2010-19 prices and market exchange rates.
2. Aggregate includes all countries in notes 4, 5, and 6, plus Mexico, but excludes Antigua and Barbuda, Barbados, Dominica, Grenada, Guyana, Haiti, St. Kitts and Nevis, St. Lucia, St. Vincent and the Grenadines, and Suriname.
3. Exports and imports of goods and nonfactor services (GNFS).
4. Includes Argentina, Bolivia, Brazil, Chile, Colombia, Ecuador, Paraguay, Peru, and Uruguay.
5. Includes Costa Rica, El Salvador, Guatemala, Honduras, Nicaragua, and Panama.
6. Includes Antigua and Barbuda, The Bahamas, Barbados, Belize, Dominica, the Dominican Republic, Grenada, Guyana, Haiti, Jamaica, St. Kitts and Nevis, St. Lucia, St. Vincent and the Grenadines, and Suriname.

TABLE 2.3.2 Latin America and the Caribbean country forecasts [1]

(Real GDP growth at market prices in percent, unless indicated otherwise)

	2021	2022	2023e	2024f	2025f	2026f	Percentage point differences from January 2024 projections: 2024f	2025f
Argentina	10.7	5.0	-1.6	-3.5	5.0	4.5	-6.2	1.8
Bahamas, The	15.4	10.8	2.6	2.3	1.8	1.6	0.5	0.2
Barbados	-1.2	13.5	4.4	3.7	2.8	2.3	-0.3	-0.2
Belize	17.9	8.7	4.7	3.4	2.5	2.5	-0.1	-0.8
Bolivia	6.1	3.6	3.1	1.4	1.5	1.5	-0.1	0.0
Brazil	4.8	3.0	2.9	2.0	2.2	2.0	0.5	0.0
Chile	11.3	2.1	0.2	2.6	2.2	2.2	0.8	-0.1
Colombia	10.8	7.3	0.6	1.3	3.2	3.1	-0.5	0.2
Costa Rica	7.9	4.6	5.1	3.9	3.7	3.7	0.0	0.1
Dominica	6.9	5.6	4.9	4.6	4.2	3.0	0.0	0.2
Dominican Republic	12.3	4.9	2.4	5.1	5.0	5.0	0.0	0.0
Ecuador	9.8	6.2	2.4	0.3	1.6	2.2	-0.4	-0.4
El Salvador	11.9	2.8	3.5	3.2	2.7	2.5	0.9	0.4
Grenada	4.7	7.3	4.8	4.3	3.8	3.2	0.5	0.3
Guatemala	8.0	4.1	3.5	3.0	3.5	3.5	-0.5	0.0
Guyana	20.1	63.3	33.0	34.3	16.8	18.2	-3.9	1.6
Haiti [2]	-1.8	-1.7	-1.9	-1.8	1.9	2.0	-3.1	-0.3
Honduras	12.5	4.0	3.6	3.4	3.3	3.4	0.2	-0.1
Jamaica	4.6	5.2	2.6	2.0	1.6	1.6	0.0	0.2
Mexico	6.0	3.7	3.2	2.3	2.1	2.0	-0.3	0.0
Nicaragua	10.3	3.8	4.3	3.7	3.5	3.5	0.5	0.0
Panama	15.8	10.8	6.5	2.5	3.5	4.0	-2.1	-1.8
Paraguay	4.0	0.2	4.7	3.8	3.6	3.6	0.0	-0.2
Peru	13.4	2.7	-0.6	2.9	2.6	2.4	0.4	0.3
St. Lucia	12.2	18.1	3.2	2.9	2.4	1.8	0.0	0.1
St. Vincent and the Grenadines	0.8	7.2	6.5	5.0	3.9	3.7	0.2	0.2
Suriname	-2.4	2.4	2.1	3.0	3.0	3.0	0.4	0.0
Uruguay	5.6	4.7	0.4	3.2	2.6	2.6	0.0	0.0

Source: World Bank.

Note: e = estimate; f = forecast. World Bank forecasts are frequently updated based on new information and changing (global) circumstances. Consequently, projections presented here may differ from those contained in other Bank documents, even if basic assessments of countries' prospects do not significantly differ at any given moment in time.

1. Data are based on GDP measured in average 2010-19 prices and market exchange rates.

2. GDP is based on fiscal year, which runs from October to September of next year.

MIDDLE EAST and NORTH AFRICA

After slowing to 1.5 percent in 2023, growth in the Middle East and North Africa (MNA) region is expected to pick up to 2.8 percent in 2024 and 4.2 percent in 2025, mainly due to a gradual resumption of oil production. The outlook for 2024 has weakened since January, partly reflecting extensions of additional voluntary oil production cuts and the ongoing conflict in the Middle East centered in Gaza. Risks to the outlook are tilted to the downside. Key downside risks include an escalation of armed conflicts, heightened local violence and social tensions, a sudden tightening in global financial conditions, more frequent or severe natural disasters, and weaker-than-projected growth in China. Conversely, stronger-than-expected activity in the United States and associated spillovers entail an important upside risk.

Recent developments

Geopolitical tensions and policy uncertainty are elevated in MNA. Human suffering and the destruction of physical capital in West Bank and Gaza arising from the conflict in the Middle East centered in Gaza are immense (World Bank and United Nations 2024). The conflict has led to wider regional repercussions, involving the Islamic Republic of Iran, Lebanon, and the Syrian Arab Republic. Attacks on shipping in the Red Sea by Houthi rebels in the Republic of Yemen have reduced transit through the Suez Canal, disrupted international trade, and heightened policy uncertainty, particularly in neighboring countries (figure 2.4.1.A).

After regional growth diminished to 1.5 percent in 2023, activity in MNA has remained weakened in the early to the middle of 2024 in both oil exporters and oil importers. In oil exporters, oil production cuts, agreed upon among the Organization of the Petroleum Exporting Countries and other affiliated oil producers (OPEC+), were extended in June 2024 by a year until the end of 2025. In addition, additional voluntary production adjustments in several OPEC+ members were also extended further, following a three-month extension in March. They agreed to maintain the additional cuts until the end of September 2024 and then gradually phase the adjustments out from October. Oil activity has been stagnant since the initial agreement of production adjustments in April 2023 (figure 2.4.1.B). Oil importers have been suffering from subdued private sector activity, partly owing to elevated inflation (figure 2.4.1.C). Several countries have also been under pressure from vulnerabilities stemming from large current account deficits and low levels of foreign exchange reserves.

Among oil exporters, declines in oil production have constrained oil activity across Gulf Cooperation Council (GCC) countries—Bahrain, Kuwait, Oman, Qatar, Saudi Arabia, and the United Arab Emirates. In Saudi Arabia, the economy contracted in the first quarter of 2024, relative to a year ago, the third consecutive quarter of output contraction. However, growth in non-oil activity has remained robust, driven by both private consumption and business investment, somewhat offsetting a contraction of oil activity.

Among other oil exporters, the Islamic Republic of Iran's growth is estimated to have increased to 5 percent in fiscal year (FY) 2023/24 (late-March 2023 to late-March 2024). Because the country is exempted from the OPEC+ agreement, oil

Note: This section was prepared by Naotaka Sugawara.

FIGURE 2.4.1 MNA: Recent developments

Tensions in the Middle East increased sharply in mid-April. The transit of ships through the Suez Canal has fallen by more than 50 percent in recent months following attacks on shipping in the Red Sea. While non-oil activity showed strong growth among oil exporters in 2022-23, private sector activity in oil importers weakened last year, with the weakening partly reflecting elevated inflation.

A. Transit of ships

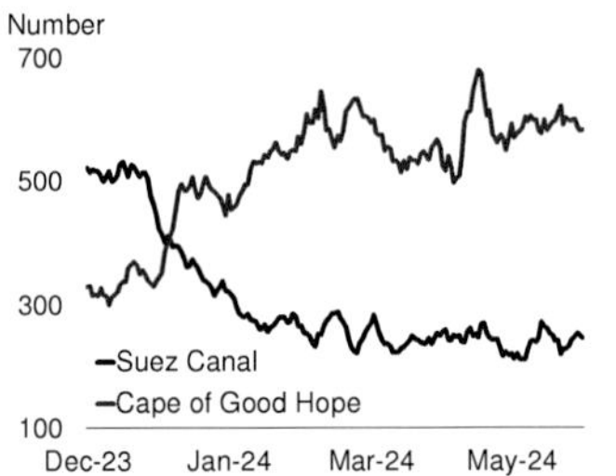

B. Gross value added in oil exporters

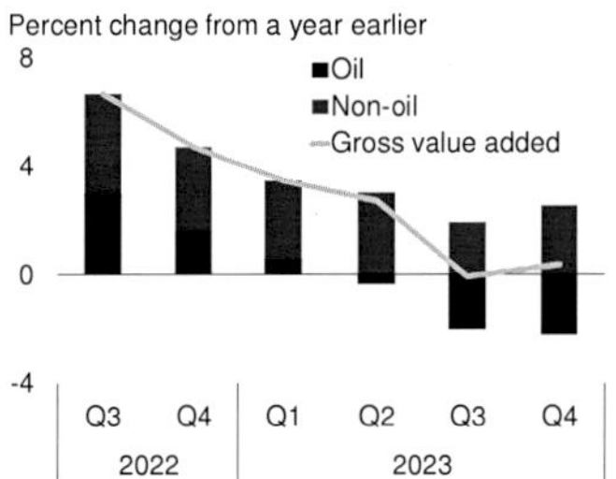

C. Industrial production in oil importers

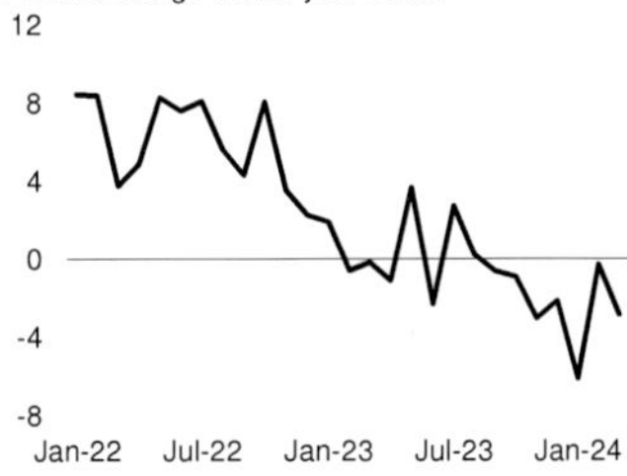

D. Inflation in oil importers

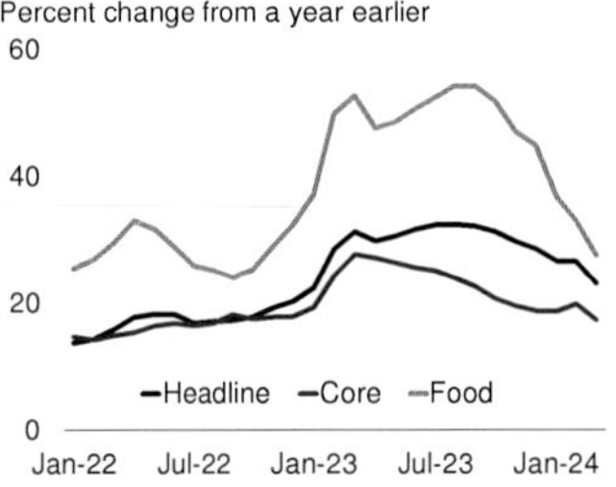

Sources: Haver Analytics; International Monetary Fund; World Bank.
Note: MNA = Middle East and North Africa.
A. Number of ships, including cargo ships and tankers, that transit the Suez Canal and the Cape of Good Hope. Data are shown as a seven-day rolling sum. Last observation is May 28, 2024.
B. Percent change in real gross value added from a year earlier, with contributions of oil (or, mining and quarrying) and non-oil (or, non-mining) activity. The aggregate is computed as a weighted average, using gross value added at 2019 prices and market exchange rates as weights. Sample includes up to eight oil exporters.
C. Percent change in industrial production from a year earlier. The aggregate is calculated as a weighted average, with value added by industry at 2015 prices and market exchange rates as weights. Last observation is March 2024. Sample includes up to four oil importers.
D. Percent change in headline consumer price, core consumer price, and food price indexes from a year earlier. The aggregate is calculated as a weighted average, using nominal GDP in U.S. dollars as weights. Last observation is March 2024. Sample includes seven oil importers.

production and exports have increased, and growth has also been robust in the non-oil sector, including services. However, oil production cuts have partly contributed to weakened activity in Iraq.

A slowdown in activity among oil importers has been less marked than in oil exporters. In the Arab Republic of Egypt, growth is set to slow to 2.8 percent in FY2023/24 (July 2023 to June 2024), 0.7 percentage point lower than the January estimate. The downward revision is partly due to weaker manufacturing activity, based on import restrictions, a downturn in the gas extractives sector operations, reduced shipping through the Suez Canal, slower investment partly owing to limited private sector credit, and a dampened recovery in tourism because of the conflict in the region.

Activity in Tunisia has halted, following a sharp contraction in agriculture during a severe drought in 2023 (World Bank 2024k). In Morocco, agricultural output contracted in early 2024 after a strong recovery in agricultural production in 2023, while services activity, particularly related to tourism, has been robust (World Bank 2023e). In West Bank and Gaza, the economy is estimated to have contracted by 6.4 percent in 2023—a downward revision of 2.7 percentage points from January. The destruction of infrastructure and productive capacity in Gaza, together with limited humanitarian assistance, has been more severe than was estimated in January.

Inflation has remained well-contained in GCC countries, as they maintain pegged exchange rates, but has been elevated in other oil exporters, particularly the Islamic Republic of Iran, and some oil importers, notably Egypt and Lebanon. In oil importers, inflation, including for food, has generally eased since mid-2023, although food price inflation remains relatively high (figure 2.4.1.D). In some cases, particularly Egypt, sharp currency depreciations have contributed to increases in inflation. As a result, policy rates in oil importers have been raised to contain inflation in early 2024.

Outlook

Growth in MNA is expected to pick up to 2.8 percent in 2024 and 4.2 percent in 2025, mainly reflecting a gradual increase in oil production since the fourth quarter of 2024 (figure 2.4.2.A; table 2.4.1). The projection for 2024 is 0.7 percentage point lower than the January forecast, reflecting the extensions of additional voluntary oil production cuts and the ongoing conflict in the region.

Growth in GCC countries is forecast to strengthen to 2.8 percent in 2024 and 4.7 percent in

2025. The extensions of oil production cuts are expected to slow output growth in 2024 (World Bank 2024l). The expected phase-out of additional cuts starting later this year is anticipated to help pick growth up next year. In Saudi Arabia, activity is forecast to increase in 2024 despite a projected decline in oil output (table 2.4.2). This growth is attributed to robust non-oil activity, driven by strong private consumption and investment, supported by fiscal and monetary policies. In 2025, a gradual resumption of oil activity is expected to raise growth.

Among other oil exporters, growth is projected to moderate in the Islamic Republic of Iran for the three fiscal years beginning in FY2024/25, while uncertainty around the outlook is elevated. The moderation partly reflects subdued global demand, the ongoing effects of international sanctions, and domestic energy shortages. In Algeria, growth is expected to be supported by the non-hydrocarbon sector in 2024 as oil production falls and to pick up in 2025 amid a recovery in agriculture (World Bank 2024m). A projected moderate recovery in the oil sector in 2025 will help strengthen growth in Iraq, following an expected output contraction in 2024. Steady growth of about 5 percent is projected for Libya, on the assumption of political stability.

Among oil importers, growth in 2024 is expected to pick up to 2.9 percent—0.3 percentage point lower than the January projection—reflecting a reassessment of the effects of the regional conflict, including on tourism. Growth is then forecast to increase to 4 percent annually in 2025-26. In Egypt, growth is projected to be 4.2 percent in FY2024/25 and 4.6 percent in FY2025/26, propelled by investment growth partly spurred by a large-scale deal with the United Arab Emirates. Private consumption is also expected to expand, supported by a recovery in remittances and a decline in inflation. Additionally, exchange rate depreciation will boost net exports. Growth in Jordan is anticipated to remain steady, at 2.6 percent per year, in 2025-26, although tourism-related activities will suffer in the short term because of the regional conflict.

In Tunisia, growth is forecast to rebound to 2.4 percent per year in 2024-25, assuming a modera-

FIGURE 2.4.2 MNA: Outlook

Growth in MNA is projected to pick up to 2.8 percent in 2024 and 4.2 percent in 2025, mainly reflecting a gradual increase in oil production. Fiscal deficits in non-GCC oil exporters and oil importers are expected to remain sizable. Although inflation is projected to fall, poverty reduction will be limited in oil importers.

A. GDP growth

B. Fiscal balances

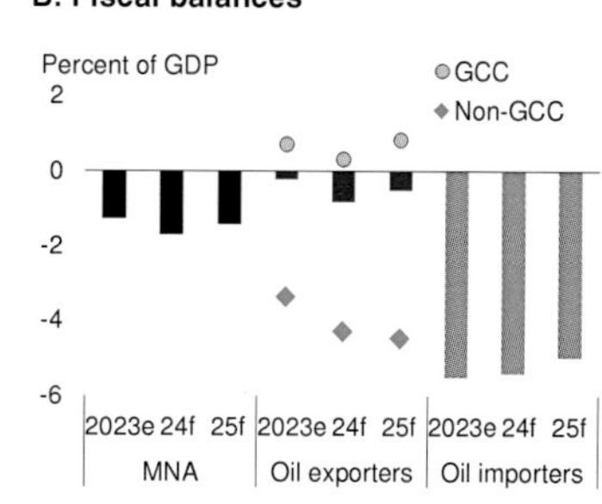

C. Headline inflation

D. Number of poor people in oil importers

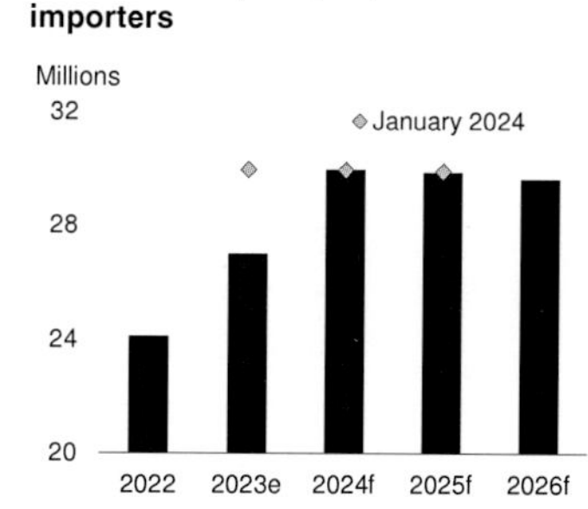

Source: World Bank.

Note: e = estimate; f = forecast; GCC = Gulf Cooperation Council; MNA = Middle East and North Africa.

A. Aggregates are calculated as weighted averages using GDP at average 2010-19 prices and market exchange rates as weights. Diamonds for January 2024 refer to data presented in the January 2024 edition of the *Global Economic Prospects* report.

B.C. Aggregates are calculated as weighted averages using nominal GDP in U.S. dollars as weights.

D. The number of poor people is defined using the lower middle-income poverty threshold of 3.65 international dollars per day in 2017 purchasing power parity. Diamonds for January 2024 refer to data presented in the January 2024 edition of the *Global Economic Prospects* report. Sample includes five oil importers.

tion of the recent drought, more benign financial conditions, and some progress in the fiscal and competition reform agendas. In Morocco, however, growth is projected to weaken to 2.4 percent in 2024, with a decline in agricultural production partly offset by a strong performance in the industrial sector, including construction—such as reconstruction from a massive earthquake last year. In Djibouti, growth is expected to moderate in 2024 to 5.1 percent and to remain steady at about this rate as the country benefits from continued demand from Ethiopia for the country's port services.

The outlook for Lebanon is uncertain, given the substantial security, political, and financial challenges the country faces. Although the economy is anticipated to grow in 2024, growth will remain weak. Inflation is anticipated to be elevated, despite some moderation, and investment will be subdued. A recovery in tourism is expected, although uncertainty is high, as tourism is subject to external and domestic shocks (World Bank 2023f). As a result, output is projected to expand by 0.5 percent in 2024, following a contraction of 0.2 percent in 2023.

Growth forecasts are also under significant uncertainty for Syria, West Bank and Gaza, and the Republic of Yemen. High uncertainty around the economic outlook in West Bank and Gaza this year reflects the severity and timeline of the conflict, changes in Israel's policies in West Bank, including those related to access to Israel's labor market, and the outcome of the clearance revenue dispute. Depending upon the outturn of these factors, the economy of West Bank and Gaza is assumed to shrink, at least, by a further 6.5 percent—with the possibility of contraction by up to 9.4 percent—in 2024 (World Bank 2024n). In Syria and the Republic of Yemen, the growth outlook is subdued and uncertain, given the ongoing conflict in the Middle East, domestic violence and unrest, and tensions in the Red Sea.

As fiscal deficits in the region are expected to widen in 2024, fiscal policy is anticipated to support growth this year, particularly in oil exporters (figure 2.4.2.B). In GCC countries, fiscal surpluses are expected to shrink as oil revenues decline and spending increases as a result of expansionary fiscal stances in several countries, including Kuwait and Saudi Arabia. Fiscal balances in other oil exporters are projected to deteriorate, partly reflecting increased spending in Algeria and Iraq. In oil importers, deficits are expected to remain elevated. In Egypt, fiscal deficits will widen if the proceedings of the recent deal with the United Arab Emirates are excluded, as interest expenses increase partly owing to tightened monetary policy and a depreciation of the exchange rate. Furthermore, it is anticipated that announced social mitigation measures, together with the negative impact on tax revenue from decreased economic activity and consumer spending, will contribute to fiscal pressures. In contrast, Morocco is envisaged to continue fiscal consolidation and see a decline in fiscal deficits. In 2025, fiscal deficits are expected to narrow marginally in the region, partly because of increases in oil revenues and gradual fiscal consolidations in several countries, including Algeria, Egypt, and Jordan.

Monetary policy in GCC countries, where exchange rates are mostly pegged to the U.S. dollar, is projected to ease in the forecast period, in tandem with expected monetary easing in the United States, supporting growth. However, among oil importers, monetary policy is envisaged to remain tight to contain inflation in 2024, before starting to ease in 2025 as inflationary pressures recede (figure 2.4.2.C).

Per capita income growth in the region is expected to rebound in the forecast period, alongside GDP growth. However, the increase in growth will be weaker in oil importers than in oil exporters, partly reflecting higher inflation in oil importers. Elevated food price inflation is also likely to continue exacerbating food insecurity, especially in economies with conflicts or social unrest (Gatti et al. 2023). As a result, only limited progress with poverty reduction is expected in oil importers (figure 2.4.2.D).

Risks

Risks to the forecast are tilted to the downside. A major downside risk is the possible escalation of armed conflicts in the region. Oil importers and countries closer to the conflicts are likely to be more negatively affected. Other downside risks to the region's growth include an increase in local violence and social tensions, a tightening of global financial conditions, more frequent natural disasters, and softer-than-expected growth in China. On the other hand, stronger-than-expected growth in advanced economies, particularly the United States, represents an important upside risk.

Prolonged, wider, or more intense conflict in the region would cause increased humanitarian and economic losses and destruction of infrastructure. Significant disruptions in oil supply could occur if the conflict widens, especially if major oil producers become heavily involved (World Bank 2024o). Adverse spillovers from escalating conflict could also damage activity in neighboring countries. The region's growth prospects could be undermined through several channels, including the effects of increased uncertainty on business and consumer confidence, a decline in tourism, capital outflows, and tighter financial conditions. An intensification of attacks on shipping in the Red Sea could weigh particularly on growth in Egypt by reducing both external accounts revenues and economic activity (Gatti et al. 2024). Disruptions in the Red Sea could also spill over to neighboring countries, including Djibouti and Saudi Arabia, dampening their export capacities (Bogetic et al. 2024).

Violence and social unrest in the region could spike because of escalating geopolitical tensions, weighing on productivity and investment (figure 2.4.3.A). More frequent or intense violent events could increase refugee flight and internal displacement of populations, adding to social tensions. An increase in the number of people affected by conflict or violence would likely worsen food insecurity, increase poverty, and hinder economic development (figure 2.4.3.B). These risks are particularly high in economies experiencing fragility or conflict and lack fiscal space to mitigate the effects of adverse developments on households, including in Syria and the Republic of Yemen (World Bank 2023g).

A tightening of global financial conditions—due, for example, to a decline in risk appetite—could lead to capital outflows and exchange rate depreciation in oil importers, particularly in those with weaker creditworthiness. As external imbalances are large in many oil importers, more limited access to foreign borrowing would further weaken growth prospects (figure 2.4.3.C). In addition, fiscal financing needs are also elevated in oil importers. Although fiscal consolidations are expected in several countries, if they are implemented abruptly and without improving revenue mobilization, such as the removal of extensive tax exemptions, and targeted support for the poor and the vulnerable, adverse growth and distributional impacts of such adjustments would be larger (Verdier et al. 2022).

Higher borrowing costs would increase debt-service burdens and widen fiscal deficits, especially

FIGURE 2.4.3 MNA: Risks

Violence has worsened in the region since the onset of the recent conflict in the Middle East centered in Gaza, and an escalation could worsen food insecurity, especially in fragile countries. In oil importers, fiscal and external financing needs are high, which makes them vulnerable to a sudden shift in global financial conditions. Additionally, commercial banks in several countries are heavily exposed to risks related to sovereign stress.

A. Incidences of political violence

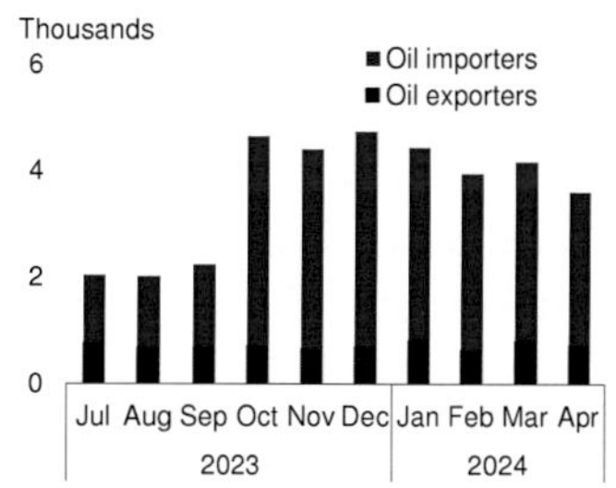

B. Prevalence of hunger

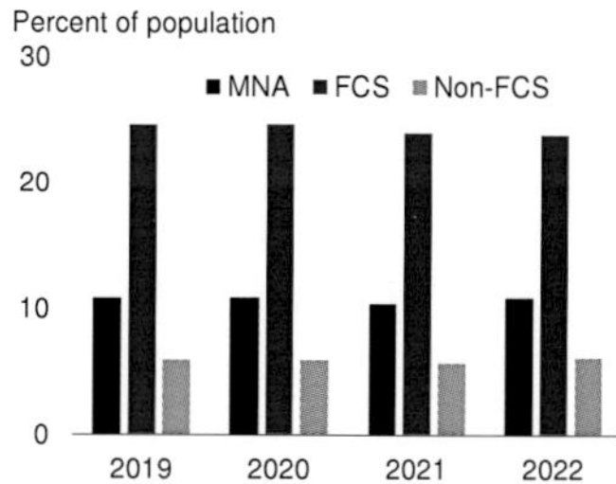

C. Financing needs in oil importers

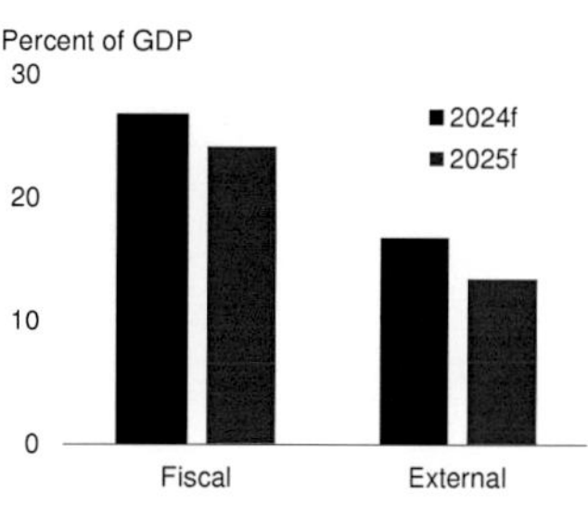

D. Commercial bank claims on government

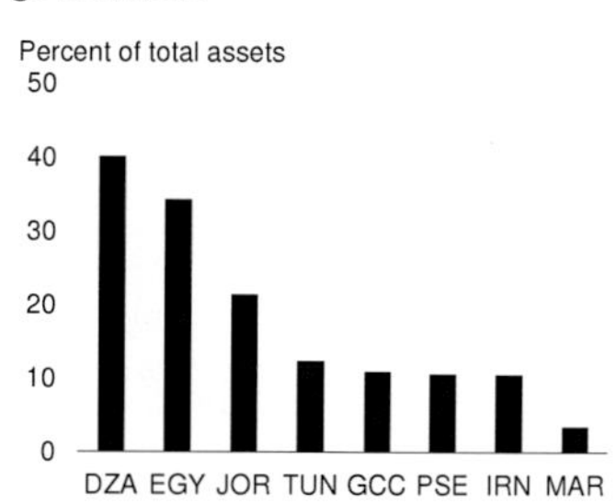

Sources: ACLED (database); Food and Agriculture Organization; Haver Analytics; International Monetary Fund; Kose et al. (2022); World Bank.

Note: f = forecast; DZA = Algeria; EGY = Arab Republic of Egypt; FCS = fragile and conflict-affected situations; GCC = Gulf Cooperation Council; IRN = Islamic Republic of Iran; JOR = Jordan; MAR = Morocco; MNA = Middle East and North Africa; PSE = West Bank and Gaza; TUN = Tunisia.

A. Total number of political violent events, including battles, explosions and remote violence, and violence against civilians. Sample includes up to 13 MNA countries, consisting of five oil exporters and eight oil importers.

B. Portion of the population that is undernourished, weighted by population in respective country groups. Sample includes up to 12 MNA countries, consisting of four FCS and eight non-FCS countries.

C. External financing needs are defined as the sum of amortization of long-term external debt, stock of short-term external debt in the previous year, and current account deficits. Fiscal financing needs are defined as a sum of short-term central government debt and fiscal deficits. Aggregates are calculated as weighted averages using nominal GDP in U.S. dollars as weights. Sample includes up to five oil importers.

D. Commercial bank claims on central or general government, in percent of total assets, including foreign and domestic assets. The GCC aggregate is calculated as a weighted average, using total assets in U.S. dollars as weights. Data are for the most recent month: March 2024 for Jordan, Morocco, and West Bank and Gaza; February 2024 for GCC countries and the Islamic Republic of Iran; December 2023 for the Arab Republic of Egypt; September 2023 for Algeria; and August 2023 for Tunisia.

in countries with high government debt and fiscal risks (Boukezia et al. 2023). These countries would be forced to reduce spending on investment and social protection, and countercyclical policy responses might be constrained. Elevated debt also increases the risk of financial instability and could weigh on growth, particularly in countries where commercial banks are exposed to sovereign debt (figure 2.4.3.D). The deterioration of market sentiment related to fiscal risks could translate into worsening bank balance sheets, adversely affecting credit to the private sector.

MNA is vulnerable to severe weather events induced by climate change, as well as other types of natural disasters such as earthquakes. The region has already experienced severe droughts and flooding, which have compromised access to basic needs, including drinking water, particularly among the poor and the vulnerable (World Bank 2023h). Increased frequency or severity of such extreme weather events would dampen food production and other agricultural activity, leading to higher food prices and exacerbating food insecurity and poverty. In countries that lack weather-resilient infrastructure, the humanitarian losses and physical damage from natural disasters related to climate change would be larger, with higher reconstruction costs.

Negative spillovers from weaker-than-expected growth in China would likely affect oil exporters through lower demand and prices for oil. Specifically, declining oil prices may lead to further reductions in oil production or an extension of current production cuts among some oil exporters, harming growth prospects in the region.

An important potential upside risk to the region's growth outlook is stronger-than-expected growth in the United States. The resulting improvement in global demand would benefit the region's exports. In oil exporters, as an increase in demand raises global oil prices, oil exporters could expand oil production, especially after the production cuts by OPEC+ members are lifted at the end of 2025. Oil importers would also gain export activity through higher external demand of their manufacturing and industrial products.

TABLE 2.4.1 Middle East and North Africa forecast summary

(Real GDP growth at market prices in percent, unless indicated otherwise)

	2021	2022	2023e	2024f	2025f	2026f	Percentage point differences from January 2024 projections: 2024f	2025f
EMDE MNA, GDP [1]	**6.2**	**5.9**	**1.5**	**2.8**	**4.2**	**3.6**	**-0.7**	**0.7**
GDP per capita (U.S. dollars)	5.0	4.5	0.2	1.5	2.9	2.4	-0.7	0.7
(Average including countries that report expenditure components in national accounts) [2]								
EMDE MNA, GDP [2]	6.3	5.9	1.5	2.8	4.2	3.6	-0.7	0.7
PPP GDP	6.3	5.7	1.8	2.9	4.2	3.6	-0.7	0.7
Private consumption	7.4	4.8	3.2	3.2	3.2	3.2	0.1	0.2
Public consumption	4.4	5.1	4.1	2.9	3.8	2.9	-0.5	0.8
Fixed investment	8.6	8.4	2.3	4.4	4.1	4.2	0.0	0.4
Exports, GNFS	6.4	11.7	1.9	3.5	6.7	5.2	-2.9	0.5
Imports, GNFS	9.3	7.9	6.0	5.5	5.3	5.1	-0.7	-0.1
Net exports, contribution to growth	-0.3	2.3	-1.2	-0.4	1.1	0.5	-1.2	0.1
Memo items: GDP								
Oil exporters [3]	6.4	6.3	1.3	2.8	4.2	3.5	-0.8	0.7
GCC countries [4]	3.6	7.5	0.7	2.8	4.7	3.5	-0.8	1.0
Non-GCC oil exporters [5]	11.9	4.2	2.4	2.7	3.4	3.5	-0.9	0.3
Oil importers [6]	5.5	3.9	2.7	2.9	4.0	4.0	-0.3	0.3

Source: World Bank.

Note: e = estimate; f = forecast; EMDE = emerging market and developing economy; GCC = Gulf Cooperation Council; GNFS = goods and non-factor services; MNA = Middle East and North Africa; PPP = purchasing power parity. World Bank forecasts are frequently updated based on new information and changing (global) circumstances. Consequently, projections presented here may differ from those contained in other Bank documents, even if basic assessments of countries' prospects do not differ at any given moment in time.

1. GDP and expenditure components are measured in average 2010-19 prices and market exchange rates. Excludes Lebanon, the Syrian Arab Republic, and the Republic of Yemen as a result of the high degree of uncertainty.
2. Aggregate includes all economies in notes 3 and 6 except Jordan, for which data limitations prevent the forecasting of GDP components.
3. Algeria, Bahrain, the Islamic Republic of Iran, Iraq, Kuwait, Libya, Oman, Qatar, Saudi Arabia, and the United Arab Emirates.
4. Bahrain, Kuwait, Oman, Qatar, Saudi Arabia, and the United Arab Emirates.
5. Algeria, the Islamic Republic of Iran, Iraq, and Libya.
6. Djibouti, the Arab Republic of Egypt, Jordan, Morocco, Tunisia, and West Bank and Gaza.

TABLE 2.4.2 Middle East and North Africa economy forecasts[1]

(Real GDP growth at market prices in percent, unless indicated otherwise)

	2021	2022	2023e	2024f	2025f	2026f	Percentage point differences from January 2024 projections: 2024f	2025f
Calendar year basis								
Algeria	3.8	3.6	4.1	2.9	3.7	3.2	0.3	1.1
Bahrain	2.6	5.2	2.6	3.5	3.3	3.4	0.2	0.1
Djibouti	4.5	3.7	6.7	5.1	5.1	5.2	0.0	-0.6
Iraq[1]	1.5	7.6	-2.9	-0.3	3.8	5.3	-4.5	0.9
Jordan	3.7	2.4	2.6	2.5	2.6	2.6	0.0	0.0
Kuwait	1.3	7.9	-0.1	2.8	3.1	2.7	0.2	0.4
Lebanon[2]	-7.0	-0.6	-0.2	0.5	..	..	..	..
Libya	153.5	1.3	-1.7	4.8	5.3	5.8	0.7	1.0
Morocco	8.0	1.3	2.8	2.4	3.7	3.3	-0.7	0.4
Oman	3.1	4.3	1.3	1.5	2.8	3.2	-1.2	-0.1
Qatar	1.6	4.2	1.8	2.1	3.2	4.7	-0.4	0.1
Saudi Arabia	4.3	8.7	-0.9	2.5	5.9	3.2	-1.6	1.7
Syrian Arab Republic[2]	1.3	-0.1	-1.2	-1.5	..	..	..	..
Tunisia	4.6	2.6	0.4	2.4	2.4	2.2	-0.6	-0.6
United Arab Emirates	4.4	7.9	3.1	3.9	4.1	4.0	0.2	0.3
West Bank and Gaza[3]	7.0	3.9	-6.4	-6.5	5.5	4.2	-0.5	0.1
Yemen, Rep.[2]	-1.0	1.5	-2.0	-1.0	1.5	..	-3.0	..
Fiscal year basis[4]	2021/22	2022/23	2023/24e	2024/25f	2025/26f	2026/27f	2024/25f	2025/26f
Iran, Islamic Rep.	4.7	3.8	5.0	3.2	2.7	2.4	-0.5	-0.5
	2020/21	2021/22	2022/23	2023/24e	2024/25f	2025/26f	2023/24e	2024/25f
Egypt, Arab Rep.	3.3	6.6	3.8	2.8	4.2	4.6	-0.7	0.3

Source: World Bank.

Note: e = estimate; f = forecast. World Bank forecasts are frequently updated based on new information and changing (global) circumstances. Consequently, projections presented here may differ from those contained in other Bank documents, even if basic assessments of economies' prospects do not significantly differ at any given moment in time.

1. Data are reported on a factor cost basis.

2. Forecasts for Lebanon (beyond 2024), the Syrian Arab Republic (beyond 2024), and the Republic of Yemen (beyond 2025) are excluded because of a high degree of uncertainty.

3. The economic outlook of West Bank and Gaza remains highly uncertain, and the growth forecast for 2024 ranges from -6.5 percent, as shown in the table, to -9.4 percent, depending upon the outturn of different factors that affect the outlook.

4. The fiscal year runs from March 21 to March 20 in the Islamic Republic of Iran; and from July 1 to June 30 in the Arab Republic of Egypt.

SOUTH ASIA

Growth in the South Asia (SAR) region is projected to slow from 6.6 percent in 2023 to 6.2 percent in 2024, mainly due to a moderation of growth in India from a high base in recent years. With steady growth in India, regional growth is forecast to stay at 6.2 percent in 2025-26. Among the region's other economies, growth is expected to remain robust in Bangladesh, though at a slower rate than in the past several years, and to strengthen in Pakistan and Sri Lanka. However, risks to the outlook remain tilted to the downside. These include disruptions in commodity markets caused by the escalation of armed conflicts, possible abrupt fiscal consolidations, financial instability stemming from the large exposure of banks to sovereign borrowers, more frequent or severe extreme weather events, and slower-than-expected growth in China and Europe. Conversely, stronger-than-projected activity in the United States and faster-than-expected global disinflation are upside risks to the forecast.

Recent developments

Growth in SAR is estimated to have increased to 6.6 percent in 2023, largely driven by faster growth in India. In early 2024, strong activity continued in India. While private sector activity picked up in several countries, including Pakistan and Sri Lanka, it remained weak. Industrial activity was disrupted in Bangladesh partly due to ongoing import restrictions, which have caused shortages of materials and intermediate goods.

In India, growth is estimated to have picked up to 8.2 percent in fiscal year (FY) 2023/24 (April 2023 to March 2024)—1.9 percentage points higher than estimated in January. Growth in industrial activity, including manufacturing and construction, was stronger than expected, alongside resilient services activity, which helped offset a slowdown in agricultural production partly caused by monsoons (figure 2.5.1.A). Growth of domestic demand remained robust, with a surge in investment, including in infrastructure, offsetting a moderation of consumption growth as post-pandemic pent-up demand eased.

Note: This section was prepared by Naotaka Sugawara.

In Bangladesh, growth is set to slow to 5.6 percent in FY2023/24 (July 2023 to June 2024) from 5.8 percent in the previous fiscal year. Government consumption and investment have supported activity, while elevated inflation has dampened real wage growth and the purchasing power of households, and weighed on private consumption. Additionally, higher borrowing costs have weighed on demand. High levels of non-performing loans in the banking sector dampened investor confidence (World Bank 2024p).

Activity in Pakistan has improved but remains subdued, with output set to expand 1.8 percent in FY2023/24 (July 2023 to June 2024), following a contraction of 0.2 percent in the previous fiscal year. Industrial production picked up in late 2023 to early 2024 after import controls were relaxed following an improvement in the country's foreign reserve positions (figure 2.5.1.B). Policy uncertainty remains elevated—despite easing from levels seen during bouts of political unceertainty over the last two years. Moreover, monetary and fiscal policies have remained tight and, together with import and capital controls aimed at fostering stability, have continued to constrain activity (World Bank 2024q). In Sri Lanka, after contracting in 2023, activity has strengthened and tourism and remittances have also recovered,

FIGURE 2.5.1 SAR: Recent developments

Growth in India has been strong, fueled by the manufacturing and services sectors. Industrial production has picked up in several countries in SAR, though credit growth has been weak. Inflation has remained generally stable in recent months, with rates in India being lower than in other parts of the region. Additionally, trade deficits have been narrowing, particularly in India.

A. Gross value added by sector, India

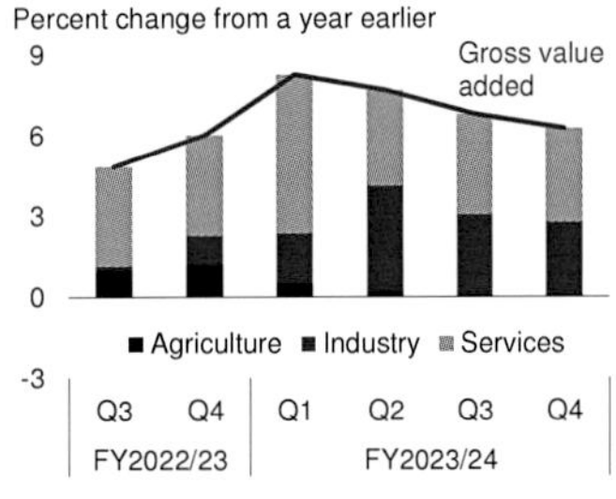

B. Industrial production and private sector credit

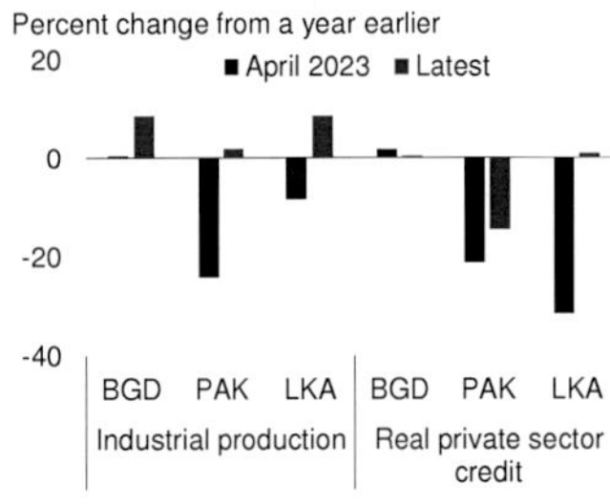

C. Headline inflation

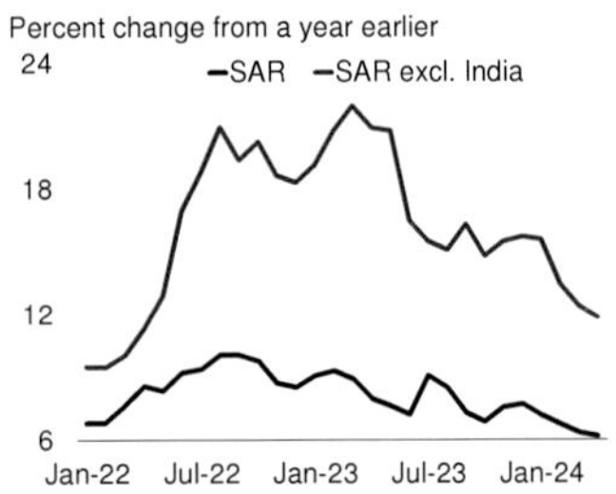

D. Goods trade balances

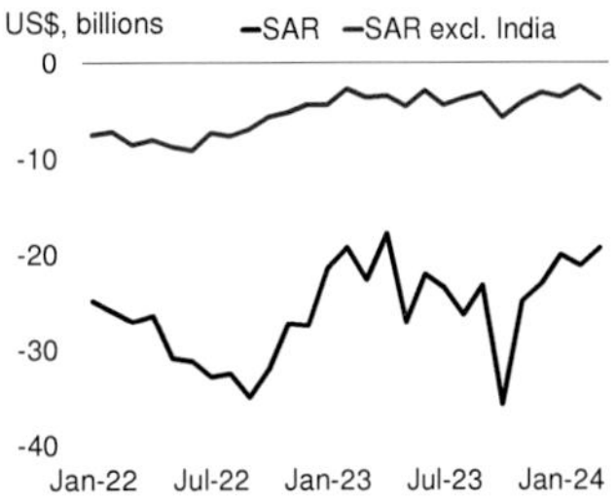

Sources: Haver Analytics; World Bank.

Note: BGD = Bangladesh; FY = fiscal year; LKA = Sri Lanka; PAK = Pakistan; SAR = South Asia.

A. Percent change in real gross value added from a year earlier, with sectoral contributions (in percentage points), in India.

B. Percent change in industrial production and real claims on the private sector by commercial banks, deflated by the consumer price index, from a year earlier. Red bars represent data for the most recent month: for industrial production, March 2024 for Pakistan and Sri Lanka, and February 2024 for Bangladesh; for private sector credit, March 2024 for all countries.

C. Percent change in headline consumer price index from a year earlier. Aggregates are calculated as weighted averages, using nominal GDP in U.S. dollars as weights. Last observation is April 2024. Sample includes up to eight countries.

D. Non-seasonally-adjusted net exports of goods, expressed in billions of nominal U.S. dollars. Last observation is March 2024. Sample includes up to six countries (Bangladesh, India, Maldives, Nepal, Pakistan, and Sri Lanka).

though they have remained below pre-pandemic levels (World Bank 2024r).

Growth in Nepal is set to rise to 3.3 percent in FY2023/24 (mid-July 2023 to mid-July 2024)—0.6 percentage point lower than projected in January—reflecting a slower recovery of non-hydropower sector activity. However, tourism and remittances have been recovering (World Bank 2024s). In Bhutan, growth is set to increase to 4.9 percent in FY2023/24 (July 2023 to June 2024)—0.9 percentage point higher than projected in January—mainly because of stronger electricity production and tourism-related activity. Growth in Maldives lost its strong momentum last year, reflecting a decline in tourist spending.

Inflation in the region has gradually declined from the peaks reached in mid-2022 (figure 2.5.1.C). In India, inflation has kept within the Reserve Bank's target range of 2 to 6 percent since September 2023. However, apart from India, regional inflation, though below peak levels, has remained elevated, reflecting persistently high food price inflation from local food supply disruptions, and increased energy prices. In Pakistan, inflation has moderated over the past year due to high base effects coupled with the stabilization of the exchange rate, but it remains high. Reflecting the persistence of inflation, policy rates have been lifted in most countries in the region.

Several developments have contributed to reductions in external imbalances. For example, trade deficits have narrowed, including in India (figure 2.5.1.D). Other factors include increases in remittances and recoveries in tourism in several countries, as well as the effects of continued import restrictions, particularly in Bangladesh. Foreign exchange reserves have increased in several countries, including Pakistan and Sri Lanka, reflecting the easing of currency pressures and receipts of official flows, but reserve levels in some countries remain low.

Outlook

Growth in SAR is projected to slow to 6.2 percent in 2024 and stay at that rate in 2025-26, mainly reflecting steady growth in India—broadly consistent with potential growth estimates in the region but weaker than the pre-pandemic longer-term averages (Kose and Ohnsorge 2023; figure 2.5.2.A). Compared with those in the January forecast, the projections are 0.6 percentage point higher for 2024 and 0.3 percentage point higher for 2025, primarily because of an upward revision in investment growth (table 2.5.1). Growth in the region excluding India is expected to pick up to 3.9 percent in 2024 and to 4.4 percent in 2026, in line with the January forecast. Inflation in the region is envisaged to moderate, supporting private consumption and contributing to monetary policy easing, although it is expected to remain elevated, particularly in Pakistan (figure 2.5.2.B).

India will remain the fastest-growing of the world's largest economies, although its pace of expansion is expected to moderate. After a high growth rate in FY2023/24, steady growth of 6.7 percent per year, on average, is projected for the three fiscal years beginning in FY2024/25 (table 2.5.2). This moderation is mainly due to a slowdown in investment from a high base. However, investment growth is still expected to be stronger than previously envisaged and remain robust over the forecast period, with strong public investment accompanied by private investment. Private consumption growth is expected to benefit from a recovery of agricultural production and declining inflation. Government consumption is projected to grow only slowly, in line with the government's aim of reducing current expenditure relative to GDP.

In Bangladesh, growth is projected to be steady, increasing slightly to 5.7 percent in FY2024/25 and 5.9 percent in FY2025/26. In addition to an increase in private consumption because of easing inflation, the implementation of large investment projects will support a pickup in overall investment. Shortages of inputs and imported goods are expected to ease gradually. A more flexible exchange rate policy is envisaged to help increase remittance inflows and reduce balance of payments pressures.

FIGURE 2.5.2 SAR: Outlook

Growth in SAR is projected to be 6.2 percent in 2024 and stay at that rate over 2025-26, mainly reflecting steady growth in India. Inflation is envisaged to decline in 2025, although fiscal deficits are expected to narrow slowly in the region. After rising in 2023-24, the number of poor people in SAR excluding India is expected to decline in 2025-26.

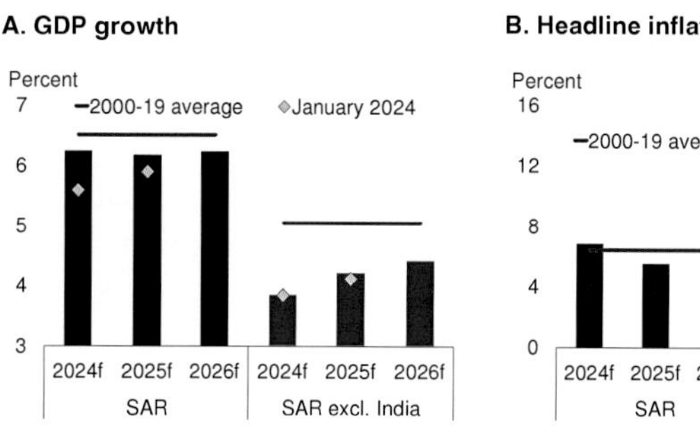

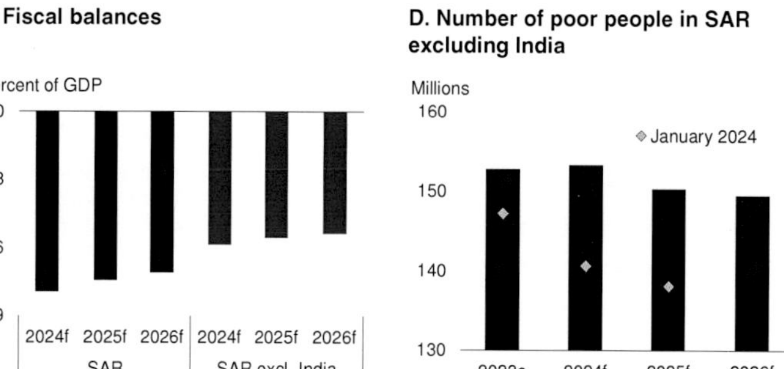

Source: World Bank.

Note: e = estimate; f = forecast; SAR = South Asia.

A. Aggregates are calculated as weighted averages, using GDP at average 2010-19 prices and market exchange rates as weights. Diamonds for January 2024 refer to data presented in the January 2024 edition of the *Global Economic Prospects* report.

B.C. Aggregates are calculated as weighted averages, using nominal GDP in U.S. dollars as weights.

D. The number of poor people is defined using the lower middle-income poverty threshold of 3.65 international dollars per day in 2017 purchasing power parity. Diamonds for January 2024 refer to data presented in the January 2024 edition of the *Global Economic Prospects* report. Sample includes four countries (Bangladesh, Bhutan, Pakistan, and Sri Lanka).

Growth in Pakistan is expected to pick up to 2.3 percent in FY2024/25 and 2.7 percent in FY2025/26. Industrial activity and confidence are projected to improve mainly due to easing import restrictions and moderating inflation, although they remain constrained largely as a result of tight macroeconomic policies. The expected increase in growth assumes continued sound macroeconomic management, progress with structural reform implementation, and continued multilateral inflows and bilateral rollovers, which would boost investor confidence.

In Sri Lanka, the economy is expected to expand by 2.2 percent in 2024—a 0.5-percentage-point upward revision from January—supported by modest recoveries in remittances and tourism. In 2025-26, growth is projected to strengthen further, reaching 3 percent in 2026, assuming successful debt restructuring negotiations and the implementation of structural reforms, which would offset the adverse impact of planned fiscal consolidation on growth.

In Nepal, growth is projected to increase to 4.6 percent in FY2024/25. Output from the hydropower sector is expected to strengthen in the forecast period, supported by robust growth in India, a major export destination. Growth is also envisaged to be boosted by an easing of monetary policy as inflation moderates. Thus, output growth in Nepal is projected to reach 5.3 percent in FY2025/26. In Bhutan, growth is projected to strengthen to 6 percent by FY2025/26, reflecting solid growth in non-hydropower industrial and services activities, in addition to firming output in the hydropower sector following the expected commissioning of a large power plant.

Growth in Maldives is projected to rise to 4.7 percent in 2024—a downward revision of 0.5 percentage point from January. Tourist spending is expected to be more moderate, as a shift in tourist demand to less expensive accommodation continues (World Bank 2024t). Planned fiscal adjustments will reduce real household income through subsidy reforms and a decline in government consumption. Growth is expected to strengthen in 2025, supported by the expansion of an international airport.

Although there are insufficient data to produce growth forecasts for Afghanistan, the economy is set to remain fragile, with high unemployment, food insecurity, and poverty. Disinflation may provide some relief to the vulnerable, but prolonged deflation would likely reduce investment and job creation and dampen activity (World Bank 2024u).

Fiscal restraint is expected to act as a modest drag on growth in the region in the forecast period. In several countries, fiscal policy is likely to tighten as part of adjustment and reform programs. In India, the fiscal deficit is projected to shrink relative to GDP, partly because of increased revenues generated by the authorities' efforts to broaden the tax base. The region's fiscal imbalances will slowly improve, although, apart from India, a reduction of fiscal deficits is expected to be smaller (figure 2.5.2.C). Nevertheless, government debt levels will remain elevated in the region. Debt-service costs are projected to be heightened in countries with the largest debt levels—including Bhutan, India, and Maldives.

Per capita income growth in the region is projected to slow to 5.1 percent in 2024-25 from 5.6 percent in 2023, before picking up to 5.2 percent in 2026. This suggests a renewed decline in poverty, but the expected pace of poverty reduction outside India in 2024-25 is slower than was projected in January, on account of weaker-than-expected growth in private consumption and fiscal adjustments that could reduce household income (figure 2.5.2.D).

Risks

Risks to the baseline forecast are tilted to the downside. These risks include commodity price spikes resulting from supply disruptions caused by the possible escalation of geopolitical tensions and intensification of armed conflicts. Other downside risks arise from high government indebtedness, including the potential need for abrupt fiscal consolidation if there are adverse developments in financial markets that increase borrowing costs or restrict the availability of finance. Climate-change-related natural disasters and weaker-than-projected growth in major trading partners are additional downside risks. Upside risks include stronger-than-expected growth in the United States and a faster-than-expected slowdown in global inflation that is not associated with weaker activity.

An intensification of armed conflicts—notably the conflict in the Middle East, attacks on shipping in the Red Sea, and Russia's invasion of Ukraine—could cause significant disruptions to food and energy supplies. Prices of these and other commodities are likely to rise as a result of increased transportation costs (World Bank 2023i). Because the share of food is larger in the consumption baskets of poor households, a surge in food prices would exacerbate poverty and food insecurity, particularly in countries with weak fiscal positions to cushion such impacts.

Elevated government debt and large debt-service burdens suggest limited fiscal buffers, highlighting the need for fiscal consolidation in many countries in the region (figure 2.5.3.A). In countries with policy programs supported by the International Monetary Fund, unwarranted delays in the implementation of fiscal adjustment plans could result in a loss of favorable investor sentiment, dampening capital inflows and investment and denting growth prospects. Meanwhile, if fiscal adjustments are implemented abruptly and opaquely, and without effective communications about the implementation, adverse effects on growth could be larger (Balasundharam et al.

2023). In addition, the share of government debt denominated in foreign currency is large in several countries in the region. Debt-service costs would rise if, for example, a decline in the global risk appetite causes depreciation of exchange rates in these countries.

High government indebtedness also increases the risk of financial instability in the region, particularly as commercial banks in several countries are heavily exposed to sovereign borrowers (figure 2.5.3.B). Market perceptions of fiscal risks could shift suddenly due to a substantial tightening of global financial conditions, driven by higher-than-expected and more persistent inflation in advanced economies and resulting higher-for-longer interest rates. The resulting reassessment of government debt sustainability and a drop in bond prices could cause a deterioration in bank balance sheets, adversely affecting economic activity. Such a tightening of global financial conditions could lead to capital outflows, reductions in foreign exchange reserves, and currency depreciations, which could heighten fiscal pressures.

More frequent or more severe extreme weather events induced by climate change could have significant consequences in the region—damaging economic growth, increasing poverty, and displacing people, particularly the poor and the vulnerable. In SAR, climate-change-related extreme weather events, including heatwaves, floods, and droughts, already occur frequently (figure 2.5.3.C). These events reduce food production, increase food prices and living costs, and make land less productive and habitable (World Bank 2024v). In addition to humanitarian losses, natural disasters can also cause massive damage to infrastructure, negatively affecting output growth. Particularly, heat waves and floods can adversely impact output directly through reduced labor productivity and investment (Acevedo et al. 2020).

In SAR, economic spillovers from outside the region tend to be limited, because the region is generally less open to international trade than other parts of the world. However, weaker-than-projected growth in major trading partners could damage growth in several countries, particularly

FIGURE 2.5.3 SAR: Risks

Government debt and financing needs are elevated in SAR, highlighting the need for fiscal consolidation in many cases. Banks in the region are heavily exposed to sovereign stress risks, which could cause instability in the financial system if they materialize. The region frequently experiences climate-change-related weather events. Weaker-than-expected activity in China could decrease receipt of intermediate goods, causing shortages in input materials and dampening activity. However, stronger-than-expected growth in the United States could benefit some countries through increased exports.

A. Fiscal financing needs, 2024

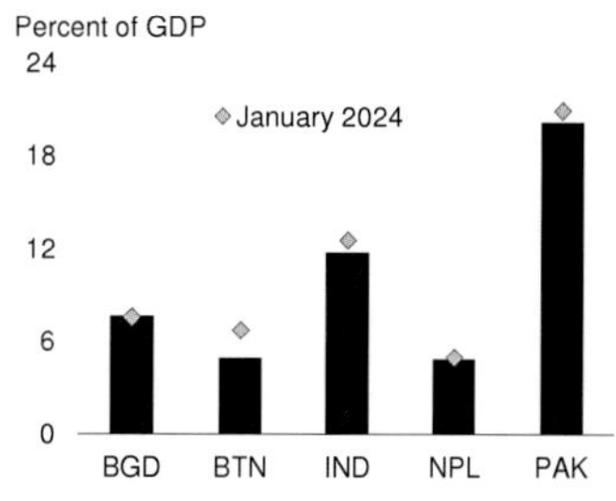

B. Commercial bank claims on government

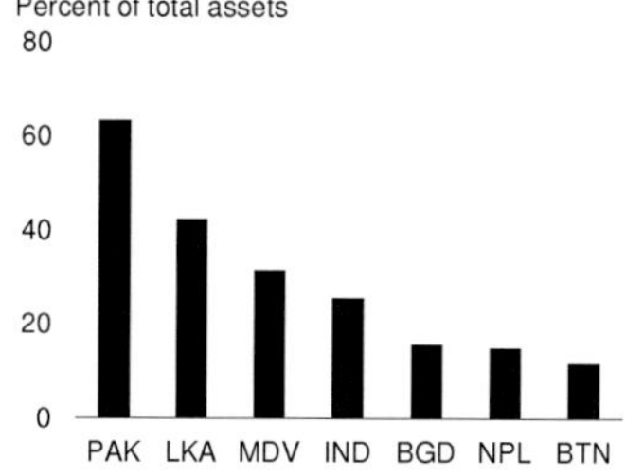

C. Frequency of extreme weather events

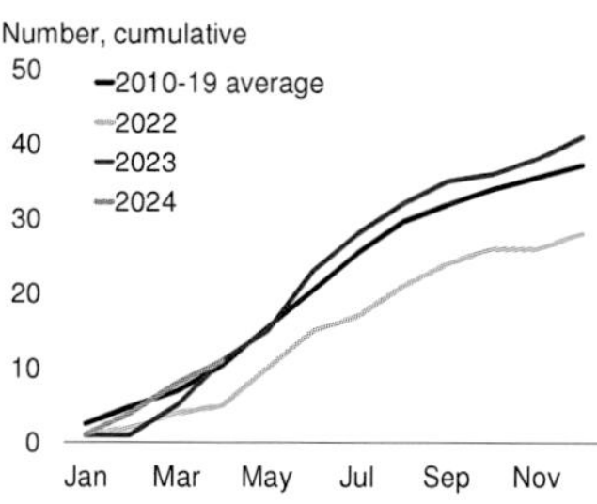

D. Trade with China and the United States

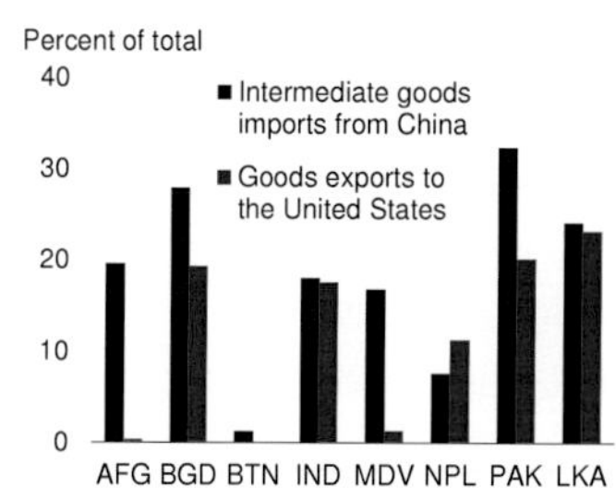

Sources: EM-DAT (database); Haver Analytics; International Monetary Fund; Kose et al. (2022); World Bank.

Note: AFG = Afghanistan; BGD = Bangladesh; BTN = Bhutan; IND = India; LKA = Sri Lanka; MDV = Maldives; NPL = Nepal; PAK = Pakistan; SAR = South Asia.

A. Fiscal financing needs are defined as the sum of short-term central government debt and fiscal deficits. Diamonds for January 2024 refer to data presented in the January 2024 edition of the *Global Economic Prospects* report.

B. Commercial bank claims on central or general government, in percent of total assets, including foreign and domestic assets. Data are for the most recent month: April 2024 for Maldives; March 2024 for Bangladesh, India, Pakistan, and Sri Lanka; December 2023 for Bhutan and Nepal.

C. Cumulative number of extreme weather events, including droughts, extreme temperatures, floods, storms, wildfire, and landslides. Last observation is April 2024. Sample includes eight countries.

D. Intermediate goods imports from China, expressed in percent of total intermediate goods imports, and goods exports to the United States, expressed in percent of total goods exports, for each country. The definition of intermediate goods is based on the 2007 version of the Harmonized System. Data are obtained from the World Integrated Trade Solution for the most recent year: 2023 for India, Maldives, and Sri Lanka; 2022 for Nepal and Pakistan; 2019 for Afghanistan; 2015 for Bangladesh; 2012 for Bhutan.

Bangladesh, Pakistan, and Sri Lanka. For example, China accounts for a high share of imports of intermediate goods in these countries, and softer-than-projected activity in China could cause a decline in receipt of intermediate goods, which would result in shortages in input materials and dampen activity (figure 2.5.3.D). In addition, countries in Europe are the main export destination for these countries, and weaker-than-expected demand in Europe, particularly the euro area, could cause a slowdown in export activity.

An upside risk to regional growth is stronger-than-projected activity in the United States. This could stimulate faster growth, especially in countries that are large exporters to the United States—including Pakistan and Sri Lanka. Another upside risk is greater progress in lowering global inflation, which could lead to faster-than-expected easing of monetary policy, reducing borrowing costs and improving the growth outlook.

TABLE 2.5.1 South Asia forecast summary

(Real GDP growth at market prices in percent, unless indicated otherwise)

	2021	2022	2023e	2024f	2025f	2026f	Percentage point differences from January 2024 projections: 2024f	2025f
EMDE South Asia, GDP[1]	**8.6**	**5.8**	**6.6**	**6.2**	**6.2**	**6.2**	**0.6**	**0.3**
GDP per capita (U.S. dollars)	7.6	4.8	5.6	5.1	5.1	5.2	0.6	0.3
(Average including countries that report expenditure components in national accounts)[2]								
EMDE South Asia, GDP[2]	8.6	5.8	6.6	6.2	6.2	6.2	0.6	0.3
PPP GDP	8.6	5.8	6.6	6.2	6.2	6.2	0.6	0.3
Private consumption	7.4	6.6	3.7	4.3	5.3	5.8	-0.6	-0.7
Public consumption	0.6	5.6	3.8	5.1	5.8	5.9	-0.4	0.4
Fixed investment	10.4	7.4	6.8	8.9	8.0	7.4	1.0	0.8
Exports, GNFS	18.3	15.8	4.7	3.1	6.3	7.4	-3.1	-0.4
Imports, GNFS	14.5	10.6	4.2	4.6	6.8	7.7	-0.9	-0.9
Net exports, contribution to growth	-0.5	0.2	-0.2	-0.6	-0.6	-0.6	-0.3	0.2
Memo items: GDP								
	2021/22	2022/23	2023/24e	2024/25f	2025/26f	2026/27f	2024/25f	2025/26f
India[3]	9.7	7.0	8.2	6.6	6.7	6.8	0.2	0.2
	2021	2022	2023e	2024f	2025f	2026f	2024f	2025f
South Asia excluding India	6.2	3.3	2.9	3.9	4.2	4.4	0.1	0.1

Source: World Bank.

Note: e = estimate; f = forecast; EMDE = emerging market and developing economy; GNFS = goods and non-factor services; PPP = purchasing power parity. World Bank forecasts are frequently updated based on new information and changing (global) circumstances. Consequently, projections presented here may differ from those contained in other Bank documents, even if basic assessments of countries' prospects do not differ at any given moment in time.

1. GDP and expenditure components are measured in average 2010-19 prices and market exchange rates. Aggregates are presented in calendar year terms. Excludes Afghanistan because of the high degree of uncertainty.

2. Aggregate excludes Afghanistan and Maldives, for which data limitations prevent the forecasting of GDP components.

3. The fiscal year runs from April 1 through March 31.

TABLE 2.5.2 South Asia country forecasts

(Real GDP growth at market prices in percent, unless indicated otherwise)

							Percentage point differences from January 2024 projections	
	2021	2022	2023e	2024f	2025f	2026f	2024f	2025f
Calendar year basis								
Afghanistan[1]	-20.7	-6.2	..	..	..	..	..	..
Maldives	37.7	13.9	4.0	4.7	5.2	4.1	-0.5	-0.3
Sri Lanka	4.2	-7.3	-2.3	2.2	2.5	3.0	0.5	0.1
Fiscal year basis[2]	2021/22	2022/23	2023/24e	2024/25f	2025/26f	2026/27f	2024/25f	2025/26f
India	9.7	7.0	8.2	6.6	6.7	6.8	0.2	0.2
	2020/21	2021/22	2022/23	2023/24e	2024/25f	2025/26f	2023/24e	2024/25f
Bangladesh	6.9	7.1	5.8	5.6	5.7	5.9	0.0	-0.1
Bhutan	-3.3	4.8	4.6	4.9	5.7	6.0	0.9	1.1
Nepal	4.8	5.6	1.9	3.3	4.6	5.3	-0.6	-0.4
Pakistan[3]	5.8	6.2	-0.2	1.8	2.3	2.7	0.1	-0.1

Source: World Bank.

Note: e = estimate; f = forecast. World Bank forecasts are frequently updated based on new information and changing (global) circumstances. Consequently, projections presented here may differ from those contained in other Bank documents, even if basic assessments of countries' prospects do not significantly differ at any given moment in time.

1. Data beyond 2022 are excluded because of a high degree of uncertainty.
2. The fiscal year runs from April 1 through March 31 in India; from July 1 through June 30 in Bangladesh, Bhutan, and Pakistan; and from July 16 through July 15 in Nepal.
3. Data are reported on a factor cost basis.

SUB-SAHARAN AFRICA

Growth in Sub-Saharan Africa is projected to pick up to 3.5 percent in 2024, and average about 4 percent in 2025-26, as inflation retreats and private consumption and investment improve. The projected recovery is somewhat weaker than January's forecast, largely reflecting the damaging effects of recent increases in political instability and conflict that have delayed recovery in parts of the region. Importantly, the expected increase in per capita income is insufficient to make significant progress on poverty alleviation in the region. Recent growth in debt-service costs has sharply narrowed fiscal space and exacerbated financing needs in many economies. Risks to the outlook remain tilted to the downside. These risks include increasing global geopolitical tensions, especially an escalation of conflict in the Middle East; a further deterioration in regional political stability; a sharper-than-expected economic slowdown in China; greater frequency and intensity of adverse weather events; and a heightened risk of government debt distress.

Recent developments

Growth in Sub-Saharan Africa (SSA) weakened to 3 percent in 2023. Growth in the region's three largest economies (Angola, Nigeria, South Africa) remained weak, holding back growth in the region. In early 2024, private sector activity picked up alongside a strengthening global economy (figure 2.6.1.A). At the same time, many economies in the region continue to struggle with weak government balance sheets, stemming partly from low revenue collection and high debt-service costs, while some also need to manage the adverse effects of currency depreciations.

Although inflation generally fell through 2023, it edged up again in early 2024, partly driven by food price inflation (figure 2.6.1.B). Continued high, and partly rising, headline inflation, particularly in several larger SSA economies (Angola, Ethiopia, Ghana, Nigeria), prompted interest rate hikes in some cases (figure 2.6.1.C). Food insecurity has remained high, with an estimated 135 million people in the region suffering from acute food insecurity in the form of a food crisis or worse conditions in 2024 (FSIN and GNAFC 2024). Prolonged droughts in parts of east Africa and floods in parts of southern Africa, as well as intense and protracted violent conflict in countries of the Sahel zone and in the Horn of Africa, have contributed to high levels of food insecurity.

In Nigeria, growth slowed to 2.9 percent in 2023. Despite ongoing macroeconomic adjustments, the economy has held up reasonably well in early 2024. Oil production has picked up since mid-2023 (figure 2.6.1.D). To rein in soaring inflation, which exceeded 30 percent year-on-year in early 2024, the central bank has tightened its monetary policy stance substantially, including by hiking the policy rate by a total of 600 basis points to 24.75 percent.

In South Africa, growth weakened to 0.6 percent in 2023. Economic activity remained subdued in early 2024 as the economy continued to struggle with a broad-based deterioration in public service delivery, including electricity supply shortages, transport bottlenecks, and a high crime rate (World Bank 2023j). Household consumption continues to be constrained by high unemployment, while investment languishes amid weak business confidence. Activity has been further dampened by necessary fiscal restraint, as public debt levels remain high, while lower global prices for the country's key commodity exports have reduced tax revenues from the mining sector.

Note: This section was prepared by Dominik Peschel.

FIGURE 2.6.1. SSA: Recent developments

Economic activity in SSA picked up in early 2024. While inflation has fallen from its late 2022 peak, it has edged up in recent months, leading to further increases in policy rates in some cases. Additionally, oil output has risen over the past year in some of the region's major producers.

A. Purchasing managers' indexes

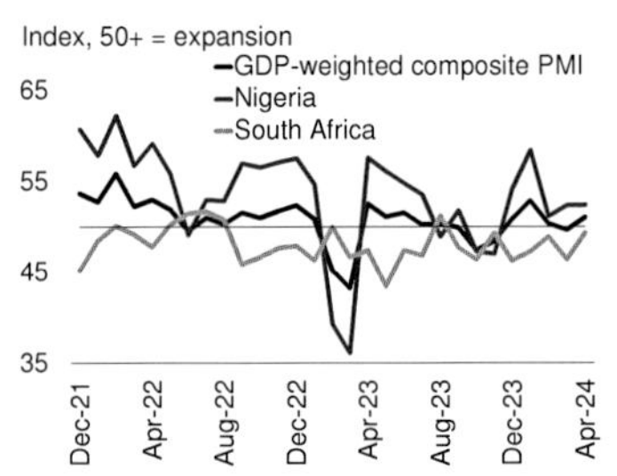

B. Consumer price inflation in SSA

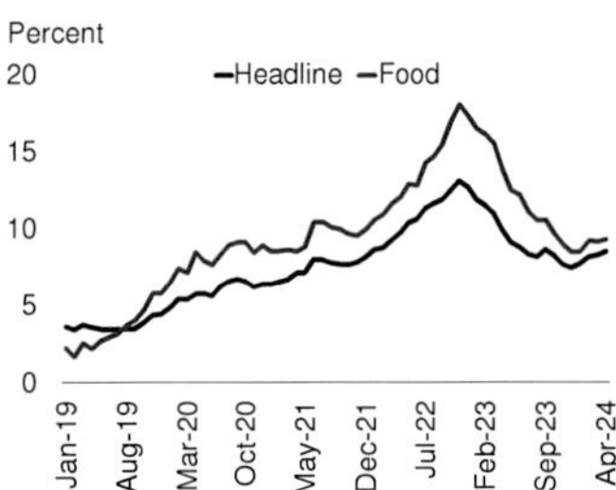

C. Monetary policy interest rates

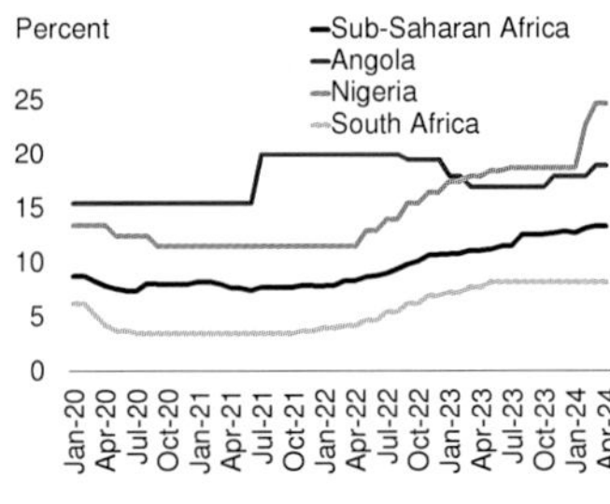

D. Oil production

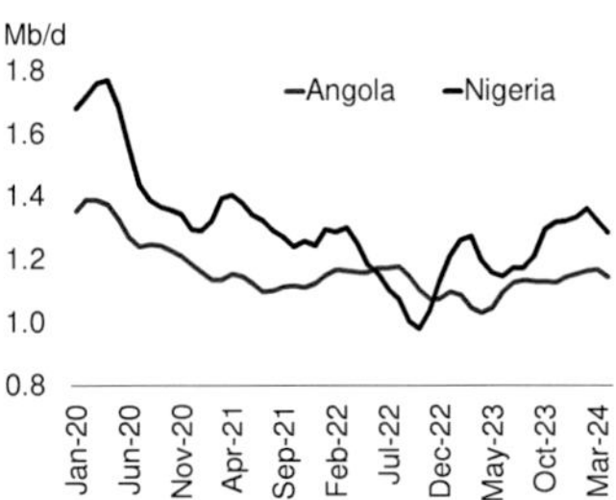

Sources: Haver Analytics; International Energy Agency; International Monetary Fund; World Bank.
Note: EMDEs = emerging markets and developing economies; GDP = gross domestic product; mb/d = million barrels per day; PMI = purchasing managers' index; SSA = Sub-Saharan Africa.
A. GDP-weighted average. Sample comprises Ghana, Kenya, Mozambique, Nigeria, South Africa, Uganda, and Zambia.
B. Change in prices from 12 months earlier. Simple averages for the sample of 19 SSA EMDEs.
C. Sample comprises 14 SSA EMDEs. Simple average for SSA.
D. Three-month moving average. Last observation is April 2024.

Growth in Angola slowed to 0.9 percent in 2023, reflecting falling oil production and a loss of dynamism in non-oil sectors. However, oil production edged up in early 2024. Inflation has risen this year, particularly for food prices.

Elsewhere in the region, the 5.7 percent growth in non-resource-rich countries in 2023 was higher than previously estimated. In Ethiopia—the region's largest agricultural-commodity producer and its most populous low-income country—growth strengthened to 7.2 percent, reflecting good harvests and strong service sector growth. In Kenya, growth also picked up in 2023, to 5.6 percent, driven by a stronger-than-expected rebound in the agricultural sector following two years of drought. Private sector activity improved further in early 2024.

In Uganda, an oil-related construction boom led to large inflows of foreign direct investment in the first quarter of 2024, supporting strong growth in the industrial sector. Increased global coffee and cocoa prices supported the agricultural sector of some economies (Côte d'Ivoire, Ethiopia, Uganda) in early 2024, although cocoa production has been disrupted by shifts in rainfall patterns and black pod disease, creating challenges for many producers (World Bank 2024w). At the same time, several economies in southern Africa (Madagascar, Malawi, Zambia, Zimbabwe) suffered from severe drought in early 2024 (OCHA 2024).

Growth in industrial-commodity exporters, excluding the three largest economies, weakened to 2.1 percent in 2023—slightly higher than the January estimate—as metal prices came down from their 2022 peak. In addition, in Zambia, a major cholera outbreak, coupled with drought conditions, weighed on economic activity in early 2024. Meanwhile, economic activity in Ghana remained subdued, reflecting the dampening effects of fiscal consolidation and high inflation on domestic demand.

Outlook

Growth in SSA is projected to pick up from 3 percent in 2023 to 3.5 percent in 2024 and about 4 percent annually in 2025-26, as fading inflationary pressures allow for interest rate cuts, which will support private consumption and investment (figure 2.6.2.A). Growth in the region's three largest economies is expected to accelerate from 1.8 percent in 2023 to 2.4 percent in 2024 and an average of 2.6 percent in 2025-26 (table 2.6.1). However, this is markedly below the region's average growth, and historical trends. Non-resource-rich economies are forecast to maintain growth above their historical average rate, while resource-rich economies recover from their slow growth in 2023, as metal prices stabilize.

Regional growth projections have been revised down from January by 0.3 percentage point for 2024 and 0.2 percentage point for 2025 (figure 2.6.2.B). Downgrades for 2024 are largest for metal exporters—many of which are fragile and conflict-affected states—with the continued slowing of growth in China expected to drag on activity in these countries. In all, forecasts have been revised down for about two-thirds of SSA economies for 2024 and for about half of them for 2025 (table 2.6.2). Upward revisions to growth forecasts are primarily for non-resource-rich economies, which are expected to benefit from further declines in fertilizer and energy prices.

FIGURE 2.6.2 SSA: Outlook

Growth is expected to accelerate in SSA over the forecast horizon, with continued robust growth in non-resource-rich economies. However, there are many downward revisions relative to January projections, particularly for metal exporters. Although per capita GDP growth is also envisaged to pick up in the forecast period, by the end of 2026 per capita GDP will still be lower than on the eve of the pandemic in 2019 in about one-quarter of SSA economies. High debt and rising interest payments are driving fiscal consolidation in many SSA economies.

A. GDP growth in SSA

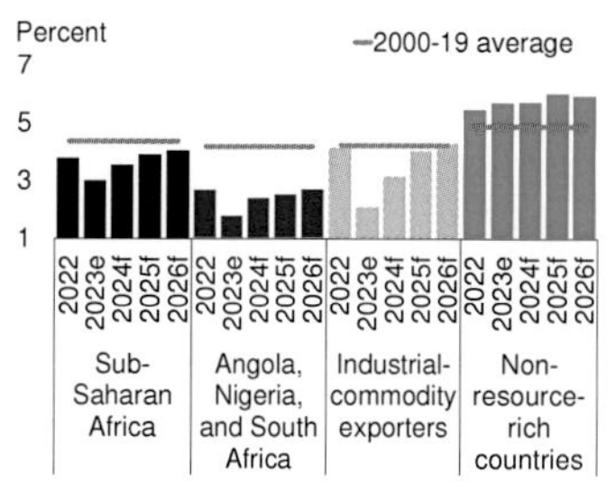

B. Growth forecast revisions for SSA since January 2024

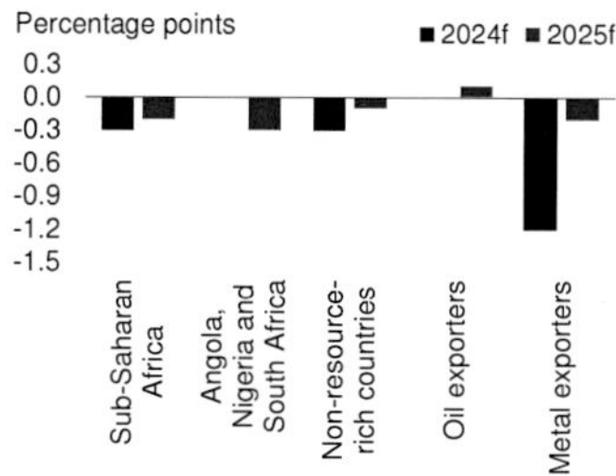

C. GDP per capita in SSA

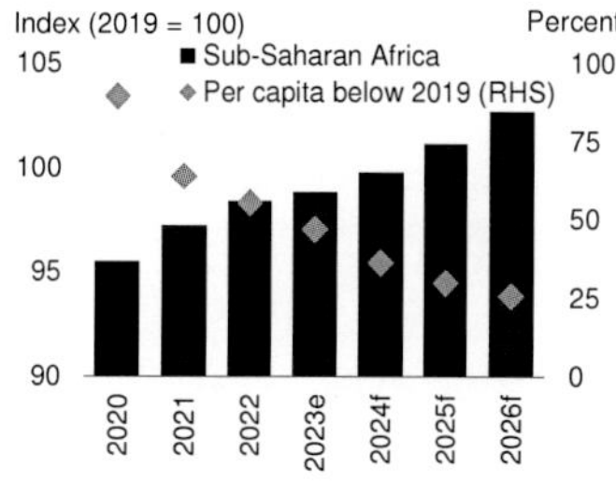

D. Fiscal balances in SSA

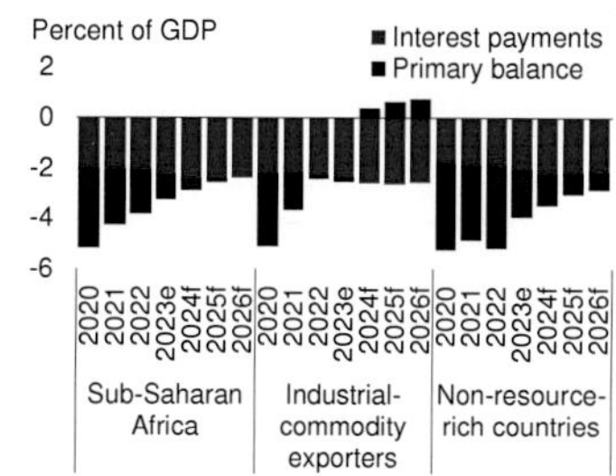

Sources: International Monetary Fund; World Bank.

Note: e = estimates; f = forecasts; SSA = Sub-Saharan Africa.

Industrial-commodity exporters excludes Angola, Nigeria, and South Africa. Non-resource-rich countries include agricultural-commodity-exporting and commodity-importing countries; excludes Chad and Sudan.

A. Aggregate growth rates calculated using constant GDP weights at average 2010-19 prices and market exchange rates.

B. Revisions relative to forecast published in the January 2024 edition of the *Global Economic Prospects* report. Oil exporters excludes Angola and Nigeria. Metal exporters excludes South Africa.

C. Proportion of SSA countries with per capita GDP below 2019.

D. Simple averages of country groupings. Sample comprises 47 SSA countries.

Growth in Nigeria is projected to pick up to 3.3 percent this year and 3.5 percent in 2025. After the macroeconomic reforms' initial shock, economic conditions are expected to gradually improve, resulting in sustained, but still-modest growth in the non-oil economy. In addition, the oil sector is expected to stabilize as production somewhat recovers. Risks to Nigeria's growth outlook are substantial, including the possibility that the tightening of monetary policy stops short of reining in inflation.

Growth in South Africa is projected to rise but remain subdued, reaching 1.2 percent in 2024 and 1.3 percent in 2025, as persistent structural constraints continue to limit near- and longer-term economic prospects. Although energy sector reforms are expected to improve energy supply in the medium term, broader reforms are necessary to lift private sector dynamism. Fiscal pressures persist on account of weak revenues, rising public sector wages, and transfers to poorly-performing state-owned enterprises. Inflation is expected to continue its gradual decline, easing cost-of-living pressures on households and supporting private consumption. Recent pension reforms that enable early access to a part of pension balances are likely to further boost consumption in late 2024, albeit to the detriment of savings.

Growth in Angola is projected to recover to 2.9 percent this year and 2.6 percent in 2025, mainly driven by a recovery in the non-oil sector. However, these growth rates are outstripped by population growth, leading to a forecast of further declines in per capita incomes. While inflation is projected to remain high in 2024 because of rising food prices and the planned further reform of fuel subsidies, monetary policy tightening—together with a restrictive fiscal stance—is expected to gradually alleviate inflationary pressures. Lower-than-expected oil prices and oil production are the chief downside risks facing this highly oil-reliant economy.

Growth in the region's industrial-commodity exporters, excluding the three largest economies, is forecast to pick up from 2.1 percent in 2023 to 3.1 percent in 2024 and 4.0 percent in 2025, as the effects of the fall in commodity prices from their 2022 peak diminishes. As inflation moderates, growth in non-mining sectors, especially services, is expected to improve in many cases. In the Democratic Republic of Congo, growth is expected to remain robust, at about 6 percent a year in 2024-25, as capacity in the mining sector expands and growth in the non-mining sector picks up. Growth is expected to improve in Ghana in 2025, after weak growth in 2024, as ongoing fiscal revenue and expenditure reforms gradually bear fruit. However, current account deficits in industrial-commodity exporters are expected to widen further.

Growth in non-resource-rich countries is projected to remain stable at 5.7 percent in 2024, before improving to 6 percent in 2025—well above historical norms—supported by declining energy and fertilizer prices. Growth of 7 percent a year is envisaged to be sustained in Ethiopia, driven by increased investment and a recovery in government consumption. In Tanzania, growth is expected to pick up to 5.4 percent in 2024 and 5.8 percent in 2025, as structural reforms gradually improve the business climate and net exports benefit from rapid growth of gold, services, and manufactured goods exports. Kenya's projected growth, improving from 5 percent in 2024 to 5.3 percent in 2025-26, reflects the country's strengthened macroeconomic framework and its regained access to international financial markets. Steady output growth of about 6.4 percent a year is also projected for Côte d'Ivoire, partly reflecting solid investment growth following oil and natural gas discoveries in the early 2020s.

Per capita gross domestic product (GDP) in SSA is expected to grow, on average, by a meager 1 percent this year and average 1.4 percent in 2025-26 (figure 2.6.2.C). While non-resource-rich economies are set to experience solid per capita GDP gains in the forecast period, the region's three largest economies will be more muted. In some countries (Angola, Central African Republic, Equatorial Guinea, Sudan) per capita GDP is projected to fall. By the end of 2026, per capita GDP in about one-quarter of SSA economies will not have recovered to pre-pandemic levels. This prolonged stunted recovery continues to inhibit progress in raising living standards and alleviating poverty.

On a positive note, declining inflation over the rest of this year should allow a gradual easing of interest rates in many SSA economies, which should boost private consumption and investment over the forecast period. At the same time, limited fiscal space, resulting from high public debt and increasing debt-service costs, is expected to weigh on public expenditure. Government debt-service costs have increased and are projected to rise further (figure 2.6.2.D). Government interest payments in the region are projected to reach 2.4 percent of GDP, on average, in 2024-25. Primary deficits, however, are forecast to shrink to 0.3 percent of GDP, on average, in 2024-25. Non-resource-rich countries are envisaged to continue running primary fiscal deficits in the forecast period, while surpluses are expected for commodity-exporting countries. However, further fiscal consolidation is likely to be needed to stabilize debt-to-GDP ratios (World Bank 2024w). Higher debt-service costs have become more challenging, especially for countries with reduced donor support and shrinking foreign exchange reserves.

Risks

Risks to the outlook are tilted to the downside. Downside risks include increasing global geopolitical tensions, especially an escalation of conflict in the Middle East; a further deterioration in regional political stability; increased frequency and intensity of adverse weather events; higher-than-expected inflation; a sharper-than-expected economic slowdown in China; and increased government debt distress, especially if elevated public debt cannot be stabilized or new sources of financing do not become available.

Many SSA economies suffer from persistent poverty and fragility that stems from festering violence and conflict, especially in the Sahel region and some neighboring countries (Ethiopia, Somalia, South Sudan), as well as the Democratic Republic of Congo (figure 2.6.3.A). Several coups d'état, including those in Gabon and Niger in 2023 and earlier ones predominantly in the Sahel region, have resulted in an escalation of political instability. Further increases in violent conflicts could not only push growth below the baseline but also result in extended humanitarian crises in many of SSA's most economically vulnerable countries.

Consumer price inflation could prove to be stickier than expected or pick up again—driven, for example, by food price inflation caused by supply disruptions, possibly triggered by an escalation of conflict in the Middle East. A sustained oil price spike caused by this conflict would not only raise food prices by increasing production and transportation costs but could also disrupt supply chains. Depending on the magnitude of conflict-related oil supply disruptions, progress on disinflation could slow notably or even reverse.

Furthermore, extreme weather events raise the likelihood of renewed upward pressure on food prices in affected economies. For instance, the current El Niño weather pattern has brought above-average rainfall and flooding to east Africa, but severe drought to southern Africa. An increase in the frequency and severity of droughts or floods would exacerbate poverty across SSA and intensify food insecurity in many countries (figure 2.6.3.B). In the longer term, climate-change-induced increases in average temperatures could hurt crop yields across the region, reducing food supplies as well as exports.

Growth in China could weaken more than expected, with adverse effects on the demand for, and prices of, many of SSA's export commodities, notably minerals and metals. SSA countries that have come to rely markedly on China as an export destination for these commodities would be hit especially hard (figure 2.6.3.C). Furthermore, slowing growth in China could lead to a further reduction in that country's investment in SSA (Chen, Fornino, and Rawlings 2024).

With public debt-service costs having surged in many SSA economies since the pandemic, the need for debt reduction in highly indebted countries has become substantial. Many SSA economies tightened their monetary policy to address rising inflation, resulting in increased financing costs. Public debt is expected to remain elevated over the forecast period (figure 2.6.3.D). If global interest rates remain high for longer than assumed in the baseline forecast, debt-service costs for SSA economies are likely to rise even further. When coupled with limited access to external financing at favorable interest rates, rising financing costs could markedly increase the risks of government debt distress—especially because debt restructuring in several SSA countries has been hampered by coordination problems among a diverse group of creditors (Bolhuis et al. 2024).

FIGURE 2.6.3 SSA: Risks

Violent events in SSA have increased since the pandemic. SSA countries, especially the region's industrial-commodity exporters, have become more dependent on China for their exports. Public debt remains high in the region, and although it is projected to moderate, interest payments as a percentage of government revenues are expected to rise further.

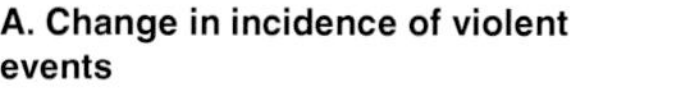

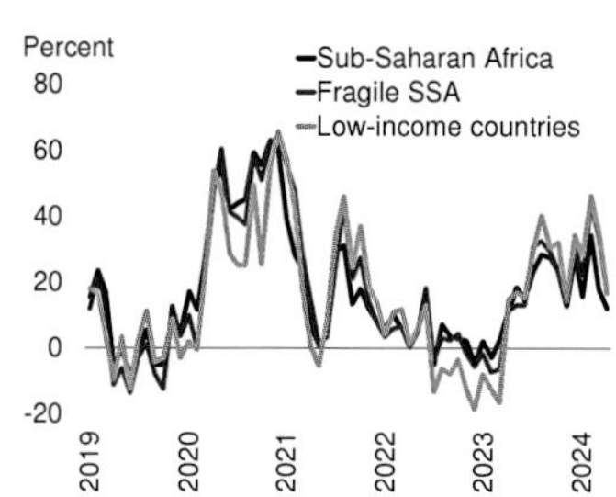

B. Food insecurity in SSA

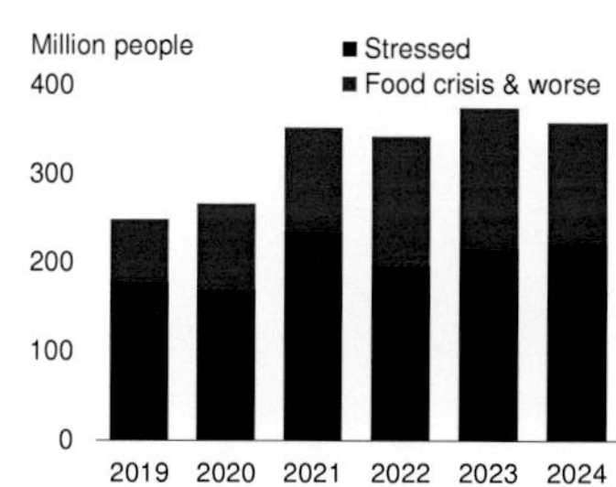

C. Share of exports to China

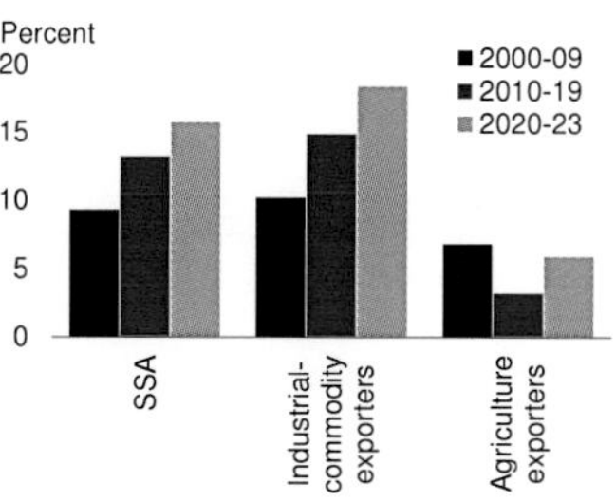

D. Public debt in SSA

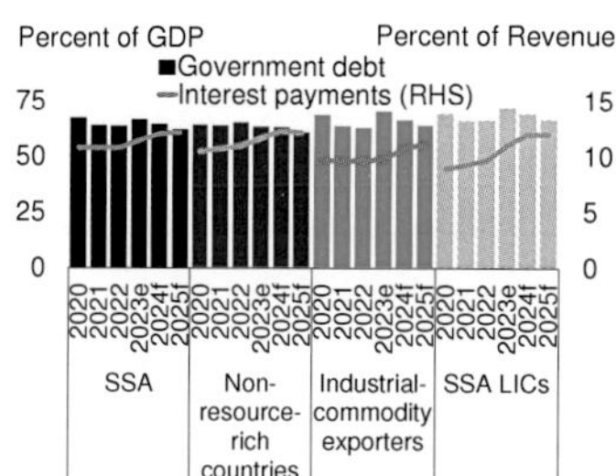

Sources: ACLED (database); FSIN and GNAFC (2023 and 2024); International Monetary Fund; World Bank.

Note: LICs = low-income countries; SSA = Sub-Saharan Africa.

A. Percent change in number of events over a year earlier. Violent events include battles, explosions, riots, and violence against civilians. Last observation is April 2024.

B. Number of people facing food security stress or food security crisis (and worse). Sample includes up to 34 countries in Sub-Saharan Africa. Data for 2022-24 are estimates.

C. Share of SSA total exports going to China. Country groupings only include SSA countries.

D. Simple averages of country groupings. Sample comprises 45 SSA countries. Industrial-commodity exporters excludes Angola, Nigeria, and South Africa. Non-resource-rich countries represent agricultural-commodity-exporting and commodity-importing countries.

TABLE 2.6.1 Sub-Saharan Africa forecast summary

(Real GDP growth at market prices in percent, unless indicated otherwise)

	2021	2022	2023e	2024f	2025f	2026f	Percentage point differences from January 2024 projections: 2024f	2025f
EMDE SSA, GDP [1]	**4.4**	**3.8**	**3.0**	**3.5**	**3.9**	**4.0**	**-0.3**	**-0.2**
GDP per capita (U.S. dollars)	1.8	1.2	0.4	1.0	1.4	1.5	-0.2	-0.1
(Average including countries that report expenditure components in national accounts) [2]								
EMDE SSA, GDP [2,3]	4.7	4.0	3.0	3.6	4.0	4.1	-0.3	-0.2
PPP GDP	4.6	4.0	2.8	3.7	4.1	4.3	-0.3	-0.2
Private consumption	4.5	4.0	2.4	3.5	3.7	3.8	-0.2	-0.1
Public consumption	5.3	2.0	0.5	2.0	1.8	1.6	0.0	-0.4
Fixed investment	8.3	7.3	5.9	5.0	6.4	6.6	-1.2	0.1
Exports, GNFS [4]	11.6	9.2	5.1	5.3	4.9	5.2	0.8	-0.3
Imports, GNFS [4]	18.1	11.3	4.0	5.5	5.1	5.3	0.8	0.3
Net exports, contribution to growth	-2.1	-1.0	0.1	-0.3	-0.3	-0.3	-0.1	-0.3
Memo items: GDP								
Eastern and Southern Africa	4.7	3.8	2.8	3.4	3.7	3.9	-0.2	-0.1
Western and Central Africa	4.0	3.8	3.2	3.8	4.1	4.2	-0.2	-0.2
SSA excluding Angola, Nigeria, and South Africa	5.0	4.9	4.2	4.6	5.2	5.3	-0.4	-0.1
Oil exporters [5]	3.2	3.2	2.5	3.1	3.4	3.6	0.0	-0.2
CFA countries [6]	4.4	4.6	3.7	4.8	5.1	4.7	-0.5	-0.2
CEMAC	1.7	3.1	1.9	2.5	2.8	3.0	-0.1	0.0
WAEMU	6.0	5.5	4.8	6.0	6.3	5.7	-0.9	-0.3
SSA3	3.9	2.7	1.8	2.4	2.5	2.7	0.0	-0.3
Nigeria	3.6	3.3	2.9	3.3	3.5	3.7	0.0	-0.2
South Africa	4.7	1.9	0.6	1.2	1.3	1.5	-0.1	-0.2
Angola	1.2	3.0	0.9	2.9	2.6	2.4	0.1	-0.5

Source: World Bank.

Note: e = estimate; f = forecast; PPP = purchasing power parity; EMDE = emerging market and developing economy. World Bank forecasts are frequently updated based on new information and changing (global) circumstances. Consequently, projections presented here may differ from those contained in other World Bank documents, even if basic assessments of countries' prospects do not differ at any given moment in time.

1. GDP and expenditure components are measured in average 2010-19 prices and market exchange rates.

2. Subregion aggregate excludes the Central African Republic, Eritrea, Guinea, Nigeria, São Tomé and Príncipe, Somalia, and South Sudan, for which data limitations prevent the forecasting of GDP components.

3. Subregion growth rates may differ from the most recent edition of Africa's Pulse (https://www.worldbank.org/en/publication/africa-pulse) because of data revisions.

4. Exports and imports of goods and nonfactor services (GNFS).

5. Includes Angola, Cameroon, Chad, the Republic of Congo, Equatorial Guinea, Gabon, Ghana, Nigeria, and South Sudan.

6. The African Financial Community (CFA) franc zone consists of 14 countries in Sub-Saharan Africa, each affiliated with one of two monetary unions. The Central African Economic and Monetary Union (CEMAC) comprises Cameroon, the Central African Republic, Chad, the Republic of Congo, Equatorial Guinea, and Gabon; the West African Economic and Monetary Union (WAEMU) comprises Benin, Burkina Faso, Côte d'Ivoire, Guinea-Bissau, Mali, Niger, Senegal, and Togo.

TABLE 2.6.2 Sub-Saharan Africa country forecasts[1]

(Real GDP growth at market prices in percent, unless indicated otherwise)

	2021	2022	2023e	2024f	2025f	2026f	Percentage point differences from January 2024 projections: 2024f	2025f
Angola	1.2	3.0	0.9	2.9	2.6	2.4	0.1	-0.5
Benin	7.2	6.3	5.8	6.0	6.0	6.0	0.0	0.0
Botswana	11.8	5.8	3.3	3.5	4.3	4.0	-0.6	0.0
Burkina Faso	6.9	1.8	3.2	3.7	3.8	4.2	-1.1	-1.3
Burundi	3.1	1.8	2.7	3.8	4.4	4.8	-0.4	-0.1
Central African Republic	1.0	0.5	0.9	1.3	1.7	1.9	-0.3	-1.4
Cabo Verde	5.6	17.1	4.8	4.7	4.7	4.6	0.0	0.0
Cameroon	3.3	3.6	3.3	3.9	4.2	4.5	-0.3	-0.3
Chad	-1.2	2.8	4.1	2.7	3.3	2.9	-0.1	0.6
Comoros	2.1	2.6	3.0	3.3	4.0	4.3	-0.2	0.0
Congo, Dem. Rep.	6.2	8.9	7.8	6.0	5.9	5.7	-0.5	-0.3
Congo, Rep.	1.0	1.5	1.9	3.5	3.7	3.2	-0.6	0.7
Côte d'Ivoire	7.1	6.2	6.0	6.4	6.4	6.3	-0.1	-0.1
Equatorial Guinea	0.3	3.8	-5.8	-4.3	-3.3	-3.6	1.8	0.6
Eritrea	2.9	2.5	2.6	2.8	3.0	3.3	-0.4	-0.3
Eswatini	10.7	0.5	4.8	4.1	3.3	2.7	1.2	0.5
Ethiopia[2]	6.3	6.4	7.2	7.0	7.0	7.0	0.6	0.0
Gabon	1.5	3.0	2.3	3.0	2.3	2.8	0.0	-0.5
Gambia, The	5.3	4.9	5.3	5.5	5.8	5.4	0.2	0.3
Ghana	5.1	3.8	2.9	2.9	4.4	4.9	0.1	0.0
Guinea	5.0	3.7	7.1	4.9	6.2	6.5	-0.9	0.0
Guinea-Bissau	6.4	4.2	4.2	4.7	4.8	4.9	-0.9	0.3
Kenya	7.6	4.9	5.6	5.0	5.3	5.3	-0.2	0.0
Lesotho	1.9	1.1	2.0	2.2	2.5	2.3	-0.3	0.4
Liberia	5.0	4.8	4.7	5.3	6.2	6.3	-0.1	0.0
Madagascar	5.7	3.8	3.8	4.5	4.6	4.7	-0.3	-0.1
Malawi	2.8	0.9	1.5	2.0	3.9	4.1	-0.8	0.6
Mali	3.1	3.5	3.5	3.1	3.5	4.5	-0.9	-1.5
Mauritania	0.7	6.4	3.4	3.8	4.5	6.3	-1.3	-1.0
Mauritius	3.4	8.9	6.8	5.0	4.1	3.9	0.4	0.5
Mozambique	2.3	4.2	5.0	5.0	5.0	4.4	0.0	0.0
Namibia	3.6	5.3	4.2	3.4	3.6	3.8	0.5	0.5
Niger	1.4	11.5	2.0	9.1	6.2	5.1	-3.7	-1.2
Nigeria	3.6	3.3	2.9	3.3	3.5	3.7	0.0	-0.2
Rwanda	10.9	8.2	8.2	7.6	7.8	7.5	0.1	0.0
São Tomé and Príncipe	1.9	0.1	-0.5	2.5	3.1	3.6	0.0	-0.2
Senegal	6.5	3.8	4.3	7.1	9.7	5.7	-1.7	0.4
Seychelles	2.5	8.9	3.3	3.5	3.4	3.4	-0.6	-0.5
Sierra Leone	4.1	3.5	3.1	3.5	4.0	4.3	-0.2	-0.3
Somalia[3]	3.3	2.4	3.1	3.7	3.9	4.0	0.2	0.1
South Africa	4.7	1.9	0.6	1.2	1.3	1.5	-0.1	-0.2
Sudan	-1.9	-1.0	-12.0	-3.5	-0.7	1.2	-2.9	-0.9
South Sudan[2]	-5.1	-2.3	-1.3	2.0	3.8	4.0	-0.3	1.4
Tanzania	4.3	4.6	5.2	5.4	5.8	6.2	-0.1	-0.3
Togo	6.0	5.8	5.4	5.1	5.4	5.6	-0.1	-0.4
Uganda[2]	3.4	4.7	5.2	6.0	6.2	6.6	0.0	-0.4
Zambia	6.2	5.2	4.0	2.7	6.1	5.9	-1.9	1.3
Zimbabwe	8.5	6.5	5.5	3.3	3.6	3.5	-0.2	0.1

Source: World Bank.

Note: e = estimate; f = forecast. World Bank forecasts are frequently updated based on new information and changing (global) circumstances. Consequently, projections presented here may differ from those contained in other Bank documents, even if basic assessments of countries' prospects do not significantly differ at any given moment in time.

1. Data are based on GDP measured in average 2010-19 prices and market exchange rates.

2. Fiscal-year-based numbers.

3. Percentage point differences are relative to the World Bank's October 2023 forecast. The January 2024 *Global Economic Prospects* did not include forecasts for Somalia.

References

Acevedo, S., M. Mrkaic, N. Novta, E. Pugacheva, and P. Topalova. 2020. "The Effects of Weather Shocks on Economic Activity: What are the Channels of Impact?" *Journal of Macroeconomics* 65 (September): 103207.

ACLED (Armed Conflict Location & Event Data Project) database. Accessed on May 31, 2024. https://acleddata.com/data-export-tool

Arteta, C., S. Kamin, and F. U. Ruch. 2022. "How Do Rising U.S. Interest Rates Affect Emerging and Developing Economies? It Depends." Policy Research Working Paper 10258, World Bank, Washington, DC.

Balasundharam, V., O. Basdevant, D. Benicio, A. Ceber, Y. Kim, L. Mazzone, H. Selim, and Y. Yang. 2023. "Fiscal Consolidation: Taking Stock of Success Factors, Impact, and Design." IMF Working Paper 23/63, International Monetary Fund, Washington, DC.

Bogetić, Ž., L. Zhao, H. Krambeck, A. Chamorro, S. Sarva, J. Matossian, and Y. Zhao. 2024. "Dire Strait: The Far-Reaching Impact of the Red Sea Shipping Crisis." MENA FCV Economic Series Brief 1, April. World Bank, Washington, DC.

Bolhuis, M., H. Mighri, H. Rawlings, I. Reyes, and Q. Zhang. 2024. *How Vulnerable Is Sub-Saharan Africa to Geoeconomic Fragmentation?* IMF Working Paper 24/83, International Monetary Fund, Washington, DC.

Boukezia, R., J. Charaoui, J. Frank, M. Harb, M. Queyranne, N. Reyes, P. F. Ryan, and A. F. Tieman. 2023. "Managing Fiscal Risks in the Middle East and North Africa." IMF Departmental Paper 2023/005, International Monetary Fund, Washington, DC.

Cai, W., G. Wang, A. Santoso, M. J. McPhaden, L. Wu, F. Jin, A. Timmermann, et al. 2015. "Increased Frequency of Extreme La Niña Events under Greenhouse Warming." *Nature Climate Change* 5 (2): 132-37.

Chen, W., M. Fornino, and H. Rawlings. 2024. Navigating the Evolving Landscape of China and Africa's Economic Engagements. IMF Working Paper 24/37, International Monetary Fund, Washington, DC.

EBRD (European Bank for Reconstruction and Development). 2023. "Transition Report 2023-24: Transitions Big and Small." European Bank for Reconstruction and Development, London.

EM-DAT (Emergency Events Database) database. Centre for Research on the Epidemiology of Disasters, UCLouvain, Brussels. Accessed on May 13, 2024. https://www.emdat.be

Freund, C. A. Mattoo, A. Mulabdic, and M. Ruta. 2023. "Is US Trade Policy Reshaping Global Supply Chains?" Policy Research Working Paper 10593, World Bank, Washington, DC.

FSIN (Food Security Information Network) and GNACF (Global Network Against Food Crises). 2024. *Global Report on Food Crises*. Rome: FSIN.

Gatti, R., F. Bennett, H. Assem, R. Lotfi, G. Mele, I. Suranov, and A. M. Islam. 2024. *Conflict and Debt in the Middle East and North Africa*. MENA Economic Update, April. Washington, DC: World Bank.

Gatti, R., D. Lederman, A. M. Islam, F. R. Bennett, B. P. J. Andree, H. Assem, R. Lotfi, and M. E. Mousa. 2023. *Altered Destinies: The Long-Term Effects of Rising Prices and Food Insecurity in the Middle East and North Africa*. MENA Economic Update, April. Washington, DC: World Bank.

IEA (International Energy Agency). 2024. "Oil Market Report." May. International Energy Agency, Paris.

Jafino, B. A., B. Walsh, J. Rozenberg, and S. Hallegatte. 2020. "Revised Estimates of the Impact of Climate Change on Extreme Poverty by 2030." Policy Research Working Paper 9417, World Bank, Washington, DC.

Kose, M. A., S. Kurlat, F. Ohnsorge, and N. Sugawara. 2022. "A Cross-Country Database of Fiscal Space." *Journal of International Money and Finance* 128 (November): 102682.

Kose, M. A., and F. Ohnsorge, eds. 2023. *Falling Long-Term Growth Prospects: Trends, Expectations, and Policies*. Washington, DC: World Bank.

Maloney, W., D. Riera-Crichton, E. I. Ianchovichina, G. Vuletin, G. Beylis, and G. Vuletin. 2023. *The Promise of Integration: Opportunities in a Changing Global Economy*. April. Washington, DC: World Bank.

OCHA (United Nations Office for the Coordination of Humanitarian Affairs). 2024. "The Humanitarian Impact of El Niño in Southern Africa." Regional Interagency Standing Committee, United Nations Office for the Coordination of Humanitarian Affairs.

Oxford Insights (database). "Government AI Readiness Index 2023." Accessed on May 31st, 2024. https://oxfordinsights.com/ai-readiness/ai-readiness-index

UNHCR (United Nations High Commissioner for Refugees). 2024. "Ukraine Situation." Flash Update #69. May 17, 2024.

Verdier, G., B. Rayner, I. Benmohamed, M. Harb, P. Muthoora, N. Reyes, L. Zhu, V. P. Koukpaizan, and C. Vellutini. 2022. "Revenue Mobilization for a Resilient and Inclusive Recovery in the Middle East and Central Asia." IMF Departmental Paper 2022/13, International Monetary Fund, Washington, DC.

Wang, B., X. Luo, Y. Yang, W. Sun, M. A. Cane, W. Cai, S. Yeh, and J. Liu. 2019. "Historical Change of El Niño Properties Sheds Light on Future Changes of Extreme El Niño." *Proceedings of the National Academy of Sciences* 116 (45): 22512-17.

World Bank. 2023a. *Which Way Forward? Navigating China's Post-Pandemic Growth Path.* China Economic Update. December. Washington, DC: World Bank.

World Bank. 2023b. *Thailand's Pathway to Carbon Neutrality: The Role of Carbon Pricing.* Thailand Economic Monitor. December. Washington, DC: World Bank.

World Bank. 2023c. *Country Climate and Development Report: Indonesia.* December. Washington, DC: World Bank.

World Bank. 2023d. "Leveraging Diaspora Finances for Private Capital Mobilization." Migration and Development Brief 39, World Bank, Washington, DC.

World Bank. 2023e. "Morocco Economic Monitor: From Resilience to Shared Prosperity." Fall. World Bank, Washington, DC.

World Bank. 2023f. "Lebanon Economic Monitor: In the Grip of a New Crisis." Fall. World Bank, Washington, DC.

World Bank. 2023g. "Yemen Economic Monitor: Peace on the Horizon?" Fall. World Bank, Washington, DC.

World Bank. 2023h. "Libya Storm and Flooding 2023: Rapid Damage and Needs Assessment." January 2024. World Bank, Washington, DC.

World Bank. 2023i. *Commodity Markets Outlook: Under the Shadow of Geopolitical Risks.* October. Washington, DC: World Bank.

World Bank. 2023j. *Safety First: The Economic Cost of Crime in South Africa.* South Africa Economic Update 14. Washington, DC: World Bank.

World Bank. 2024a. *Back on Track? The Imperative of Investing in Education.* Pacific Economic Update. March. Washington, DC: World Bank.

World Bank. 2024b. *Commodity Markets Outlook.* April. Washington, DC: World Bank.

World Bank. 2024c. *Firm Foundations of Growth.* East Asia and Pacific Economic Update. April. Washington, DC: World Bank.

World Bank. 2024d. *Ukraine: Third Rapid Damage and Needs Assessment; February 2022—December 2023.* February. Washington, DC: World Bank.

World Bank. 2024e. "Ukraine: Growth Foundations Development Policy Operation; March 2024." Report PD000047, Macroeconomics, Trade and Investment Europe and Central Asia, World Bank, Washington, DC.

World Bank. 2024f. "Invigorating Growth." Western Balkans Regular Economic Report 25. Spring. World Bank, Washington, DC.

World Bank. 2024g. "Unleashing the Power of the Private Sector." Europe and Central Asia Economic Update. April. World Bank, Washington, DC.

World Bank. 2024h. *Greening the Economy of Europe and Central Asia.* February. Washington, DC: World Bank.

World Bank. 2024i. *Net Zero Energy by 2060: Charting Europe and Central Asia's Journey Toward Sustainable Energy Futures.* February. Washington, DC: World Bank.

World Bank. 2024j. "Revitalizing Growth: An Urgent Agenda for Latin America and the Caribbean." World Bank, Washington DC.

World Bank. 2024k. "Tunisia Economic Monitor: Renewed Energy to the Economy." Spring. World Bank, Washington, DC.

World Bank. 2024l. "Gulf Economic Update: Unlocking Prosperity: Transforming Education for Economic Breakthrough in the GCC." Spring. World Bank, Washington, DC.

World Bank. 2024m. "Algeria Economic Update: Investing in Data for Diversified Growth." Spring. World Bank, Washington, DC.

World Bank. 2024n. "Impacts of the Conflict in the Middle East on the Palestinian Economy." May. World Bank, Washington, DC.

World Bank. 2024o. *Commodity Markets Outlook.* April. Washington, DC: World Bank.

World Bank. 2024p. "Bangladesh Development Update." April. World Bank, Washington, DC.

World Bank. 2024q. "Pakistan Development Update: Fiscal Impact of Federal State-Owned Enterprises." April. World Bank, Washington, DC.

World Bank. 2024r. "Sri Lanka Development Update: Bridge to Recovery." April. World Bank, Washington, DC.

World Bank. 2024s. "Nepal Development Update: Nepal's Economy on a Recovery Path but Private Investment Remains Low." April. World Bank, Washington, DC.

World Bank. 2024t. "Maldives Development Update: Scaling Back & Rebuilding Buffers." May. World Bank, Washington, DC.

World Bank. 2024u. "Afghanistan Development Update: Navigating Challenges: Confronting Economic Recession and Deflation." April. World Bank, Washington, DC.

World Bank. 2024v. *South Asia Development Update: Jobs for Resilience.* April. Washington, DC: World Bank.

World Bank. 2024w. *Africa's Pulse: Tackling Inequality to Revitalize Growth and Reduce Poverty in Africa.* April. Washington, DC: World Bank.

World Bank and United Nations. 2024. "Gaza Strip Interim Damage Assessment." Summary Note, March 29. World Bank, Washington, DC.

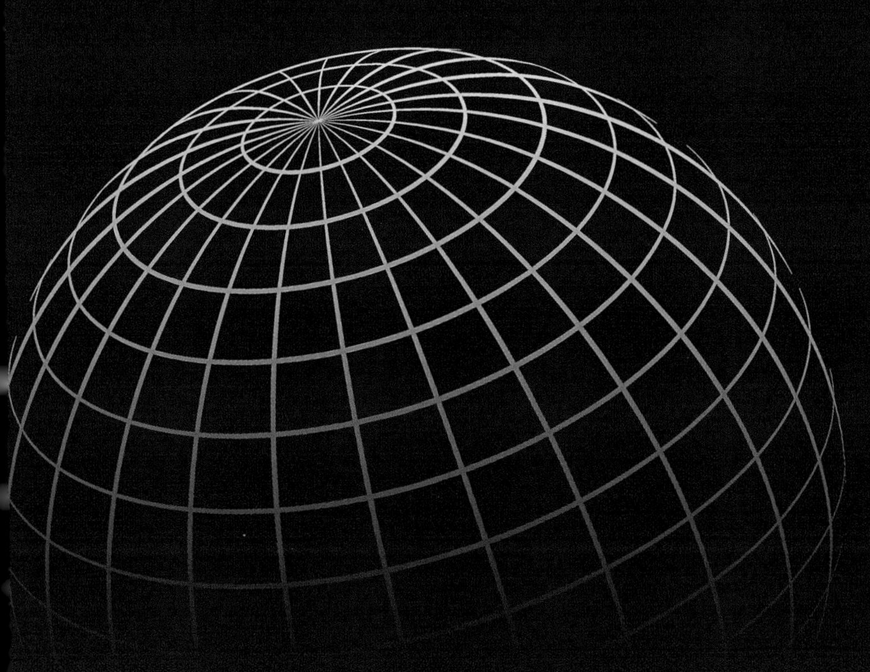

CHAPTER 3

HARNESSING THE BENEFITS OF PUBLIC INVESTMENT

A significant acceleration in investment is essential if emerging market and developing economies (EMDEs) are to achieve key development goals and tackle the challenges associated with climate change. Investment—public as well as private—tends to fuel a virtuous cycle of development, boosting growth, improving productivity, and reducing poverty. In EMDEs, however, investment growth has seen a sustained slowdown since the global financial crisis and is expected to remain weak in the coming years. Policy action is necessary to reverse this trend. Public investment averages about one-quarter of total investment in the median EMDE—a modest share. Yet it can be a powerful policy lever to help ignite growth, including by helping to catalyze private investment. This chapter offers a comprehensive assessment of public investment and its macroeconomic effects in EMDEs. It finds that public investment in these economies has experienced a historic slowdown in the past decade. In EMDEs with ample fiscal space and a record of efficient government spending, on average, scaling up of public investment by one percent of GDP can increase output by up to 1.6 percent over five years. Public investment also crowds in private investment and boosts productivity, promoting long-run economic growth in these economies. To maximize the impact of public investment, EMDEs should undertake wide-ranging policy reforms to improve public investment efficiency—by, among other things, strengthening governance and fiscal administration—and create fiscal space through revenue and expenditure measures. The global community can play an important role in facilitating these reforms—particularly in lower-income developing countries—through financial support and technical assistance.

Introduction

The scale of global investment needed to meet the Sustainable Development Goals (SDGs) and achieve commitments made under the Paris Agreement is enormous. Emerging market and developing economies (EMDEs) need to invest an estimated $2.4 trillion per year, and low-income countries (LICs) have especially hefty investment gaps (World Bank 2024; figure 3.1.A). By some estimates, to meet climate change objectives and other development goals, LICs require annual investment of 8 percent of GDP through 2030 (Rozenberg and Fay 2019; World Bank 2023a).[1] Infrastructure capital investment spending needs and maintenance costs related to SDGs vary across EMDE regions and are particularly high in Sub-Saharan Africa (figure 3.1.B). LICs have especially large infrastructure gaps related to the provision of basic public services such as electricity, transportation, clean water, basic sanitation, and health, while the quality of existing EMDE infrastructure in some sectors (transport, for example) is much lower than that in advanced economies (figures 3.1.C and 3.1.D).

Compounding the challenge, since the global financial crisis, investment has been in a broad-based and prolonged slump, as economic growth slowed and the external macroeconomic environment deteriorated. In EMDEs, average total investment growth decelerated from about 10 percent per year in the 2000s to 5 percent in the 2010s—the slowest average pace in the past three decades (figure 3.1.E).[2] Investment growth accelerations, which are associated with multiple macroeconomic benefits, also became less common in the past decade (World Bank 2024). Going forward, prospects for investment in EMDEs remain subdued (figure 3.1.F; chapter 1).

To address their substantial development needs and boost growth, EMDEs will need both public and private investment.[3] Public investment has the

Note: The chapter was prepared by Amat Adarov with contributions by Valerie Mercer-Blackman. Other contributors include Joseph Mawejje, Nikita Perevalov, and Naotaka Sugawara. Some of the analytical work draws from the background paper by Adarov, Clements, and Jalles (forthcoming).

[1] For a recent assessment of investment gaps see also G20-IEG (2023), Hallegatte et al. (2018), IPCC (2022), Kose and Ohnsorge (2024), UNEP (2023), and Vorisek and Shu (2020).

[2] Investment in the context of this chapter refers to gross fixed capital formation and comprises public and private investment. The decline in investment growth is extensively discussed in Kose and Ohnsorge (2024), World Bank (2023a), and World Bank (2024a).

[3] Public investment in this chapter refers to general government gross fixed capital formation. Investment data are in constant U.S. dollar terms. More formally, public investment includes the total net value of general government acquisitions of fixed assets during a given period and changes in the valuation of non-produced non-financial assets, such as land improvements. The main source of the data for public investment is the Investment and Capital Stock Dataset (IMF 2021a). For the post-2019 period, the data are complemented by the estimates using Haver Analytics and World Bank's WDI databases.

FIGURE 3.1 Infrastructure investment needs and investment growth

The scale of global investment needed to meet the Sustainable Development Goals and achieve commitments made under the Paris Agreement is enormous. To meet climate change objectives and other development goals, LICs require annual investment of 8 percent of GDP through 2030. Investment needs are particularly high in Sub-Saharan Africa. Compounding the challenge, in EMDEs, average investment growth decelerated from about 10 percent per year in the 2000s to 5 percent in the 2010s and is likely to remain subdued.

A. Investment needs for a resilient and low-carbon pathway, 2022-30

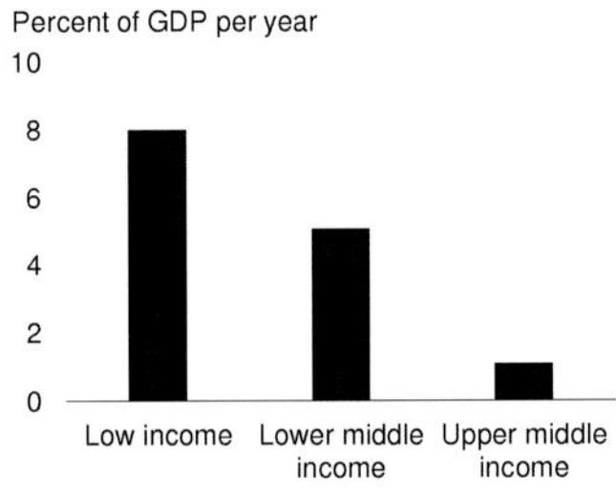

B. Capital and maintenance needs in infrastructure sectors related to SDGs, by region

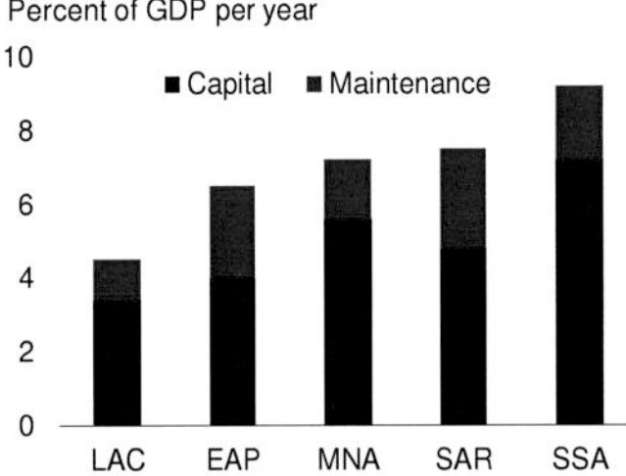

C. Access to infrastructure

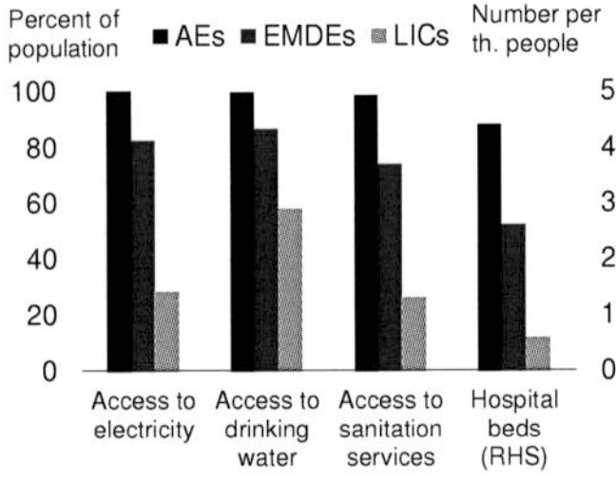

D. Quality of transport infrastructure

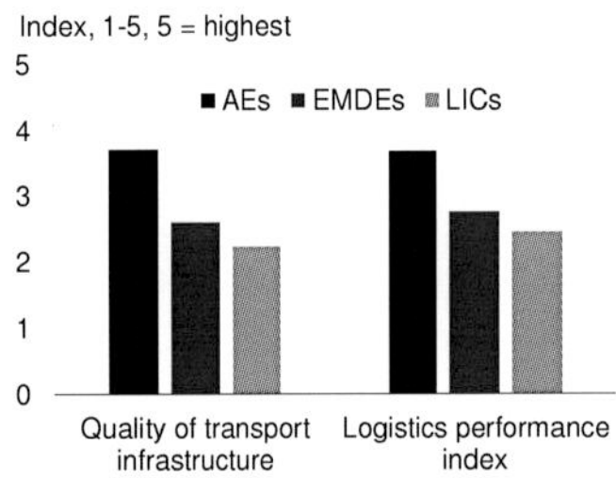

E. Average annual investment growth

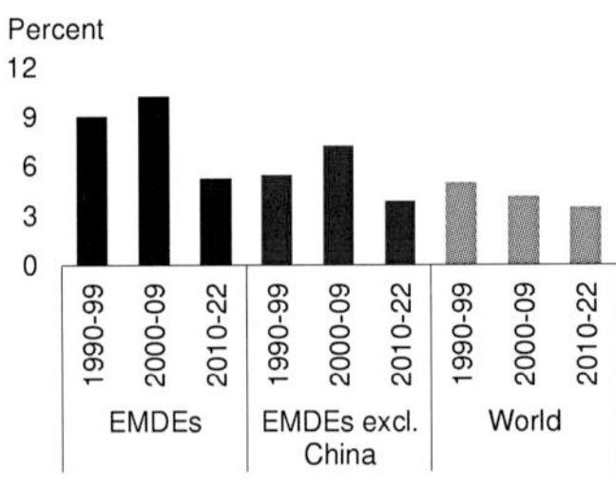

F. Investment growth forecasts

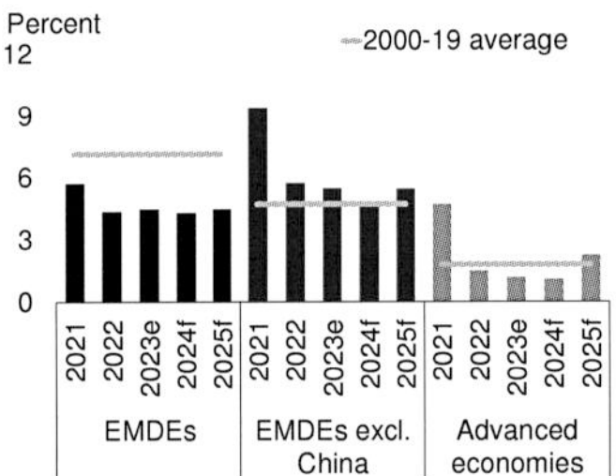

Sources: Feenstra, Inklaar, and Timmer (2015); Haver Analytics; Rozenberg and Fay (2019); WDI (database); World Bank.

Note: e = estimate; f = forecast; AEs = advanced economies; EAP = East Asia and Pacific; EMDEs = emerging market and developing economies; LAC = Latin America and the Caribbean; LICs = low-income countries; MNA = Middle East and North Africa; SAR = South Asia; SDGs = Sustainable Development Goals; SSA = Sub-Saharan Africa.

A. Estimates of the annual investment needs to build resilience to climate change and put countries on track to reduce emissions by 70 percent by 2050. Depending on data availability, estimates include investment needs on transport, energy, water, urban adaptations, industry, and landscape.

B. Average annual spending needs on electricity, transport, water and sanitation, flood protection, and irrigation during 2015-30. Country sample includes low- and middle-income countries, as defined in the technical appendix of Rozenberg and Fay (2019).

C. 2013-23 averages of the percent of the population with access to electricity, access to minimally adequate drinking water, access to basic sanitation facilities, and 2013-23 averages of the number of hospital beds available per 1,000 people. Sample includes 34 advanced economies and up to 104 EMDEs, of which 19 are LICs.

D. 2013-23 averages. The indexes range from 1 to 5 (5 = highest). Quality of transport infrastructure reflects perceptions of the quality of trade and transport related infrastructure. Logistics performance index reflects perceptions of the overall quality of logistics. Sample includes 34 advanced economies and 100 EMDEs, of which 19 are LICs.

E. Investment growth averages are calculated using GDP weights at average 2010-19 prices and market exchange rates. Sample includes up to 103 economies, including 68 EMDEs.

F. Aggregates are calculated using investment weights at average 2010-19 prices and market exchange rates.

potential to be a strong policy lever that can help ignite growth and crowd in private investment. Public investment typically includes capital expenditures on connectivity infrastructure (roads, bridges, telecommunications networks), public hospitals and schools, energy facilities, and other infrastructure—all of which can act as building blocks to enhance firm productivity, promote the flow of capital and labor, facilitate the exchange of goods and services, and foster human capital development. In other words, beyond its short-term demand effects, public investment can have positive supply-side impacts, raising the productive capacity of the economy and private sector competitiveness, supporting economic growth in the long term.[4]

Public investment can play an important role in the economy for multiple reasons. Infrastructure investment offers a helpful lens for articulating this. First, infrastructure projects often involve substantial upfront costs and maintenance expenditures without necessarily generating a commercially viable revenue stream. Second, infrastructure sectors with especially large sunk costs and economies of scale may also exhibit natural monopoly properties: that is, there are often only a few efficient market participants given high barriers to entry. Some of these projects in advanced economies can be undertaken by the private sector with appropriate regulation. However, in EMDEs, the private sector often lacks access to finance and the technical capabilities to develop critical infrastructure effectively. Third, some capital services may also have the characteristics of public goods, meaning they are non-excludable and non-rival—they can be used by many simultaneously without the ability to exclude non-payers. This might complicate their provision by the private sector.

In addition, governments are also generally seen as more creditworthy than private companies, given their power to tax; their ownership of large-scale assets that can serve as collateral for borrowing; and greater capacity to pool the necessary

[4] Public investment may also trigger sustained investment accelerations associated with multiple positive macroeconomic effects (World Bank 2024).

resources to execute large-scale infrastructure investment projects.[5]

A combination of these factors means that the private sector in EMDEs may not always be best-placed to deliver some types of public infrastructure effectively and ensure equitable or universal access by the population without some form of government intervention. This is especially so in the case of public health care, water provision, electricity transmission, public transportation, and recreation spaces (parks, for example). Provision of such infrastructure can also help lower poverty and inequality, build resilience against climate change and natural disasters, and promote inclusive economic development (Schwartz et al. 2020). This may strengthen the case for public investment, extending it far beyond pure economic growth effects, though the benefits can be difficult to quantify precisely, and alternative approaches (such as regulation), as well as different forms of public-private sector interaction related to investment, may help address specific market failures in certain circumstances.

That said, investment, whether public or private, can also lead to undesired outcomes if mismanaged. Specifically for public investment, there can be negative fiscal implications: the construction and upkeep of public infrastructure can involve massive costs, which could lead to large fiscal deficits and debt-related risks. Public sector inefficiencies can also undermine investment projects, especially in countries with weak governance and limited capacity for fiscal administration. In the worst case, public investment could yield infrastructure that is both unproductive and costly to maintain, resulting in negative net macroeconomic effects over an extended period. Furthermore, public investment could crowd out private investment in some circumstances, especially when public sector is inefficient and/or when scaling up is sizable and fast-paced. These challenges are particularly relevant for EMDEs, many of which have weak institutions, public sector inefficiencies, and limited fiscal resources.[6]

Against this background, this chapter presents a detailed study of the macroeconomic implications of public investment focusing on EMDEs. It addresses the following questions:

- How has public investment evolved in EMDEs?
- What is the impact of public investment on output and private investment?
- What policies can EMDEs adopt to bolster public investment and harness the benefits from it?

Contributions. The chapter contributes to the literature in several ways:

- *Reviewing public investment trends with a focus on EMDEs.* The chapter provides a thorough assessment of public investment trends in EMDEs and reviews the evolution of public investment growth during major adverse events, including recessions and financial crises. It considers a large set of countries and examines heterogeneity as well as commonalities across EMDE country groups and regions.
- *Assessing macroeconomic implications of public investment in EMDEs.* The chapter offers a comprehensive account of the macroeconomic effects of public investment. To this end, it provides a broad synthesis of the existing literature and estimates the effect of public investment on output—known as the public investment multiplier—using a new approach to identify public investment shocks. This approach can be applied to a broad sample of countries. The chapter analyses the macroeconomic conditions and structural characteristics that help bolster the effects of public invest-

[5] For the role of public investment in the provision of infrastructure see Aschauer (1989a,b), Ramey (2021), Schwartz et al. (2020); for constraints faced by private investment see IMF (2021b), Kose and Ohnsorge (2024), World Bank (2023a); for the borrowing capacity of governments see Martinez et al. (2023).

[6] For the fiscal impact of public investment, see Afonso and Alves (2023), Berg et al. (2012); for public sector inefficiencies in the context of investment, see Chakraborty and Dabla-Norris (2011), Dabla-Norris et al. (2012); for unproductive public infrastructure, see Pritchett (2000); and for the role of public investment in crowding out private investment, see Aschauer (1989a) and Cavallo and Daude (2011).

ment, and examines the impact of public investment on private investment, productivity, and potential output.

- *Outlining key policy interventions to increase public investment and enhance its benefits in EMDEs.* In light of the insights from the empirical analysis, the chapter presents a high-level summary of policies in EMDEs to boost public investment and to maximize its positive macroeconomic effects. It considers the current capacity of EMDEs to engage in government investment without undermining fiscal sustainability as well as structural challenges critical for ensuring investment efficiency and opportunities for greater international support.

Main findings. The chapter offers the following key findings:

Public investment growth in EMDEs slowed sharply over the past decade. Public investment growth in EMDEs halved from an average of 10 percent per year over 2000-09 to about 5 percent over 2010-22. More generally, public investment growth tended to slow following adverse events such as recessions and financial crises. Recessions also have scarring effects: public investment in the average EMDE contracted by about 4 percent during recessions (a drop of 9 percentage points from the pre-recession trend) and remained subdued for an extended period. Given the significant infrastructure needs of EMDEs, the broad-based decline in public investment growth is worrisome—particularly because it has been accompanied by a slowdown in private investment and in light of greater reliance of EMDEs on government investment. In particular, over the past decade, public investment comprised about 7 percent of GDP in EMDEs (compared with an average of 4 percent in advanced economies).

Public investment has the strongest impact on output when it occurs in countries with ample fiscal space and high government efficiency. Effective public investment can stimulate economic growth in EMDEs—for an average EMDE, scaling up of public investment equivalent to one percent of GDP leads to an increase in output of 1.1 percent after five years. However, its effectiveness hinges on government efficiency and fiscal space.[7] In countries with higher public investment efficiency or low fiscal sustainability concerns, an increase in public investment equivalent to one percent of GDP can increase output by up to 1.6 percent in the medium term—over the horizon of five years.[8] In countries with low public investment efficiency and high public debt, the output effects of public investment are positive but not statistically significant.

Public investment can have broader benefits: mobilizing private investment, enhancing productivity, and generating potential output gains. Public investment can have significant crowding-in effects on private investment. In EMDEs, a scaling up of public investment by one percent of GDP leads to an increase in private investment by up to 2.2 percent over the horizon of five years, on average. In the EMDE sample with available data, an equivalent increase in public investment can increase labor productivity by 1.9 percent and total factor productivity by 0.8 percent over the medium term. Potential output in response to these positive public investment shocks increases by up to 1.1 percent over the same period. These results offer empirical support for the arguments in favor of long-run supply-side transmission channels of public investment.

Pursuing a "Three Es" package of policy priorities can help harness the benefits of public investment in EMDEs. Specific policy interventions to increase public investment and secure the benefits from it depend on individual country circumstances, but three broadly applicable

---

[7] Fiscal space can be affected by government debt sustainability, balance sheet composition, external and private sector debt, and market perceptions of sovereign risk (see Kose et al. 2022). The chapter's empirical analysis uses the public-debt-to-GDP ratio as a proxy for fiscal space, though the amount of fiscal space for a given debt-to-GDP ratio may vary depending on country circumstances.

[8] In more technical terms, public investment efficiency is defined as the fraction of public investment that translates into effective public capital stock (Pritchett 2000). This entails the strength of institutions, quality of the design and implementation of public investment projects, effectiveness of procurement systems, among other factors (see also Kim, Fallov, and Groom 2020). The chapter uses several measures of public investment efficiency (see a detailed discussion in the sections on methodology and policy implications).

policy interventions—the "Three Es"—emerge as priorities for EMDEs:

- *Expansion of fiscal space.* Limited fiscal space not only impedes the ability of a government to scale up public investment, but also undermines its effectiveness. This is because additional public spending in countries with weak fiscal positions may lead to a heavier tax burden, greater sovereign risk, and higher borrowing costs weakening private sector activity. Estimates suggest that the effect of public investment on output in countries with large fiscal space is up to one percentage point higher than in countries with small fiscal space, on average.[9] Policy measures that help expand fiscal space are a priority for EMDEs as many of them suffer from elevated fiscal deficits and debt levels. EMDEs often have constrained revenue mobilization capacity and limited scope to (re)allocate budgetary resources to public investment. They should therefore undertake reforms to improve tax collection efficiency, enhance fiscal frameworks, and curtail unproductive spending.

- *Efficiency of public investment.* Public investment efficiency is paramount for reaping the full benefits of public investment. A wide range of policy interventions can be employed by EMDEs to improve the efficiency of public investment. Tackling corruption, poor governance, and limited capacity of fiscal administration are all important, as is improving public investment project management frameworks. These policies can be complemented by initiatives to prioritize public investment projects with the greatest potential to mobilize private investment and spark productivity gains, such as health, education, digital networks, and renewable energy infrastructure projects. In some cases, effective public-private partnerships can also help achieve the twin objectives of efficiency gains and mobilization of private capital. Estimates suggest that in EMDEs with high public investment efficiency, an increase in public investment by one percent of GDP may lead to an increase in output of up to 1.6 percent in the medium term (about one-half percentage point higher than the average effect in EMDEs). By contrast, in countries with the lowest efficiency, the output effects of public investment are lower and not statistically significant.[10]

- *Enhanced global support.* Developing countries with limited fiscal space and deep structural challenges, especially LICs, need external support to undertake comprehensive reforms critical for ensuring the effectiveness of public investment and to embark on large-scale public investment projects addressing vast infrastructure gaps. Coordinated financial support and effective technical assistance are both imperative for accelerating structural reforms and improving investment prospects. Given challenging macroeconomic conditions and the growing urgency of tackling climate change, delivering the green transition, and making progress toward other sustainable development goals, enhanced support from the international community will be vital for these countries.

Evolution of public investment

Public investment growth in EMDEs. Public investment growth has evolved notably over the past three decades. In the 1990s, public investment in EMDEs was growing at a much higher pace relative to advanced economies to a large extent on account of robust growth in China. This was followed by exceptionally high public investment growth in the 2000s which witnessed a period of macroeconomic stability, rapid economic integration, and reduction of poverty, amid elevated commodity prices (figures 3.2.A

[9] The high-debt and low-debt states are defined using the smooth transition function in the estimations (see annex 3.2). For a median EMDE, a low-debt state over the sample period corresponds to about 30 percent of GDP and a high-debt state corresponds to about 80 percent of GDP.

[10] Here, the high and low levels of public investment efficiency correspond to the top and bottom quartiles of the public infrastructure efficiency index used in the estimation of public investment multipliers—see annex 3.2 and estimation results.

FIGURE 3.2 Public investment patterns in EMDEs

Average annual public investment growth in EMDEs halved, dropping from 10 percent in the 2000s to 5 percent in the 2010s—the slowest average pace over the past three decades. Private investment growth in EMDEs also decelerated significantly, from 11 percent per year in the 2000s to 7 percent in the following decade The slowdown was broad-based across EMDE regions and country groups. In EMDEs, public investment tends to play a greater role than in advanced economies: it accounted for about 7 percent of GDP on average in EMDEs in the past decade, versus about 4 percent of GDP in advanced economies.

A. Public investment growth

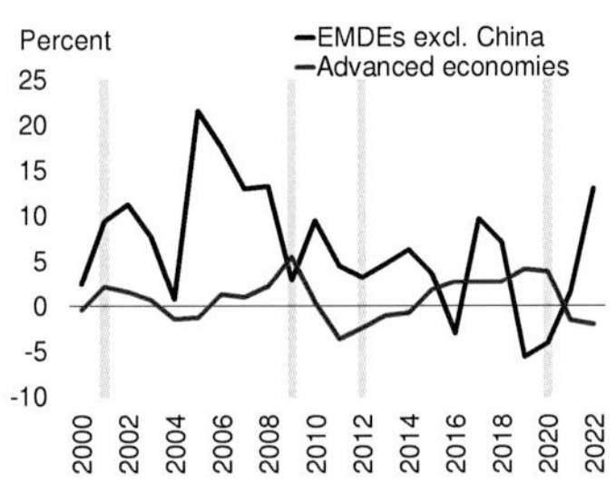

B. Public investment growth by decade

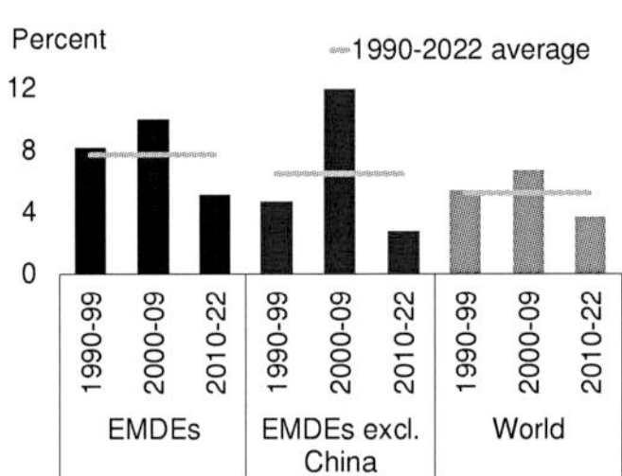

C. Private investment growth

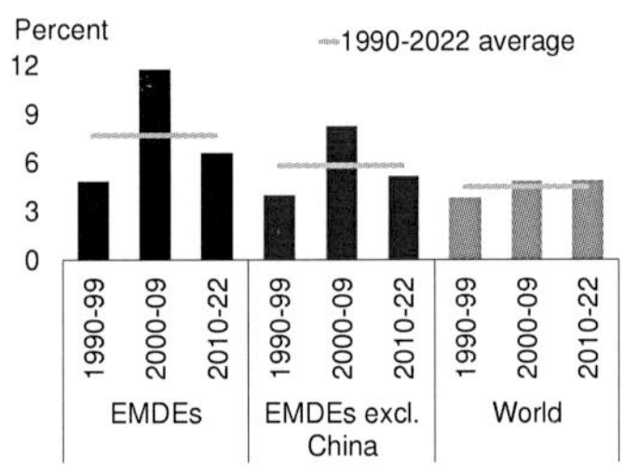

D. Public investment growth by EMDE group

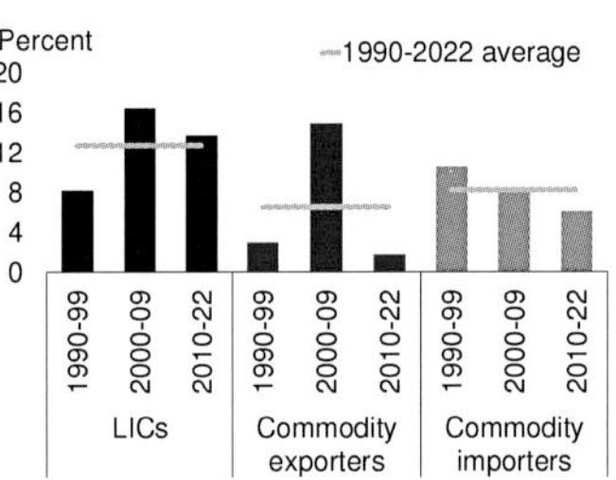

E. Public investment growth by EMDE region

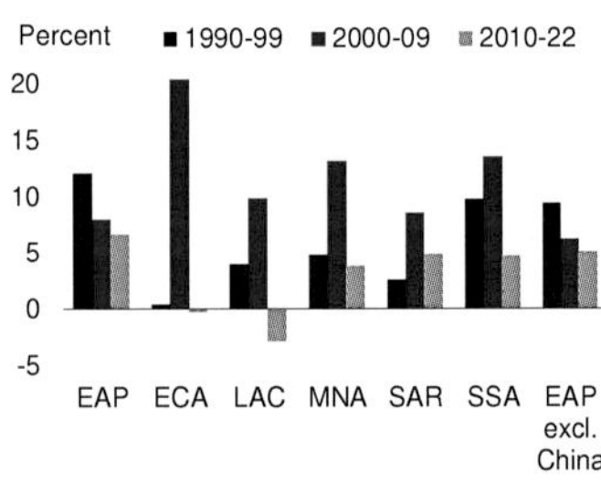

F. Public investment as a share of GDP

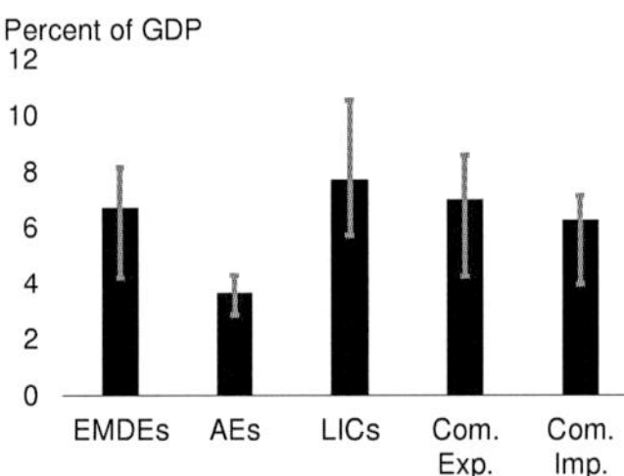

Sources: Haver Analytics; Investment and Capital Stock Dataset (IMF 2021a); WDI (database); World Bank.

Note: AEs = advanced economies; EMDEs = emerging market and developing economies; Com. Exp. = commodity-exporting EMDEs; Com. Imp. = commodity-importing EMDEs; EAP = East Asia and Pacific; ECA = Europe and Central Asia; LAC = Latin America and the Caribbean; LICs = low-income countries; MNA = Middle East and North Africa; SAR = South Asia; SSA = Sub-Saharan Africa. Public investment growth is calculated with countries' public investment in constant international dollars as weights.

A. Shaded areas indicate global recessions (in 2009 and 2020) and slowdowns (in 2001 and 2012), as defined in Kose, Sugawara, and Terrones (2020). Sample includes 27 EMDEs and 12 advanced economies.

B.D.E. Average annual public investment growth. Sample includes up to 162 economies, of which 126 are EMDEs, 23 are LICs, 76 are commodity-exporting EMDEs, 50 are commodity-importing EMDEs. Sample includes 12 EAP, 19 ECA, 28 LAC, 15 MNA, 8 SAR, and 44 SSA countries.

C. Average annual private investment growth, calculated with countries' private investment in constant international dollars as weights. Sample includes up to 162 economies, of which 126 are EMDEs.

F. Bars show means and whiskers show interquartile ranges for 2010-22 by group. Sample includes up to 36 advanced economies and 126 EMDEs.

and 3.2.B). The latter also resulted in accelerated public investment growth in commodity-exporting EMDEs.

However, public investment growth plunged after the global financial crisis, contracting in advanced economies and decelerating significantly in EMDEs. Average annual public investment growth in EMDEs halved, dropping from 10 percent in the 2000s to 5 percent in the 2010s—the slowest average pace over the past three decades (figure 3.2.B). This slowdown was associated with multiple factors: weaker economic growth in EMDEs in the aftermath of the global financial crisis; the worsening of global macroeconomic environment resulting in the slowdown of trade and capital flows; heightened economic uncertainty; geopolitical tensions; tight financial conditions; increased debt levels eroding fiscal space and requiring consolidation; and highly volatile commodity prices. The pandemic global recession further worsened the macroeconomic backdrop. Government expenditures to contain the pandemic, provide support to vulnerable population groups and the private sector were prioritized, resulting in cutbacks and delays in public investment spending. The decline in public investment growth was also accompanied by a broad-based slowdown in private investment growth in EMDEs, decelerating from 11 percent per year in the 2000s to 7 percent in the 2010-22 period (figure 3.2.C).

Trends across EMDE groups and regions. Public investment growth in commodity-exporting EMDEs—which was much higher than that in other EMDEs through the 2000s—has slumped as global commodity prices declined, adversely affecting these countries' public finances (figure 3.2.D). Over this period, public investment in LICs, on average, grew much faster than in other EMDEs.

The weakening of public investment in the past decade was broad-based across EMDE regions. The decline was especially notable in Europe and Central Asia, Latin America and the Caribbean, and the Middle East and North Africa, where fiscal challenges were compounded by the sustained decline in commodity prices leading to falls in revenues and adjustments in government spending in commodity-exporting countries (figure 3.2.E).

Public investment dynamics around adverse events. An event study analysis suggests that recessions and financial crises in EMDEs often cause prolonged dips in public investment (box 3.1). In recessions, public investment contracts by about 4 percent (a decline of about 9 percentage points relative to periods of economic stability) and remains subdued for an additional two years after the initial shock. Currency crises are also associated with a decline of about 6 percent in public investment during the crisis year, while debt and banking crises tend to have the largest impact in the year that follows the crisis—with public investment contracting by 3.5 and 3 percent, respectively.

Public-investment-to-output ratios. In EMDEs, public investment tends to play a greater role than in advanced economies: it accounted for about 7 percent of GDP on average in EMDEs in the past decade, versus about 4 percent of GDP in advanced economies (figure 3.2.F). Although public investment shares are similar across EMDE regions and country groups, LICs and commodity-exporting EMDEs have public investment ratios slightly higher than other EMDEs.

Public investment tends to play a larger role in EMDEs because the private sector is generally weaker in EMDEs than it is in advanced economies. It often lacks the capacity or willingness to invest in large infrastructure projects, partly because of greater uncertainty and perceived risks. EMDEs thus tend to rely on the public sector to deliver necessary infrastructure to a larger extent than advanced economies. Moreover, domestic and international creditors often see EMDE governments as more creditworthy than local private investors, given their power to tax, their ownership of significant assets that can serve as collateral, and their capacity to pool the resources needed to execute large-scale projects (Martinez et al. 2023).

Public investment-growth nexus: Channels of transmission

Public investment can be a potent policy tool to promote economic growth. The literature documents that public investment has a positive impact on growth in the medium term, but the range of the estimated public investment multipliers varies widely (see box 3.2 for a detailed discussion). Because of data constraints and methodological challenges, estimates of public investment multipliers for EMDEs are especially limited. Studies show that the economic effects of public investment may be influenced by various factors, such as public investment efficiency, fiscal space, trade openness, currency regime, informality, financial development, the phase of the business cycle, and macroeconomic uncertainty.

The heterogeneity of the output impacts of public investment reflects the effectiveness of the transmission channels through which public investment operates:

- *Short-term aggregate demand effects.* Public investment has the potential to support economic activity by boosting aggregate demand in the short term. This positive impact, however, is at least partly offset by the associated fiscal effects on the real economy, because public investment in principle is funded via taxation, debt issuance, or reallocation of government expenditure. In addition, the multiplier effect is weakened by purchases of investment goods abroad and depends on the import intensity of investment ("leakage effect"). Rapid scaling up of public investment, depending on its funding source and efficiency, may fuel fiscal imbalances and thereby undermine growth prospects (Bom and Ligthart 2014a; Romp and de Haan 2005).

- *Long-run aggregate supply effects.* Public investment has the potential to directly increase the productive capacity of an economy by fostering enhanced productivity of private fixed capital and labor through the provision of public infrastructure. For instance, new roads and bridges can increase the overall competitiveness of an economy by enabling connectivity or reducing its cost (Aschauer 1989b; Romp and de Haan 2005; Straub 2011).

- *Crowding-in or crowding-out of private investment.* Public investment can *crowd in* private investment directly by requiring the use of private capital in the implementation of an investment project, for instance, via public-private partnerships. Public investment can also enable infrastructure that raises returns on private capital—for instance, roads and communications infrastructure—thereby encouraging private sector investment (Aschauer 1989a; Eden and Kraay 2014). Public investment helps to reduce uncertainty and risks associated with large private investment projects, especially infrastructure projects requiring massive upfront costs but longer payback periods (IMF 2021b). However, public investment may also *crowd out* private investment, especially when fiscal space is limited and additional fiscal stimulus raises sovereign risk and borrowing costs for the private sector (Abiad, Furceri, and Topalova 2016; Erenburg and Wohar 1995; Huidrom et al. 2020). The net effect on the private sector depends on the balance between these opposing factors, which, in turn, is influenced by fiscal space and the quality of public investment.

- *Efficiency and quality of public investment.* Scaling up of public investment may not necessarily result in an equivalent increase in the value of productive public capital (Pritchett 2000). Some of the resources are lost during the investment process because of weak governance, corruption, coordination issues, and poor design and implementation of investment projects. There may also be diminishing returns on additional public investment, though this depends on a country's circumstances and the merits of specific projects. In the worst case, poor investment may yield infrastructure that is unproductive and yet requires a continuous stream of fiscal resources to maintain, thereby hurting long-term growth prospects (Chakraborty and Dabla-Norris 2011; Dabla-Norris et al. 2012). In part, this also relates to the composition of public investment: not all projects contribute equally to growth.[11]

- *Public capital maintenance costs.* More generally, depreciating public capital stocks require additional short- and long-run maintenance. The associated costs may lead to additional fiscal strains that undermine long-term positive growth effects. Meanwhile, inadequate or untimely maintenance of public capital could lead to even larger social and economic costs associated with infrastructure failures (Schwartz et al. 2020).[12] The strength of this channel is intertwined with the efficiency channel, as low-quality public investment is more likely to yield infrastructure that is prone to larger or more frequent upkeep costs.

- *Sustainability of growth.* Public investment—though not always the only solution—can also play an important role in delivering public goods or services that may not be privately profitable, such as public health care and education, water and energy transmission, and national security. This type of public investment can be instrumental for facilitating sustainable and inclusive growth through its positive effects on human capital development, social inclusion, environmental impacts (Foster et al. 2023; Mazzucato and Semieniuk 2017; Turnovsky 2015; Zachmann et al. 2012).

[11] As a related matter, there are challenges associated with the measurement and valuation of public investment at a disaggregated level—identifying infrastructure-related spending and composition of public investment by capital asset types (see also ADB 2017 and Fay et al. 2019b). This hinders the assessment of the macroeconomic effects by individual categories of public investment and types of infrastructure—likely to be heterogeneous (see a meta-analysis in Foster et al. 2023).

[12] Governments may also have stronger incentives to spend on new investment projects rather than on maintenance as the former is more visible and attractive from an electoral perspective (De Haan and Klomp 2013).

Macroeconomic implications of public investment

Database and methodology

Database. The database used in the estimation of the macroeconomic effects of public investment draws from several sources. Public investment, private investment, and capital stock data are from the International Monetary Fund's Investment and Capital Stock Dataset (IMF 2021a). Public debt data are retrieved from the World Bank's Fiscal Space Database (Kose et al. 2022). Public investment efficiency data are obtained from several sources: IMF (2021b) Fiscal Monitor database, Devadas and Pennings (2018), and Dabla-Norris et al. (2012). Potential output data are sourced from Kilic Celik et al. (2023). GDP and inflation series are from the IMF's World Economic Outlook database. Labor productivity and total factor productivity data are from Penn World Table 10.01. The resulting dataset comprises up to 129 EMDEs, spanning the period 1980-2019 (see table A3.2.1 for the sample composition).[13]

Methodology. The major challenge in the estimation of the macroeconomic effects of public investment is associated with the bidirectional causality between public spending and economic growth (Canning and Pedroni 2008). Several approaches have been developed in the literature to address this problem. However, the methods devised to date have certain caveats that limit their application to the large sample of EMDEs (see annex 3.1 for an overview). This section summarizes the new approach used in the analysis to identify the changes in public investment that are not affected by macroeconomic conditions (public investment shocks), and the methodology deployed to estimate the effect of these shocks on output (in other words, public investment multipliers) and other macroeconomic variables.

- *Identification of public investment shocks.* The chapter identifies public investment shocks as episodes of large changes in cyclically adjusted public investment (technical details are provided in annex 3.1 and Adarov, Clements, and Jalles, forthcoming). This framework removes the component of public investment associated with transitory macroeconomic dynamics (the business cycle) and focuses only on episodes of large discretionary public investment. This approach is easy to replicate and can be applied to a broad sample of countries. This enables an analysis of heterogeneity across countries and the effects of public investment conditional on country characteristics and macroeconomic conditions.

- *Estimation of public investment multipliers.* The responses of output to identified public investment shocks are estimated using the local projections method (Jordà 2005). The results are reported in the form of impulse response functions showing the effects on real GDP (cumulative change in percent relative to the year preceding the public investment shock) of public investment shocks equivalent to one percent of GDP. These effects are examined over a five-year horizon following a shock. A similar approach is used to estimate the impact of public investment on potential output, productivity, and other macroeconomic variables. Annex 3.2 provides further details on the estimation methodology, data, and robustness checks.

Results

Growth effects of public investment in EMDEs. Public investment shocks lead to positive output responses that remain highly statistically significant at the horizon of five years (figure 3.3.A). An increase in public investment equivalent to one percent of GDP is associated with a gradual increase in output from 0.4 percent after one year, reaching 1.1 after five years.[14] The output effects of public investment tend to be smaller in the

[13] The sample composition and time coverage are determined entirely by the data availability. In particular, the current version of the Investment and Capital Stock Dataset (IMF 2021a), providing consistent disaggregated series for public and private investment, covers the period 1960-2019.

[14] The responses are the cumulative changes relative to the year before the public investment shock, in percent. The results are confirmed using robustness checks (see annex 3.2 for details).

FIGURE 3.3 Macroeconomic impacts of public investment in EMDEs

An increase in public investment equivalent to one percent of GDP in EMDEs is associated with a gradual increase in output from 0.4 percent after one year, reaching 1.1 percent after five years. Potential output in response to public investment shocks increases by 1.1 percent after five years. This effect is associated with a boost in productivity—by up to 0.8 percent for total factor productivity and 1.9 percent for labor productivity over the medium term. A scaling up of public investment by one percent of GDP leads to an increase in private investment by up to 2.2 percent over the horizon of five years, on average. Public investment multipliers tend to be larger in recessions.

A. Impact on output

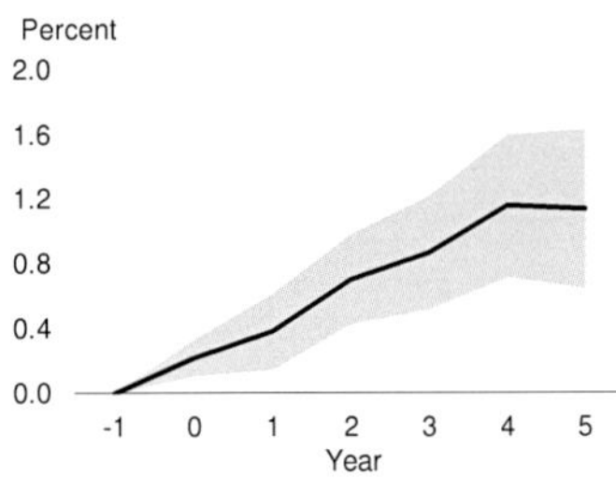

B. Impact on potential output

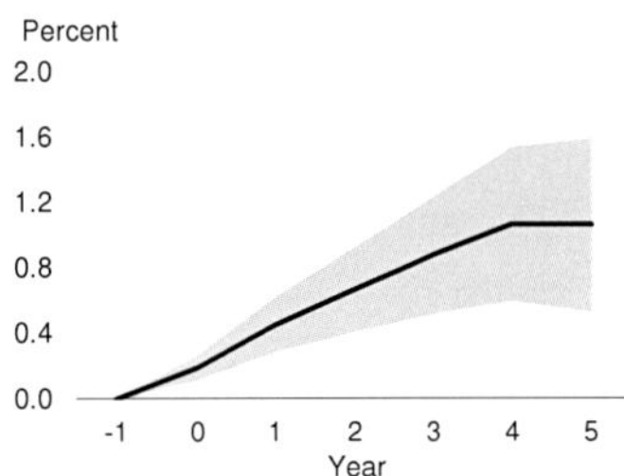

C. Medium-run impact on productivity and inflation

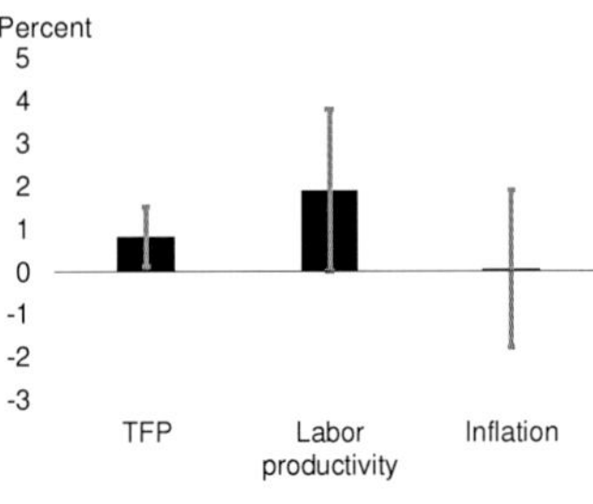

D. Impact on private investment

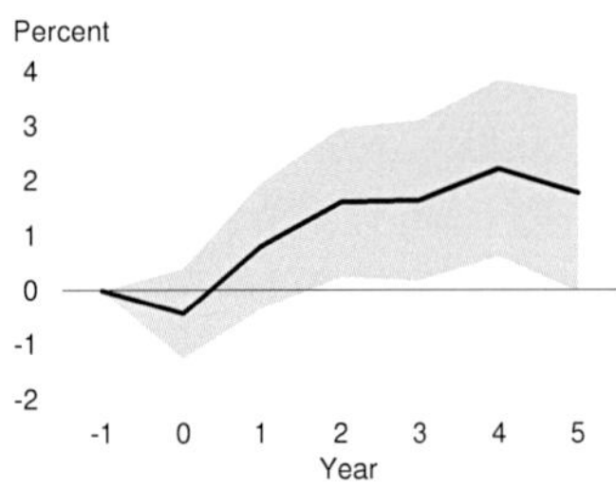

E. Impact on output in recessions

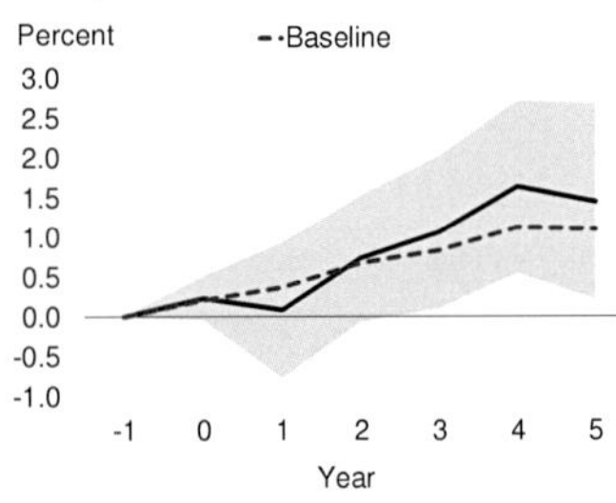

F. Impact on output in expansions

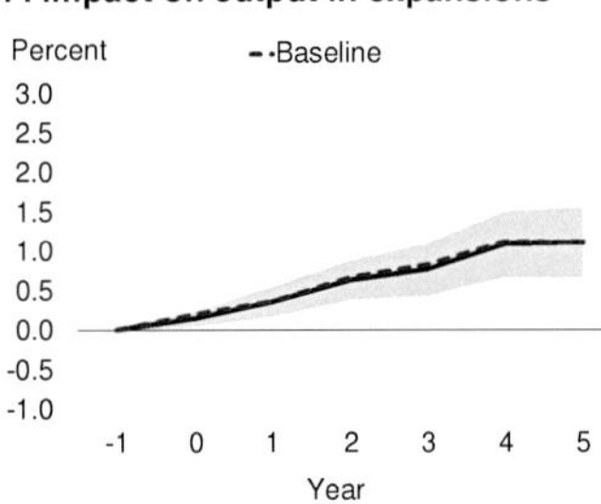

Source: World Bank.

Note: CPI = consumer price index; EMDEs = emerging market and developing economies; TFP = total factor productivity. Sample includes up to 129 EMDEs. Responses of variables (cumulative change in year *t* relative to year *t* = -1, in percent) to a public investment shock equivalent to one percent of GDP; *t* = 0 is the year of the shock. Shaded areas denote 90 percent confidence bands, based on standard errors clustered at the country level.

A. Response of real GDP to a public investment shock.

B. Response of real potential GDP to a public investment shock.

C. Responses of TFP, labor productivity, and CPI to a public investment shock after five years based on local projections. Bars indicate the point estimates, whiskers indicate 90 percent confidence intervals.

D. Response of real private investment to a public investment shock.

E.F. Response of real GDP to a public investment shock in recessions and expansions, defined as periods of negative and positive real GDP growth. Dashed lines indicate the baseline unconditional responses.

short run, but increase over the long term as supply-side effects on productivity and productive capacity fully manifest themselves, consistent with the literature (Leduc and Wilson 2012; Ramey 2021). In the short run, offsetting fiscal effects, impact of leakage through imports, possible transitory crowding out of private investment, private sector capacity constraints, and the time needed to adjust consumption and production may dampen the effects of public investment.[15] The estimated effects are broadly in line with public investment multipliers reported in existing empirical studies on EMDEs (box 3.2).[16]

The analysis suggests that *potential* output also increases steadily in response to public investment. In a sample of EMDEs with the available data, a one percent of GDP rise in public investment leads to an increase in potential output peaking at about 1.1 percent over five years (figure 3.3.B).[17] This effect is associated with a concurrent boost in productivity—by up to 0.8 percent for total factor productivity and 1.9 percent for labor productivity over the medium term (figure 3.3.C). The impact of public investment surges on output does not lead to a corresponding increase in inflation. These findings support the hypothesis that public investment can increase output through both short-term aggregate demand and longer-run aggregate supply channels, thereby boosting potential output (Ramey 2021).

Impact on private investment. An important impact of public investment occurs via the crowding-in effect on private investment. An increase in public investment equivalent to one percent of GDP induces an increase in private

[15] Similar results are reported in recent empirical studies (for instance, Abiad, Furceri, and Topalova 2016; Furceri and Li 2017; Ilzetzki, Mendoza, and Végh 2013).

[16] Public investment multiplier estimates reported in the literature vary widely for EMDEs and tend to be larger in advanced economies. Gechert and Rannenberg (2018) and Vagliasindi and Gorgulu (2021) in a meta-analysis show the average value of public investment multiplier across studies of about 1.5—slightly larger than the value estimated in the chapter for EMDEs. Public investment multipliers are larger than public consumption multipliers; the latter are not statistically significant from zero (see table B3.2.1 for studies reporting similar findings).

[17] The sample size for the exercises with potential output and productivity is smaller because of data availability, and is not directly comparable to the baseline results, which use the full EMDE sample.

investment by up to 2.2 percent at the horizon of five years (figure 3.3.D). The estimates also suggest a possible crowding-out effect on impact; however, the effect is small, not statistically significant from zero, and is reversed within a year.

The crowding-in effect on private investment is in line with the estimates reported in the literature (see, for instance, Eden and Kraay 2014; Furceri and Li 2017). In this regard, the results provide empirical support for policies to mitigate private investment slowdown through a scaling up of public investment. This effect could operate through several transmission channels. An increase in public capital can raise the return on private capital by facilitating connectivity (for instance, roads and bridges), thereby facilitating private sector investment (Aschauer 1989a, Eden and Kraay 2014). Public investment reduces uncertainty and risks associated with private investment in large infrastructure projects and may also directly crowd in private investment via public-private partnerships (IMF 2021b).

The role of the business cycle. Public investment multipliers, on average, are greater in magnitude during recessions than during expansions. A one percent of GDP increase in public investment yields an increase in output by 1.1 percent in times of expansion after five years. An equivalent public investment shock in recessions leads to an increase in output by up to 1.6 percent over the same period. However, the estimates during recessions are characterized by notable heterogeneity across countries, resulting in wider confidence bands (figures 3.3.E and 3.3.F). These results are consistent with the empirical literature reporting larger government spending multipliers in recessions.[18]

The position of an economy in the business cycle may affect the size of the multiplier for several reasons. In expansions, public spending stimulus may be less effective because, if the economy is operating close to full capacity, an additional increase in public spending is less likely to crowd in private sector resources.[19] In contrast, economic slack during recessions enables public investment to mobilize unused private sector capacity (Batini et al. 2014). Public spending during recessions may also help mitigate unemployment and improve market confidence, and is less likely to be accompanied by increasing inflation and interest rates (Auerbach and Gorodnichenko 2012; Ghassibe and Zanetti 2022).

In practice, however, EMDEs often have limited fiscal resources for public investment projects during recessions and crises. In fact, public investment tends to contract during economic distress (see box 3.1). "Shovel-ready" investment projects may help revive economic activity and crowd in private investment during economic downturns as long as they are well-planned and executed, and do not undermine fiscal sustainability; such projects and conditions, however, may not always be present.

Implications of fiscal space. EMDEs with lower fiscal sustainability concerns, as measured by public-debt-to-GDP ratios (indicating larger fiscal space), experience much stronger positive impacts of public investment: output increases by up to 1.6 percent five years after a public investment shock equivalent to one percent of GDP. Conversely, public investment in countries with high and rising debt (implying limited fiscal space) appears to be ineffective: the estimated public investment multipliers are lower and not statistically significant (figures 3.4.A and 3.4.B).[20] While changes in public-debt-to-GDP ratios only partly reflect fiscal space dynamics, these results nevertheless imply that the effect of public investment on output in countries with large fiscal

[18] Larger public investment multipliers in recessions are reported in Auerbach and Gorodnichenko (2012 and 2013); Caggiano et al. (2015); Furceri and Li (2017); Honda et al. (2020); Riera-Crichton et al. (2015). That said, such estimates may not be fully robust with significant heterogeneity across countries (Ramey 2019).

[19] That said, during expansions public investment also has a positive effect on output in EMDEs. This is in line with the view that EMDEs often have underutilized capacity because of infrastructure gaps, limited access to finance constraining the ability of the private sector to expand production capacity, and unused available labor resources, which can be engaged in expansions through public investment.

[20] These results thus are in line with the literature, arguing that in countries with high debt, public spending multipliers can be insignificant or even negative (Huidrom et al. 2020; Ilzetzki Mendoza, and Végh 2013).

FIGURE 3.4 Effects of public investment on output conditional on country characteristics

EMDEs with lower fiscal sustainability concerns, as measured by public-debt-to-GDP ratios, experience much stronger positive impacts of public investment: output increases by up to 1.6 percent over the horizon of five years. Conversely, public investment in countries with high and rising debt appears to be ineffective. The estimates suggest a greater effect on GDP in response to public investment shocks in EMDEs with the highest efficiency, culminating in an increase in output of about 1.6 percent after five years. In countries with the lowest efficiency, the effects of public investment are lower and not statistically significant (albeit still positive). Public investment multipliers in capital-scarce economies tend to be larger.

A. Large fiscal space

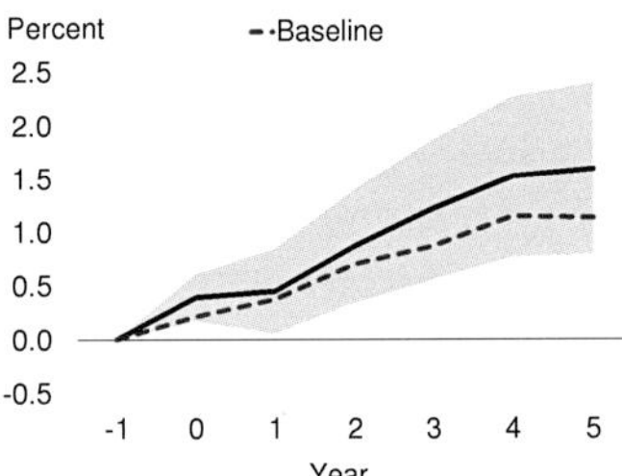

B. Small fiscal space

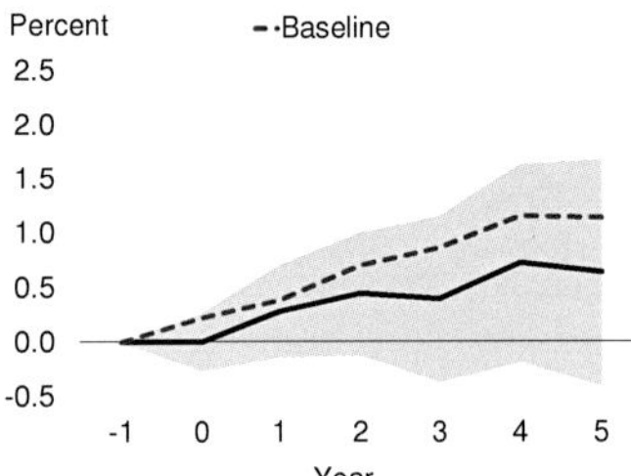

C. High investment efficiency

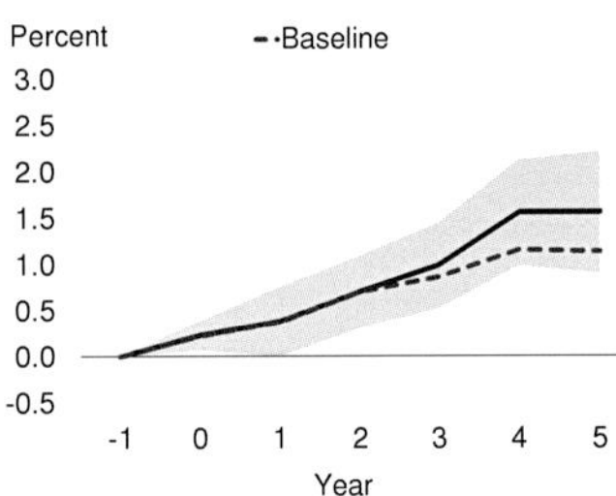

D. Low investment efficiency

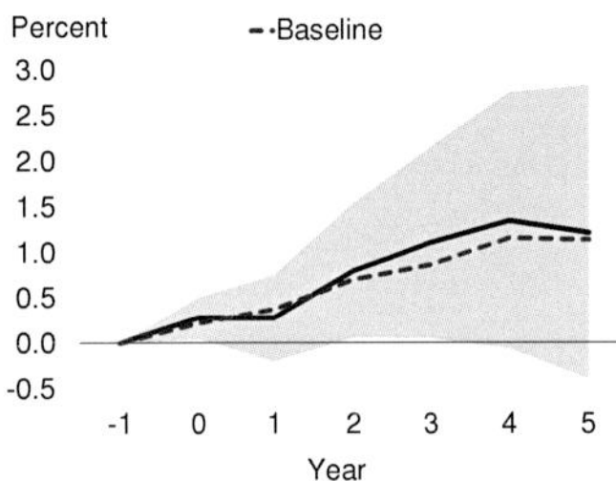

E. Small public capital stock

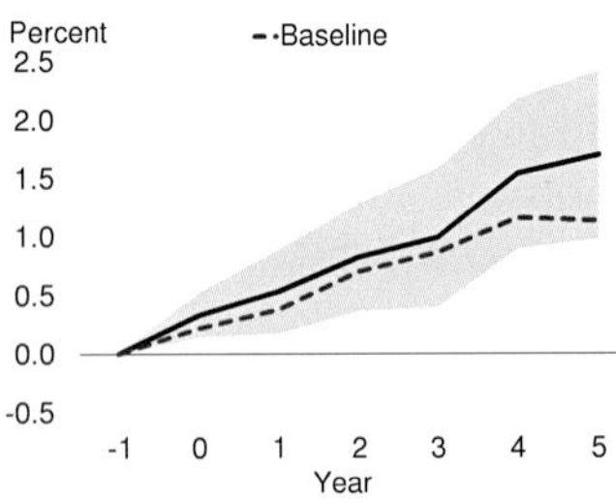

F. Large public capital stock

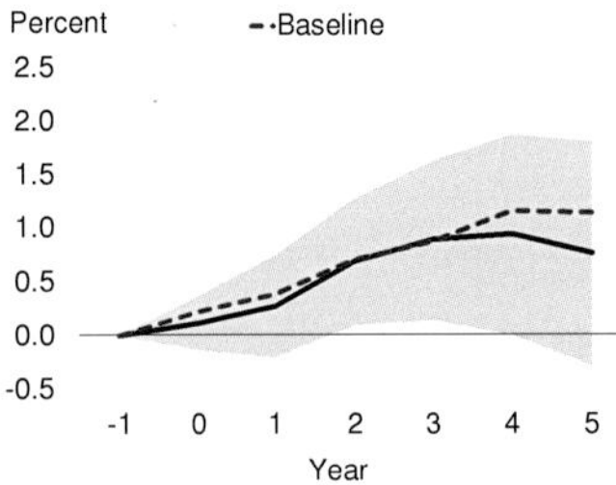

Source: World Bank.

Note: EMDEs = emerging market and developing economies. Responses of real GDP (cumulative change in year *t* relative to year *t* = -1, in percent) to a public investment shock equivalent to one percent of GDP; *t* = 0 is the year of the shock. Shaded areas denote 90 percent confidence bands, based on standard errors clustered at the country level. Dashed lines indicate the baseline unconditional responses. Sample includes up to 129 EMDEs.

A.B. Large-fiscal space and small-fiscal space responses are based on local projections with the smooth transition function that uses public-debt-to-GDP ratio as the conditioning variable. Large fiscal space state corresponds to the transition function value of 1, reflecting historically lowest debt ratio for a given country, and small fiscal space state corresponds to the transition function value of 0, reflecting the highest debt ratio for a given country in public investment shock years (the debt ratios of about 30 and 80 percent of GDP for a median EMDE, respectively).

C.D. High-efficiency and low-efficiency samples are based on the top and bottom quartiles of the IMF (2021b) public infrastructure efficiency index, which ranges from 0 to 100 (the values above 81 and below 47, respectively).

E.F. Small public capital stock and large public capital stock responses are based on local projections with the smooth transition function that uses public-capital-stock-to-GDP ratio as the conditioning variable to capture historically lowest and highest capital stock ratios of a given country in public investment shock years (the values of public capital stock of 68 and 113 percent of GDP for a median EMDE, respectively).

space is up to one percentage point higher than in countries with small fiscal space, on average.[21]

Fiscal space influences the output effects of public investment through two channels. The first is associated with the effects on private sector, as additional public spending in countries with weak fiscal positions may lead to lower disposable income of liquidity-constrained households, as well as increased tax burdens for the private sector in the future (which may also be anticipated). The second channel relates to the interest rate effect, as scaling up of government expenditures in countries with high levels of debt may lead to higher international interest rate spreads, on account of higher sovereign risk and inflation, thus increasing borrowing costs for the private sector (Blanchard 1990; Huidrom et al. 2020; Sutherland 1997).

Infrastructure investment projects, given their large upfront costs and long time horizons, are often financed by borrowing rather than from current government revenues. Larger fiscal space implies that the sovereign has more capacity to service its borrowing and therefore is more creditworthy, allowing it to finance such investment at a lower interest rate.

Public investment efficiency. Efficiency of public investment plays a crucial role in driving its growth effects.[22] The estimates suggest a greater effect on GDP in response to public investment shocks in EMDEs with the highest efficiency,

[21] The high-debt and low-debt states are defined using the smooth transition function that reflects the historical dynamics of public-debt-to-GDP ratios on a country-by-country basis. For a median EMDE, a low-debt state over the sample period corresponds to about 30 percent of GDP and a high-debt state corresponds to about 80 percent of GDP for EMDEs that experienced a public investment shock.

[22] The analysis uses the IMF (2021b) public infrastructure efficiency index, which is a cross-sectional index available for 120 countries (including 93 EMDEs), produced using the data envelopment analysis. The index ranges from 0 to 100, with higher values indicating better efficiency (the distribution is shown in figure 3.7.A). The model was also estimated using the Devadas and Pennings (2018) infrastructure efficiency index and the Dabla-Norris et al. (2012) public investment management index, available for 69 EMDEs in the sample. Estimations using alternative measures also suggest statistically insignificant and lower output effects of public investment in low-efficiency economies (table A3.2.4).

culminating in an increase in output of about 1.6 percent after five years—one-half percentage point higher than the effect of public investment in EMDEs with the lowest efficiency (figures 3.4.C and 3.4.D). In countries with the lowest efficiency, the effects of public investment are lower and not statistically significant (albeit still positive).

These results are consistent with empirical studies using other samples and methods, and provide support for the argument that low public investment efficiency is problematic.[23] Poor design, evaluation, and implementation of investment projects, including issues with corruption and governance, can deplete valuable fiscal resources without necessarily increasing the quantity or quality of public infrastructure that supports growth (Dabla-Norris et al. 2012; IMF 2014; Pritchett 2000). Therefore, well-designed public investment management processes are essential to ensure the effectiveness of public investment.

Public capital stock scarcity. The impact of public investment on output also varies with the initial level of the public capital stock (figures 3.4.E and 3.4.F). The magnitude and statistical significance of public investment multiplier tends to decrease with the level of public capital stock relative to GDP, consistent with expectations of diminishing marginal returns to capital. Specifically, a one percent of GDP increase in public investment is associated with a 1.7 percent increase in GDP after five years in capital-scarce countries. This contrasts with 0.9 percent (not statistically significant in the medium term) when the public-capital-stock-to-GDP ratio is high. Similar results are found in empirical studies using other samples and methods (for instance, Izquierdo et al. 2019).

Heterogeneity across EMDEs. In higher-income EMDEs, positive public investment shocks lead to strong and persistent impacts on output. In LICs, however, the effects on output are characterized by a wide dispersion, which translates to much lower statistical significance of public investment multipliers. Small sample size may play a part, but this could also be the result of lower efficiency in their public investment. That said, the average effect tends to be larger in LICs than in higher-income EMDEs, reaching up to 1.7 percent over the horizon of five years after a public investment shock equivalent to one percent of GDP (figures 3.5.A and 3.5.B). Public investment effects are slightly lower in commodity-exporting EMDEs than in other EMDEs (figures 3.5.C and 3.5.D).

FIGURE 3.5 Effects of public investment on output by EMDE groups

In higher-income EMDEs, public investment shocks lead to strong and persistent impacts on output. In LICs, however, the effects on output are characterized by a wide dispersion, which translates to much lower statistical significance of public investment multipliers. That said, the average effect tends to be larger in LICs than in higher-income EMDEs, reaching up to 1.7 percent over the horizon of five years after a public investment shock. Public investment effects are slightly lower in commodity-exporting EMDEs than in other EMDEs.

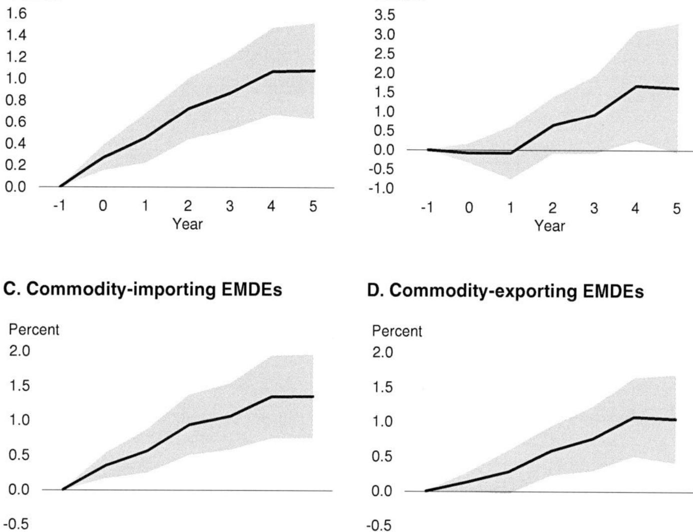

Source: World Bank.

Note: EMDEs = emerging market and developing economies; LICs = low-income countries. Responses of real GDP (cumulative change in year t relative to year t = -1, in percent) to a public investment shock equivalent to one percent of GDP; t = 0 is the year of the shock. Sample includes 129 EMDEs, of which 23 are LICs, 48 are commodity exporters, and 81 are commodity importers. Shaded areas denote 90 percent confidence bands, based on standard errors clustered at the country level.

[23] See Cavallo and Daude (2011); Furceri and Li (2017); IMF (2014); Izquierdo et al. (2019); Leduc and Wilson (2012); Leeper et al. (2010).

Policies to improve the macroeconomic benefits of public investment

The need for additional public investment has grown in the last two decades, accentuated by objectives to deliver the SDGs, address climate change, and recover from multiple shocks. Public investment has a potential to mobilize private investment and to help spur economic growth. However, the analysis suggests its beneficial effects are muted when fiscal space is constrained and when government spending is inefficient. This has important policy implications for EMDEs, many of which suffer from elevated debt levels, deep structural challenges, and weak institutions. Furthermore, many EMDEs, especially LICs, have limited financial and technical capacity to advance the needed reforms; significant and timely support from the international community will be necessary.

While policies to promote public investment and boost its effectiveness should be tailored to individual country circumstances, there are three overarching priorities that are relevant for all EMDEs—the package of "Three Es": *expansion of fiscal space, efficiency of public investment,* and *enhanced global support.*

Expansion of fiscal space

Fiscal space—the room in a government's budget that allows it to engage in expenditures without jeopardizing the sustainability of its financial position or the stability of the economy—is a critical concept when considering public investment (Kose et al. 2022). Options to boost fiscal space are arguably more limited in EMDEs than in advanced economies, as they quickly come up against fiscal sustainability limits. On the revenue side, the tax collection and administration capacity in EMDEs is generally more constrained than in advanced economies. On the expenditure side, a high share of the budget allocated to interest spending on accumulated debt implies that fewer budget resources are available to spend on social and economic needs, including investment in infrastructure.

Policy interventions that can help expand fiscal space include reforms to strengthen debt management and fiscal frameworks, domestic revenue mobilization, and optimal allocation of public expenditure.

Domestic revenue mobilization

Many EMDEs suffer from weaknesses in mobilizing fiscal revenues, which are critical for securing fiscal space and delivering priority spending. Tax collection and administration capacity in EMDEs is generally more limited than in advanced economies. EMDEs, especially LICs, tend to lag advanced economies in the size of government tax revenues relative to GDP (figure 3.6.A). This also reflects, in part, the difficulty in establishing monitoring and compliance processes for broad direct income taxation (Besley and Persson 2014).

Options for greater revenue mobilization in the short term may be limited in EMDEs. Deep structural factors may influence tax collection capacity, including the resources available to tax and the level of economic informality (Bird, Martinez Vazquez, and Torgler 2008; Waseem 2018). Increasing tax rates as a part of a comprehensive fiscal reform may not always be politically or administratively feasible in the near term. However, efforts to broaden the tax base without raising statutory rates can go a long way in closing loopholes and simplifying tax collection. Inefficient tax expenditures—tax breaks, deductions, credits, and other exemptions granted to certain favored sectors or groups of taxpayers—constitute a significant challenge in some EMDEs. Eliminating these expenditures or at a minimum, transparently including their cost in the budget, can lead to more effective use of limited fiscal resources.

Reforms to improve tax policies and administration. Better tax administration can help tap underutilized sources of revenue (World Bank 2023b). Progress in tax administration could be aided, for example, by improving the management of the taxpayer registry, tax dispute resolution, transparency, and accountability functions. The simplicity of the tax structure itself can aid its administration. For example, a uniform sales tax on businesses may foster compliance and reduce opportunities to exploit loopholes. Trade taxes at the border, such as value-added taxes, can take advantage of automated customs management systems for international trade and transport operations (UNCTAD 2022).[24]

Adoption of new technologies. Implementation of new technologies to process tax payments and monitor tax compliance can aid revenue mobilization (Gupta et al. 2017). For instance, wider adoption of mobile payment systems can help simplify tax payment processes in EMDEs, which helps gain efficiency in tax revenue collection, particularly for direct taxes (Dom et al. 2022). The implementation of mobile money platforms has helped reduce property tax evasion in Tanzania, and has been used to facilitate filing tax returns and increase non-tax revenue collection in Kenya and the Philippines (Arewa and Davenport 2022).

Reallocation of public spending

Although debt-service payments and other non-discretionary spending items reduce fiscal room for public investment, EMDEs generally also have some scope for increasing public sector spending efficiency. For example, reducing distortive subsidies can achieve greater allocative efficiency of public spending. Governments often choose to subsidize certain domestic industries to bolster their competitiveness, for national security interests, or to promote development in specific regions.

However, artificially propping up certain sectors through subsidies distorts market dynamics, diverts resources toward less efficient firms and industries, creates unfair advantages, and discourages competition, which ultimately impedes structural adjustments within the economy (World Bank 2023c). Globally, though estimates vary, subsidies for fossil fuels, agriculture, and fisheries are large, amounting to US$1.25 trillion per year, or more than one percent of global GDP according to a recent

FIGURE 3.6 Fiscal space in EMDEs

EMDEs, especially LICs, tend to lag advanced economies in the size of government tax revenues relative to GDP. Government debt in EMDEs escalated significantly in 2020-23 to 65 percent of GDP—about 20 percentage points higher than the average over the previous two decades. EMDEs with higher interest payments tend to have lower public-investment-to-GDP ratios. Borrowing costs have risen sharply since 2020, as inflation and interest rates increased globally.

A. Fiscal revenues

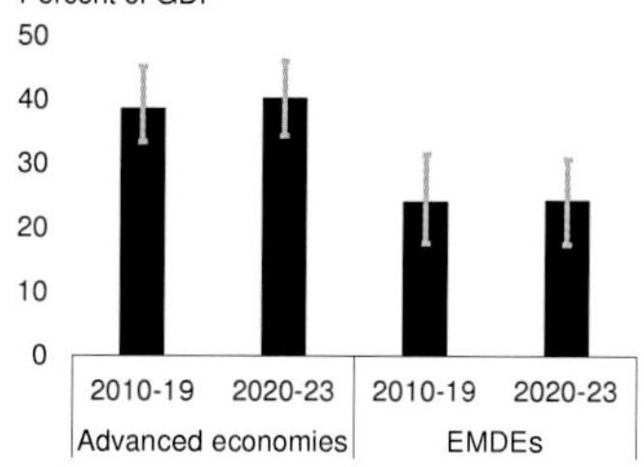

B. Government debt in EMDEs

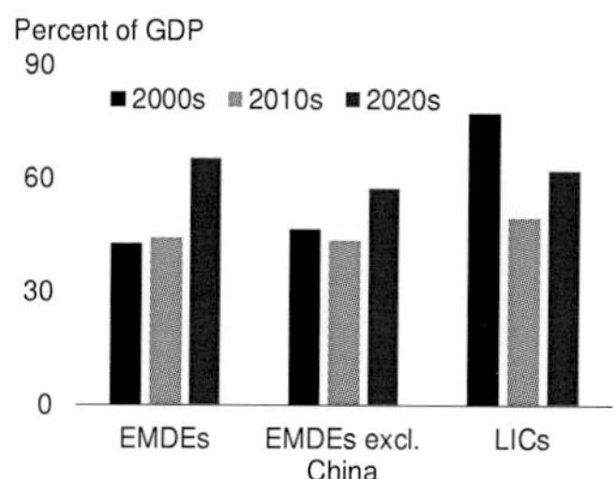

C. Public investment and net interest payments in EMDEs in the 2010s

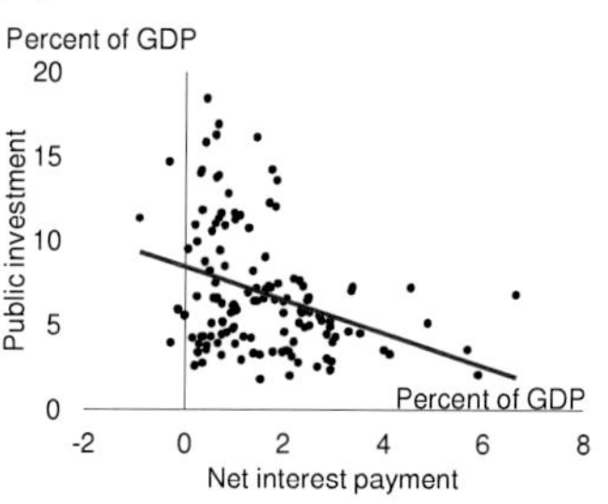

D. Interest payments and rates in EMDEs

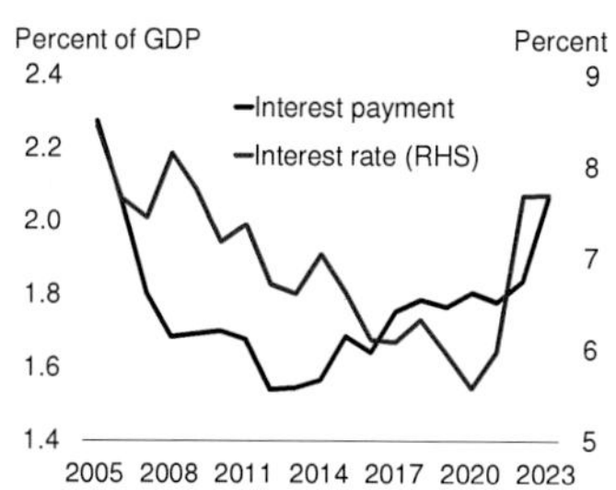

Sources: International Monetary Fund; Kose et al. (2022); World Bank.

Note: EMDEs = emerging market and developing economies; LICs = low-income countries.

A. Bars show group medians of the countries' period average fiscal revenues in percent of GDP. Whiskers indicate interquartile ranges. Sample includes up to 41 advanced economies and 154 EMDEs.

B. Aggregates are computed as weighted averages with nominal GDP in U.S. dollars as weights. Data for the 2020s cover 2020-23. Sample includes up to 153 EMDEs, including 23 LICs.

C. Relationship between public investment and net interest payments, computed as differences between primary balances and fiscal balances (in percent of GDP). Correlation coefficient is -0.34, statistically significant at the 1 percent level, based on data for 130 EMDEs.

D. Interest payment refers to net interest payment, and interest rate refers to long-term interest rate. Sample includes up to 149 EMDEs for interest payment and 77 EMDEs for interest rate.

assessment (Damania et al. 2023). Such subsidies—popular in many EMDEs—can considerably reduce fiscal space, in addition to often being poorly targeted and distortionary. This can be done by using gradual increases in regulated gasoline and diesel prices, liberalizing fuel markets, reforming the excise tax on fuel, and introducing a carbon tax (Parry, Black, and Vernon 2021). Removing subsidies can be politically contentious. Nevertheless, some countries have been able to undertake fuel subsidy reforms. For example, Mexico was able to remove the fuel subsidy and turn fuel taxes into a net

[24] In particular, the UNCTAD Automated System for Customs Data (ASYCUDA)—an integrated customs management system for international trade and transport operations—increasingly adopted by countries globally, helps improve fiscal governance and revenue administration efficiency.

fiscal revenue source (Arlinghaus and van Dender 2017).

Improving debt management and fiscal frameworks

Debt financing via bond issuance and loans from domestic and international borrowers allows governments to mobilize more resources for large-scale infrastructure projects, while spreading the costs of investment over time. However, incurring more public debt may be difficult: many countries have come up against borrowing limits. Government debt in EMDEs escalated significantly over 2020-23 to 65 percent of GDP—about 20 percentage points higher than the average over the previous two decades (figure 3.6.B).

In a time of elevated interest rates, higher debt levels are associated with larger debt-service costs, limiting the budgetary resources for public investment. When debt service is high, the first reaction in liquidity-constrained EMDEs is often to cancel or postpone public investment projects. Indeed, EMDEs with higher interest payments tend to have lower public-investment-to-GDP ratios (figure 3.6.C). Borrowing costs have risen sharply since 2020, as inflation and interest rates increased globally, increasing debt servicing obligations for many EMDEs (figure 3.6.D).

Credible, stable, and predictable fiscal frameworks can help to increase fiscal space by generating the capacity for the government to take on more debt without undermining sustainability. Improved public debt management, the implementation of medium-term expenditure frameworks, the introduction of effective fiscal rules, and the establishment or strengthening of institutions for building fiscal buffers (such as stabilization funds) can all reinforce fiscal discipline.

Public debt management. Implementing best practices in debt management regarding liquidity, maturity, currency, and coupon payment arrangements can reinforce EMDEs' capacity to borrow. Good public management makes government financing less vulnerable to short-term changes in market sentiment, exchange rate and interest rate fluctuations, and other shocks (Kose et al. 2021). Accurate and transparent monitoring of government balance sheets and contingent government liabilities is also important for effective debt management.

Medium-term expenditure frameworks. The adoption of multiyear planning frameworks helps to strengthen the credibility and transparency of budgetary process and establishes a formal connection between budgets and broad macroeconomic and fiscal policy objectives. This can help contain budgetary inertia, overspending, and near-term bias in budgeting. This is particularly important for the planning of public infrastructure projects that require medium-term financing commitments and large upfront costs.

Fiscal rules and stabilization funds. Fiscal rules can help reduce the influence of political actors by setting transparent numerical limits. Successful implementation of effective fiscal rules allows a government to establish credibility with its creditors, which can improve borrowing capacity and avoid the risks of sudden spending cuts during crises. Flexible fiscal rules that exclude public investment from the regulatory constraints on fiscal aggregates may help prevent abrupt investment cuts during fiscal adjustment periods (Guerguil, Mandon, and Tapsoba 2017; Rajaram et al. 2014; Schwartz et al. 2020). However, there may be trade-offs between flexibility and clarity. Fiscal rules have been implemented successfully in many EMDEs; examples include Chile and Indonesia. Well-designed fiscal rules and stabilization funds with strong institutional frameworks are especially important for commodity exporters, as they help mitigate the volatility and procyclicality that can result from exposure to commodity price volatility (Gill et al. 2014; World Bank 2024). Some EMDEs have been able to significantly expand fiscal space in recent years amid a low global growth environment. For example, Jamaica was successful in reducing its debt burden by introducing transparent fiscal rules and implementing its medium-term fiscal framework (Arslanalp et al. 2024).

Efficiency of public investment

Public investment efficiency is critical for realizing the macroeconomic benefits of public investment. In technical terms, public investment efficiency is defined as the ratio between the actual increment of public capital and the amount spent (Pritchett 2000). The extent to which each dollar spent on public investment translates into a dollar of productive public capital depends on many factors, including the quality of institutions, the effectiveness of fiscal planning and execution, the quality of project evaluation, and the speed of implementation of public investment projects (Dabla Norris et al. 2012; Schwartz et al. 2020). In the worst case, low-quality public investment processes may result in "white elephant" infrastructure projects that are very costly to build and maintain, while bringing only limited economic returns.

EMDEs, especially LICs, generally lag advanced economies in terms of public investment efficiency (figures 3.7.A and 3.7.B). Institutional weaknesses such as government corruption, regulatory bottlenecks, and inefficient procurement systems are closely linked to low efficiency of public investment (Rajaram et al. 2014). Over recent decades, in the average EMDE, there has been little progress in improving the quality of institutions that are critical for overall public investment efficiency, including control of corruption and the strength of regulatory quality (figures 3.7.C and 3.7.D). According to some estimates, in EMDEs, over one-third of public investment may be lost because of inefficiency (Schwartz et al. 2020).

Public investment management is critical for the successful implementation of large-scale public investment projects with long development cycles and high risks, such as sustainable infrastructure projects. Robust risk management processes, along with transparent and well-monitored procurement frameworks, are particularly important for crowding in private investment for infrastructure projects (Davoodi 1998; Kim, Fallov, and Groom 2020). Besides structural reforms to enhance the quality of institutions, effective public investment management frameworks are also important to improve public investment efficiency, including at the project level.[25] Moreover, lack of human

[25] Public investment management frameworks developed by the World Bank and the IMF provide a taxonomy of essential policy elements to effective public investment management process (IMF 2018; Kim, Fallov, and Groom 2020; Rajaram et al. 2014).

FIGURE 3.7 Public investment efficiency

EMDEs, especially LICs, generally lag advanced economies in terms of public investment efficiency. Over recent decades, in the average EMDE, there has been little progress in improving the quality of institutions that are critical for overall public investment efficiency, including control of corruption and the strength of regulatory quality.

A. Public infrastructure efficiency

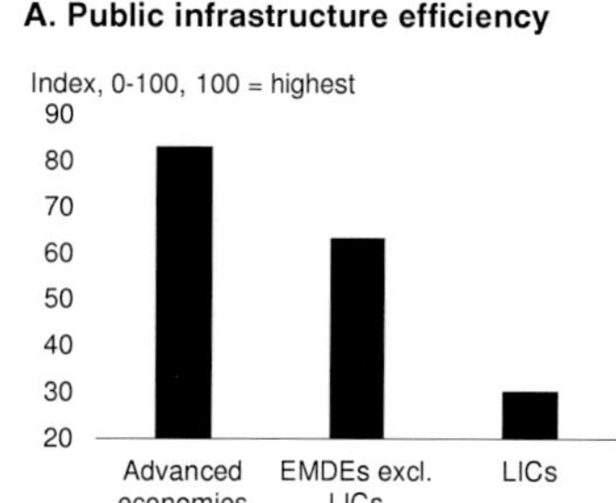

B. Public investment management

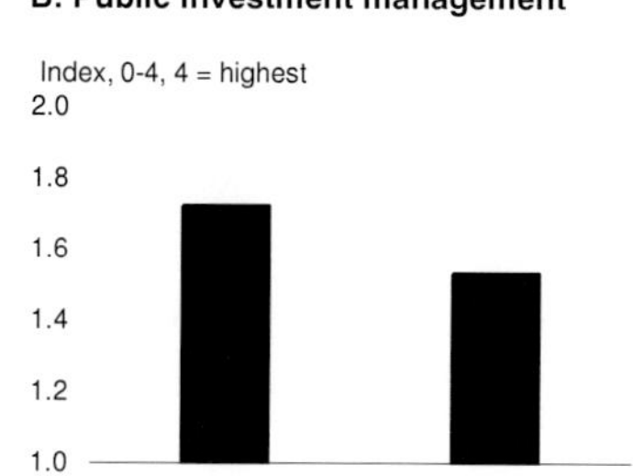

C. Control of corruption

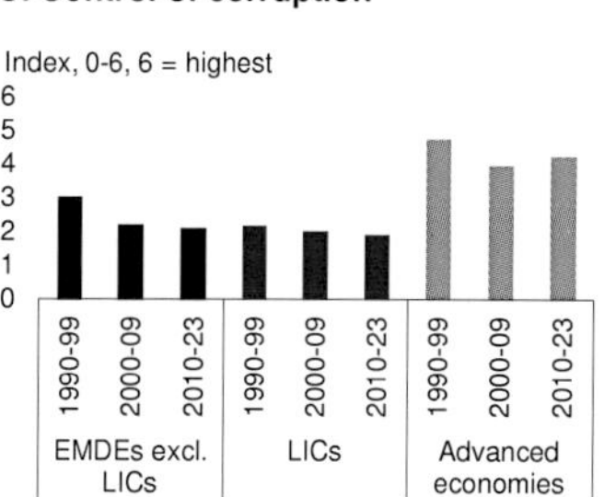

D. Law and order

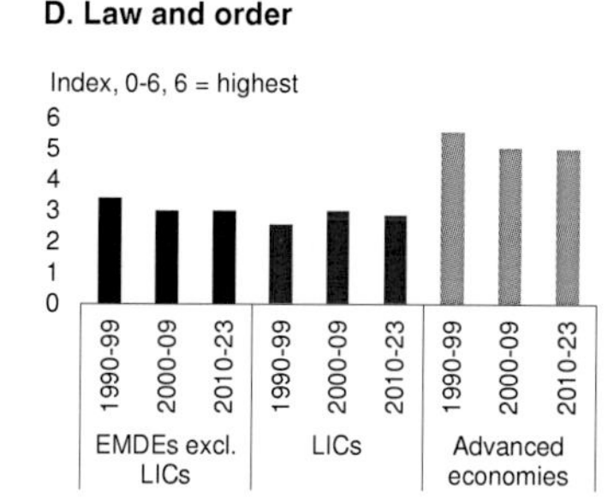

Sources: Dabla-Norris et al. (2012); IMF (2021b); International Country Risk Guide (ICRG); World Bank.

Note: EMDEs = emerging market and developing economies; LICs = low-income countries.

A. Bars show group medians of the IMF (2021b) public infrastructure efficiency index. The index is based on data envelopment analysis (see table A3.2.3). Sample includes 27 advanced economies and 93 EMDEs, of which 15 are LICs.

B. Group medians of the Dabla-Norris et al. (2012) public investment management index. Sample includes 69 EMDEs, of which 16 are LICs.

C.D. Bars show group medians of institutional quality index values. The indexes are International Country Risk Guide's Control of Corruption and Law and Order. Sample includes 36 advanced economies and 97 EMDEs, of which 17 are LICs.

resources to design and manage a project often results in slow budget execution rates, which are intrinsically related to low efficiency. Poor execution often reduces returns on public investment. This is a particular challenge for many LICs and small states (chapter 4).

Public investment project management frameworks

Improvements in public investment project management frameworks can enhance the efficiency of public investment and avoid cost overruns, which are common in large projects. For instance, in a study of 258 transportation projects, Flyvbjerg et al. (2004) showed that costs were initially underestimated in nine out of ten cases.

International organizations have developed a range of frameworks to strengthen public investment management. For instance, the World Bank's public investment management framework helps countries assess the strengths and weaknesses of their public investment practices through eight features: guidance, appraisal, independent review, selection, implementation, adjustment, operation, and evaluation (Rajaram et al. 2014). Similarly, the IMF's Public Investment Management Assessment framework allows for a diagnostic assessment of the efficiency of the government procedures to provide infrastructure assets and identify shortcomings and reform priorities (IMF 2018). This framework also envisions a detailed list of key practices comprising planning, allocation, and implementation of projects, along with cross-cutting enabling factors.

Allocation. Effective public investment planning requires consolidated public investment programs aligned with long-run strategic economic priorities. A transparent, open, and well-monitored procurement process can help keep investment costs under control.

Implementation. Effective implementation of public investment projects requires full and timely financing, monitoring, and operational management processes. Risk management systems are also important and should include contingency planning for economic, design, technological, environmental, and other risk factors (Kim, Fallov, and Groom 2020). Digital innovations can improve spending efficiency, transparency, accountability, and public finance management more broadly (Amaglobeli et al. 2023; Gupta et al. 2017). The benefits of digitization in public investment management are already evident in many EMDEs. For example, in Honduras and Thailand, the use of digital technology has improved transparency and accountability in public infrastructure investments (World Bank 2020).

Maintenance, monitoring, and evaluation. Proper maintenance, and careful monitoring and evaluation are essential to improve the efficiency of public investment projects. Governments should include sufficient funds in medium-term budgets to ensure that public assets put in place are appropriately operated and maintained. This lengthens the life of these assets and thus the quality of the services provided. Moreover, transparent and systematic monitoring of projects, and evaluation of project implementation, can improve the assessment of the benefits and costs of public investment, for example, help to identify the reasons for cost overruns, the social and economic benefits derived from the project. This is particularly important for countries with less experience implementing large-scale investment projects, and when the projects are financed through external borrowing (World Bank 2021).

Public-private partnerships

Public-private partnerships (PPPs) can be important in enabling governments to gain greater efficiency by leveraging private sector resources. Besides directly crowding in private capital, in principle PPPs can help governments share project risks and delegate project operations to the private sector, which may be more efficient from a commercial standpoint. For example, private sector investment in infrastructure, or private participation in infrastructure (PPI), may lead to better spending efficiency if innovations at the design and construction stage underpin lower maintenance and operation costs. Moreover, charging fees for use of services can help depoliticize public service delivery and thus improve public perception. For example, paying tolls for the use of a road that is clearly well-maintained may be perceived as more transparent than paying the equivalent tax.

PPI has been increasing throughout the 1990s and 2000s in EMDEs, with more than 300 projects ongoing every year and an annual investment value of almost two percent of GDP, on average (figure 3.8.A). However, PPI declined significantly in the past decade. The number of PPI projects dropped by almost two-thirds. PPI engagement is especially low in LICs with just a handful of projects operating across these countries in any given year (figure 3.8.B).

Despite substantial efforts in many EMDEs to set up appropriate institutional structures to attract PPI, the evidence on the effective savings from PPI has been mixed (Fabre and Straub 2023). PPP agreements sometimes end up costing society more than the benefits they produce, as these come most of the time with either explicit or implicit guarantees, funded by the government. This can lead to future public liabilities, which can be especially problematic when they are not explicitly accounted for in public budget (Herrera et al. 2023). Moreover, by letting private investors take on the projects, the public sector can sometimes forego the benefits associated with the stream of operational revenues (Engel, Fischer, and Galetovic 2013 and 2014; Fabre and Straub 2023).

The complexity and long-term nature of projects involving the private sector often leads to demands for renegotiation. This can significantly raise costs over the life of the project. Governments are often less able to renegotiate a favorable contract, reflecting the limited choice of private sector partners in EMDEs willing and able to develop bankable projects. For example, a series of renegotiations of transport PPI in some EMDEs led to taxpayers essentially bailing out firms for a significant share of highway construction costs (Moore, Straub, and Dethier 2014).

Even if intentions and agreements on both sides are aligned, getting the contract terms right to account for all risks can be daunting for the private sector partner. Infrastructure investments can involve sizeable sunk costs, making managing risk and uncertainty one of the most important factors in attracting private financing. Elevated global uncertainty over the last decade has undermined the appetite of the private sector to invest in infrastructure. Many types of risks could hamper the flow of investment financing and implementation, including project-specific risks, as well as regulatory risks (Bonaglia et al. 2015). While the private sector seeks a return on investment, governments find themselves caught between cost recovery and affordability. Therefore, if the affordability of the service is a priority, governments would need to subsidize the gap to ensure it is attractive to private investors. This may imply trade-offs regarding coverage which could make the project less advantageous from a development perspective (Fay, Martimort, and Straub 2019a).

FIGURE 3.8 Private sector participation in infrastructure

PPI has been increasing throughout the 1990s and 2000s, with more than 300 projects ongoing every year and an annual investment value of almost two percent of GDP, on average. However, PPI declined significantly in the past decade. The number of PPI projects dropped by almost two-thirds. PPI engagement is especially low in LICs with just a handful of projects operating across these countries in any given year.

A. PPI trends in EMDEs

B. PPI trends in LICs

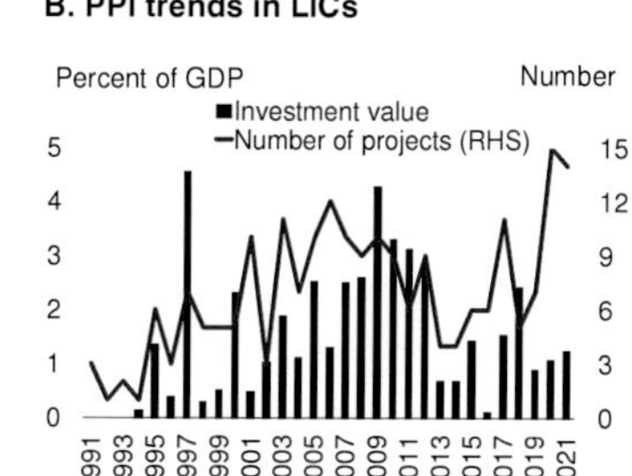

Sources: International Monetary Fund; World Bank (PPI Database).

Note: EMDEs = emerging market and developing economics; LICs = low-income countries; PPI = private participation in infrastructure. Sample includes up to 128 EMDEs, of which 24 are LICs. Bars show average values of PPI investment in percent of GDP. Lines show the total number of PPI projects in a given year.

Nonetheless, private sector participation can come in different forms. With new technologies that create network externalities, many services that used to be traditionally funded or provided through public investment can now be provided by the private sector (such as information and communication technology, digital, finance, and sections of the energy supply chain). These are areas in which public intervention in the form of appropriately designed regulation can correct various market failures such as the ones mentioned above, with the risks and rewards borne by the private sector. In this way, public involvement can ensure that outcomes are aligned with social welfare criteria, even when investment is undertaken by private entities.

More generally, policy interventions to promote macroeconomic stability, strengthen banking sector regulation and supervision, improve the legal and contractual environment to protect the rights of creditors and borrowers, and enhance project de-risking can all help bolster private sector participation in development. Besides PPPs, certain types of public infrastructure can be acquired by institutional investors, which could generate additional financing for the government and might facilitate the efficiency of operation and maintenance.

Given that EMDEs often have relatively weak domestic private sectors, attracting foreign financing, particularly greenfield investment, can increase competition in domestic markets and raise efficiency. Besides providing private capital, foreign investors can help improve efficiency through technology spillovers and competitive business management practices, and can facilitate integration into global production networks. However, positive spillovers from foreign direct investment to the domestic economy tend to depend on the quality of the regulatory environment, skills endowment, and absorptive capacity (Farole and Winkler 2014). Domestic investor partners are also important because they contribute local know-how, so policy makers could encourage programs that link domestic firms with foreign firms.

Enhanced global support

Many EMDEs, especially LICs, have deep structural challenges and limited fiscal space. Without external support, they may not be able to embark on significant public investment. Considering their large investment needs in an environment of sustained growth slowdowns and growing challenges (including the need to address climate change and deliver the SDGs), there is an urgent need for enhanced support from the global community to accelerate structural policy interventions and improve their investment prospects (see Chrimes et al. 2024; G20-IEG 2024).

The international community, including multilateral organizations, can play a critical steering role in facilitating globally coordinated policies to mobilize resources toward urgent public investment in EMDEs and ensure their effective use. Of particular importance is financial support to fund those priority public investment projects that have the greatest potential to mobilize private investment, facilitate equitable access to critical public infrastructure, address climate change mitigation and adaptation needs, facilitate the green transition, and boost long-run productivity through human capital development.

International organizations have also developed a range of frameworks to help strengthen public investment management. In addition to the World Bank's public investment management framework (Rajaram et al. 2024) and the IMF's Public Investment Management Assessment framework (IMF 2018), other initiatives have been utilized: the IMF-World Bank Public-Private Partnership Fiscal Risk Assessment Model, which assesses the fiscal costs and risks of PPPs, and the framework for better infrastructure governance by the Organisation for Economic Co-operation and Development (OECD 2017). Policy advice and capacity development across the public investment management process could increase efficiency and improve borrowing capacity.

For countries with limited fiscal space and restrained access to financial markets, including highly vulnerable small states and countries facing fragility and conflict, official development assistance in the form of grants or concessional lending may be the only feasible source of continued funding. International organizations could help unlock financing for the riskier phase of greenfield investment projects (Arezki and Sy 2016). They can also provide essential expertise in project preparation to EMDEs, thus helping to solve the often-cited problem of lack of capacity to prepare a pipeline of bankable projects (Arezki et al. 2017).

Besides stepping up financial aid to countries in need, the international community should also actively push ahead with the debt restructuring and relief processes to adapt to the changing sovereign debt landscape given the increasing number of creditors and growing complexity of debt instruments (World Bank 2024).

Conclusion

Significant investment is necessary for EMDEs to address structural challenges, including to tackle climate change and make progress toward achieving SDGs. This requires redoubled policy efforts to mobilize both public and private resources. Empirical analysis in this chapter suggests that raising public investment can help trigger a virtuous cycle of development via positive supply-side and demand-side effects: crowding in private investment, enhancing productivity, and boosting economic growth.

However, the effectiveness of public investment hinges on whether it is efficient and whether there is adequate fiscal space. If a government has room to spend without jeopardizing its fiscal sustainability, and public investment projects are selected and implemented well, EMDEs can raise output by up to 1.6 percent in the medium term for every one percent of GDP increase in public investment. The estimates in the chapter consider the direct effect on output from public investment. However, public investment can also provide other benefits that are difficult to quantify, for example ensuring equitable access to essential public goods and services, as well as improving quality of life.

Proactive support from the global community could help jump-start virtuous development cycles in EMDEs, particularly those that are fiscally constrained and have weak public spending efficiency. High debt levels in EMDEs in the wake of the COVID-19 pandemic compound the challenges for these countries in advancing reforms and boosting productive investment (World Bank 2022). This strengthens the case for timely and substantive support from the global community.

While reforms need to be tailored to specific country circumstances and aligned with their long-term development strategies, three overarching policy priorities are critical for EMDEs—the package of "Three Es": expansion of fiscal space, efficiency of public investment, and enhanced global support.

Expansion of fiscal space. Given limited capacity for revenue mobilization and reallocation of public resources toward public investment, policy makers in EMDEs need to undertake reforms to improve tax collection efficiency, enhance fiscal frameworks, and prioritize public spending with an eye on productive public investment projects.

Efficiency of public investment. EMDEs should enhance the efficiency of public investment—maximize the quality and quantity of productive public capital that each dollar of public investment yields. This requires reforms to tackle corruption and poor governance, and to improve public investment project management frameworks. Project selection should focus on advancing those investments which have the greatest potential to mobilize private investment, spark productivity gains, and facilitate green transition—in particular, health, education, digital networks, and renewable energy infrastructure projects.

Enhanced global support. Many EMDEs with limited fiscal space and deep structural issues, especially LICs, may not be able to finance beneficial large-scale public investment projects and implement the wide range of necessary reforms to improve the efficiency of public investment without additional help. With investment gaps particularly large in such countries, enhanced financial support and technical assistance from the global community are essential. The findings of this chapter underscore the importance of reforms to strengthen public investment management frameworks and improve institutions. Financial support may therefore be most effective if it helps improve the fiscal sustainability of the recipient country and the efficiency of its public investment.

Increasing investment in EMDEs is a crucial component of delivering strong, sustainable growth in these countries. Yet despite large investment gaps, investment growth has been weakening. Public investment has an important role to play, in its own right as well as to help catalyze private sector investment. Creating the conditions for effective and efficient public investment should therefore be a priority both for domestic policy makers and for the international community.

BOX 3.1 Public investment dynamics around adverse events

Public investment growth tends to decline sharply during recession years—by about 9 percentage points relative to periods of economic stability, on average, and remains subdued for an additional two years after the initial shock. Public investment also generally contracts after financial crises hit. These effects reflect the diversion of fiscal resources toward immediate stabilization needs, disruptions in financial markets and higher borrowing costs, lower fiscal revenues following contraction in private sector activity.

Introduction

In emerging market and developing economies (EMDEs), public investment weakened significantly after the 2007-09 global financial crisis and the associated recession. Public investment growth in EMDEs decelerated from an average of 10 percent in the 2000s to 5 percent in the 2010s. More generally, during recessions and crises public investment might be expected to weaken, as fiscal revenues decline and governments may prioritize countercyclical public consumption policies over public investment. However, countries with sufficient fiscal space could in principle embark on additional scaling up of public investment as part of a countercyclical fiscal support package. Similarly, natural disasters may damage or destroy infrastructure such as roads and bridges, requiring public investment to rebuild it.

In order to find commonalities in the dynamics of public investment around potentially disruptive events, this box addresses the following question: How does public investment growth evolve around shock events—specifically, recessions, financial crises, and natural disasters?

To this end, this box examines the trajectory of public investment growth around these adverse episodes—during the event and across three-year windows either side of it. The analysis is based on a sample of 117 EMDEs over 1970-2019. Only countries with sufficient data in the windows around events are included in the sample for each event study. The data for public investment growth are from the International Monetary Fund's Investment and Capital Stock Dataset (IMF 2021a). Recession years are defined as years with negative real per capita income growth. Natural disasters data are from the EM-DAT the International Disaster Database. The data for financial crises, including systemic banking crises, debt crises, and currency crises, are from the Systemic Banking Crises Database II (Laeven and Valencia 2020). The mean response for the sample is shown along with the 90-percent confidence bands (figure B3.1.1).

Recessions

During a recession, the adverse macroeconomic effects exerting a downward pressure on investment in general might be partly offset by a boost in government spending, including public investment, in an effort to provide fiscal stimulus to the economy, particularly given that the empirical evidence points at larger output effects of public investment during recessions than expansions. That said, the event study analysis suggests that on average, recessions have an adverse impact on public investment growth, with effects lasting well beyond the shock episode itself. Public investment contracts by 4 percent on average in a recession year—a decline of about 9 percentage points relative to public investment growth in the year before a recession (figure B3.1.1.A). Public investment growth remains lower for two more years after the initial shock. Recessions triggered by financial crises are associated with deeper negative effects, with public investment contracting by about 6 percent in the year of the recession.

Government revenues in recessions decline as a result of lower economic activity. At the same time, during economic downturns, EMDEs often choose to prioritize immediate needs such as macroeconomic stabilization, unemployment relief, and support to firms and households. These measures take precedence over public investment projects. The combination of lower revenue and increased spending often leads to deterioration of fiscal space in the aftermath of recessions, constraining the government's ability to invest in infrastructure.

Financial crises

Systemic banking, currency, and debt crises have an adverse impact on public investment growth and are generally followed by quicker public investment

Note: The analysis in this box draws from Adarov et al. (forthcoming).

BOX 3.1 Public investment dynamics around adverse events (*continued*)

FIGURE B3.1.1 Public investment dynamics around adverse events

In recessions, public investment contracts by about 4 percent and remains subdued for additional two years after the initial shock. Currency crises are also associated with a decline of about 6 percent in public investment during the crisis year, while debt and banking crises tend to have the largest impact in the year that follows the crisis—with public investment contracting by 3.5 and 3 percent, respectively. There are no statistically significant changes in public investment growth associated with natural disasters.

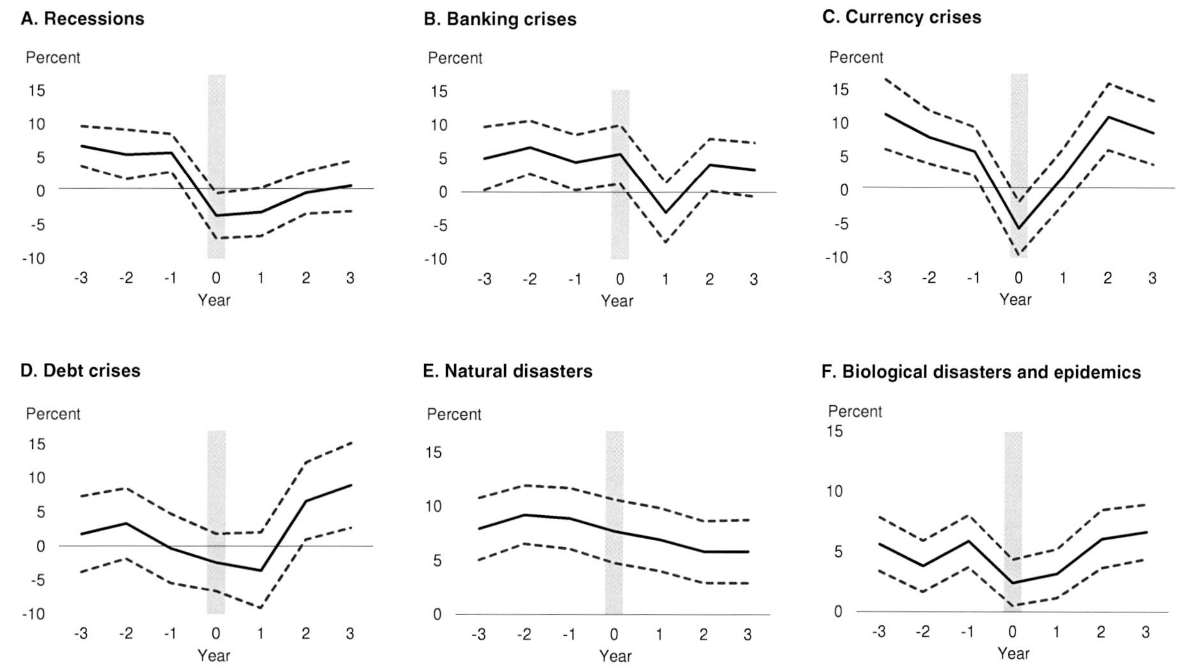

Sources: EM-DAT (database); Investment and Capital Stock Dataset (IMF 2021a); Laeven and Valencia (2020); World Bank.

Note: Public investment refers to general government gross fixed capital formation in billions of constant 2017 international dollars. Sample includes 117 EMDEs over the period 1970-2019. Gray areas indicate the event year. Solid lines indicate mean public investment growth, dashed lines indicate 90 percent confidence bands.

recoveries relative to recessions (figures B3.1.1.B-D). Debt and banking crises have the deepest adverse effect in the year that follows the initial shock, with public investment contracting by 3.5 and 3 percent, respectively. Public investment growth declines in the run-up to a debt crisis itself, as markets respond to the deteriorating fiscal position before the crisis actually crystallizes. On average, public investment growth remains in negative territory in the year following a debt crisis—unlike systemic banking crises and currency crises (figure B3.1.1.D).

Like in recessions, governments during financial crises may prioritize short-term measures aimed at macroeconomic stabilization rather than long-term infrastructure investment spending. Furthermore, financial crises can disrupt credit markets, making it more challenging and expensive for governments to borrow, leading to a decline in government investment (Laeven and Valencia 2018; Reinhart and Rogoff 2011).

Currency crises are associated with a sharper drop in public investment than other types of financial crises—a 6 percent contraction on average in the year of the shock. Currency crises, in addition to the adverse effects discussed above, can also lead to a reduction in external financing, as international lenders become concerned about repayment risk demanding higher risk premiums. Currency crises may also increase the cost of imported goods and services needed for public investment projects, making them more expensive to undertake.

BOX 3.1 Public investment dynamics around adverse events (*continued*)

That said, currency and banking crises are associated with faster recoveries of public investment growth, compared with more entrenched adverse effects associated with recessions and debt distress episodes. The latter have more direct and profound adverse effects on the fiscal positions, necessitating cuts or delays in discretionary government spending—including sizable public investment projects—during the shock episodes, as well as lasting impact on the sovereign's creditworthiness, which affects the ability of the government to tap financial markets in the longer run.

Natural disasters

Analysis of the evolution of investment around natural disasters incorporates the years in which geophysical, climatological, and biological disasters (including epidemics) occurred. Whether considering each event type separately, or on aggregate, there are no statistically significant changes in public investment growth (figure B3.1.1.E). Two opposing forces at work might explain this result: while disasters cause physical damage to infrastructure and have a negative impact on public investment, the affected economy may also invest more to recover from the consequences of the disaster. Only in the case of biological disasters does public investment register a slowdown in growth—perhaps as budget resources are diverted to spending on health-related public services and relief to the affected populations—but even this effect is not statistically significant (figure B3.1.1.F).

Conclusion

Negative macroeconomic shocks tend to have adverse effects on the fiscal positions of EMDEs, including expenditure patterns. This translates to lower public investment growth. During recessions, public investment tends to contract, remaining low for an additional two years after the initial shock. In response to systemic banking crises, currency, and debt crises, public investment growth also declines. Although decelerations during currency crises are more severe, investment reductions during debt crises are typically more prolonged, extending up to two years. Thus, while empirical evidence supports the conjecture that scaling up of public investment tends to generate greater output effects in recessions, in practice EMDEs find it challenging to prioritize public investment owing to limited borrowing capacity and restrained fiscal revenues during periods of macroeconomic distress.

BOX 3.2 Macroeconomic impacts of public investment: A literature review

Public investment is viewed by some policy makers as a powerful policy tool that can help promote economic growth. However, empirical evidence on the impact of public investment on growth is mixed. The empirical work to date suggests that the impact of public investment on growth tends to be greater in countries with better government spending efficiency, larger fiscal space, greater trade openness, lower economic informality, greater financial and economic development, as well as during recessions and periods of elevated uncertainty.

Introduction

Public investment is often viewed as one of the important policy tools that can accelerate growth, as well as address pressing infrastructure needs. At the same time, sceptics argue that public spending in general is inefficient, especially in emerging market and developing economies (EMDEs) with greater institutional challenges, and public investment therefore is wasteful. The literature on the subject matter has been rapidly evolving, and the evidence presented to date is rather sporadic with the size of the public investment multipliers—the change in output in response to a unit-increase in public investment—varying significantly across studies. This box synthesizes the growing literature on the topic and explores the following questions:

- What are the implications of public investment for output growth?
- What factors and country characteristics influence the impact of public investment on growth?

Theoretical foundations

The early literature examined the effects of government investment on economic growth in the context of the endogenous growth model, in which public capital enters the production function as one of the productive inputs (Aschauer 1989a,b; Barro 1990; Barro and Sala-i-Martin 1992; Futagami, Morita, and Shibata 1993; Glomm and Ravikumar 1994; Turnovsky 1997). Subsequent studies built on this framework, incorporating features such as aid-funded public investment, infrastructure networks, and public debt accumulation to facilitate a more nuanced analysis of the transmission channels of public investment to growth (Adam and Bevan 2006; Berg et al. 2010; Chatterjee and Turnovsky 2007; Agenor 2010; Berg et al. 2012). More recently, Chakraborty and Dabla-Norris (2011) studied the quality of public investment and distortionary effects of corruption within a general equilibrium growth model.

Empirical estimates of public investment multipliers

While the empirical work on total public spending multiplier across a broad range of countries is voluminous, the subset of the literature that distinguishes public investment multipliers is limited and primarily focuses on advanced economies. In general, there is an emerging consensus that public investment tends to have a positive growth impact in the medium term (Auerbach and Gorodnichenko 2013; Eden and Kraay 2014; Furceri and Li 2017; Izquierdo et al. 2019; Ilzetzki, Mendoza, and Végh 2013; Leduc and Wilson 2012). However, there remains considerable variation in the estimates of output elasticity to public investment; in a meta-analysis of 68 studies, Bom and Ligthart (2014b), report that the range is -1.7 to 2.0. In reviews of the literature, Gechert and Rannenberg (2018) and Vagliasindi and Gorgulu (2021) also report that public investment multiplier estimates range widely with an average of about 1.5. Table B3.2.1 provides a comprehensive review of public investment multipliers in the literature over the past two decades.

Empirical work focusing on EMDEs has been especially scarce, given data constraints and methodological challenges in identifying public investment shocks (see annex 3.1 for a discussion of existing identification frameworks). Nevertheless, limited research on EMDEs also documents important growth impacts of public investment. For instance, Miyamoto et al. (2020) report an increase in output by 0.4 percent over four years for a sample of 39 EMDEs. Ilzetzki, Mendoza, and Végh (2013) estimate a public investment multiplier of 0.6 on impact, increasing to 1.6 in the longer run, for a panel of 24 developing countries. Furceri and Li (2017) report smaller magnitudes for a sample of 79 EMDEs: a 10-percent increase in public investment induces

BOX 3.2 Macroeconomic impacts of public investment: A literature review *(continued)*

growth of 0.4 percent over four years. Smaller effects are reported in Warner (2014) using a sample of 124 EMDEs: a change in public investment equivalent to one percent of GDP is found to spur only meagre output growth in the short run (0.1 percent) with no significant effect in the long run. The observed wide range of estimates of multipliers has prompted additional inquiry into the factors that may explain these differences.

Factors affecting the size of public investment multipliers

Macroeconomic conditions. In a synthesis review, Izquierdo et al. (2019) note that a position of economy in the business cycle, the degree of exchange rate flexibility, debt levels, and the monetary policy stance are important determinants of the size of multipliers. In this regard, the literature indicates that multipliers tend to be larger during recessions (Auerbach and Gorodnichenko 2012 and 2013; Honda et al. 2020; Riera-Crichton, Vegh, and Vuletin 2015). Ramey (2019) notes that these results may not be fully robust given their sensitivity to the sample composition and the methodology. Further, the output effects tend to be larger in supply-driven recessions compared with those in demand-driven recessions (Ghassibe and Zanetti 2022). The multipliers are found to be larger during periods of monetary policy easing and elevated macroeconomic uncertainty, particularly, when nominal interest rates are at very low levels and reach the "zero lower bound" (Christiano, Eichenbaum, and Rebelo 2011; Gbohoui 2021).

Country structural characteristics. Multipliers tend to be greater in countries with a fixed exchange rate regime, low levels of debt, greater trade openness, and lower economic informality (Colombo et al. 2022; Honda, Miyamoto, and Taniguchi 2020; Huidrom et al. 2020; Ilzetzki, Mendoza, and Végh 2013). Financial development and economic development are also positively associated with the size of spending multipliers (Ilzetzki, Mendoza, and Végh 2013; Koh 2017).

Initial stock of public capital. Public investment multipliers are greater in countries with a lower level of initial public capital stock (Izquierdo et al. 2019). Excessive levels of public capital stock and investment may be detrimental for growth if resources are diverted away from more productive uses or crowd out private investment (Canning and Pedroni 2008; Devarajan, Swaroop, and Zou 1996). Contrary to these studies, Honda, Miyamoto, and Taniguchi (2020) find that, in a sample of low-income countries (LICs), output effects of public investment are greater in economies with higher initial capital stock, and conjecture that in LICs the private sector may not be responsive to fiscal policy shocks when initial capital stock is too low.

Public investment efficiency. The quality of the public investment management process is important to reap the positive macroeconomic effects of public capital. The public investment management process encompasses multiple aspects, including project development, implementation, monitoring, and evaluation (Dabla-Norris et al. 2012). Gupta et al. (2014) compute "efficiency adjusted" public capital stocks and find that the growth effects of efficient public investment are higher. Positive impacts of higher efficiency of public investment are also documented in other empirical studies (Berg, Portillo, and Yang 2013; Cavallo and Daude 2011; Furceri and Li 2017; Izquierdo et al. 2018; Leduc and Wilson 2012; Leeper, Walker, and Yang 2010; Miyamoto et al. 2020).

Conclusion

The literature is generally in agreement that public investment tends to have positive impacts on economic growth, particularly in the longer run. The wide dispersion of the estimated magnitudes of public investment multipliers, however, motivated research that sought to reconcile the heterogeneity. Findings suggest that country-level characteristics—including public investment efficiency, debt levels, capital scarcity—and prevailing macroeconomic conditions at the time of public investment shocks impact the size of the multiplier. Methodological and sample differences may also explain some variation in results across studies. That said, the evidence on the impact of public investment on output in EMDEs is limited to date, owing in large part to associated data constraints. This important topic warrants further research to better inform the policies to stimulate economic growth and mobilize private investment.

BOX 3.2 Macroeconomic impacts of public investment: A literature review (*continued*)

TABLE B3.2.1 Output effects of public investment: Summary of the literature

Study	Public investment multiplier	Sample	Methodology	Notes
Abiad et al. (2016)	0.4 (year 0) – 1.4 (year 4)	17 OECD economies; 1985-2013	Local projections with forecast error shocks	Output growth in response to a one percent of GDP increase in public investment. Larger multipliers in low-growth episodes and in countries with high spending efficiency.
Auerbach and Gorodnichenko (2012)	2.12 (peak response over 20 quarters)	the United States; 1947-2008	SVAR with forecast error shocks	Cumulative output effect in dollars in response to a one dollar increase in public investment. Larger multipliers in recessions that in expansion.
Barry et al. (2018)	0.16 (quarter 1) – 1.10 (quarter 12)	Cameroon; 1999-2015	SVAR with Blanchard and Perotti (2002) identification	Cumulative change in output in percent, in response to a one percent increase in public investment. Statistically insignificant for most of the forecast horizon and in the longer run.
Bom and Ligthart (2014b)	0.08 (short run) – 0.12 (long run)	68 studies over 1983-2008	Meta-regression analysis	Meta-regression estimates of output elasticity of public capital based on studies utilizing a production-function approach. Impact on output growth in response to a one percent increase in public capital.
David (2017)	0.1 (quarter 0) – 2.1 (quarter 20)	Paraguay; 1998-2015	SVAR with Blanchard and Perotti (2002) identification	Output growth in percent, in response to a 1 percent increase in public investment. Larger multipliers for public investment than for public consumption.
Deleidi et al. (2020)	[0.9 – 1.2] in year 0; [1.9 – 3.4] in year 6	11 euro area countries; 1970-2016	Local projections	Output growth in response to a one percent increase in public investment. Smaller multipliers in the pre-2007 period. The ranges of individual country estimates are in parentheses.
Demetriades and Mamuneas (2000)	[0.36 – 2.06] in the short run; [0.36 – 1.97] in the long run	12 OECD countries; 1972-91	Simultaneous equations system	Output elasticities. Impact on output of a one percent increase in public capital. The ranges of individual country estimates are in parentheses.
Eden and Kraay (2014)	1.5 (year 1)	39 low-income countries (IDA borrowers)	2SLS with Kraay (2012) identification	Output increase in dollars in response to a one dollar increase in public investment. Lower multiplier using OLS estimation (0.2).
Elkhdari et al. (2018)	0.3 (year 1) – 1.2 (year 5) 0.5 (year 1) – 1.8 (year 5)	Algeria; 2008-15 9 MNA countries; 2000-15	SVAR with Blanchard and Perotti (2002) identification;	Output growth in response to a one percent increase in capital expenditures. Larger multipliers during periods with negative output gaps.
Espinoza and Senhadji (2011)	0.2-0.3 in the short term; 0.6-1.1 in the long term	Gulf Cooperation Council countries; 1975-2009	Panel models	Output growth in response to a 15 percent increase in capital expenditures. Larger multipliers for public investment than for public consumption.
Furceri and Li (2017)	0.2 (year 1) – 0.4 (year 4)	79 EMDEs; 1990-2013	Local projections with forecast error shocks	Output growth in response to a 10 percent increase in public investment. Larger multipliers during economic slack, in closed economies, in countries with fixed exchange rates, lower public debt, and higher investment efficiency.
Gbohoui (2021)	0.55 (year 0) – 0.07 (year 2) 0.22 (year 0) – 0.56 (year 2)	Advanced economies; 1996-2019 EMDEs; 1990-2019	Local projections with forecast error shocks	Output growth in response to a one percent of GDP increase in public investment. Larger multipliers during heightened uncertainty.
Gechert and Rannenberg (2018)	0.6	98 empirical studies	Meta-regression analysis	Output growth in response to a one percent of GDP increase in public investment. Larger multipliers during economic downturns.
Gonzales-Garcia et al. (2013)	0.12 (year 0) – 0.44 (after 4 years)	Eastern Caribbean Currency Union; 1994-2009	SVAR with Blanchard and Perotti (2002) identification	Cumulative output growth in response to a one percent of GDP increase in public investment. Larger multipliers for public investment than for public consumption (the latter are not statistically significant).

BOX 3.2 Macroeconomic impacts of public investment: A literature review (*continued*)

TABLE B3.2.1 Output effects of public investment: Summary of the literature

Study	Public investment multiplier	Sample	Methodology	Notes
Honda et al. (2020)	0.1 (year 1) – 0.2 (year 2)	42 low-income countries; 1995-2017	Local projections with forecast error shocks	Output growth in response to a one percent of GDP increase in public investment. Larger multipliers in recessions, under a fixed exchange rate regime, in countries with better institutions.
Ilzetzki et al. (2013)	0.4 (quarter 0) – 1.5 (quarter 20) 0.6 (quarter 0) – 1.6 (quarter 20)	High income countries; 1985-2013 Developing countries; 1985-2013	SVAR with Blanchard and Perotti (2002) identification	Cumulative output multipliers (ratio of cumulative increase in output and cumulative increase in public investment). Larger multipliers in countries with fixed exchange rates, closed economies, countries with low debt (not stat. significant in high-debt countries).
IMF (2014)	0.4 (year 0) – 1.5 (year 4)	Advanced economies; 1985-2013	Local projections with forecast error shocks	Output response to a one percent of GDP increase in public investment. Larger multipliers during low growth and in countries with higher spending efficiency.
	(1) 0.3 in year 0 – 0.5 in year 4; (2) 0.5 in year 0 – 0.9 in year 4	Developing economies; 1990-2013	Local projections with shocks based on Corsetti et al. (2013) and Kraay (2012)	Output response to a one percent of GDP increase in public investment. Shock identification: (1) Corsetti et al. (2013) approach based on fiscal rules; (2) Kraay (2012) methodology based on official development assistance.
Izquierdo et al. (2019)	0.2 – 1.4 after two years	31 European countries; U.S. states; Argentine provinces	Local projections with Blanchard and Perotti (2002), forecast error, and IV identification	Output growth in response to a one percent increase in public investment. Larger multipliers in countries with low public capital stock; statistically insignificant multipliers in countries with low spending efficiency.
Jong-A-Pin and de Haan (2008)	Ranging from about -2.5 to 2.5	21 OECD countries; 1960-2001	VAR	Output elasticity of public capital at the horizon of 20 years. Output growth in response to a one percent increase in public capital.
Minea and Mustea (2015)	0.53 (year 1) – 1.18 (year 10)	Mediterranean countries; 1980-2012	PVAR	Cumulative output growth in response to a one percent increase in public investment. Heterogeneous multipliers across country groups within the sample: larger in Asian, smaller in African countries.
Miyamoto et al. (2020)	0.2 (year 0) – 1.2 (year 4) 0.2 (year 0) – 0.5 (year 4)	17 advanced economies 39 EMDEs	Local projections with forecast error shocks	Output growth in response to a one percent of GDP increase in public investment. Statistically insignificant in low-income countries. Larger multipliers in countries with better governance.
Petrovic et al. (2021)	0.7 – 0.8 (after one year)	10 Central and Eastern European countries	Local projections and SVAR with Blanchard and Perotti (2002) identification	Cumulative output growth in percent in response to a one percent increase in public investment. Larger multipliers in low-growth periods.
Puig (2014)	1.03 over two years	Argentina; 1993-2012	SVAR	Increase in output in dollars in response to a one dollar increase in public investment. Greater impact of public investment than public consumption.
Rafiq and Zeufack (2012)	2.7 in recessions; 2.0 in expansions (year 1)	Malaysia; 1981-2004	SVAR with Blanchard and Perotti (2002) identification	Output growth in response to a one percent increase in public investment. Greater impact of public investment than public consumption.
Warner (2014)	0.14 (year 0)	124 EMDEs; 1960-2011	OLS	Output per capita growth in response to a one percent increase in public investment. Insignificant impact in the long run.

Source: World Bank.
Note: 2SLS = two-stage least squares; EMDEs = emerging market and developing economies; IDA = International Development Association; IV = instrumental variables approach; MNA = Middle East and North Africa; OECD = Organisation for Economic Co-operation and Development; OLS = ordinary least squares; PVAR = panel vector autoregression; SVAR = structural vector autoregression; VAR = vector autoregression.

ANNEX 3.1 Identification of public investment shocks

This annex provides technical details on the new methodology utilized in this chapter to identify public investment shocks and reviews alternate identification methods adopted in the existing literature.

Review of public spending shock identification frameworks

To gauge the extent to which public spending shocks—including public investment—impact economic growth, it is first necessary to identify changes in public spending that are independent of prevailing macroeconomic conditions.[26] To date, the main methods deployed to tackle this identification challenge are the structural vector autoregression (SVAR) estimation with recursive identification, frameworks relying on instrumental variables, the narrative approach, and identification based on forecast errors.

- *SVAR with recursive identification of public spending shocks.* The relatively prevalent SVAR approach employs recursive identification schemes and other parameter restrictions to pin down unexpected public spending shocks. Specifically, the Cholesky decomposition exploits an assumption that government spending does not respond to macroeconomic shocks in the same period (Blanchard and Perotti 2002). A drawback is that this rationale becomes less compelling at an annual frequency, yet availability of higher frequency data is often constrained, especially for EMDEs.
- *Official lending as an instrument for exogenous public spending.* This approach, pioneered by Kraay (2012, 2014) uses data on official creditor loan disbursements to identify public spending shocks in the recipient country based on the lag between loan approval and subsequent disbursements to isolate a component insulated from contemporaneous macroeconomic developments. However, this framework is only applicable to countries that are recipients of official development assistance and requires the calculation of "predicted" disbursements for each loan.
- *Military spending as an instrument for exogenous public spending.* Building on the "natural experiment" framework proposed by Barro (1981), the narrative approach, developed in Ramey and Shapiro (1998), Ramey (2011a, 2011b), and Ramey and Zubairy (2018), uses fluctuations in governments' military expenditures—assumed to be driven by external geopolitical factors as opposed to domestic macroeconomic conditions—to isolate exogenous changes in public spending. This approach, however, would not work well for EMDEs, in which military spending is typically less prone to fluctuation. More broadly, a pitfall of this method is that the resulting growth responses may be largely attributable to the military spending sub-component as opposed to more general fiscal stimulus.
- *Forecast errors in public spending as a proxy for fiscal shocks.* In more recent empirical research, Auerbach and Gorodnichenko (2012, 2013) use differences between actual public spending and the level predicted by professional forecasters to identify unanticipated public spending shocks.[27] The methodology has the advantage of overcoming the issue of fiscal foresight, whereby, anticipated fiscal policy changes may be incorporated into current economic decisions (Forni and Gambetti 2010; Leeper, Richter, and Walker 2012, 2013). However, this approach relies on the availability and quality of public spending forecast data. Additional caveats relate to the nature of fiscal projections: first, they may not

[26] Failure to do so would obfuscate the "pure" effect of public spending on output, given the bidirectional relationship between economic activity and fiscal policy. For instance, a change in economic growth can affect government spending through fiscal policy responses or the operation of automatic stabilizers. The objective of public spending shock identification methods is to identify a component of government spending that is exogenous with respect to the economic conditions.

[27] This approach was utilized recently in Abiad et al. (2016), Furceri and Li (2017), Honda et al. (2020), and Miyamoto et al. (2020) to estimate unconditional and state-dependent public spending multipliers.

be fully orthogonal to past macroeconomic trends; and second, they rely on subjective, heterogeneous assumptions about future macroeconomic developments.

An approach based on cyclically adjusted public spending

This chapter applies a new approach introduced in Adarov, Clements, and Jalles (forthcoming) to identify public spending shocks, separately for public investment and public consumption. The methodology builds on the work of Alesina and Ardagna (1998, 2010) and related studies that assess the macroeconomic effects of changes in cyclically adjusted fiscal variables. Conceptually, the approach is consistent with the literature arguing that large and apparent scaling up of public investment tends to reflect exogenous decisions by the public authorities (Deleidi, Iafrate, and Levrero 2020; Warner 2014). The shock identification framework for public investment involves four steps:

1. For each country, output elasticities of public investment are estimated by regressing the logarithm of real public investment on the logarithm of real GDP.

2. Measures of potential output, GDP^{pot}, are obtained via a Hodrick-Prescott filter. Alternative filters, including the Baxter-King, Christiano-Fitzgerald, and the Hamilton (2018) filters, are used as a robustness check.

3. Cyclically adjusted real public investment (*CAPI*) is then computed as follows:

$$CAPI = PI\left(\frac{GDP^{pot}}{real\,GDP}\right)^{\varepsilon_{PI}} \quad (3.1.1)$$

where *PI* is real public investment and ε_{PI} is the output elasticity computed in step 1.

4. For each country *i*, measures of public investment shocks *(PIS)* are constructed as the variable that takes the value of one when a country's first difference of *CAPI* exceeds its country-specific mean by one standard deviation:

$$PIS = 1\ if\ \Delta CAPI_{it} > \overline{\Delta CAPI_i} + SDCAPI_i, 0\ otherwise \quad (3.1.2)$$

Focusing on country-level public investment adjustments greater than one standard deviation is in the spirit of Alesina and Ardagna (2010), who argue that honing in on large fiscal adjustments helps identification of changes in fiscal variables that are induced by discretionary policy, rather than influenced by the business cycle. Some examples of the episodes identified using this approach include rapid scaling up of public investment in Poland in 2005-06 and 2018, in Brazil in 2007, and Morocco in 2008. In Poland, the episodes followed significant EU fund inflows and reforms as part of its EU integration.[28] In Brazil, the episode followed the launch of the Growth Acceleration Program—a major infra-structure program including investment projects and policies to boost growth. In Morocco, the episode involved major public investment in infrastructure projects, such as the Green Morocco Plan to bolster the agricultural sector and the expansion of the Tanger Med port.

This approach to the identification of public investment shocks has several advantages. Given the focus only on large episodes of public investment increases, the results are more robust to imperfections in measuring the effect of the business cycle on fiscal variables, as small changes in cyclically adjusted public spending are excluded from the estimation. The proposed framework eschews certain limitations of existing identifica-tion methods that rely on data that are not publicly available (for instance, methods based on government spending forecast errors) or yield estimates for a limited set of countries (for instance, frameworks relying on narrative shock identification or quarterly-frequency data). As such, identification of disaggregated public spending shocks—public investment and public consumption—can be undertaken for a broad sample of countries with available annual data. The large sample, in turn, facilitates estimation of multipliers conditional on country characteristics.

In contrast to one-size-fits-all approaches, this framework accounts for heterogeneity across countries by considering the magnitude of public spending shocks within country-specific historical contexts. This is an important feature in the

[28] See also World Bank (2024) for a review of associated investment accelerations, and IMF (2023) for a discussion of the role of EU funding for boosting public investment in Poland.

analysis of EMDEs, which may exhibit fiscal procyclicality (commodity exporters) or budgetary process-driven volatility of public spending (LICs).[29] The approach can be expanded to allow for time-varying or state-dependent thresholds.

At the same time, a few caveats should be noted. First, issues related to endogeneity and fiscal foresight may persist, despite focusing on large cyclically adjusted public spending innovations to mitigate business cycle effects. Second, the methodology relies on the measure of potential output, which are generally estimated with a certain degree of imprecision. Third, the measure of public investment shock is a binary variable and does not yield an estimate of a multiplier directly in regression. Rather, the output effects need to be interpreted in the context of the average change in public investment for the effective sample subject to the shock, rescaling to obtain the public investment multiplier values.

ANNEX 3.2 Estimation of public investment multipliers

This annex discusses the methodological framework to estimate the effects of public investment on output and other macroeconomic variables.

Estimation framework for unconditional public investment multipliers

Responses of real GDP to public investment shocks are estimated using the local projections method proposed by Jordà (2005). The method lends itself to the analysis in this chapter, given that fiscal shocks are already orthogonalized and do not need further identification, as would be required for vector autoregression (VAR) models. There are distinct advantages to this approach, which has been endorsed by Auerbach and Gorodnichenko (2012) and Romer and Romer (2019) as a flexible alternative to VAR models.[30] First, it does not impose dynamic restrictions and obviates the need to estimate the equations for dependent variables other than the variable of interest, thereby economizing on the number of estimated parameters. Second, it is well-suited to estimating nonlinear effects of public investment conditional on country-characteristics (state-dependent multipliers). Third, it is relatively simple to deal with correlation in error terms—a likely complication in cross-country analysis. Against this background, the following baseline specification is estimated:[31]

$$\log(y_{i,t+k}) - \log(y_{i,t-1}) = \alpha_i + \tau_t + \beta_k shock_{i,t} + \theta X_{i,t} + \varepsilon_{i,t} \quad (3.2.1)$$

in which $k=0,\ldots,5$ is the forecast horizon in years; $\log(y_{i,t+k}) - \log(y_{i,t-1})$ represents the cumulative change in real GDP (in percent) over the forecast horizon; α_i and τ_t are country and time fixed effects to account for time-invariant country heterogeneity and global factors (such as the world business cycle or oil price movements); $X_{i,t}$ is a set of control variables including—as in Abiad, Furceri, and Topalova (2016) and Furceri and Li (2017)—two lags of the shocks and two lags of real GDP growth.[32] To control for outliers, data points above the 99th percentile and below the 1st percentile are dropped in the estimations.

The coefficient β_k denotes the response of output in each period k to a public investment shock at $t=0$, $shock_{i,t}$, identified using the methodology described in annex 3.1. Specifically, it measures the average cumulative real GDP change in period $t+k$ relative to period $t-1$ (in percent), in response to the public investment shock for the effective sample—the sample of countries used in the estimation. To ease interpretation, the estimated coefficients are scaled by the average change in

[29] See also a related discussion in De Haan and Klomp (2013) and Wiese, Jong-A-Pin, and de Haan (2018).

[30] See Plagborg-Møller and Wolf (2021) for a discussion on the trade-offs between VARs and local projections.

[31] The specification is based on the local projections model widely used in empirical literature on public spending multipliers—for instance, Abiad, Furceri, and Topalova (2015); Furceri and Li (2017); Honda, Miyamoto, and Taniguchi (2020); Miyamoto et al. (2020). A similar approach was also used in other empirical studies examining the impact of policy shocks (for instance, in De Haan and Wiese 2022).

[32] Among other robustness checks—discussed in this annex—the model is also estimated with additional control variables to examine the omitted variable bias, dropping lagged real GDP growth, and using the generalized method of moments estimator to address possible bias arising from the lagged dependent variable.

public investment as a percent of GDP for the effective sample that experienced the public investment shock, so that the impulse responses can be interpreted as the change in output (in percent) in response to a one percent of GDP increase in public investment.[33] The model is estimated for the broadest sample of countries available for robustness (table A3.2.1). For some exercises, however, the sample size is much smaller (for instance, for potential output, productivity estimations, subgroups of EMDEs), and thus the results are not directly comparable and should be interpreted with caution.

Descriptive statistics summarizing average changes in output and public investment during public investment shock episodes are reported in table A3.2.2. Impulse response functions are obtained by plotting the estimated multipliers for $k = 0,\ldots,5$, with 90 percent confidence bands computed using robust standard errors clustered at the country level.

Estimation framework for state-dependent public investment multipliers

To examine heterogeneity across country groups (for instance, categorized using income levels, commodity exporter status, degree of public investment efficiency) and discrete macroeconomic states (negative and positive economic growth periods), the model is estimated separately for each subsample. State-dependent multipliers, conditional on the values of continuous time-varying variables, are estimated using a local projections framework with a smooth transition function:[34]

$$\log(y_{i,t+k}) - \log(y_{i,t-1}) = \alpha_i + \tau_t + \beta_k^L F(z_{i,t})\,\text{shock}_{i,t} + \beta_k^H [1 - F(z_{i,t})]\,\text{shock}_{i,t} + \theta X_{i,t} + \varepsilon_{i,t} \tag{3.2.2}$$

$$\textit{with } F(z_{i,t}) = \frac{\exp(-\gamma z_{i,t})}{1+\exp(-\gamma z_{i,t})}, \gamma > 0$$

in which $z_{i,t}$ is the value of a conditioning variable, normalized to have zero mean and unit variance.[35]

The coefficients β_k^L and β_k^H capture the output impact of public investment shocks at each horizon k for the state characterized by low values of a conditioning variable, $F(z_{i,t}) \approx 1$ when z goes to minus infinity; and the state characterized by high values of a conditioning variable, $1 - F(z_{i,t}) \approx 1$ when z goes to plus infinity.

This approach is equivalent to the smooth transition autoregressive model developed by Granger and Teräsvirta (1993). The advantage of this methodology is twofold. First, it permits a direct test of whether the effect of public investment varies across high and low levels of a given conditioning variable. Second, it allows the effect of public investment shocks to change smoothly between the levels of a conditioning variable by considering a continuum of states to estimate the impulse response functions, thus making the responses more stable and precise. To compute multipliers conditional on the public capital scarcity and fiscal space, equation (3.2.2) is estimated using the following conditioning variables for $F(z_{it})$: (1) Gross government debt as a share of GDP, as a proxy for fiscal space; (2) Public capital stock as a share of GDP, to examine the implications of capital scarcity. Variable definitions are provided in table A3.2.3.

Robustness

A range of robustness checks were carried out, and results were corroborative of baseline findings. These included testing alternatives for public investment shock identification, sensitivity checks to the choice of statistical filters, robustness checks to the sample period, and model specifications (selected results are reported in table A3.2.4):

Sensitivity checks for public spending shock parameterization and statistical filters. Given that the identification of public investment shocks may be sensitive to the choice of the statistical filters or the cut-off level to isolate large changes in public investment, alternative threshold levels and filters were explored, including the Baxter-King, Christiano-Fitzgerald, and Hamilton filters.

[33] It is a standard approach in the empirical literature on spending multipliers to use an ex post conversion using the average public-spending-to-GDP ratio. As argued in Ramey and Zubairy (2016), this may however introduce a bias if the public-spending-to-GDP ratio varies significantly over the sample period.

[34] The same approach was used to estimate state-dependent public spending multipliers in Abiad et al. (2015); Furceri and Li (2017); Honda et al. (2020); Miyamoto et al. (2020).

[35] The weights assigned to each regime vary between 0 and 1 according to the weighting function so that can be interpreted as the probability of being in a given economic state. Following the literature that uses a similar approach, (Abiad et al. 2015 and Furceri and Li 2017), the parameter is set to 1.5, while the results do not change materially when other values are used.

The results are not statistically different from the baseline results. The focus only on large changes in cyclically adjusted public investment also mitigates the imprecision in the estimation of potential output. Using higher threshold levels to identify public investment shocks comes at the cost of lower number of shock episodes, resulting in less precise estimates.

Sensitivity to country fixed effects. A possible bias from estimating the baseline model using country fixed effects stems from the fact that the error term may have a non-zero expected value on account of the interaction between fixed effects and country-specific developments (Teulings and Zubanov 2014). Estimates excluding country fixed effects are similar to the baseline results.

Omitted variables and the choice of estimator. The baseline model was estimated with additional variables, introduced to control for inflation and trade openness. The results indicate no large differences relative to the baseline. As an additional check, the model was estimated dropping the lagged dependent variable. Results are also robust to using generalized method of moments as the estimator. As an alternative, the identified public investment shocks were also used as an instrument for a change in public investment as a share of GDP, in two-stage least squares (2SLS) estimation, yielding very similar results.

Sensitivity to the sample period and the sample composition. In order to examine whether the effects of public investment may have changed in the aftermath of the global financial crisis, the multipliers were estimated also for the pre-2007 period, with the findings confirming the baseline results. As a sensitivity check, the estimations were also carried out using the same common sample of countries across all empirical exercises, however this results in less reliable estimates on account of a much smaller sample, with larger error bands.

TABLE A3.2.1 Sample used in the estimation of public investment multipliers

Emerging market and developing economies (EMDEs)
Albania, Algeria, Angola, Antigua and Barbuda, Argentina, Armenia, Azerbaijan, The Bahamas, Bahrain, Bangladesh, Barbados, Belize, Benin, Bhutan, Bolivia, Bosnia and Herzegovina, Botswana, Brazil, Brunei Darussalam, Bulgaria, Burkina Faso, Burundi, Cabo Verde, Cambodia, Cameroon, Central African Republic, Chad, Chile, China, Colombia, the Comoros, the Democratic Republic of Congo, the Republic of Congo, Costa Rica, Côte d'Ivoire, Djibouti, Dominica, the Dominican Republic, Ecuador, the Arab Republic of Egypt, El Salvador, Equatorial Guinea, Eritrea, Eswatini, Ethiopia, Fiji, Gabon, The Gambia, Georgia, Ghana, Grenada, Guatemala, Guinea, Guinea-Bissau, Guyana, Haiti, Honduras, Hungary, India, Indonesia, the Islamic Republic of Iran, Iraq, Jordan, Kazakhstan, Kenya, Kuwait, Lao PDR, Lebanon, Lesotho, Liberia, Libya, Madagascar, Malawi, Malaysia, Maldives, Mali, Mauritania, Mauritius, Mexico, Moldova, Mongolia, Montenegro, Morocco, Mozambique, Myanmar, Namibia, Nepal, Nicaragua, Niger, Nigeria, North Macedonia, Oman, Pakistan, Panama, Papua New Guinea, Paraguay, Peru, the Philippines, Poland, Romania, the Russian Federation, Rwanda, São Tomé and Príncipe, Saudi Arabia, Senegal, Serbia, the Seychelles, Sierra Leone, South Africa, Sri Lanka, St. Kitts and Nevis, St. Lucia, St. Vincent and the Grenadines, Sudan, the Syrian Arab Republic, Tajikistan, Tanzania, Thailand, Togo, Tunisia, Uganda, Ukraine, the United Arab Emirates, Uruguay, Uzbekistan, Viet Nam, the Republic of Yemen, Zambia.

Source: World Bank.

TABLE A3.2.2 Summary statistics for public investment shocks

Variable	Value
Number of economies	129
Public investment shock = 1	
Number of observations	557
Mean real GDP growth (percent)	4.48
Mean public investment (percent of GDP)	8.11
Mean change in public-investment-to-GDP ratio (percentage points)	2.68
Public investment shock = 0	
Number of observations	3804
Mean real GDP growth (percent)	3.79
Mean public investment (percent of GDP)	6.76
Mean change in public-investment-to-GDP ratio (percentage points)	-0.43

Source: World Bank.

Note: Summary statistics for the sample of 129 EMDEs used in the estimation of public investment multipliers, differentiating between periods with and without public investment shocks.

TABLE A3.2.3 Definitions of data used and sources

Variable	Definition	Source
Real public investment	General government investment (gross fixed capital formation) in billions of national currency deflated using the GDP deflator	Investment and Capital Stock Dataset (IMF 2021a)
Real private investment	Private investment (gross fixed capital formation), in billions of national currency deflated using the GDP deflator	Investment and Capital Stock Dataset (IMF 2021a)
Real GDP	Gross domestic product, in billions of national currency deflated using the GDP deflator	IMF World Economic Outlook Database
Potential GDP	Index derived from real potential output growth estimated using the production function approach	Potential growth database (Kilic Celik et al. 2023)
Inflation	Growth rate of consumer price index, in percent	IMF World Economic Outlook Database
Labor productivity	Real GDP per average annual hours worked by persons engaged	Penn World Table 10.01
Total factor productivity	Total factor productivity in constant national prices (2017 = 1)	Penn World Table 10.01
Public debt	General government debt, percent of GDP	World Bank's Fiscal Space Database (Kose et al. 2022)
Public infrastructure efficiency index (IMF 2021b)	Public infrastructure efficiency index constructed based on the data envelopment analysis using the volume and quality of infrastructure as output, and public capital stock and per capita GDP as input variables	IMF (2021b)
Public infrastructure efficiency index (Devadas and Pennings 2018)	Infrastructure efficiency index constructed as a weighted average of the quality of electricity, water, and road infrastructure	Devadas and Pennings (2018)
Public investment management index (PIMI)	Index based on country performance scores in public investment project appraisal, selection, implementation, and evaluation	Dabla-Norris et al. (2012)
Public capital stock	General government capital stock, percent of GDP	Investment and Capital Stock Dataset (IMF 2021a)

Source: World Bank.

TABLE A3.2.4 Selected additional results and robustness checks

Model	Public investment multiplier	
	t = 1	*t = 5*
Baseline specification	0.4***	1.1***
IV (2SLS) estimation using public investment shocks to instrument public investment	0.4***	1.0***
GMM estimation	0.5**	0.8**
Dropping country fixed effects	0.4***	1.5***
Dropping lagged real GDP growth variable	0.3**	1.1***
Pre-global financial crisis period only (1980-2007)	0.3*	0.9***
Additional control variables: two lags of inflation and trade-to-GDP ratio	0.4**	1.1***
Alternative fiscal space specification		
Large increase in debt-to-GDP ratio (upper quartile = above 3.7)	0.3	0.7
Large decrease in debt-to-GDP ratio (lower quartile = below -3.2)	0.5*	1.4***
Alternative public investment efficiency measures		
Low efficiency: Dabla-Norris et al. (2012) PIMI below the sample mean	0.1	0.9
High efficiency: Dabla-Norris et al. (2012) PIMI above the sample mean	0.4***	1.2***
Low efficiency: Bottom quartile of Devadas and Pennings (2018) Infrastructure Efficiency index	0.2	0.3
High efficiency: Top quartile of Devadas and Pennings (2018) Infrastructure Efficiency index	0.2*	1.0***
Low efficiency: Bottom quartile of CPIA Public Sector Management and Institutions index	0.3	0.6
High efficiency: Top quartile of CPIA Public Sector Management and Institutions index	0.4**	1.1***

Source: World Bank.
Note: 2SLS = two-stage least squares; CPIA = Country Policy and Institutional Assessment; GMM = generalized method of moments; IV = instrumental variables approach; PIMI = Public Investment Management Index. The table shows responses of real GDP (cumulative change in year t relative to year $t = -1$, in percent) to a public investment shock equivalent to one percent of GDP; $t = 0$ is the year of the shock. ***, **, and * indicate statistical significance at the 1, 5, and 10 percent levels, respectively.

References

Abiad, A., D. Furceri, and P. Topalova. 2016. "The Macroeconomic Effects of Public Investment: Evidence from Advanced Economies." *Journal of Macroeconomics* 50: 224-40.

Adam, C., and D. Bevan. 2006. "Aid and the Supply Side: Public Investment, Export Performance, and Dutch Disease in Low-Income Countries." *The World Bank Economic Review* 20 (2): 261-90.

Adarov, A., M. Chinn, H. Ito, and K. Stamm. Forthcoming. "Investment Trends, Structure, and Patterns." In *Promoting Investment Growth*, edited by A. Adarov. Washington, DC: World Bank.

Adarov, A., B. Clements, and J. T. Jalles. Forthcoming. "Growth Effects of Public Investment and Public Consumption: The Role of the Business Cycle, Fiscal Space, and Efficiency." Forthcoming.

Afonso, A., and J. Alves. 2023. "Does Government Spending Efficiency Improve Fiscal Sustainability?" *European Journal of Political Economy*, 102403.

Agenor, R. 2010. "A Theory of Infrastructure-Led Development." *Journal of Economics Dynamics and Control* 34 (5): 932-50.

Alesina, A., and S. Ardagna, 2010. "Large Changes in Fiscal Policy: Taxes versus Spending." In J. Brown (ed.), Tax Policy and the Economy (University of Chicago Press), 24.

Alesina, A., S. Ardagna, and J. Galí. 1998. "Tales of Fiscal Adjustment." *Economic Policy* 13 (27): 489-545.

Amaglobeli, D., R. de Mooij, A. Mengistu, M. Manabu Nose, et al. 2023. "Transforming Public Finance Through GovTech." IMF Staff Discussion Note, SDN/2023/04.

Arewa, M., and S. Davenport. 2022. "The Tax and Technology Challenge." In *Innovations in Tax Compliance: Building Trust, Navigating Politics, and Tailoring Reform*, edited by R. Dom, A. Custers, S. Davenport, and W. Prichard, 171-204. Washington, DC: World Bank.

Arezki, R., P. Bolton, S. Peters, F. Samama, and J. Stiglitz. 2017. "From Global Savings Glut to Financing Infrastructure." *Economic Policy* 32 (90): 221-61.

Arezki, R., and A. Sy. 2016. "Financing Africa's Infrastructure Deficit: From Development Banking to Long-term Investing." *Journal of African Economies* 25 (suppl_2): ii59-ii73.

Arlinghaus, J., and K. van Dender. 2017. "The Environmental Tax and Subsidy Reform in Mexico." OECD Taxation Working Paper 31, OECD Publishing, Paris.

Arslanalp, A., B. Eichengreen, and P. Blair Henry. 2024. "Sustained debt reduction: The Jamaica exception" Paper presented to the Spring 2024 edition of the Brookings Papers on Economic Activity, Washington DC.

Aschauer, D. 1989a. "Does Public Capital Crowd Out Private Capital?" *Journal of Monetary Economics* 24 (2): 171-88.

Aschauer, D. 1989b. "Is Public Expenditure Productive?" *Journal of Monetary Economics* 23 (2): 177-200.

Asian Development Bank. 2017. *Meeting Asia's Infrastructure Needs.* Manila: Asian Development Bank.

Auerbach, A. J., and Y. Gorodnichenko. 2012. "Measuring the Output Responses to Fiscal Policy." *American Economic Journal: Economic Policy* 4 (2): 1-27.

Auerbach, A. J., and Y. Gorodnichenko. 2013. "Fiscal Multipliers in Recession and Expansion." In Fiscal Policy after the Financial Crisis, edited by A. Alesina and F. Giavazzi, 63-102. Chicago: University of Chicago Press.

Barro, R. J. 1981. "Output Effects of Government Purchases." *Journal of Political Economy* 89 (December): 1086-1121.

Barro, R. J. 1990. "Government Spending in a Simple Model of Endogenous Growth." *Journal of Political Economy* 95: 103-26.

Barro, R., and X. Sala-I-Martin. 1992. "Public Finance in Models of Economic Growth." *The Review of Economic Studies* 59 (4): 645-61.

Barry, M., C. Chen, K. Kalonji, M. Sow, M. MacDonald, D. P. Tchakoté, and J. Jellema. 2018. Cameroon Country Report (No. 18/256). International Monetary Fund, Washington, DC.

Batini, N., L. Eyraud, A. Weber, and L. Forni. 2014. "Fiscal Multipliers: Size, Determinants, and Use in Macroeconomic Projections." IMF Technical Notes and Manuals 2014/004, International Monetary Fund, Washington, DC.

Berg, A., J. Gottschalk, R. Portillo, and L. Zanna. 2010. "The Macroeconomics of Medium-Term Aid Scaling-Up Scenarios." IMF Working Paper 10/160, International Monetary Fund, Washington, DC.

Berg, A., R. A. Portillo, E. F Buffie, C. A. Pattillo, and L. Zanna. 2012. "Public Investment, Growth, and Debt Sustainability: Putting Together the Pieces Together." IMF Working Papers 2012/144, International Monetary Fund, Washington, DC.

Berg, A., Portillo, R., and S. C. Yang, 2013. "Public Investment in Resource-Abundant Developing Countries." *IMF Economic Review* 61: 92-129.

Besley, T., and T. Persson. 2014. "Why Do Developing Countries Tax So Little?" *Journal of Economic Perspectives* 28 (4): 99-120.

Bird, R. M., J. Martinez-Vazquez, and B. Torgler. 2008. "Tax Effort in Developing Countries and High Income Countries: The Impact of Corruption, Voice and Accountability." *Economic Analysis and Policy* 38 (1): 55-71.

Blanchard, O. J., and R. Perotti. 2002. "An Empirical Characterization of the Dynamic Effects of Changes in Government Spending and Taxes on Output." *Quarterly Journal of Economics* 117 (4): 1329-68.

Blanchard, O. J. 1990. "Comment: can severe fiscal contractions be expansionary? Tales of two small European countries." *NBER Macroeconomics Annual 1990* , 5 : 111-16.

Bom, P., and J. Ligthart. 2014a. "Public Infrastructure Investment, Output Dynamics, and Balanced Budget Fiscal Rules." *Journal of Economic Dynamics and Control* 40: 334-54.

Bom, P., and J. Ligthart. 2014b. "What Have we Learnt from Three Decades of Research on the Productivity of Public Capital?" *Journal of Economic Surveys* 28 (5): 889-916.

Bonaglia, F., R. Della Croce, M. Moseley, F. R. Nunez. 2015. "Risk and Return Characteristics of Infrastructure Investment In Low-Income Countries." 4th Meeting of the G20 Development Working Group, 14-16 September 2015, Antalya, Türkiye.

Caggiano, G., E. Castelnuovo, V. Colombo, and G. Nodari. 2015. "Estimating Fiscal Multipliers: News from a Nonlinear World." *Economics Journal* 125 (584): 746-76.

Canning, D., and P. Pedroni. 2008. "Infrastructure, Long-Run Economic Growth and Causality Tests for Cointegrated Panels." *The Manchester School* 76 (5): 504-27.

Cavallo, E., and C. Daude. 2011. "Public Investment in Developing Countries: A Blessing or a Curse?" *Journal of Comparative Economics* 39: 65-81.

Chakraborty, S., and E. Dabla-Norris. 2011. "The Quality of Public Investment." *The B.E. Journal of Macroeconomics* 11 (1): 1-29.

Chrimes, T., B. Gootjes, M.A. Kose, and C. Wheeler. 2024. *The Great Reversal: Prospects, Risks, and Policies in International Development Association (IDA) Countries.* Washington, DC: World Bank.

Christiano, L., M. Eichenbaum, and S. Rebelo, 2011. "When Is the Government Spending Multiplier Large?" *Journal of Political Economy* 119 (1): 78-121.

Colombo, E., D. Furceri, P. Pizzuto, and P. Tirelli. 2022. "Fiscal Multipliers and Informality." IMF Working Paper No. 2022/082, International Monetary Fund, Washington, DC.

Corsetti, G., K. Kuester, A. Meier, and G. J. Müller. 2013. "Sovereign Risk, Fiscal Policy, and Macroeconomic Stability." *Economic Journal* 123 (566): F99-F132.

Dabla-Norris, E., J. Brumby, A. Kyobe, et al. 2012. "Investing in Public Investment: an Index of Public Investment Efficiency." *Journal of Economic Growth* 17: 235-66.

Damania, R., E. Balseca, C. De Fontaubert, et al. 2023. *Detox Development: Repurposing Environmentally Harmful Subsidies.* World Bank, Washington, DC.

David, A. 2017. "Fiscal Policy Effectiveness in a Small Open Economy: Estimates of Tax and Spending Multipliers in Paraguay." IMF Working Paper, WP/17/16, International Monetary Fund, Washington, DC.

Davoodi, H., and V. Tanzi. 1998. "Roads to Nowhere: How Corruption in Public Investment Hurts Growth." Economic Issues Series, number 12. International Monetary Fund, Washington, DC.

De Haan, J., and J. Klomp. 2013. "Conditional Political Budget Cycles: A Review of Recent Evidence." *Public Choice* 157: 387-410.

De Haan, J., and R. Wiese. 2022. "The Impact of Product and Labour Market Reform on Growth: Evidence for OECD Countries Based on Local

Projections." *Journal of Applied Econometrics* 37 (4): 746-70.

Deleidi, M., F. Iafrate, and E. S. Levrero. 2020. "Public Investment Fiscal Multipliers: An Empirical Assessment for European Countries." *Structural Change and Economic Dynamics* 52: 354-65.

Demetriades, P. O., and T. P. Mamuneas. 2000. "Intertemporal Output and Employment Effects of Public Infrastructure Capital: Evidence from 12 OECD Economies." *Economic Journal* 110 (465): 687-712.

Devadas, S., and S. Pennings. 2018. "Assessing the Effect of Public Capital on Growth: An Extension of the World Bank Long-Term Growth Model." Policy Research Working Paper WPS 8604, World Bank Group, Washington, DC.

Devarajan, S., V. Swaroop, and H. Zou. 1996. "The Composition of Public Expenditure and Economic Growth." *Journal of Monetary Economic* 37 (2): 313-44.

Dom, R., A. Custers, S. Davenport, and W. Prichard. 2022. "Innovations in Tax Compliance: Building Trust, Navigating Politics, and Tailoring Reform." World Bank, Washington, DC.

Eden, M., and A. Kraay. 2014. ""Crowding in" and the Returns to Government Investment in Low-Income Countries." Policy Research Working Paper Series 6781, The World Bank, Washington, DC.

Elkhdari, M., M. Souissi, and M. A. Jewell. 2018. "Empirical Estimation of Fiscal Multipliers in MENA Oil-Exporting Countries with an Application to Algeria." IMF Working Papers 2018/124, International Monetary Fund, Washington, DC.

EM-DAT (database). The International Disaster Database. https://www.emdat.be

Engel, E., R. Fischer, and A. Galetovic. 2013. "The Basic Public Finance of Public-Private Partnerships." *Journal of the European Economic Association* 11 (1): 83-111.

Engel, E., R. Fischer, and A. Galetovic. 2014. *The Economics of Public-Private Partnerships: A Basic Guide.* Cambridge University Press.

Erenburg, S. J., and M. E. Wohar. 1995. "Public and Private Investment: Are There Causal Linkages?" *Journal of Macroeconomics* 17 (1): 1-30.

Espinoza, R. A., and A. S. Senhadji. 2011. "How Strong are Fiscal Multipliers in the GCC? An Empirical Investigation." IMF Working Paper, WP/11/16. International Monetary Fund, Washington, DC.

Eyraud, H. D., A. Peralta, et al. 2021. "Private Finance for Development: Wishful Thinking or Thinking Out of the Box?" IMF Departmental Paper No 2021/011. International Monetary Fund, Washington, DC.

Fabre, A., and S. Straub. 2023. "The Impact of Public Private Partnerships (PPPs) in Infrastructure, Health and Education." *Journal of Economic Literature* 61 (2): 655-715.

Farole, T., and D. Winkler, eds. 2014. *Making Foreign Direct Investment Work for Sub-Saharan Africa: Local Spillovers and Competitiveness in Global Value Chains. Directions in Development.* Washington, DC: World Bank.

Fay, M., H. Lee, M. Mastruzzi, S. Han, and M. Cho. 2019b. "Hitting the Trillion Mark—A Look at How Much Countries Are Spending on Infrastructure." Policy Research Working Paper Series 8730, The World Bank, Washington, DC.

Fay, M., D. Martimort, and S. Straub. 2019a. "Funding and Financing Infrastructure: The Joint-Use of Public and Private Finance." *Journal of Development Economics* 150, 102629.

Feenstra, R. C., R. Inklaar, and M. P. Timmer. 2015. "The Next Generation of the Penn World Table." *American Economic Review* 105 (10): 3150-82.

Foster, V., N. Gorgulu, D. Jain, S. Straub, and M. Vagliasindi. 2023. "The Impact of Infrastructure on Development Outcomes: A Meta-Analysis." Policy Research Working Paper Series 10350, The World Bank, Washington, DC.

Furceri, D., and B. Li. 2017. "The Macroeconomic (and Distributional) Effects of Public Investment in Developing Economies." IMF Working Paper 17/217, Washington, DC.

Futagami, K., Y. Morita, and A. Shibata. 1993. "Dynamic Analysis of an Endogenous Growth Model with Public Capital." *The Scandinavian Journal of Economics* 95 (4): 607-25.

Flyvbjerg, B., M. K. Skamris Holm, and S. L. Buhl. 2004. "What Causes Cost Overrun in Transport Infrastructure Projects?" *Transport Reviews* 24 (1): 3-18.

Forni, M., and L. Gambetti. 2010. "Fiscal Foresight and the Effects of Government Spending." CEPR Discussion Paper, 049.

G20 (Group of Twenty)-IEG (Independent Expert Group). 2023. *The Triple Agenda: A Roadmap for Better, Bolder, and Bigger MDBs.* Report of the Independent Expert Group.

G20 (Group of Twenty)-IEG (Independent Expert Group). 2024. *Implementing MDB Reforms: A Stocktake.* Report of the Independent Expert Group.

Gbohoui, W. 2021. "Uncertainty and Public Investment Multipliers: The Role of Economic Confidence." IMF Working Papers 2021/272, International Monetary Fund, Washington, DC.

Gechert, S., and A. Rannenberg. 2018. "Which Fiscal Multipliers are Regime-Dependent? A meta-regression analysis." *Journal of Economic Surveys* 32: 1160-82.

Ghassibe, M., and F. Zanetti. 2022. "State Dependence of Fiscal Multipliers: the Source of Fluctuations Matters." *Journal of Monetary Economics* 132: 1-23.

Gill, I. S., I. Izvorski, W. van Eeghen, and D. De Rosa. 2014. *Diversified Development: Making the Most of Natural Resources in Eurasia.* Washington, DC: World Bank.

Glomm, G., and B. Ravikumar. 1994. "Public Investment in Infrastructure in a Simple Growth Model." *Journal of Economic Dynamics and Control* 18 (6): 1173-87.

Gonzales-Garcia, J., A. Lemus, and M. Mrkaic, 2013. "Fiscal Multipliers in the ECCU," IMF Working Paper No. 2013/117. International Monetary Fund, Washington, DC.

Granger, C. W. J., and T. Terasvirta. 1993. "Modeling Nonlinear Economic Relationships." New York: Oxford University Press.

Guerguil, M., P. Mandon, and R. Tapsoba. 2017. "Flexible Fiscal Rules and Countercyclical Fiscal Policy." *Journal of Macroeconomics* 52: 189-220.

Gupta, S., A. Kangur, C. Papageorgiou, and A. Wane. 2014. "Efficiency-Adjusted Public Capital and Growth." *World Development* 57: 164-78.

Gupta, S., M. Keen, A. Shah, and G. Verdier eds. 2017. *Digital Revolutions in Public Finance.* USA: International Monetary Fund.

Hallegatte, S., C. Brandon, R. Damania, Y. Lang, J. Roome, J. Rozenberg, and A. Tall. 2018. "The Economics (and Obstacles to) Aligning Development and Climate Change Adaptation: A World Bank Contribution to the Global Commission on Adaptation." Discussion Paper, Global Commission on Adaptation, Rotterdam, Netherlands.

Hamilton, J. D. 2018. "Why You Should Never Use the Hodrick-Prescott Filter." *The Review of Economics and Statistics* 100 (5): 831-43.

Herrera, M., V. Foster, A. Musacchio, T. Ter-Minassian, and B. Turkgulu. 2023. *Off the Books: Understanding and Mitigating the Fiscal Risks of Infrastructure.* Washington, DC: World Bank.

Huidrom, R., M. A. Kose, J. Lim, and F. Ohnsorge. 2020. "Why Do Fiscal Multipliers Depend on Fiscal Positions?" *Journal of Monetary Economics* 114 (1): 109-25.

Honda, J., H. Miyamoto, and M. Taniguchi. 2020. "Exploring the Output Effect of Fiscal Policy Shocks in Low Income Countries." IMF Working Papers 2020/012, International Monetary Fund, Washington, DC.

Ilzetzki, E., E. G. Mendoza, and C. A. Végh. 2013 "How Big (Small?) are Fiscal Multipliers?" *Journal of Monetary Economics*, 60 (2): 239-254.

IDA (International Development Association). 2024. *Financing the Future: IDA's Role In The Evolving Global Aid Architecture.* Development Finance, the World Bank Group. Washington, DC.

IEG (Independent Evaluation Group). 2021. *World Bank Support for Public Financial and Debt Management in IDA-Eligible Countries.* World Bank Publications—Books. The World Bank Group, 35361.

IMF (International Monetary Fund). 2014. *World Economic Outlook, October 2014: Legacies, Clouds, Uncertainties."* International Monetary Fund, Washington, DC.

IMF (International Monetary Fund). 2018. "Public Investment Management Assessment Review and Update." May. International Monetary Fund, Washington, DC.

IMF (International Monetary Fund). 2021a. "Investment and Capital Stock Dataset." Macroeconomic and Financial Data, International Monetary Fund, Washington, DC. https://data.imf.org/?sk=1ce8a55f-cfa7-4bc0-bce2-256ee65ac0e4

IMF (International Monetary Fund). 2021b. *Fiscal Monitor, April 2021: A Fair Shot.* International Monetary Fund, Washington, DC.

IMF (International Monetary Fund). 2023. Poland. Technical Assistance Report—Public Investment Management Assessment. IMF Country Report No. 22/321. International Monetary Fund, Washington, DC.

IPCC (Intergovernmental Panel on Climate Change). 2022. "Climate Change 2022: Mitigation of Climate Change." IPCC Sixth Assessment Report. Cambridge, U.K., and New York: Cambridge University Press.

Izquierdo, A., R. E. Lama, J. Medina, J. P. Puig, D. Riera-Crichton, C. Vegh, and G. Vuletin. 2019. "Is the Public Investment Multiplier Higher in Developing Countries? An Empirical Investigation." NBER Working Papers 26478.

Jong-A-Pin, R., and J. de Haan, 2008. "Time-varying Impact of Public Capital on Output: New evidence based on VARs for OECD countries." EIB Papers 3/2008.

Jordà, O. 2005. "Estimation and Inference of Impulse Responses by Local Projections." *American Economic Review* 95: 161-82.

Kilic Celik, S., M. A. Kose, F. Ohnsorge, and F. U. Ruch. 2023. "Potential Growth: A Global Database." Policy Research Working Paper 10354, World Bank, Washington, DC.

Kim, J. H., J. A. Fallov, and S. Groom. 2020. *Public Investment Management Reference Guide.* Washington, DC: World Bank.

Koh, W. C. 2017. "Fiscal Multipliers: New Evidence from a Large Panel of Countries." *Oxford Economic Papers* 69 (3): 569-90.

Kose, A. M., S. Kurlat, F. Ohnsorge, and N. Sugawara. 2022. "A Cross-Country Database of Fiscal Space." *Journal of International Money and Finance*, 128, 102682.

Kose, A. M., P. Nagle, F. Ohnsorge, and N. Sugawara. 2021. *Global Waves of Debt: Causes and Consequences.* Washington, DC: World Bank.

Kose, A. M., and F. Ohnsorge, eds. 2024. *Falling Long-Term Growth Prospects: Trends, Expectations, and Policies.* Washington, DC: World Bank.

Kose, A. M., Sugawara, N., and M. E. Terrones. 2020. "Global Recessions." Policy Research Working Paper No. 9172. World Bank, Washington, DC.

Kraay, A. 2012. "How Large Is the Government Spending Multiplier? Evidence from World Bank Lending." *The Quarterly Journal of Economics* 127 (2): 829-87.

Kraay, A. 2014. "Government Spending Multipliers in Developing Countries: Evidence from Lending by Official Creditors." *American Economic Journal: Macroeconomics* 6 (4): 170-208.

Laeven, L., and F. Valencia. 2018. "Systemic Banking Crises Revisited." IMF Working Paper No. 18/206, International Monetary Fund, Washington, DC.

Laeven, L., and F. Valencia. 2020. "Systemic Banking Crises Database II." *IMF Economic Review* 68 (2): 307-61. Palgrave Macmillan; Washington, DC: International Monetary Fund.

Leduc, S., and D. Wilson. 2012. "Roads to Prosperity or Bridges to Nowhere? Theory and Evidence on the Impact of Public Infrastructure Investment." NBER Working Papers 18042.

Leeper, E. M., A. W. Richter, and T. B. Walker. 2012. "Quantitative Effects of Fiscal Foresight." *American Economic Journal: Economic Policy* 4 (2): 115-44.

Leeper, E. M., T. B. Walker, and S. Yang. 2013. "Fiscal Foresight and Information Flows." *Econometrica* 81 (3): 1115-45.

Leeper, E., T. Walker, and S. Yang. 2010. "Government Investment and Fiscal Stimulus." *Journal of Monetary Economics* 57: 1000-12.

Martinez, L., F. Roch, F. Roldán, and J. Zettelmeyer. 2023. "Sovereign Debt." In *Research Handbook of Financial Markets,* edited by R. S. Gürkaynak and J. H. Wright. 378-405. Northampton, MA: Edward Elgar Publishing.

Mazzucato, M., and G. Semieniuk. 2017. "Public Financing of Innovation: New Questions." *Oxford Review of Economic Policy* 33 (1): 24-48.

Minea, A., and L. Mustea. 2015. "A Fresh Look at Fiscal Multipliers: One Size Fits it All? Evidence from the Mediterranean Area." *Applied Economics* 47 (26): 2728-44.

Miyamoto, H., et al. 2020. "Growth Impact of Public Investment and the Role of Infrastructure Governance." In *Well Spent,* edited by Schwartz, F. et al. Washington, DC: International Monetary Fund.

OECD (Organisation for Economic Co-operation and Development). 2017. "Getting Infrastructure Right: A Framework for Better Governance." Paris: OECD.

Parry, I., S. Black, and N. Vernon. 2021. "Still Not Getting Energy Prices Right: A Global and Country Update of Fossil Fuel Subsidies." IMF Working Paper No. 21/236, International Monetary Fund, Washington, DC.

Petrović, P., M. Arsić, and A. Nojković. 2021. "Increasing Public Investment Can be an Effective

Policy in Bad Times: Evidence from Emerging EU Economies." *Economic Modelling* 94: 580-97.

Plagborg-Møller, M., and C. K. Wolf. 2021. "Local Projections and VARs Estimate the Same Impulse Responses." *Econometrica* 89: 955-80.

Pritchett, L. 2000. "The Tyranny of Concepts: CUDIE (Cumulated, Depreciated, Investment Effort) is Not Capital." *Journal of Economic Growth* 5(4): 361-84.

Puig, J. 2014. "Multiplicador del Gasto Público en Argentina." *Económica* 60 (2014): 188-210.

Rafiq, S., and A. Zeufack. 2012. "Fiscal Multipliers over the Growth Cycle: Evidence from Malaysia." World Bank Policy Research Working Paper, 5982. World Bank, Washington, DC.

Rajaram, A., K. Kaiser, T. M. Le, J. H. Kim, and J. Frank, eds. 2014. *The Power of Public Investment Management: Transforming Resources into Assets for Growth.* Washington, DC: World Bank.

Ramey, V. A. 2011a. "Can Government Purchases Stimulate the Economy?" *Journal of Economic Literature*, 49 (3): 673-85.

Ramey, V. A. 2011b. "Identifying Government Spending Shocks: It's All in the Timing." *Quarterly Journal of Economics*, 126 (1): 51-102.

Ramey, V. A. 2019. "Ten Years after the Financial Crisis: What Have We Learned from the Renaissance in Fiscal Research?" *Journal of Economic Perspectives* 33 (2): 89-114.

Ramey, V. A. 2021. "The Macroeconomic Consequences of Infrastructure Investment." In *Economic Analysis and Infrastructure Investment*, edited by Glaeser E. L., and J. M. Poterba, 219-76, Chicago: University of Chicago Press.

Ramey, V. A., and M. D. Shapiro. 1998. "Costly Capital Reallocation and the Effects of Government Spending," in Carnegie-Rochester Conference Series on Public Policy 48: 145-94.

Ramey, V. A., and S. Zubairy. 2018. "Government Spending Multipliers in Good Times and in Bad: Evidence from US Historical Data." *Journal of Political Economy* 126 (2): 850-901.

Reinhart, C. M., and K. S. Rogoff. 2011. "From Financial Crash to Debt Crisis." *American Economic Review* 101 (5): 1676-1706.

Riera-Crichton, D., C. A. Vegh, and G. Vuletin. 2015. "Procyclical and Countercyclical Fiscal Multipliers: Evidence from OECD Countries." *Journal of International Money and Finance* 52(C): 15-31.

Romer, C. D., and D. H. Romer. 2010. "The Macroeconomic Effects of Tax Changes: Estimates Based on a New Measure of Fiscal Shocks." *American Economic Review* 100 (3): 763-801.

Romp, W. E., and J. de Haan. 2005. "Public Capital and Economic Growth: A Critical Survey." European Investment Bank (EIB) Papers, Luxembourg 10 (1): 41-70.

Rozenberg, J., and M. Fay, eds. 2019. *Beyond the Gap: How Countries Can Afford the Infrastructure They Need While Protecting the Planet.* Washington, DC: World Bank.

Schwartz, G., M. Fouad, T. Hansen, and G. Verdier, eds. 2020. *Well Spent: How Strong Infrastructure Governance Can End Waste in Public Investment.* Washington, DC: International Monetary Fund.

Straub, S. 2011. "Infrastructure and Development: A Critical Appraisal of the Macro-level Literature" *The Journal of Development Studies* 47(5): 683-708.

Sutherland, A. 1997. "Fiscal Crises and Aggregate Demand: Can High Public Debt Reverse the Effects of Fiscal Policy?" *Journal of Public Economics* 65: 147-62.

Teulings, C. N., and N. Zubanov. 2014. "Is Economic Recovery a Myth? Robust Estimation of Impulse Responses." *Journal of Applied Econometrics* 29 (3): 497-514.

Turnovsky, S. 1997. "Fiscal Policy in a Growing Economy with Public Capital." *Macroeconomic Dynamics* 1 (3): 615-39.

Turnovsky, S. 2015. "Economic Growth and Inequality: The Role of Public Investment." *Journal of Economic Dynamics and Control* 61: 204-21.

UNCTAD (United Nations Conference for Trade and Development). 2022. *ASYCUDA Compendium 2022: Digital connectivity.*

UNEP (United Nations Environment Programme). 2022. *State of Finance for Nature. Time to Act: Doubling Investment by 2025 and Eliminating Nature-Negative Finance Flows.* Nairobi: United Nations Environment Programme.

Vagliasindi, M., and N. Gorgulu. 2021. "What Have We Learned about the Effectiveness of Infrastructure Investment as a Fiscal Stimulus? A Literature Review." Policy Research Working Paper Series 9796, The World Bank.

Vorisek, D., and S. Yu. 2020. "Understanding the Cost of Achieving the Sustainable Development Goals." Policy Research Working Paper 9146, World Bank, Washington, DC.

Warner, A. 2014. "Public Investment as an Engine of Growth." IMF Working Paper 14/148, International Monetary Fund, Washington, DC.

Waseem, M. 2018. "Taxes, Informality and Income Shifting: Evidence from A Recent Pakistani Tax Reform." *Journal of Public Economics* 157: 41-77.

Wiese, R., R. Jong-A-Pin, and J. de Haan. 2018. "Can Successful Fiscal Adjustments only be Achieved by Spending Cuts?" *European Journal of Political Economy* 54 (C): 145-66.

World Bank. 2020. "Enhancing Government Effectiveness and Transparency: The Fight Against Corruption." Washington, DC: World Bank.

World Bank. 2021. "World Bank Support for Public Financial and Debt Management in IDA-Eligible Countries." Independent Evaluation Group. Washington, DC: World Bank.

World Bank. 2022. *Global Economic Prospects.* January. Washington, DC: World Bank.

World Bank. 2023a. *Global Economic Prospects.* January. Washington, DC: World Bank.

World Bank. 2023b. "World Bank Support for Domestic Revenue Mobilization: An Independent Evaluation." Independent Evaluation Group. Washington, DC: World Bank.

World Bank. 2023c. *Unfair Advantage: Distortive Subsidies and Their Effects on Global Trade.* Washington, DC: World Bank.

World Bank. 2024. *Global Economic Prospects.* January. Washington, DC: World Bank.

World Bank—WDI (World Development Indicators) database. "World Development Indicators." https://databank.worldbank.org/source/world-development-indicators

Zachmann, G., E. Calthrop, A.-D. Riess, and A. Kolev. 2012. *Investment and Growth in the Time of Climate Change.* Brussels, Belgium: Bruegel.

CHAPTER 4

FISCAL CHALLENGES IN SMALL STATES

Weathering Storms, Rebuilding Resilience

The COVID-19 pandemic and the global shocks that followed have worsened fiscal and debt positions in small states, intensifying their already substantial fiscal challenges—especially the need to manage more frequent climate change-related natural disasters. Forty percent of the 35 emerging market and developing economies (EMDEs) that are small states are at high risk of debt distress or already in it, roughly twice the share for other EMDEs. Larger fiscal deficits since the pandemic reflect increased spending to support households and firms, and weaker revenues. To improve their fiscal sustainability and resilience to future shocks, small states need to strike a balance between maintaining adequate fiscal buffers and increasing investments in human capital and climate change-resilient infrastructure. Comprehensive fiscal reforms are essential. First, small states' revenues, which are highly volatile and dependent on sometimes unreliable sources, should be drawn from a more stable and secure tax base. Second, spending efficiency needs to be improved, especially on transfers to public enterprises, subsidies, and the public wage bill. Third, these changes should be complemented by reforms to fiscal frameworks, including better utilization of fiscal rules and sovereign wealth funds. Finally, to help these countries stay on sustainable fiscal paths, well-coordinated and targeted global policies are also needed. Policies supported by the global community can help improve fiscal policy management, provide technical assistance, address debt challenges, and bolster funding for small states to invest in climate change resilience and adaptation, and other priority areas.

Introduction

The pandemic and subsequent global shocks hit small states—those with a population of around 1.5 million or less—particularly hard (World Bank 2023a). Small states experienced some of the deepest contractions and slowest recoveries of all emerging market and developing economies (EMDEs). Governments appropriately implemented wide-ranging and often large spending measures to support firms and households. These, together with weaker revenue, led to a substantial widening of fiscal deficits, adding to already high and rising levels of public debt.

These developments are especially troubling against the backdrop of significant longstanding development and fiscal policy challenges (figure 4.1; World Bank 2023a). Since 2000, annual growth of GDP per capita in small states has on average been 2.6 percentage points slower than in other EMDEs and barely kept pace with advanced economies. Recent fiscal consolidation efforts have helped narrow deficits in some cases. Yet in many small states fiscal positions remain precarious, increasing risks to fiscal sustainability. This chapter therefore examines fiscal policy challenges in the context of developments before and since the onset of the pandemic.

Small states, located in every World Bank region of the world and with sometimes large exclusive economic zones that span vast areas of the world's oceans, are highly heterogenous, comprising a mix of high- and middle-income countries as well as some fragile and conflict-affected situations (table 4.1). However, the fiscal challenges they face reflect important common underlying vulnerabilities that raise their exposure to adverse exogenous shocks (UNCTAD 2022; World Bank 2023a). Trade openness is much higher in small states than other EMDEs, while economic activity, including exports, is highly concentrated in a few sectors of comparative advantage. High openness and lack of diversification leave the fortunes of small state economies dependent on developments in key sectors—notably tourism and some commodity sectors—resulting in higher output volatility than in other EMDEs (Briguglio and Vella 2018).

The experience of small states during the pandemic underscores their structural vulnerabilities. Tourism, which accounts for higher shares of economic activity and export earnings than in other EMDEs, was devastated. Some small states, moreover, rely heavily on exports of a narrow range of commodities such as oil and gas, the prices of which plummeted in 2020. Many small states also rely on remittances for much of their external income, but these were severely affected by pandemic-related restrictions on international labor mobility and the decline in demand for

Note: This chapter was prepared by Samuel Hill and Jeetendra Khadan.

labor in host economies. Advanced economies and many EMDEs experienced robust recoveries as the global recovery took hold. For small states, however, the economic and fiscal consequences have endured.

Many small states are tropical islands, which are highly vulnerable to costly natural disasters, particularly storms and other weather-related events that have become more frequent with climate change (Heinen, Khadan, and Strobl 2019). As a result, small states face substantial climate change adaptation challenges that are compounded by a lack of resources to invest in resilient infrastructure (Jafino et al. 2020; UNEP 2023; World Bank forthcoming). Small states also face the risk of a sustained deterioration in productive capacity. Some of them face existential threats from rising sea levels and coastal erosion—particularly those with predominately low-lying areas such as Kiribati, Maldives, the Marshall Islands, and Tuvalu (Vousdoukas et al. 2023).

Greater economic volatility brings adverse fiscal consequences, including more volatile and less predictable revenues and expenditures (Hnatkovska and Köhler-Geib 2018). Narrow tax bases and high dependence on other, less stable forms of revenue—notably various types of sovereign rents and external grants—amplify the challenge of revenue volatility. With limited fiscal buffers and opportunities to borrow, spending can be sensitive to revenue swings, and prone to booms and busts. Fiscal space can deteriorate rapidly in response to large external shocks, leading to procyclical fiscal policy.

Government spending, relative to GDP, is on average much higher in small states than in other EMDEs, irrespective of income group. Government operations in small states suffer from diseconomies of scale, which increase the costs of providing public goods and services. This is exacerbated by the higher costs of supporting dispersed populations, including small communities located far away from major centers and separated by significant expanses of sea or land. A reliance on imported goods, which are typically more expensive because of the remoteness of small states, adds to input costs. Geographic dispersion and remoteness are negatively associated with public spending efficiency (World Bank 2023b). Moreover, with limited private sector activity, governments often need to provide a wider range of services, including through state-owned enterprises (SOEs)—and at subsidized prices—putting further upward pressure on public spending (Dornan et al. 2013; Reyes-Tagle et al. 2022).

Reflecting their substantial development challenges, small states face significant additional spending pressures to meet Sustainable Development Goals (SDGs; Tiedemann et al. 2021). Their limited institutional capacity, human capital, and sometimes underutilization of technology exacerbate the challenges of fiscal management (Schwartz and Beuermann 2021). They can make the provision of government goods and services more inefficient and more expensive, and encumber the collection of taxes and other revenues. Inadequate resources can also add to challenges with fiscal planning and execution.

After the significant deterioration in the debt sustainability of small states in recent years, the need to strengthen fiscal policy is now perhaps the most important economic challenge they face. Forty percent (14) of the 35 small states are rated as being in, or at high risk of, debt distress, roughly double the proportion of other EMDEs. The strengthening of fiscal policy is particularly critical in small states given the outsized role it plays in macroeconomic stabilization and promoting external balance, given the absence in most cases of exchange rate flexibility.

Against this backdrop, the chapter addresses the following questions:

- How have fiscal positions in small states evolved since the decade preceding the COVID-19 pandemic?
- What are the main causes of the deterioration in fiscal positions?
- What are the policy priorities for improving fiscal positions?

Contributions. The chapter contributes to the literature in three ways.

- *Systematic review of fiscal positions.* The chapter presents the first systematic review of the fiscal positions of small states. It identifies the key trends in debt, fiscal balances, and government revenues and expenditures in small states before and after the pandemic and assesses the fiscal challenges that these countries now face.

- *Comprehensive analysis of small states.* The chapter presents an analysis of a broad sample of up to 35 EMDE small states that cuts across economic structures, and geographic and income groups, drawing out the many common economic and fiscal challenges they face. The large sample also makes possible a richer comparative analysis—including of opportunities for reform—than previous studies, complementing country-focused assessments. This is informed by extensive comparisons across groups of small states defined by structural features that impact fiscal outcomes, including export structures and size.

- *New insights from analytical frameworks.* The chapter derives new empirical insights from a range of analytical frameworks. It finds that following a natural disaster or global recession fiscal outcomes in small states have tended to deteriorate more markedly than in other EMDEs. In addition, persistent fiscal deficits have been a key driver of higher small states' debt, while small states' deficits have tended to narrow after increases in debt—but only slightly.

Main findings. The chapter presents the following key findings.

Natural disasters and global recessions weaken small states' fiscal and debt positions. An event analysis shows that both types of event significantly weaken fiscal balances and increase government debt, relative to GDP, in small states. For example, three years after a large natural disaster or global recession, fiscal balances deteriorate by around 1.8 percentage points. Three years after a global recession, debt ratios increase by 3.5 percentage points and three years after a natural

FIGURE 4.1 Small states and other economies: Output growth and structural characteristics

GDP per capita growth in small states has significantly lagged other EMDEs and barely kept pace with advanced economies, underscoring their significant development challenges. Small states' trade openness and relatively high exposure to natural disasters leave them more vulnerable to external shocks, with associated higher output and government revenue and spending volatility. Debt sustainability in small states has substantially worsened in the aftermath of the COVID-19 pandemic.

A. GDP per capita growth, 2000-23

Percent
5
4
3
2
1
0
Small states
EMDEs excl. small states
Advanced economies

B. Average cost and frequency of natural disasters

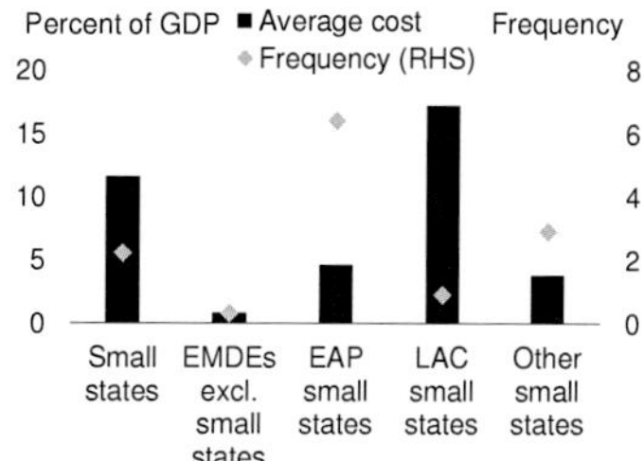

C. Trade openness

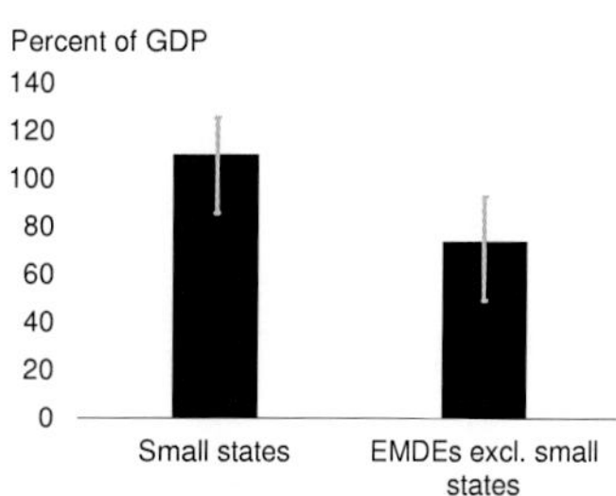

D. Output volatility

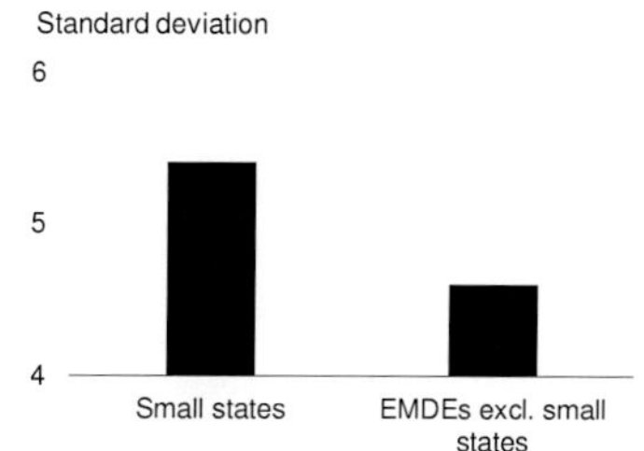

E. Revenue and expenditure volatility

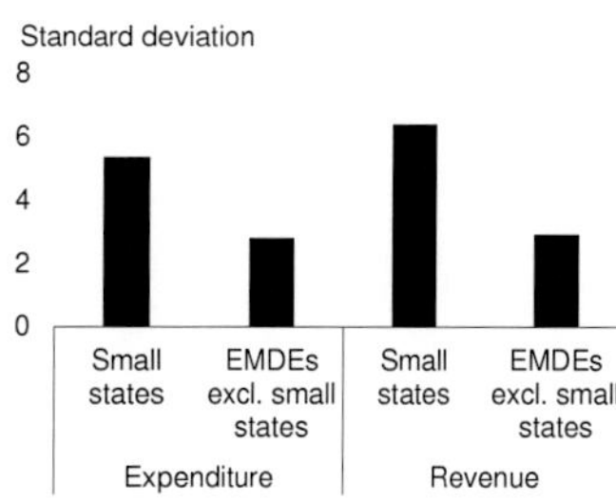

F. Risk of debt distress

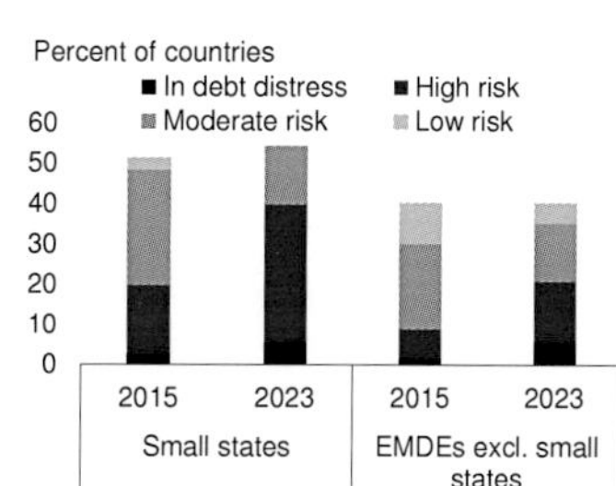

Sources: EM-DAT (database); International Monetary Fund; WDI (database); WEO (database); World Bank.

Note: EAP = East Asia and Pacific; EMDEs = emerging market and developing economies; LAC = Latin America and the Caribbean.

A. GDP weighted average annual GDP per capita growth for groups of countries. Sample includes 34 small states, 111 other EMDEs and 37 advanced economies. Guyana is excluded.

B. Frequency is the average number of natural disasters per year, adjusted by land mass, for the period 2000-22. Unit of frequency is the number of natural disasters per year per one hundred thousand square kilometers. Average cost of natural disasters per year as percent of GDP for 24 small states and 93 other EMDEs. EAP small states include 8 economies, LAC small states include 11 economies, and other small states include 5 economies. Natural disasters include droughts, storms, floods, extreme temperatures, earthquakes, volcanic activity, and wildfires.

C. Average ratio of trade (exports plus imports of goods and services) to GDP, 2000-22, for 27 small states and 114 other EMDEs. Whiskers indicate interquartile range.

D. Standard deviation of annual real GDP growth in 34 small states and 115 other EMDEs for the period 2000-23.

E. Standard deviation of annual change in revenue and expenditure to GDP ratios in 35 small states and up to 117 other EMDEs for the period 2000-23.

F. Shares of small states and other EMDEs in overall debt distress or at risk of debt distress, based on the published Joint World Bank-International Monetary Fund Debt Sustainability Framework for Low-Income Countries as of March 30, 2024. Sample includes up to 19 small states and 48 other EMDEs.

disaster, by 6 percentage points. Moreover, both types of event are found to have larger adverse impacts on small states than other EMDEs

Debt burdens have expanded rapidly. Government debt in small states averaged 57 percent of GDP between 2011 and 2023, 10 percentage points higher than in other EMDEs. Over this period, average debt in small states increased by around 11 percentage points of GDP. About one third of the debt build-up occurred after the onset of the COVID-19 pandemic, reflecting the economic and broader damage it inflicted. Although debt rose more in tourism-dependent small states the increase in debt was widespread, occurring in around two-thirds of small states.

Persistent fiscal deficits have been a key driver of the increase in debt burdens. The increase in government debt-to-GDP ratios is largely due to sizeable fiscal deficits, alongside interest costs, which since 2011 have, on average, offset the debt -reducing effects of GDP growth. Since the pandemic, the debt build-up has reflected a marked widening in deficits together with large output contractions and sometimes slow economic recoveries. Even with some recent consolidation efforts, about three-quarters of small states reported weaker primary balance ratios in 2020-23 than their five-year pre-pandemic average.

Spending is up and revenues are down since the pandemic. Before the pandemic, government spending in small states was already high—averaging 39 percent of GDP between 2011 and 2019, well above the average of 27 percent in other EMDEs. Average spending increased by 4 percentage points of GDP in small states from 2019 to 2020, more than the increase of 2.6 percentage points in other EMDEs. Average revenues in small states were 36 percent of GDP during 2011-19, compared with 25 percent in other EMDEs. The pandemic had a somewhat delayed but sustained negative impact on revenues in small states: they fell by almost one percentage point of GDP between 2019 and 2023, compared with a similar increase in other EMDEs, reflecting a sharp downturn in economic activity followed by slow recoveries that lagged behind other EMDEs.

Comprehensive fiscal reforms are necessary. The experience of the pandemic illustrates small states' structural vulnerabilities to large shocks and their related development challenges. Small states' fiscal frameworks should therefore be even more resilient than those of other EMDEs. Evidence suggests that stronger fiscal frameworks are essential to buttress government balance sheets against large shocks, and they should be complemented by reforms to promote economic growth and strengthen resilience. Reforms targeting both expenditure and revenue streams can reverse deteriorating fiscal positions while building resilience for the future. These include improving spending efficiency, enhancing domestic revenue mobilization particularly tax revenues, to reduce reliance on volatile and less sustainable revenue sources, and establishing well-designed, flexible, but enforceable rules-based fiscal frameworks with ample buffers to more effectively respond to external shocks and manage volatility. The international community has important roles to play in supporting small states in all these areas, particularly in bolstering resilience against larger and more frequent climate change-related natural disasters.

The remainder of the chapter is organized as follows. First, the impact of natural disasters and global recessions on fiscal positions in small states is analyzed. Second, the evolution of fiscal positions in small states is examined, both in the years leading up to the pandemic and in the subsequent period, and the drivers of the rise in debt burdens and fiscal deficits are identified. Finally, the chapter considers the policies needed to address these challenges, drawing on successful experiences in small states and other EMDEs.

Fiscal vulnerability to shocks

Small states are especially vulnerable to natural disasters and global economic shocks. Although exposure varies, many small states are among the most disaster-prone countries in the world. Climate change is exacerbating this vulnerability, leading to more frequent and intense disasters that result in large economic losses (Guo and

Quayyum 2020; Rustomjee 2016; WMO 2023). The high degrees of openness and narrow export bases of small states also make them vulnerable to global economic developments such as recessions, commodity price changes, and financial market fluctuations (Acevedo, Cebotari, and Turner-Jones 2013).[1]

Natural disasters. Natural disasters adversely affect fiscal balances and debt ratios by reducing economic growth and government revenues, and increasing government spending (Cabezon et al. 2019; Lee, Zhang, and Nguyen 2018; Melecky and Raddatz 2011). For example, it has been estimated that following an average hurricane shock, tax revenues in a sample of Caribbean small states dropped by up to 5.3 percent in the short-term because of reduced economic activity, especially in private consumption (Auffret 2003; Mohan and Strobl 2021). Revenues from transactions in goods and services and international trade are especially vulnerable to tropical storms—one of the most damaging kinds of shock faced by small island states (Mohan and Strobl 2021). After a disaster, higher government spending is needed to finance emergency relief efforts and reconstruction (Cabezon et al. 2019; Lis and Nickel 2009). These increases in government spending are sustained for at least two years after the shock (Ouattara and Strobl 2013). Tropical storms have also increased government debt in some small states, particularly to external creditors (Cavallo et al. 2024; Mohan and Strobl 2020).

Global recessions. Global recessions can significantly worsen countries' fiscal positions, with debt ratios rising for up to five years after the start of a recession (Kose et al. 2021). During global recessions, pressure on real household incomes in advanced economies can lead to cuts in spending on international travel, on which many small states depend heavily. For example, the 2009 global recession significantly reduced government revenues in tourism-reliant Caribbean small states, contributing to sharp increases in their fiscal deficits (Mercer-Blackman and Melgarejo 2013). Global recessions are often associated with job losses or reduced wages in advanced economies, which can also decrease remittance flows to small states that rely on them, leading to reductions in consumer spending and consumption-based tax revenues. In addition, higher social spending is often required to support vulnerable groups during global recessions, exacerbating already strained public finances in small states.

Natural disasters and global recessions weaken small states' fiscal and debt positions. An event analysis of global recessions and natural disasters since 2000 shows that both types of event significantly weaken fiscal balances and increase government debt, relative to GDP, in small states (figure 4.2).[2] For example, on average, large natural disasters are associated with a 0.7 percentage point deterioration in the fiscal balance and a 2.4 percentage points increase in the debt ratio in the year of the shock, with the deterioration of both measures continuing in the subsequent two years. Fiscal balances initially deteriorate even more in the year of a global recession, around 3 percentage points, on average, but the impact is less persistent than in the case of natural disasters. In the year of a global recession debt ratios rise by around 8 percentage points but then begin to decline. Comparing the persistence of shocks, three years after natural disasters, fiscal balances deteriorate by 1.8 percentage points, similar to a global recession. However, three years after a natural disaster, debt ratios increase by 6 percentage points, more than the 3.5 percentage points increase following a global recession. Thus, natural disasters appear to have a more persistent adverse impact on small states' fiscal positions. Finally, both natural disasters and global recessions are found to have larger adverse impacts on small states than other EMDEs. In particular, on average, in the third year after such shocks fiscal balances had weakened and debt-to-GDP ratios had increased by more in small states than other EMDEs.

[1] In contrast, over the past decade or so, small states have typically been less affected by other events such as domestic financial crises, armed conflict, and wars.

[2] Alternative methods for the event analysis including regression analysis were explored but not used owing to data limitations.

FIGURE 4.2 Fiscal outcomes around major events in small states and other EMDEs

Average fiscal positions in small states have deteriorated markedly following natural disasters and global recessions, with fiscal balances weakening and debt increasing relative to GDP. Three years after such shocks, on average, fiscal balances have weakened by more and debt increased further in small states than in other EMDEs.

A. Small states: Change in fiscal balances around large natural disasters

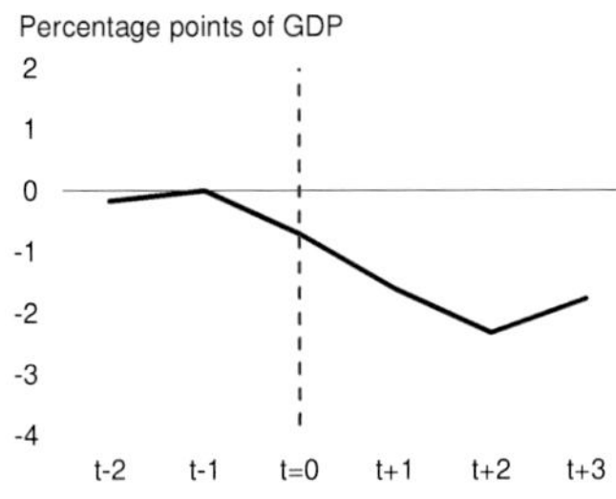

B. Small states: Change in government debt around large natural disasters

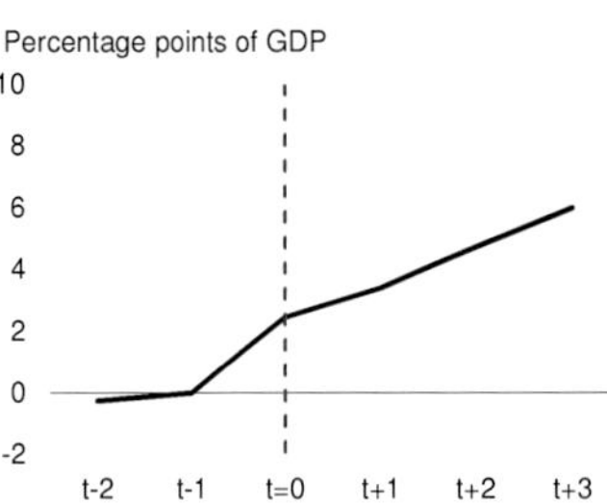

C. Small states: Change in fiscal balances around global recessions

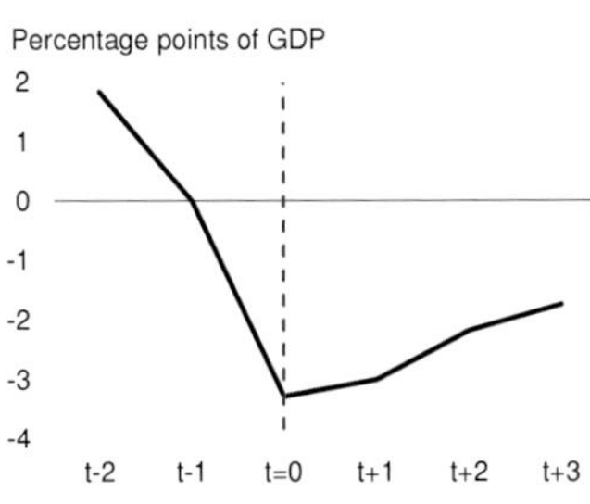

D. Small states: Change in government debt around global recessions

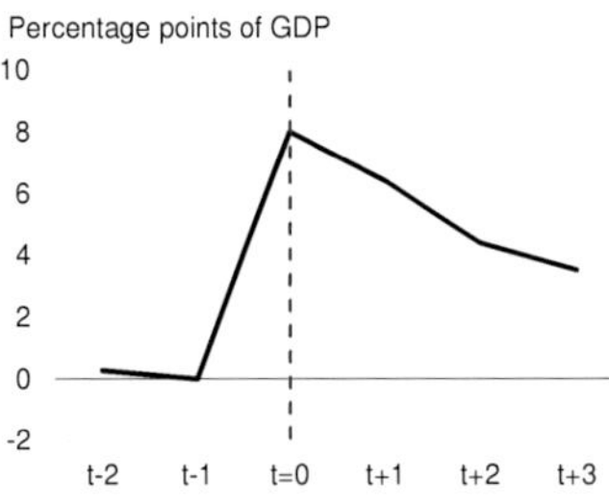

E. Change in fiscal balances three years after major events

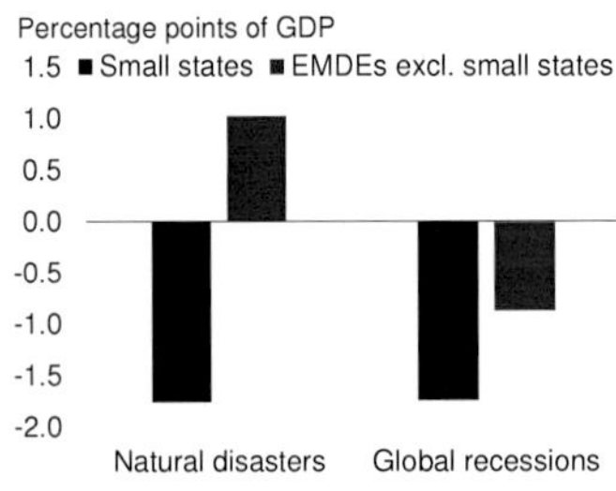

F. Change in government debt three years after major events

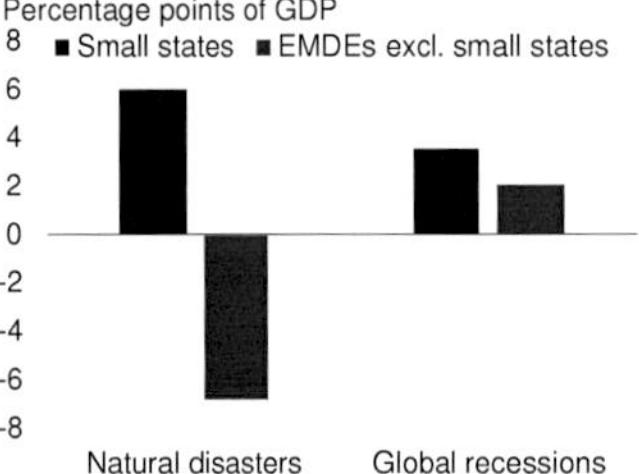

Sources: EM-DAT (database); WEO (database); World Bank.

Note: EMDEs = emerging market and developing economies. Panels show differences in average fiscal balance and debt as a percent of GDP in EMDEs compared with those in the year preceding events occurring in year *t=0*. Events include global recessions (2009 and 2020) or natural disasters resulting in damages of at least 5 percent of GDP. Natural disasters include droughts, earthquakes, extreme temperatures, floods, storms, volcanic activity, and wildfires. In five cases where natural disasters coincide with global recessions, they are attributed to either natural disaster or global recession events and not both, to avoid double counting. Results are robust to alternative assumptions.

A.B. Difference in average fiscal balance and debt as a percent of GDP in small states compared to year preceding a natural disaster occurring in period *t=0*. Based on a sample of 24 natural disasters in small states for the period 2000-22.

C.D. Difference in average fiscal balance and debt as a percent of GDP in small states compared to year preceding global recessions occurring in period *t=0*. Based on a sample of 34 small states.

E.F. Difference in average fiscal balance and debt as a percent of GDP in EMDEs three years after global recessions and a natural disaster resulting in damages of at least 5 percent of GDP compared to year preceding the shock. Based on a sample of up to 34 small states and 111 other EMDEs.

Evolution of fiscal positions in small states

The pandemic shock hit small states harder than other EMDEs, largely because of prolonged disruptions to global tourism (World Bank 2023a). Collectively small states contracted by about 11 percent in 2020, much more than other EMDEs (figure 4.3). Moreover, although they constitute only one quarter of EMDEs in number, in 2020 small states accounted for more than half of the largest economic contractions across all EMDEs. Contractions were particularly large in tourism-dependent economies, including The Bahamas, Fiji, and Maldives. Recoveries from the pandemic have also been slower in small states, particularly in the East Asia and Pacific (EAP) region, where reopening after the pandemic was delayed and the revival of tourism was slow. In some small states, output continued to contract through 2022. By 2023 average output across small states was around 5 percent higher than before the pandemic, in 2019, far below the 15 percent increase in other EMDEs.

With the tailwinds from the pandemic recovery fading, growth across small states is projected to slow this year and next. The pandemic has left substantial economic scaring on small states, with GDP projected to be around 7 percent below pre-pandemic trends in 2024 and with no expectation that this loss will be recovered in the next two years. Moreover, medium-term growth prospects are declining in some small states as underlying growth drivers, notably investment, weaken, in the face of more frequent and severe natural disasters, and climate change (World Bank 2024a).

Conceptual framework

The main drivers of government debt, relative to GDP, can be identified by applying an accounting decomposition (World Bank 2023c). Specifically, the change in the debt-to-GDP ratio in any period can be separated into contributions from the primary fiscal balance—the difference between revenue and non-interest expenditures—interest costs on debt, output growth, and other factors including inflation.

Such a decomposition is used to analyze the drivers of the average debt-to-GDP ratio in small states for the period 2011-23, and then separately for the pre-pandemic period 2011-19 and the period 2019-23, to examine the initial impact of the pandemic (annex 4.1). A representative sample of 32 small states, determined by data availability, are included in the exercise. To examine the possible path and drivers of debt in the next few years, a decomposition is also applied for the period 2023-26, using forecasts from the International Monetary Fund's (IMF's) April 2024 *World Economic Outlook*.

Evolution of debt

Government debt in small states averaged 57 percent of GDP between 2011 and 2023, 10 percentage points higher than in other EMDEs (figure 4.4). In small states, as in other EMDEs, average government debt has risen markedly since 2011. It was rising even before the pandemic, but there was a sharp acceleration when the pandemic hit (Sirimaneetham 2022). Although the debt-to-GDP ratio has moderated in the last few years, it remains higher than in the pre-pandemic period. The debt build-up reflects persistent fiscal deficits as well as the growth collapse caused by the pandemic.

Widespread rise in government debt

Between 2011 and 2023, average government debt in small states increased by about 11 percentage points of GDP. Although this increase was smaller than in other EMDEs, the average debt-to-GDP ratio in small states in 2023, at 61 percent, remained higher than in other EMDEs. The debt build-up was also widespread, occurring in about 60 percent of small states. Where it fell, this was often the result of surging revenues from sovereign rents, grants, or other non-tax revenues; in other cases, it reflected debt restructuring linked to IMF-supported policy programs. Reflecting the widespread debt build-up, the proportion of small states saddled with high debt rose from around one-third in 2011 to one-half in 2023; throughout the period it was higher than for other EMDEs.

About two-thirds of the increase in debt between 2011 and 2023 occurred before the pandemic. In 2011-19, government debt rose relative to GDP because of lingering adverse effects of the Global Financial Crisis and a variety of country-specific factors such as natural disasters, increased borrowing to fund large projects, and sharp falls in commodity prices for some commodity exporters. Debt rose markedly in Samoa and Vanuatu following large, damaging storms in 2012 and 2015 respectively. In Eswatini, a drought in 2015 added to fiscal challenges. Debt also rose significantly among metal and oil exporters, including Suriname, around 2015, when falling gold and oil prices curtailed revenues.

FIGURE 4.3 Output since the COVID-19 pandemic in small states and other EMDEs

The pandemic disproportionately impacted small states, with an average economic contraction of about 11 percent in 2020, much greater than in other EMDEs. Tourism-dependent small states were hit particularly hard. Recoveries have also been slower in small states: their output in 2023 was only 5 percent higher than in 2019, far below the 15 percent increase in other EMDEs. Moreover, output in small states is set to continue on a lower path than expected before the pandemic.

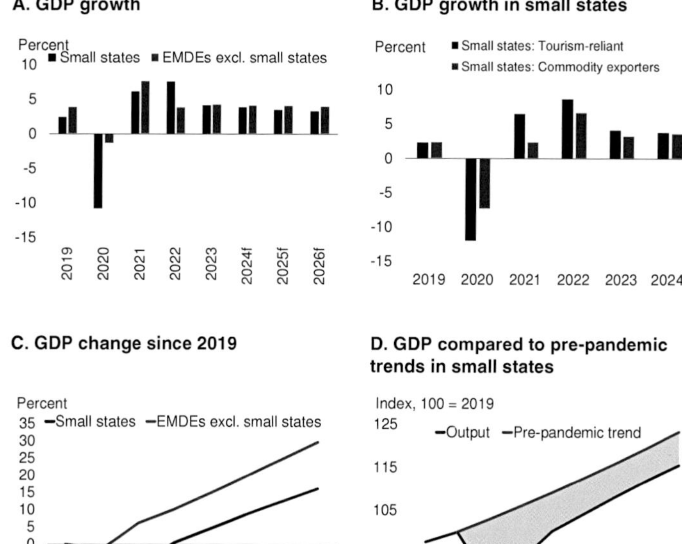

Source: World Bank.

Note: f = forecast; EMDEs = emerging market and developing economies. Guyana is excluded from the small states sample.

A.-C. Country groups are GDP weighted at average 2010-19 prices and market exchange rates. Data for 2024-26 are World Bank forecasts. Based on a sample of up to 34 small states and 119 other EMDEs.

B. Small states commodity exporters include 13 economies and tourism-reliant small states include 22 economies.

D. Blue line indicates GDP outcomes and current World Bank forecasts. Red line indicates the counterfactual had GDP grown in line with forecasts in the January 2020 *Global Economic Prospects*, extended at constant growth rates beyond 2022. Based on a sample of up to 34 small states.

FIGURE 4.4 Government debt in small states and other EMDEs

Following a gradual rise since 2011, the average government debt-to-GDP ratio in small states increased sharply at the onset of the COVID-19 pandemic. While it has since declined, it remains higher than before the pandemic and in other EMDEs. Increases in debt among small states have been widespread. Small states rely more heavily on official borrowing than other EMDEs and have lower debt-carrying capacity, with debt risk ratings triggered at lower average debt levels.

A. Government debt

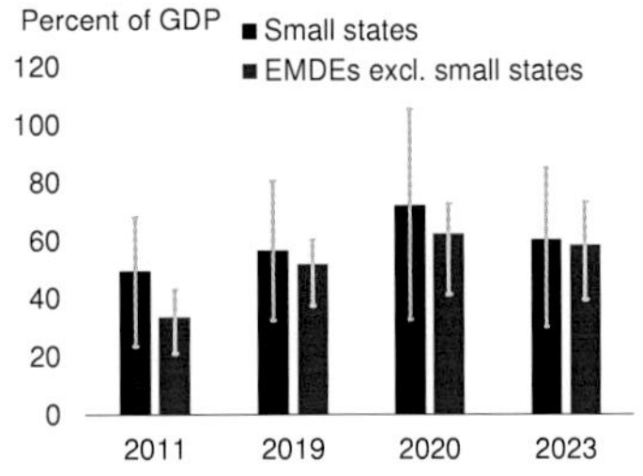

B. Shares of small states and other EMDEs with high public debt

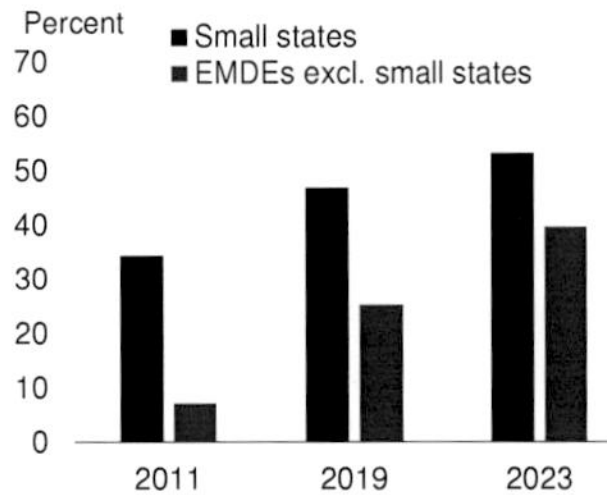

C. Composition of external public debt by creditor

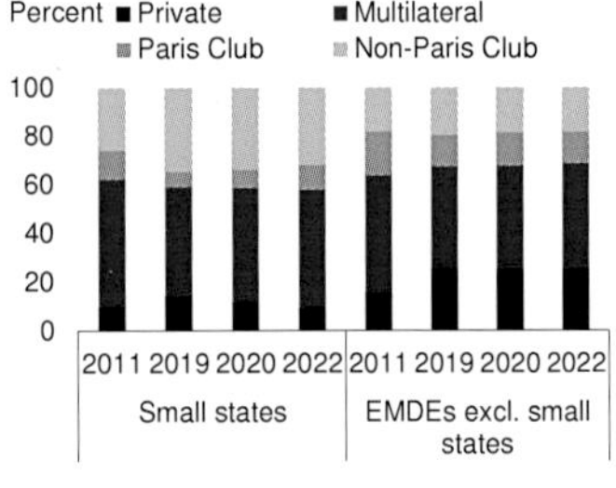

D. Debt level by debt sustainability rating

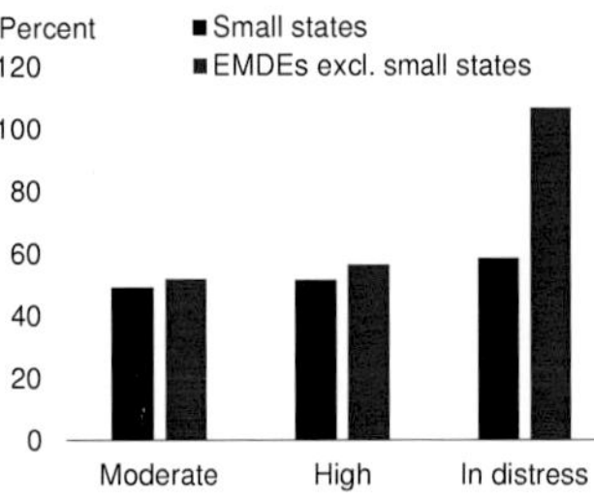

Sources: International Debt Statistics (GDDS database); International Monetary Fund; WEO (database); World Bank.

Note: EMDEs = emerging market and developing economies.

A. Average government debt to GDP ratio for 32 small states and 111 other EMDEs. Whiskers indicate interquartile range.

B. Bars show the percentage of small states and other EMDEs with debt to GDP ratios of at least 60 percent for 32 small states and 111 other EMDEs.

C. Average share of public and publicly guaranteed external debt by type of creditor for 22 small states and 100 other EMDEs.

D. Average debt as a percent of GDP in 2023 for countries classified at different levels of debt risk ratings, based on the published Joint World Bank-International Monetary Fund Debt Sustainability Framework for Low-Income Countries as of March 30, 2024. Sample includes up to 19 small states and 48 other EMDEs.

At the onset of the pandemic-induced recession, in 2020, government debt in the average small state jumped by 15 percentage points of GDP, much more than in other EMDEs, before moderating by around 12 percentage points by 2023. In 2020, non-grant-reliant small states experienced a particularly large increase in debt. Although the pandemic was the main factor driving debt higher, natural disasters also contributed—including a volcanic eruption in St. Vincent and the Grenadines in 2021.

Deficit-driven government debt buildup

The sharp increase in the average government debt-to-GDP ratio in small states between 2011 and 2023 reflected rising primary fiscal deficits and interest costs, which together outweighed the debt-reducing effects of real growth and other factors (figures 4.5 and 4.6). In countries where the debt ratio increased, the contribution from fiscal deficits varied, but in most cases it was greater than one-half. However, debt drivers varied somewhat before and following the pandemic. From 2011 to 2019, solid growth was sufficient to offset primary deficits. In contrast, between 2019 and 2023, widening fiscal deficits overwhelmed the debt-reducing effects of growth, which shrank on account of the pandemic induced contractions in output and slow recoveries.

Between 2023 and 2026, average government debt in small states is projected to moderate by around 2 percentage points to 58 percent of GDP, supported by economic growth that is expected to partially offset persistent primary deficits. In most countries, projected growth over this period exceeds the pre-pandemic average, reflecting tailwinds from the pandemic recovery. If growth falls short of expectations, however, there is a risk of weaker fiscal outcomes. Even if the projections materialize, average debt in small states, relative to GDP, would remain a little above its pre-pandemic level.

Reliance on official creditors

Governments in small states have limited access to borrowing from domestic or foreign private sources, so they often rely heavily on official sources (World Bank 2023a, 2023d). Reflecting their considerable development challenges, 14 of the 35 small states are eligible for concessional financing through the World Bank's International Development Association (IDA), with an additional seven classified as IDA-blend countries. Reliance on official borrowing reflects generally low creditworthiness and underdeveloped domestic financial systems—particularly in the smallest and poorest economies and in fragile and conflict-affected small states. Government borrowing from private sources is often reliant on local commercial banks. Several factors influence the ability of governments to borrow from private creditors, including a country's macroeconomic stability and a government's record in meeting its financial obligations (Reinhart, Rogoff, and Savastano 2003). The debt-carrying capacity of small states tends to be smaller than that of other EMDEs, partly reflecting structural constraints on economic growth and susceptibility to external shocks (World Bank 2023b). This is underscored by the fact that higher risk ratings from debt sustainability analyses are on average triggered at lower debt levels in small states than in other EMDEs.

On average, in 2022, small states owed around 90 percent of their external public debt to official creditors, more than they did on the eve of the pandemic—and well above the 75 percent average share for other EMDEs. A little less than half of small states' external debt is owed to multilateral creditors. The remaining approximately 40 percent is owed to bilateral creditors including a diverse mix of Paris and non-Paris Club members, the latter including notably China. In some small states, loans owed to Chinese entities account for a substantial share of total external debt (Horn, Reinhart, and Trebesch 2021).[3] The large share of official borrowing reduces rollover risks and enables access to concessional terms in many cases. However, limited access to private borrowing narrows the options for small states to meet their significant financing needs.

Evolution of primary deficits

Persistent primary deficits

In small states primary fiscal deficits have persisted since before the pandemic. Between 2011 and 2023, there was an average primary deficit in small states of 1.4 percent of GDP, with about 70 percent of small states having primary deficits on average. Small states reliant on commodity exports had, on average, a primary deficit of 4 percent of GDP compared with an average primary surplus of 0.5 percent of GDP in their commodity-importing peers. Commodity exporters' fiscal and external positions were severely affected by commodity-price shocks during this period (Al-Sadiq, Bejar, and Ötker-Robe 2021). The fiscal positions of small states also differed among regions, with small states in EAP and Latin America and the Caribbean (LAC) having deficits smaller than other regions. Micro states—which typically have an outsized reliance on external grants and other non-tax revenue—on average reported primary surpluses.

The pandemic-induced recession dealt a severe blow to fiscal balances in small states (figure 4.7).

FIGURE 4.5 Contributors to increases in government debt in small states

The rise in government debt, relative to GDP, in small states since 2011 primarily reflects large and persistent fiscal deficits alongside interest costs. Although economic growth provided significant offsets to primary deficits during the pre-pandemic period, widening fiscal deficits between 2019 and 2023 overwhelmed the effects of growth, weakened by the COVID-19 pandemic. Debt is expected to fall modestly relative to GDP in the near term, with economic growth partially offsetting continued fiscal deficits.

A. Contributions to change in average debt-to-GDP ratio, 2011-23

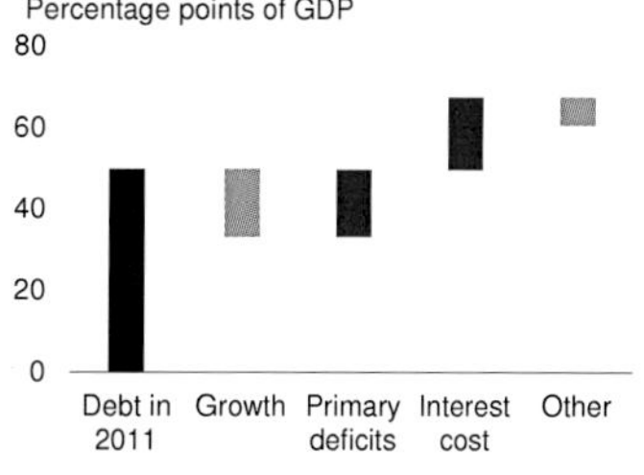

B. Contributions to change in average debt-to-GDP ratio, 2011-19

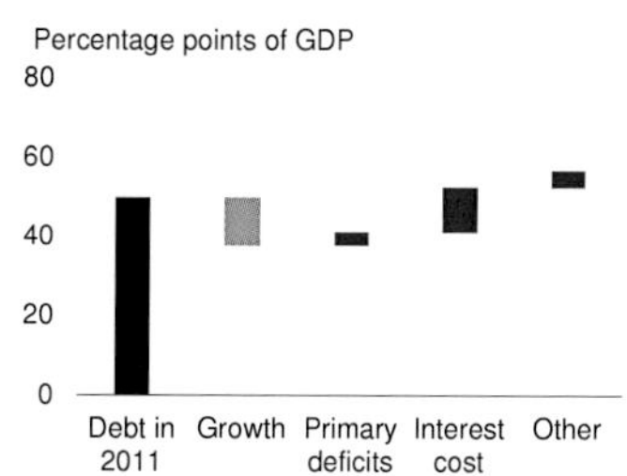

C. Contributions to change in average debt-to-GDP ratio, 2019-23

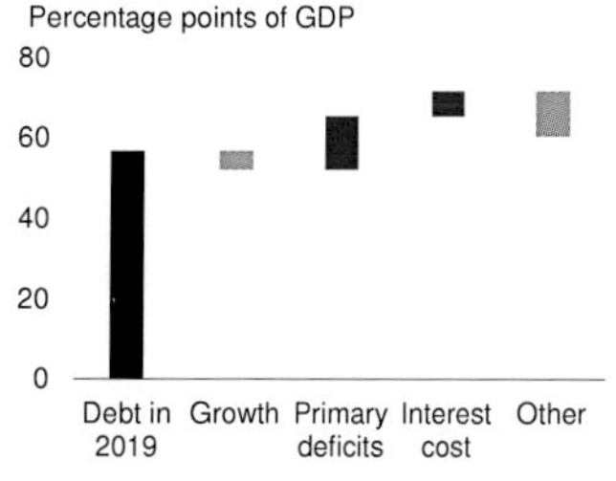

D. Contributions to change in average debt-to-GDP ratio, 2023-26

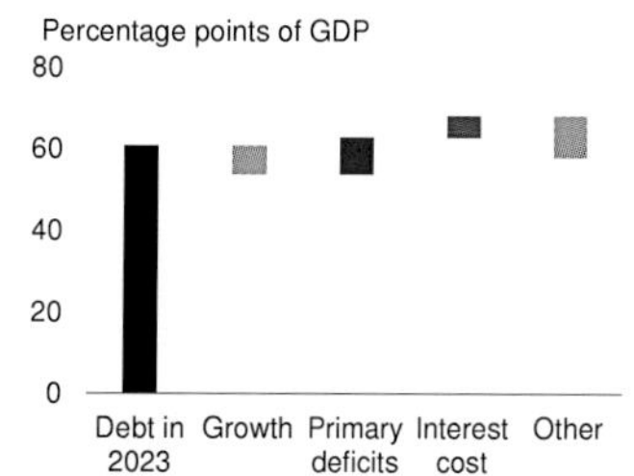

Sources: WEO (database); World Bank.
Note: Contributions to changes in debt-to-GDP ratios. See annex 4.1 for further details. "Other" factors include exchange rate depreciation, inflation, privatization proceeds, the materialization of contingent liabilities and other ad-hoc changes to debt stocks.
A.-C. Orange bars indicate debt-decreasing contributions and red bars indicate debt-increasing contributions. Sample includes 32 small states.
D. Orange bars indicate debt-decreasing contribution and red bars indicate debt-increasing contribution. The decomposition is based on forecasts from the April 2024 *World Economic Outlook*. Sample includes 32 small states.

[3] According to estimates by Horn, Reinhart, and Trebesch (2021), external debt owed to China as a share of GDP exceeded 25 percent in three small states: Djibouti, Maldives, and Tonga.

FIGURE 4.6 Fiscal balances in small states and other EMDEs

Fiscal balances in small states deteriorated markedly, on average, at the onset of the pandemic and, despite narrowing since 2020, average deficits in 2023 were larger than those in other EMDEs. Moreover, since the pandemic fiscal balances have been weaker than pre-pandemic averages in most small states. However, fiscal balances have varied significantly among small states, with deficits in EAP and LAC smaller than elsewhere; commodity-exporting small states having larger deficits; and micro states, reliant on external grants, having primary surpluses.

A. Overall fiscal balance

Percent of GDP
■ Small states
■ EMDEs excl. small states

B. Primary fiscal balance

Percent of GDP
■ Small states
■ EMDEs excl. small states

C. Share of EMDEs with weaker primary balances in 2020-23 than before the pandemic

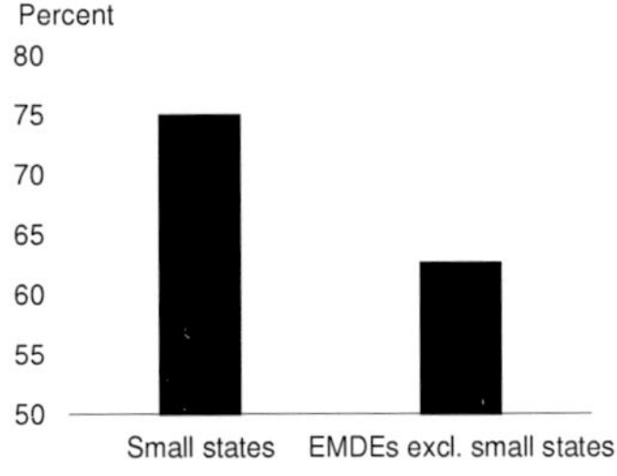

D. Average primary balance in small states, by region, 2011-23

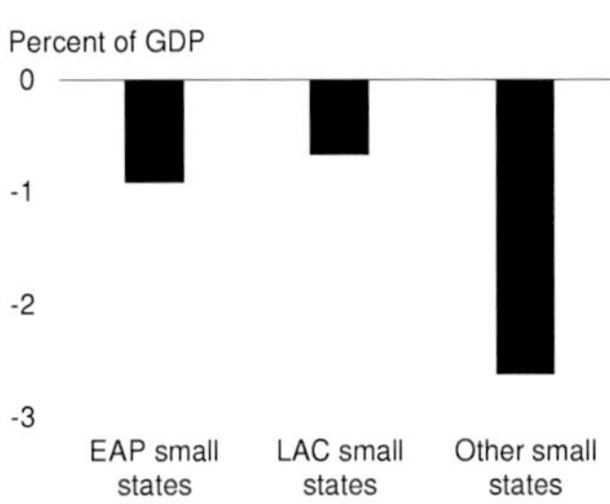

E. Average primary balance in small states, by trade composition, 2011-23

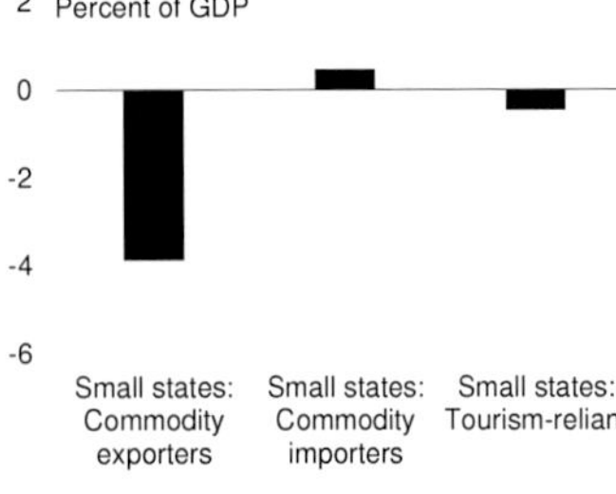

F. Average primary balance in small states, by population size, 2011-23

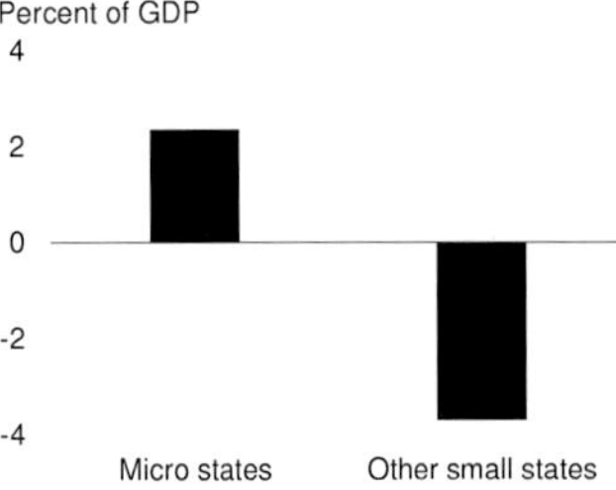

Sources: WEO (database); World Bank.

Note: EAP = East Asia and Pacific; EMDEs = emerging market and developing economies; LAC = Latin America and the Caribbean.

A. Panel shows the average overall fiscal balance as a percent of GDP for a sample of 32 small states and 110 other EMDEs.

B. Panel shows the average primary fiscal balance as a percent of GDP for a sample of 32 small states and 110 other EMDEs.

C. Bars show the percent of countries with weaker primary balances as a percent of GDP in 2020-23 than the average for the period 2015-19. Sample includes 32 small states and 112 other EMDEs.

D.-F. Bars show the average primary balance over the period 2011-23.

D. EAP small states include 10 economies, LAC small states include 11 economies, and other small states include 11 economies.

E. Small states commodity exporters include 13 economies, small states commodity importers include 19 economies, and tourism-reliant small states include 20 economies.

F. Micro states have a population of less than 200,000. Micro states include 12 economies, and other small states include 20 economies.

Before the pandemic, from 2011 to 2019, small states' primary deficits averaged 0.6 percent of GDP. In contrast, between 2020 and 2023, they averaged 3.3 percent of GDP, an increase of more than 2 percentage points. Of this increase, about three-quarters is attributed to higher spending and the remainder to lower revenue. Even though growth rebounded in 2021-23, small states continued to post larger primary deficits than other EMDEs. In 2023, small states' primary deficits averaged 2.1 percent of GDP, compared with less than 1 percent of GDP in other EMDEs. Moreover, around three-quarters of small states reported weaker primary balance ratios in 2020-23 than their 5-year pre-pandemic average, a greater share than other EMDEs.

Evolution of government revenues

Revenue levels

Small states' government revenues-to-GDP ratios are on average markedly higher than other EMDEs. However, in small states, revenue ratios have yet to recover to pre-pandemic levels. Revenue ratios averaged 36 percent of GDP, between 2011 and 2019, with revenues particularly buoyant in micro states reflecting rising grants and non-tax revenues. The average revenue ratio declined from 2020 to 2023, to a level of almost one percentage point below their pre-pandemic levels. In contrast, revenues in other EMDEs had fully recovered by 2022. Among small states, between 2011 and 2023, commodity exporters had lower revenues than their commodity-importing peers. Revenues in the EAP region and in micro states were more than double those in other small states, largely reflecting their reliance on grants and non-tax revenue. Overall, small states exhibit significant variation in revenue ratios, and unlike other EMDEs, these do not always correlate closely with income levels.

Revenue composition and volatility

Small states rely more on non-tax revenues than other EMDEs. Small states, especially micro states, derive significant revenues from a variety of sometimes unusual non-tax revenue sources such as fishing licenses and citizenship-by-investment programs. Excluding grants, non-tax revenue

FIGURE 4.7 Contributors to changes in primary balances in small states and other EMDEs

Increases in average primary deficits in small states since the pandemic reflect higher government expenditures, and to a lesser extent, weaker revenues. The contributions to widening deficits from increased spending and weaker revenues in small states have both been greater than in other EMDEs.

A. Revenue, primary spending, and primary balance in small states

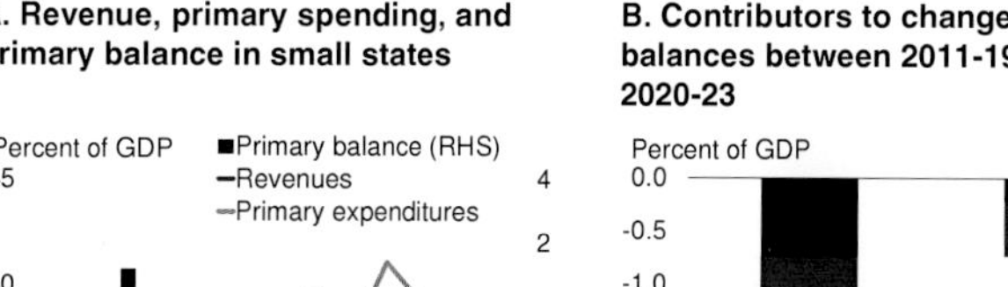

B. Contributors to changes in primary balances between 2011-19 and 2020-23

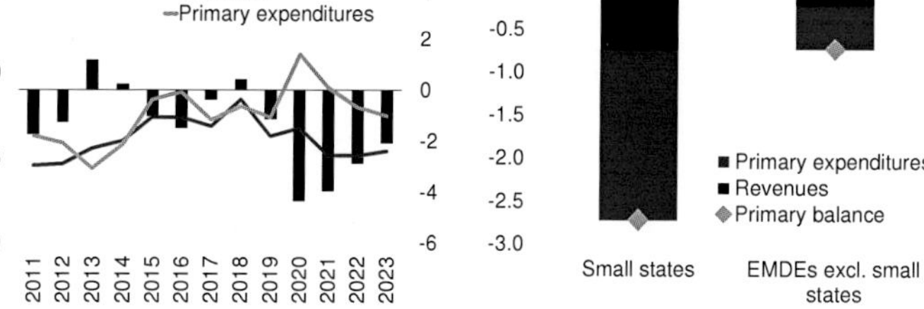

Sources: WEO (database); World Bank.

Note: EMDEs = emerging market and developing economies.

A. Average primary balance, revenues, and primary expenditures as a percent of GDP for a sample of 32 small states.

B. Bars show the contributions of changes in average primary balances as a percent of GDP from changes in revenues and primary expenditures for a sample of 32 small states and up to 110 other EMDEs.

averaged around 34 percent of total revenues in small states during 2011-22, 10 percentage points higher than in other EMDEs (figure 4.8). However, there is significant variation in the level of such revenues across small states, being generally higher in EAP, especially in the smallest Pacific Island economies, and commodity importers. In some cases, large marine territories and small populations enable significant revenue to be derived from sovereign rents, notably selling fishing access rights in their exclusive economic zones, shipping licenses, and economic citizenship programs (Cover-Kus 2019).

Grants, from bilateral and multilateral donors, are markedly higher in Pacific Island small states—particularly micro states—than in other EMDEs, and they provided timely fiscal support during the pandemic (World Bank 2023d). On average, grants amounted to almost 7 percent of GDP in small states between 2011 and 2022, compared with 2 percent of GDP in other EMDEs. Grants accounted for 17 percent of total revenues in small states during 2011-22—about twice the share in other EMDEs. In EAP small states, grants amounted to 14 percent of GDP in this period, compared with just 1.6 percent of GDP in LAC and 3.3 percent of GDP in other small states. In some cases, sustained large grants reflect ongoing bilateral assistance arrangements. For example, under the Compacts of Free Association, the United States provides financial assistance to the Marshall Islands, the Federated States of Micronesia, and Palau. The terms are renegotiated intermittently with a new agreement reached in 2023 on extending economic assistance for 20 years, thereby avoiding a fiscal cliff in the recipient countries (Lum 2023). Grants have also featured more prominently in some small states' revenues in the aftermath of natural disasters.

From 2011 through 2022, tax revenues in small states averaged 20 percent of GDP, 5 percentage points higher than in other EMDEs. Although direct and indirect taxes accounted for similar shares of tax revenues, on average, in small states as in other EMDEs, there were notable differences in the shares of specific taxes (figure 4.9). Most notably, trade taxes contributed almost one-quarter of tax revenues in small states, more than double the 11 percent share in other EMDEs. Small states' outsized trade revenue share stems from their high economic openness and the relative ease, for island states, of collecting taxes on imported goods (Borg 2006). Additionally, taxes on consumption of goods and services accounted for a smaller proportion of revenue in small states—40 percent—than in other EMDEs—52 percent. However, the contributions of income and property taxes in small states were similar to those in other EMDEs—about 35 and 1.5 percent, on average, respectively.

Notable differences in tax composition also exist among small states. In LAC small states, only about one-quarter of tax revenues come from direct taxes, less than in other small states, particularly those in EAP, primarily because of deficiencies in personal income tax collection (Acosta-Ormaechea, Pienknagura, and Pizzinelli 2022). In tourism-reliant small states, consumption taxes are far more important than in commodity-exporting small states. Finally, in micro states, where trade openness is greater than in other small states, trade taxes account for an outsized share of tax revenue.

FIGURE 4.8 Government revenue in small states and other EMDEs

Although small states have higher average ratios of total government revenue and tax revenue to GDP than other EMDEs, they are more reliant on non-tax revenues. Their revenue sources vary widely, including sovereign rents such as sales of fishing access rights, shipping licenses, and economic citizenship programs. Revenues are particularly high in EAP, and commodity-importing small states, and in micro states. Small states revenues are also more volatile than in other EMDEs.

A. Government revenue

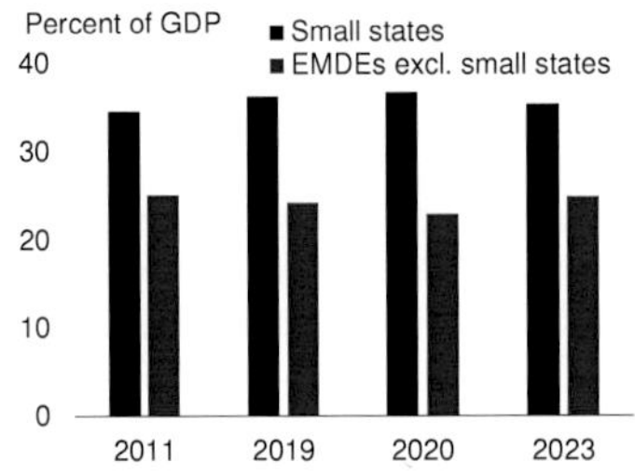

B. Composition of government revenue, 2011-22

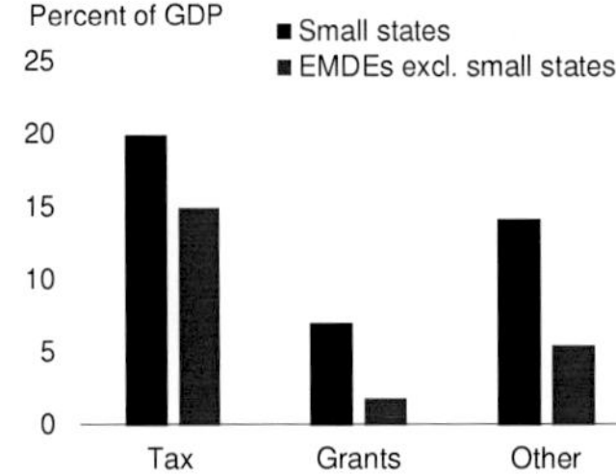

C. Government revenue, by region, 2011-23

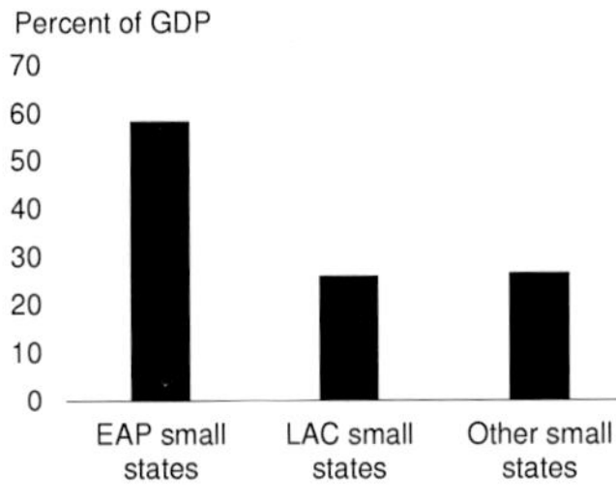

D. Government revenue, by trade composition, 2011-23

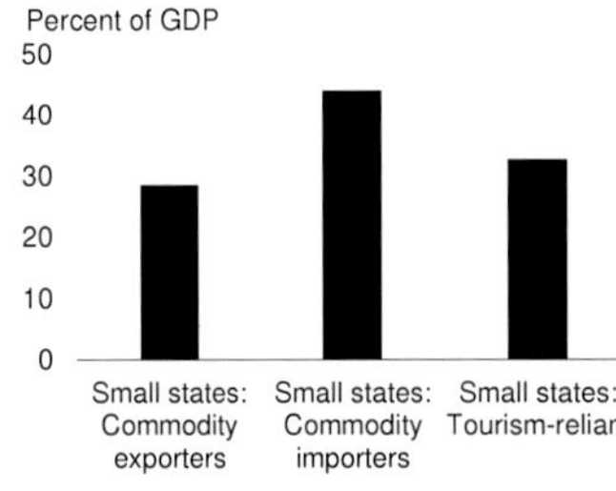

E. Government revenue, by population size, 2011-23

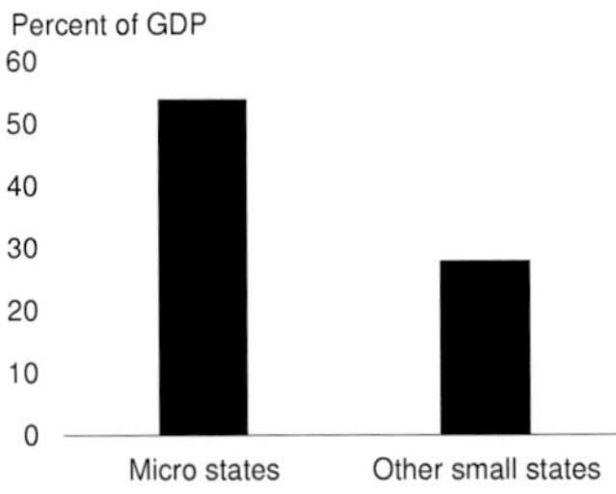

F. Volatility of government revenue, 2000-23

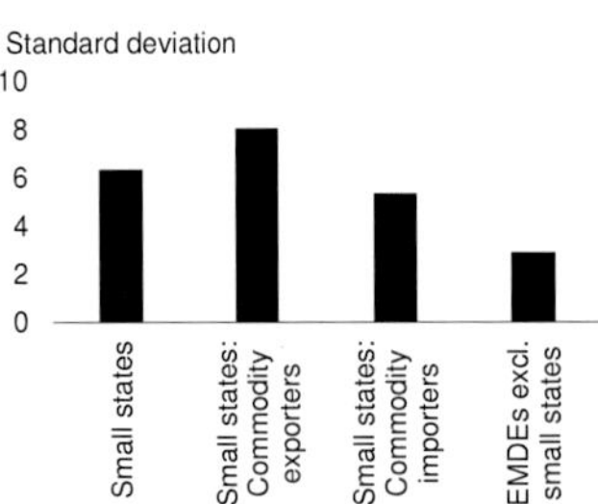

Sources: GFS (database); WEO (database); World Bank.

Note: EAP = East Asia and Pacific; EMDEs = emerging market and developing economies; LAC = Latin America and the Caribbean.

A. Panel shows average revenue to GDP ratios in 32 small states and 110 other EMDEs.

B. Bars show the average revenue to GDP ratios for the period 2011-22. Small states include 34 economies, and EMDEs excluding small states include 97 economies.

C.-E. Bars show the average revenue to GDP ratios for the period 2011-23.

C. EAP small states include 13 economies, LAC small states include 11 economies, and other small states include 11 economies.

D. Small states commodity exporters include 13 economies, small states commodity importers include 22 economies, and tourism-reliant small states include 22 economies.

E. Micro states have a population of less than 200,000. Micro states include 14 economies, and other small states include 21 economies.

F. Standard deviation of annual change in revenue to GDP ratios in 35 small states and 113 other EMDEs for the period 2000-23. Small states commodity exporters include 13 economies, and small states commodity importers include 22 economies.

Government revenues in small states tend to be relatively volatile because of the vulnerability of these economies to external shocks, including natural disasters and movements in commodity prices (Reyes-Tagle, Silvani, and Ospina 2022). Revenue from income taxes, which accounts for more than one-third of tax revenues, are particularly sensitive to shifts in output triggered by such shocks. Furthermore, the unpredictability of such revenue sources as grants and sovereign rents tends to amplify volatility, contributing to procyclicality and increasing risks to fiscal sustainability (Talvi and Vegh 2005). Both commodity-importing and commodity-exporting small states experience higher revenue volatility than other EMDEs.

Evolution of government expenditure

Spending levels

Between 2011 and 2023, government expenditures in small states averaged 40 percent of GDP, 13 percentage points of GDP higher than in other EMDEs (figure 4.10). In small states, they grew by 3 percentage points of GDP, on average, from 2011 to 2019, rising in more than half of them, especially in micro states, where expenditures on wages and goods and services both increased significantly. In contrast, government expenditure in other EMDEs was relatively stable between 2011 and 2019. There were significant differences in the level of spending among small states, with primary expenditures being relatively high in the EAP region (partly because of the prevalence of micro states), commodity importers, and micro states.

Small states' total government spending increased to 45 percent of GDP in 2020, its highest level during 2011-23, 4 percentage points higher than in 2019, and 16 percentage points higher than in other EMDEs. This reflected both the contraction in GDP and continued growth in spending including higher outlays on healthcare and efforts to counter the economic effects of the pandemic (figure 4.11; Fordelone, Tortora, and Xia 2022). By 2022, expenditures in small states had returned to pre-pandemic levels, but remained significantly higher than in other EMDEs. In 2023, small states' expenditure averaged 41 percent of GDP, compared with 28 percent of GDP in other EMDEs.

Spending composition and volatility

In small states, both capital and primary current expenditures have been relatively high. Primary expenditures in small states averaged 38 percent of GDP between 2011 and 2023—12 percentage points higher than in other EMDEs. Primary spending was notably higher for small states in the EAP region—partly because of the prevalence of micro states—relative to other small states during 2011-23. Small states' interest payments on government debt were on a par with those in other EMDEs, averaging almost 2 percent of GDP, but with significant variation among small states, ranging from negligible amounts for some countries to as high as 4.2 percent of GDP for Suriname—nearly one-fifth of its government's revenue. Capital expenditure in small states averaged 7 percent of GDP during 2011-22, higher than in other EMDEs.

Primary current expenditure in small states is mainly driven by the public wage bill and expenditures on goods and services. During 2011-22, together these were equivalent to 22 percent of GDP, 10 percentage points higher than in other EMDEs. Wage bills were particularly large, relative to GDP, in small states—some 5 percentage points of GDP higher than in other EMDEs—partly reflecting diseconomies of scale in the provision of public goods and services (Cas and Ota 2008). However, wage bills varied significantly among small states: in EAP, they were nearly double those in other regions; commodity importers had wage bills 6 percentage points higher than commodity exporters; and micro states had wage bills 4 percentage points higher than other small states. There are also expenditure variations across income groups in small states. For example, high-income small states have lower wage bills than other small states and other EMDEs, while lower-middle-income small states allocate less budget resources to investment, in favor of goods and services, than other small states and their other EMDE counterparts.

Expenditure volatility is higher in small states than in other EMDEs, and slightly higher for commodity importers within small states.

FIGURE 4.9 Tax revenue composition in small states and other EMDEs

Compared with other EMDEs, in small states trade taxes account for a higher share of tax revenues and consumption taxes a lower share. However, there is substantial variation in the composition of tax revenue among small states, with income taxes accounting for a higher share of revenue in EAP, while in other regions and in tourism-dependent small states consumption taxes are more important.

A. Composition of tax revenue, 2011-22

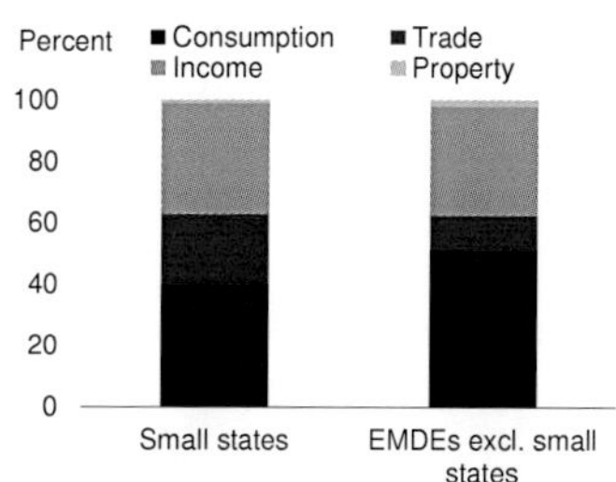

B. Composition of tax revenue by region, 2011-22

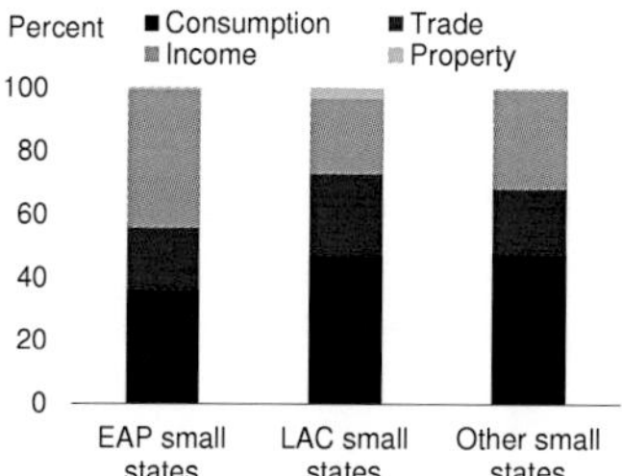

C. Composition of tax revenue by trade composition, 2011-22

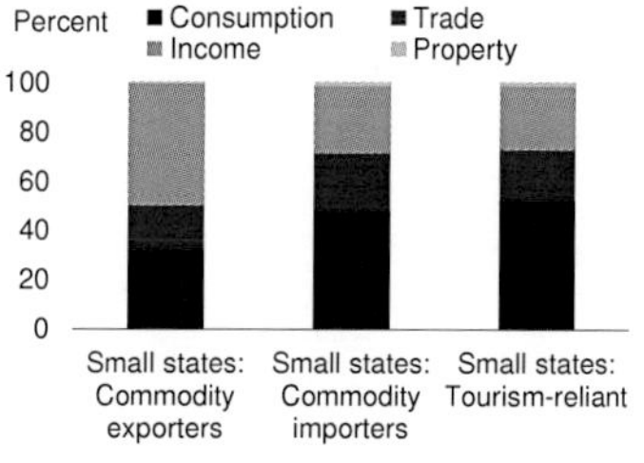

D. Composition of tax revenue by population size, 2011-22

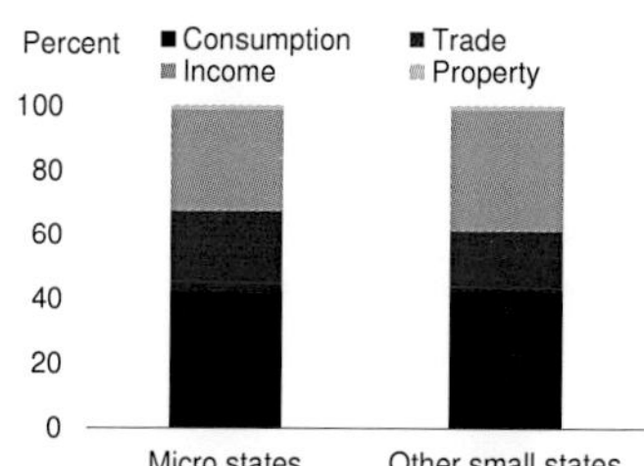

Sources: GFS (database); International Monetary Fund; World Bank.

Note: EAP = East Asia and Pacific; EMDEs = emerging market and developing economies; LAC = Latin America and the Caribbean.

A.-D. Bars show average consumption, trade, income, and property taxes as share of total tax revenues for period 2011-22.

A. Sample includes 28 small states and 95 other EMDEs.

B. EAP small states include 11 economies, LAC small states include 8 economies, and other small states include 9 economies.

C. Small states commodity exporters include 9 economies, small states commodity importers include 19 economies, and tourism-reliant small states include 21 economies.

D. Micro states have a population of less than 200,000. Micro states include 12 economies, and other small states include 16 economies.

Fiscal policy options in small states

Increased fiscal deficits and higher public debt in the aftermath of the pandemic, in a context of continued exposure to large external shocks including from climate change, present a significant challenge to fiscal sustainability in small states (Cevik and Nanda 2020; Clayton and Rosenblatt 2024; Khadan 2019; Khadan and Deonarine 2019). This is especially so given small states' high reliance on external borrowing and stocks of

FIGURE 4.10 Government expenditure in small states and other EMDEs

Government expenditure in small states, relative to GDP, is substantially higher than in other EMDEs. It increased at the onset of the pandemic before easing somewhat between 2020 and 2023. Capital expenditure in small states is higher than in other EMDEs. Primary current expenditure in small states is largely driven by the public wage bill and expenditures on goods and services, both of which were significantly higher than in other EMDEs during 2011-22. Across regions, government expenditures in small states are highest in EAP. The volatility of expenditures is higher in small states, particularly commodity importers, than in other EMDEs.

A. Government expenditure

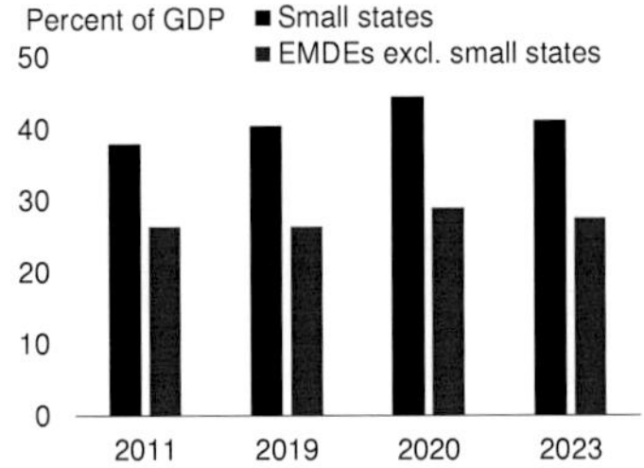

B. Composition of government expenditure, 2011-22

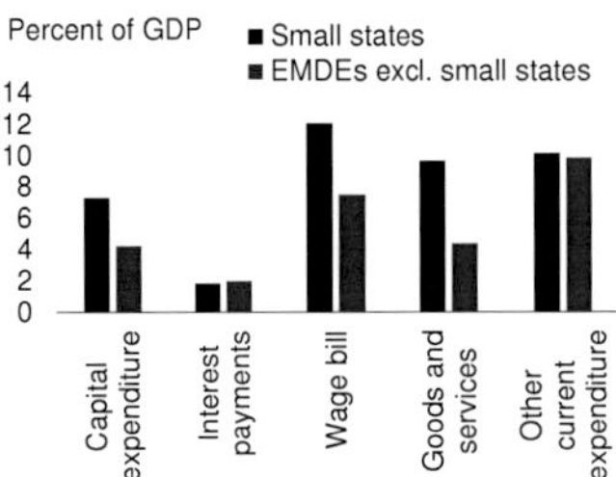

C. Primary expenditure by region, 2011-23

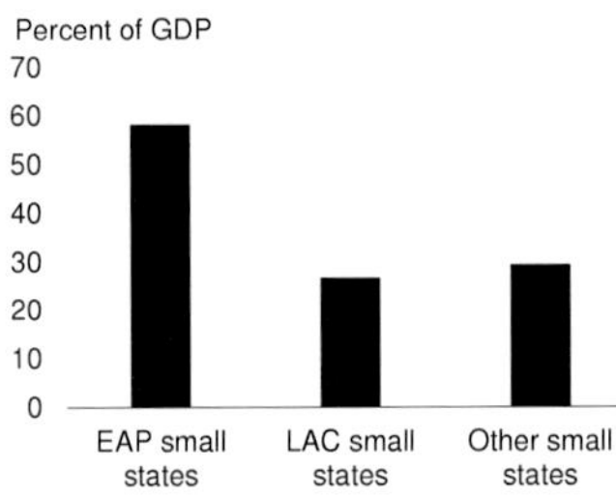

D. Primary expenditure by trade composition, 2011-23

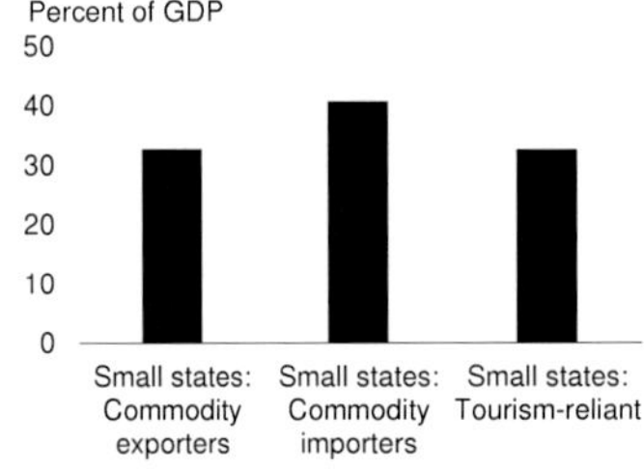

E. Primary expenditure by population size, 2011-23

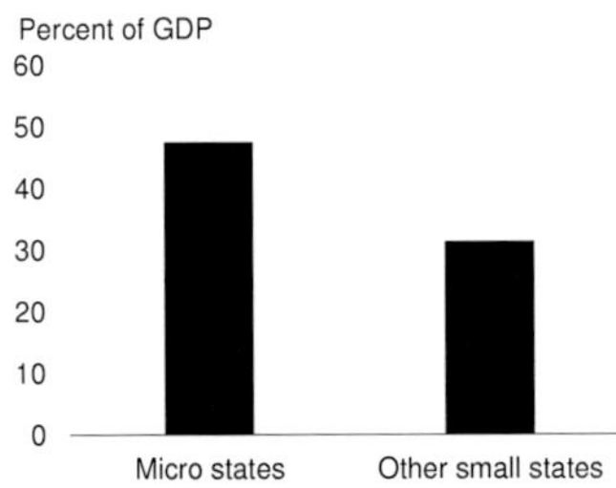

F. Volatility of expenditure, 2000-23

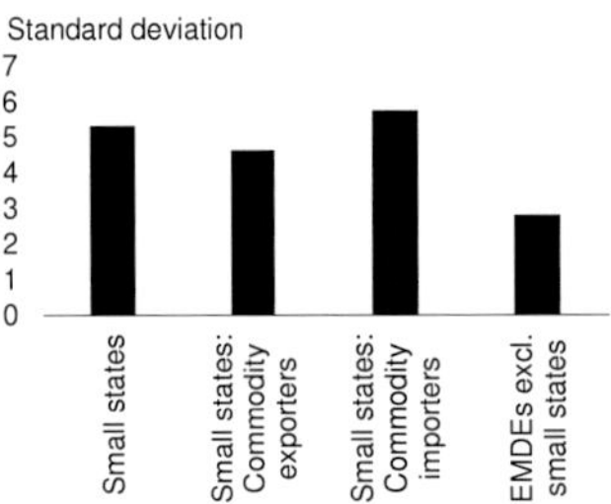

Sources: GFS (database); International Monetary Fund; WEO (database); World Bank.

Note: EAP = East Asia and Pacific; EMDEs = emerging market and developing economies; LAC = Latin America and the Caribbean.

A. Average total expenditure to GDP ratios in 35 small states and 112 other EMDEs.

B. Average total expenditure to GDP ratios by major component of government spending for the period 2011-22. Sample includes 19 small states and 80 other EMDEs.

C.-E. Average primary expenditure to GDP ratios over the period 2011-23.

C. EAP small states include 10 economies, LAC small states include 11 economies, and other small states include 11 economies.

D. Small states commodity exporters include 13 economies, small states commodity importers include 19 economies, and tourism-reliant small states include 20 economies.

E. Micro states have a population of less than 200,000. Micro states include 12 economies, and other small states include 20 economies.

F. Standard deviation of annual change in total expenditure to GDP ratios in 35 small states and 117 other EMDEs for 2000-23. Small states commodity exporters include 13 economies, and small states commodity importers include 22 economies.

foreign currency denominated debt. Fresh econometric analysis underscores these challenges (annex 4.2). An investigation of the fiscal reaction function in small states—which captures how the primary fiscal balance reacts to changes in debt—finds that fiscal policy takes corrective actions in response to rising debt ratios, but only in a muted manner (table A4.2.2). The substantial fiscal impact of such external shocks as global recessions and natural disasters underscores the need for reforms of both revenue and expenditure policies, as appropriate for different countries, supported by rules-based fiscal frameworks aimed at bolstering resilience.

An important reason small states face significant revenue challenges is their generally narrow tax bases—reflecting high economic concentration and, in some cases, reliance on a limited range of taxes—and weak tax administration. Although non-tax sources can generate substantial revenues that may provide a buffer against shocks, these revenues can be highly volatile and subject to risks of being unsustainable—including risks from climate change. Pacific Island economies, for example, face the threat of substantial tuna-catch revenue losses in the coming decades as tuna migration patterns are impacted by rising greenhouse gas emissions (Bell et al. 2021). Economic citizenship programs may experience sudden stops reflecting changes in immigration policies in other countries, and they can lead to reputational risks (Gold and Myrvoda 2017). In many small states international trade taxes, including import tariffs, have traditionally been an important source of revenue because they are relatively easy to enforce at the border. However, as small states lower import duties, their revenues could fall further (Khadan and Hosein 2015). Finally, some small states have adopted aggressive tax regimes designed to attract foreign financial flows, featuring zero or low corporate tax rates or other arrangements that severely limit the tax obligations of foreign entities. These can undermine revenue mobilization. They can also create compliance and transparency risks, and undermine anti-money laundering and combatting terrorism financing efforts (UNCTAD 2024). Additionally, these types of low-tax regimes are at risk from the global minimum tax initiative, which aims to create a fairer international tax system and curb tax avoidance.

Small states' spending requirements are substantially higher than those of other EMDEs partly because of diseconomies of scale in the provision of goods and services and greater vulnerability to natural disasters (Horscroft 2014). Substantial additional spending will be needed to meet the SDGs in small states. Tiedemann et al. (2021), for example, examine spending needs to meet SDGs across five key physical infrastructure and social sectors in a representative sample of small states, taking account of their greater exposure to natural disasters and higher costs of delivering goods and services. Estimated median additional annual spending for small states between 2019 and 2030 is 6.7 percent of 2030 GDP, with higher spending than this needed in poorer countries.

Small states today are characterized by increasingly unsustainable public debt levels, high fiscal volatility, reliance on less secure revenue sources, and high public spending. Restoring sustainability and stability will require action to achieve several policy priorities. These include domestic resource mobilization with an emphasis on increasing the tax share of revenue; increasing spending efficiency; and strengthening fiscal frameworks to boost resilience. Particularly for poorer small states, these efforts need to be complemented by continued external financial support, as well as fiscal capacity building. Such support should focus on the most critical development challenges, including strengthening education, healthcare, and social protection systems, and tackling the substantial threats posed by climate change.

FIGURE 4.11 Composition of government expenditure in small states and other EMDEs

The share of capital expenditure in total government expenditures was slightly higher in small states than in other EMDEs during 2011-22. While varying greatly, small states' interest payments were on average comparable to those of other EMDEs, and, as in other EMDEs, they increased markedly between 2019 and 2023. Small states spend more on health and education, as well as public investment, than other EMDEs.

A. Current and capital expenditure, 2011-22

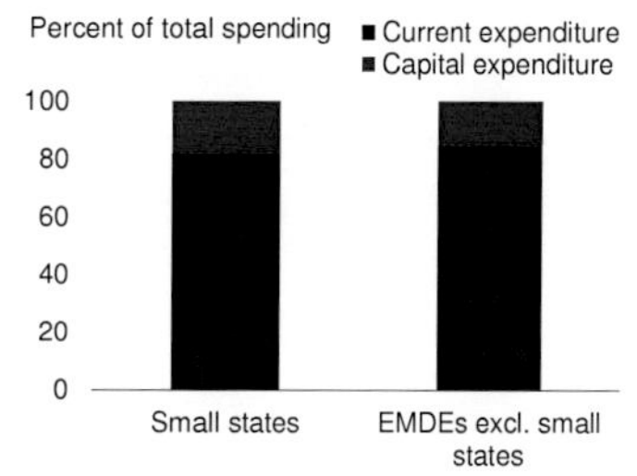

B. Net interest payments

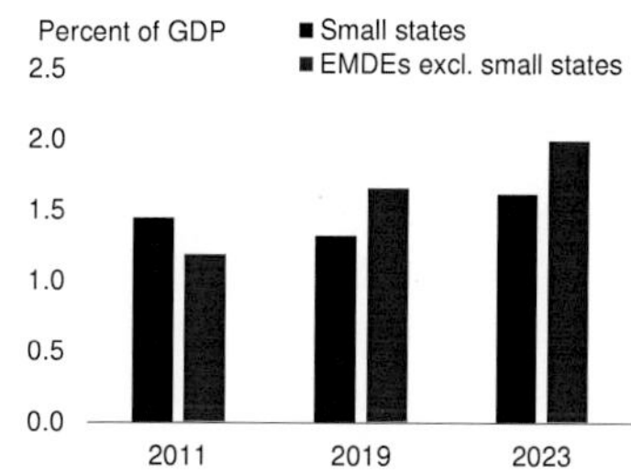

C. Composition of expenditure, 2011-21

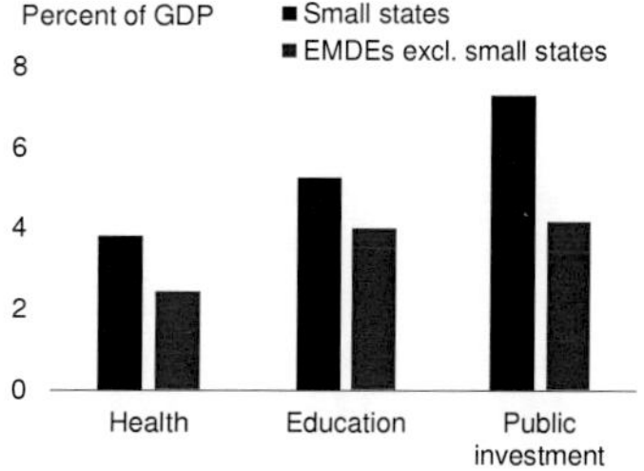

D. Expenditure on healthcare and education by region, 2011-21

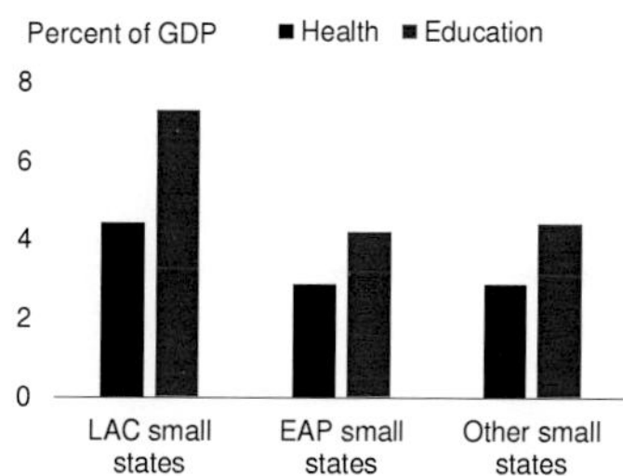

Sources: GFS (database); International Monetary Fund; WDI (database); WEO (database); WHO (database); World Bank.

Note: EAP = East Asia and Pacific; EMDEs = emerging market and developing economies; LAC = Latin America and the Caribbean.

A. Panel shows the share of major components of total spending for 19 small states and 81 other EMDEs for the period 2011-22.

B. Average net interest payments as a percent of GDP for 32 small states and 110 other EMDEs.

C. Average expenditures on health, education, and public investment as a percent of GDP in 31 small states and 116 other EMDEs for the period 2011-21.

D. Average expenditures on health and education as a percent of GDP for the period 2011-21. EAP small states include 10 economies, LAC small states include 11 economies, and other small states include 10 economies.

Domestic revenue mobilization

Although small states benefit from higher average government revenue, relative to GDP, than other EMDEs, there is scope to mobilize greater revenue, particularly from taxes, which would lessen reliance on other revenue sources. Estimates for a sample of small states indicate shortcomings in tax effort—the difference between actual and potential tax revenue, estimated on the basis of economic structural features (McNabb, Danquah, and Tagem 2021). As in other EMDEs, average tax effort in small states lags advanced economies highlighting the scope to boost revenue (figure 4.12). Moreover, there is substantial variation across small states, with tax effort lower among commodity exporters compared with their peers. Increasing tax revenue in small states requires broadening tax bases; in some cases, introducing taxes that are widely used in other EMDEs; strengthening tax collection, including by improving the efficiency of tax administration and modernizing the technology used; and considering raising tax rates where appropriate.

FIGURE 4.12 Domestic revenue mobilization in small states and other EMDEs

Small states rely much more on grants and other non-tax revenues than other EMDEs but there is scope to mobilize additional tax revenues, particularly in commodity exporters, where tax effort lags behind that of peers. Additional tax revenues could be generated by better harnessing technology to support tax collection and, in some cases, by increasing value-added tax rates.

A. Composition of total revenues, 2011-22

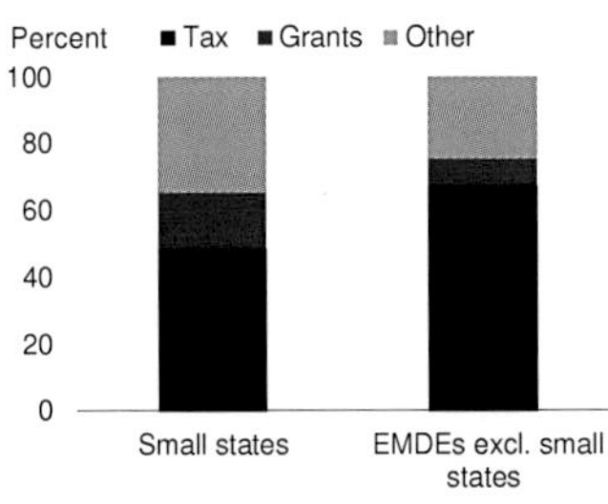

B. Tax effort

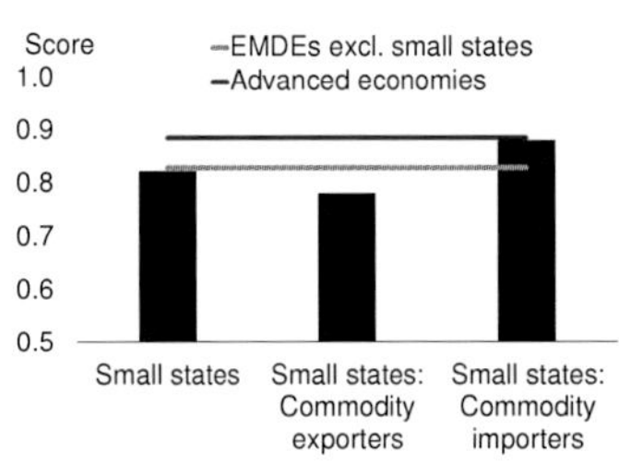

C. Share of electronic tax filing, 2021

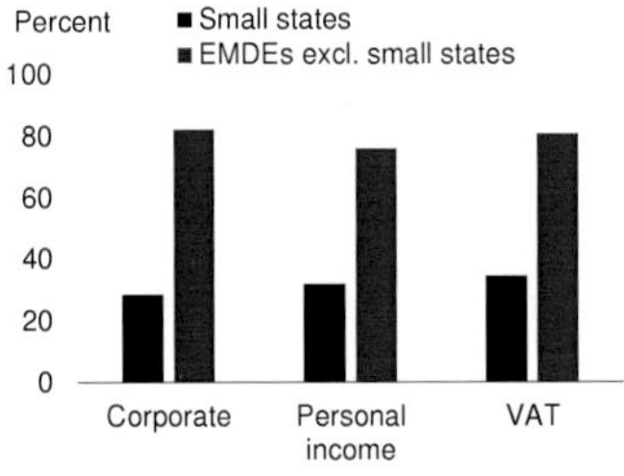

D. VAT rates, 2024

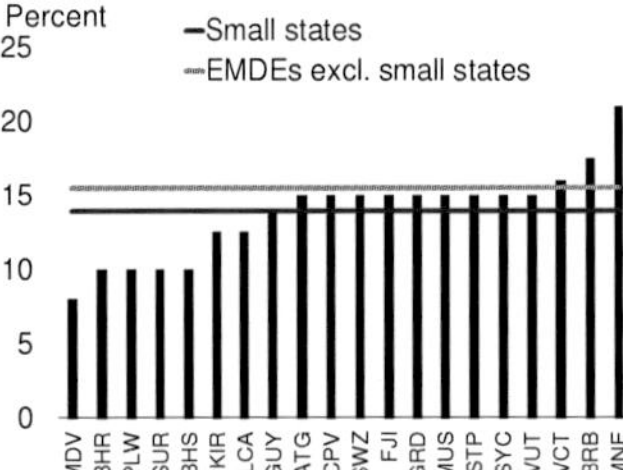

Sources: Ernst and Young (database); GFS (database); International Monetary Fund; ISORA (database), McNabb, Danquah, and Tagem (2021); PWC (database); World Bank.

Note: ATG = Antigua and Barbuda; BHR = Bahrain; BHS = The Bahamas; BRB = Barbados; CPV = Cabo Verde; EMDEs = emerging market and developing economies; FJI = Fiji; GRD = Grenada; GUY = Guyana; KIR = Kiribati; LCA = St. Lucia; MDV = Maldives; MNE = Montenegro; MUS = Mauritius; PLW = Palau; STP = São Tomé and Príncipe; SUR = Suriname; SWZ = Eswatini; SYC = Seychelles; VCT = St. Vincent and the Grenadines; VAT = Value-added tax; VUT = Vanuatu.

A. Panel shows average composition of total revenue by major component in 34 small states and 97 other EMDEs for the period 2011-22.

B. Tax effort reflects the difference between actual and potential tax revenue. Tax potential estimates are latest available for each country based on the true random effects method reported in McNabb, Danquah, and Tagem (2021). Sample includes 14 small states, 8 small states commodity exporters, 6 small states commodity importers, 35 advanced economies, and 98 EMDEs excluding small states.

C. Panel shows share of tax returns filed electronically, for different tax types. Based on a sample of up to 18 small states and 57 other EMDEs for 2021.

D. Panel shows standard VAT rates as of March 2024. EMDEs excluding small states include 81 economies.

Tax policy. Following the trend in other EMDEs, a growing number of small states have introduced value-added taxes (VATs), including recently Palau, São Tomé and Príncipe, and Suriname. VATs offer several advantages over alternatives. They are generally more efficient than taxes on income and international trade. When they are appropriately designed, implemented, and enforced, they can generate significant revenue. Although such broad-based consumption taxes can be regressive, with adverse implications for equity, evidence suggests that this need not be the case, particularly in developing countries, where there is a higher propensity among affluent households to consume goods and services in the formal sector where the VAT is applied (Bachas, Gadenne, and Jensen 2023). Moreover, any regressive effect of VATs can be offset through transfers to poorer households. In small states currently lacking VATs—including Brunei, Marshall Islands and Timor-Leste, where tax revenues are amongst the lowest of all small states—they could be introduced to bolster revenue. Similarly, income taxes—a cornerstone of revenue in most countries and which are typically progressive—could be introduced in The Bahamas and Vanuatu (IMF 2023a, IMF 2024).

VATs and other cornerstone taxes can be exploited more effectively in small states. As a result of tax design and enforcement issues, the average Pacific Island economy collects only about half of its potential VAT revenue (Sy et al. 2022). In addition, VAT rates in small states average 14 percent, around 2 percentage points lower than the average in other EMDEs. This suggests that there is scope to lift VAT rates to increase revenue, as done in Fiji in 2023 when the VAT rate was increased from 9 to 15 percent, while maintaining exemptions for essential items. Small states where VAT rates are well below peers and other EMDEs include The Bahamas and Maldives. Income taxes could also be better utilized in small states to boost revenue and support distribution objectives. Although high corporate income tax rates can hinder competitiveness and discourage investment, there is scope to increase these rates where they are particularly low.

Widespread exemptions and zero rating of certain goods and services give rise to significant foregone revenue, distortions, and complications for tax collection, for example in some LAC small states (Schlotterbeck 2017). Although such exemptions are often intended to support development goals, including progressive redistribution and investment promotion, they are often arbitrary in many respects, opaque and non-transparent—and less effective than other policy options. They need to be carefully reviewed and, unless justified, removed, and governance frameworks should be strengthened to make it more difficult to grant exemptions in the first place (World Bank 2023e).

Tax administration. Strong tax administrations are essential for enforcement and revenue collection. In small states, tax administrations often suffer from organizational inefficiencies, out-of-date systems, and low capacity (Kidd 2010; Schlotterbeck 2017). They are also often obligated to administer a variety of government fees and service charges, which can distract from core tax enforcement and collection functions. Tax administrations in small states also typically lack scale—particularly in micro states, where in several instances there are fewer than 100 staff working in tax and customs administration. Semi-autonomous and integrated organizational approaches that minimize administrative duplication can help maximize efficiency (Junquera-Varela et al. 2019). While a dedicated office for large taxpayers may be infeasible, particularly in micro states, it is essential that adequate resources are mobilized to ensure compliance by large taxpayers, including foreign-owned businesses with ready access to professional advice on how to minimize their tax obligations. More fundamentally, successful tax administration requires a broad consensus that the tax system is fair (Martínez-Vazquez, Sanz-Arcega, and Tránchez-Martín 2023).

A wide variety of digital technologies have been used by tax administrations around the world to improve taxpayer experiences, enhance internal tax and customs operations, strengthen tax compliance, reduce costs, and bolster revenue collection (Junquera-Varela et al. 2022; Nose and Mengistu 2023; Oyebola and Tourek 2023). Digital technologies can also be a vital aid with audits and detecting fraud. Tax administrations in small states have continued to implement new technologies, but in many cases a lack of investment in systems, and broader institutional and digital connectivity constraints, prevent countries from taking full advantage of them (Reyes-Tagle, Silvani, and Ospina 2022). On average, rates of electronic filing of tax returns for income tax and VAT remain markedly lower than in other EMDEs, but they vary significantly across small states, highlighting the opportunity to expand electronic filing in many of them. In some small states virtually all tax returns are filed electronically, which has helped boost revenues, including in Barbados and Mauritius (IMF 2022a, 2023b). In others—including Antigua and Barbuda and Belize—the rate is much lower. Experience shows that integrating digital technologies into tax administration increases tax revenue and reduces the tax compliance gap. For instance, a 50 percent increase in electronic filing adoption can lift tax revenues by 1.6 percent of GDP, while the introduction of mandatory electronic filing can boost revenues by as much as 5 percent of GDP (Nose and Mengistu 2023).

Structural policies. In EMDEs, pervasive informality hinders tax collection (Ohnsorge and Yu 2022). There tends to be less informality in small states than in other EMDEs, reflecting the greater role of the public sector, including as an employer. Even so, measures to reduce informality in small states would support tax collection and yield other benefits (Khadan and Ruprah 2022).

Expenditure efficiency

The public sector in small states tends to be larger than it is in other EMDEs, in part because the government's fixed costs—for administration and infrastructure, for example—represent a larger proportion of the overall economy than is the norm in larger economies. As a result, higher public spending levels in small states can be partially justified by diseconomies of scale (Horscroft 2014). Yet they also reflect expenditure inefficiencies that can weigh on fiscal sustainability (figure 4.13; Afonso and Alves 2023).

Spending efficiency scores, which measure the distance between observed input-output combinations and an estimated efficiency frontier, indicate that there is room for small states to improve spending efficiency in the provision of education and healthcare, and in investment. Enhancing institutional quality is one way of boosting expenditure efficiency. Thus in growth-enhancing public investment projects, inefficiencies may arise from a lack of good governance frameworks, inadequate project appraisals, weak implementation capacity, and corruption (Schwartz et al. 2020).

FIGURE 4.13 Expenditure efficiency in small states and other economies

Small states spend more, relative to GDP, on social development and infrastructure investment than other EMDEs, but do not achieve superior outcomes. Several factors, including weak governance and implementation challenges, contribute to inefficiencies in public projects. Small states, particularly commodity exporters, spend significant amounts on subsidies, especially for energy consumption. Digital connectivity is particularly poor in small states in EAP and SSA, but significantly better in small states in LAC than in other EMDEs.

A. Healthcare, education expenditures and human development outcomes, 2011-21

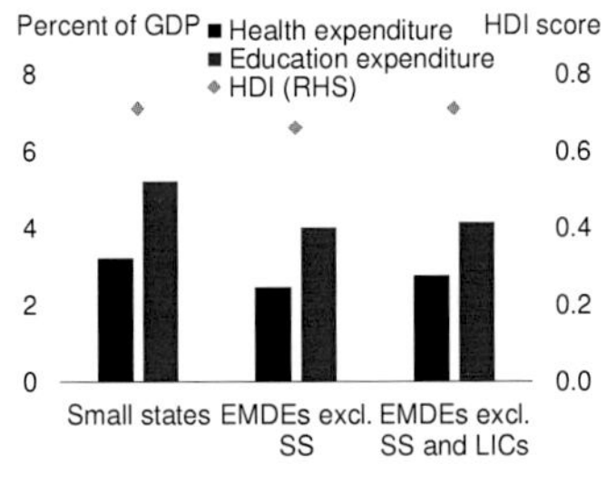

B. Spending efficiency, 2010-20

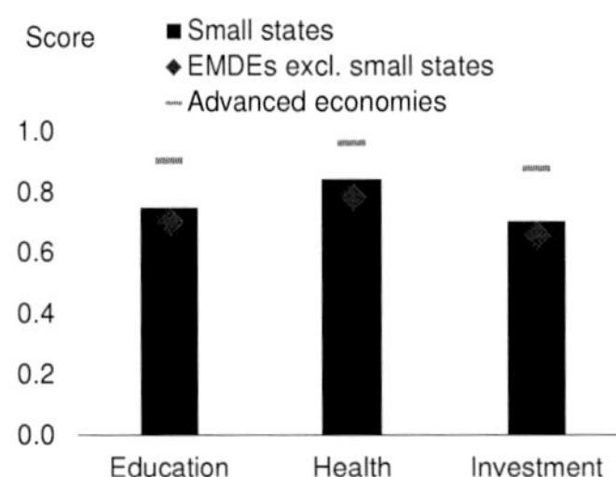

C. Energy subsidies, 2022

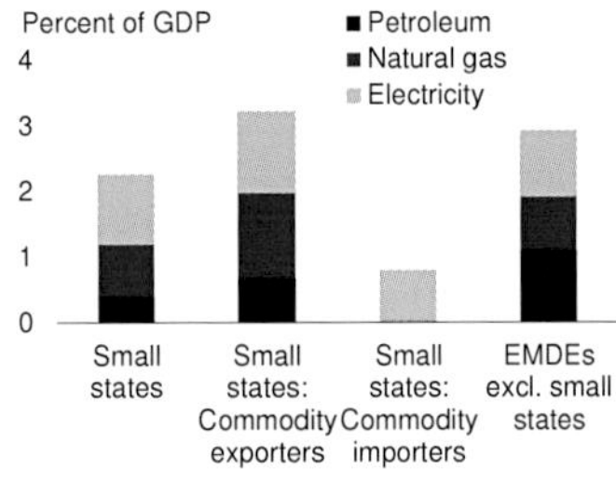

D. Digital connectivity, 2019

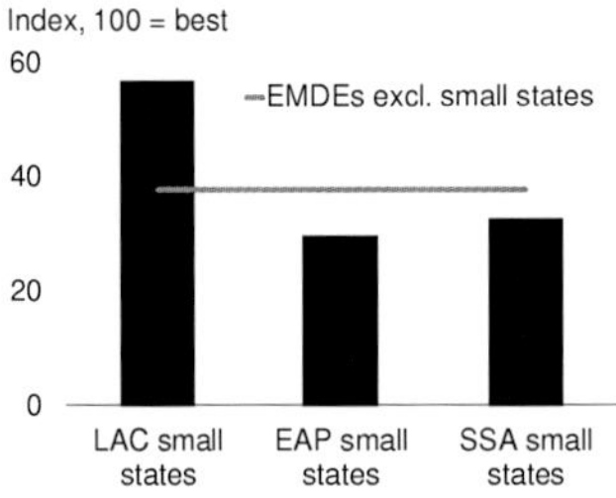

Sources: Black et al. (2023); Cantu-Bazaldua (2021); GFS (database); Herrera et al. (forthcoming); WDI (database); World Bank.

Note: EAP = East Asia and Pacific; EMDEs = emerging market and developing economies; LAC = Latin America and the Caribbean; LICs = Low-Income Countries; SS = Small states; SSA = Sub-Saharan Africa.

A. Panel shows the Human Development Index (HDI) score for 2021 and average health and education expenditures as a percent of GDP for 30 small states and 104 EMDEs excluding small states for the peirod 2011-21.

B. Bars show average efficiency score for up to five different methodologies for 35 small states for health, 6 small states for education, and 8 small states infrastructure investment for the period 2010-20 from Herrera et al. (forthcoming). Sample includes 32 advanced economies and up to 111 EMDEs excluding small states.

C. Bars show average explicit subsidies as a percent of GDP by energy type in 2022. Sample includes 20 small states, 12 small states commodity exporters, 8 small states commodity importers, and 113 EMDEs excluding small states.

D. Digital connectivity is a composite measure of Internet access of the population, international bandwidth per Internet user, and latency rate (a measure of network performance). Bars and line show medians of country groups. Sample includes 13 EAP small states, 11 LAC small states, 6 SSA small states, and 117 EMDEs excluding small states.

Small states spend more on social development, without achieving superior outcomes than other EMDEs. For example, small states' expenditures on education and healthcare is about 2 percentage points of GDP higher than in other EMDEs at comparable income levels, while their Human Development Index (HDI) scores are broadly similar. Small states could more effectively leverage technology to improve expenditure efficiency (Favaro 2008). Public expenditures in small states are also more rigid than other EMDEs, with a significant share allocated to subsidies, numerous public enterprises, the public wage bill, and resources needed to respond to natural disasters (Alichi, Shibata, and Tanyeri 2021; World Bank 2023b). The large wage bills in small states, which have tended to ratchet upward during economic upswings without offsetting downward adjustments in downturns, exacerbates fiscal vulnerabilities for these countries (Mitchell, James, and Wickham 2019).

Subsidies. As in other EMDEs, governments in some small states provide generous fuel and energy subsidies that often favor high-income households and underpin a range of sometimes poorly targeted social welfare programs (Del Granado, Coady, and Gillingham 2012; Black et al. 2023). Small states' energy subsidies, relative to GDP, are on average slightly lower than in other EMDEs, but in small-state commodity exporters they are markedly higher. Some small states have begun to phase out fuel and other subsidies since the pandemic. For example, Suriname, a commodity exporter, has begun to phase out its large fuel and energy subsidies, whose value in 2022 has been estimated at 5.3 percent of GDP (IMF 2023c). Reducing these poorly targeted subsidies can help governments increase spending in critical areas such as healthcare, education, and climate-resilient infrastructure. Winding back fossil-fuel subsidies can also support other policy objectives, notably encouraging investment in renewable energy, mitigating climate change, and reducing pollution.

State-owned enterprises. SOEs are a major source of spending pressure and fiscal risk in small states. The outsized role of the public sector in providing goods and services has led to a prolifera-tion of SOEs in many small states. Small states in LAC are some of the most densely populated countries with SOEs in the Western Hemisphere (Reyes-Tagle et al. 2022). SOEs are generally unprofitable, inefficient, and poorly managed, requiring large fiscal transfers and posing cash flow and contingent liability risks to their governments. In some small states, governments are required to cover annual losses of SOEs amounting to as much as 9 percent of GDP (Reyes-Tagle et al. 2022). The pandemic has further increased fiscal risks from SOEs, including from national airlines in some Pacific Island small states that suffered from the collapse in tourism (Balasundharam et al. 2021). State-owned utility companies usually are also among those that pose large fiscal risks. For example, in São Tomé and Príncipe, the public electricity and water company accumulated arrears amounting to around one-third of GDP in 2022 (World Bank 2023f). Weak fiscal governance is one of the key factors contributing to the inefficiency of SOEs. Policymakers should prioritize bolstering the financial management of these entities, emphasizing robust transparency and accountability frameworks, including through community service obligation mechanisms, and consolidation and privatization where appropriate (Reyes-Tagle et al. 2022).

Aside from phasing out poorly targeted subsidies and transfers, to improve spending efficiency, policy makers in small states should improve public financial management and public investment management (see chapter 3). They can enhance the effectiveness of education spending by developing and implementing evidence-based and carefully costed initiatives that target specific improvements in learning outcomes. Greater regional cooperation may also help them reduce overhead costs, including relating to some administrative tasks (World Bank 2023b). The impact of health spending can be strengthened by focusing on high-return investments—including prevention and primary health care—and ensuring value for money in large expenditure areas such as human resources and pharmaceuticals. Finally, policy makers need to exploit emerging opportunities from innovations in digital connectivity to reduce service-delivery costs and expand telehealth and similar services.

Robust fiscal frameworks

Small states need resilient fiscal frameworks. Large external shocks, such as natural disasters, global recessions, pandemics, and commodity-price shifts, have had long-lasting impacts on debt and fiscal positions in small states, and are likely to continue doing so (Lee, Zhang, and Nguyen

FIGURE 4.14 Fiscal performance and fiscal frameworks

Government revenue and expenditure in small states over the past decade were characterized by volatile growth, leaving limited fiscal buffers in many cases, as indicated by levels of public debt and primary balances. Shortcomings in fiscal management may reflect, in part, the relatively low proportion of small states with fiscal rules, fiscal councils, and sovereign wealth funds, and the relatively low quality of governance.

A. Revenue and expenditure growth in small states

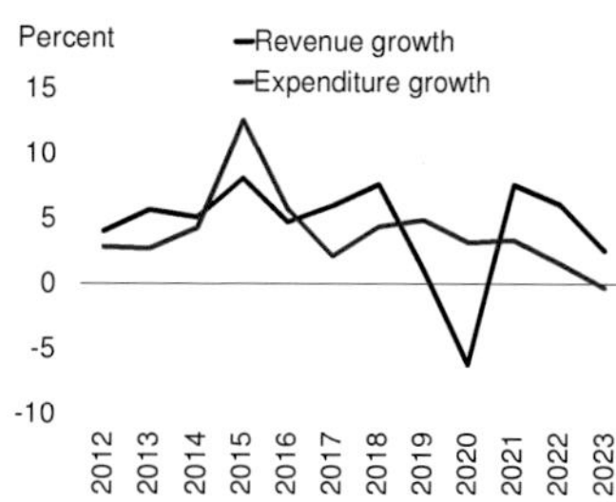

B. Public debt and primary fiscal balances in small states, 2020-23

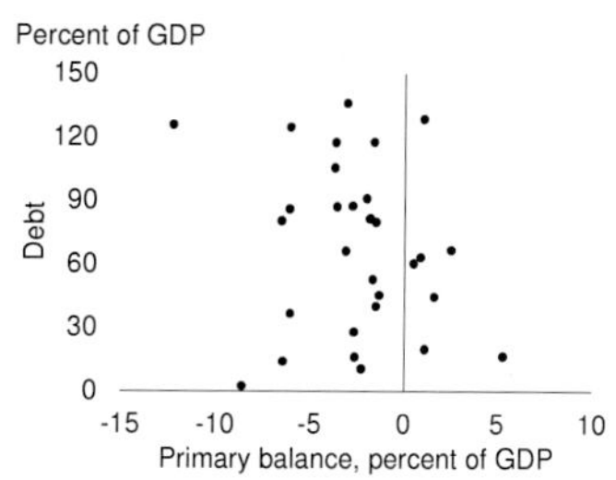

C. Share of economies with fiscal rules, 2021

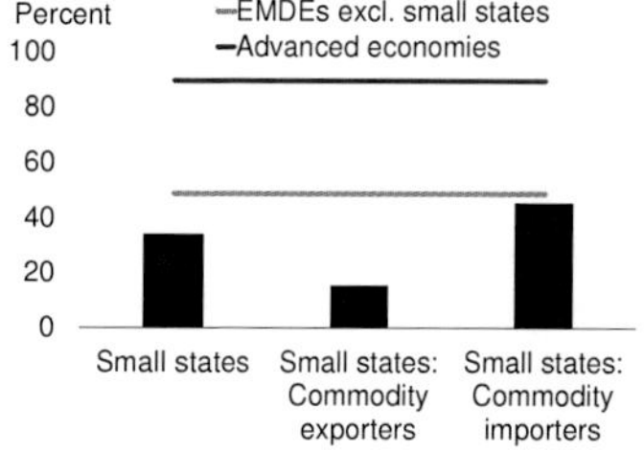

D. Share of economies with fiscal councils, 2021

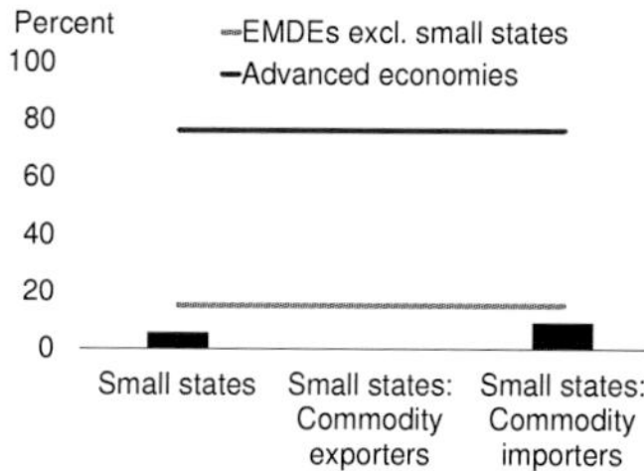

E. Share of economies with sovereign wealth funds, 2022

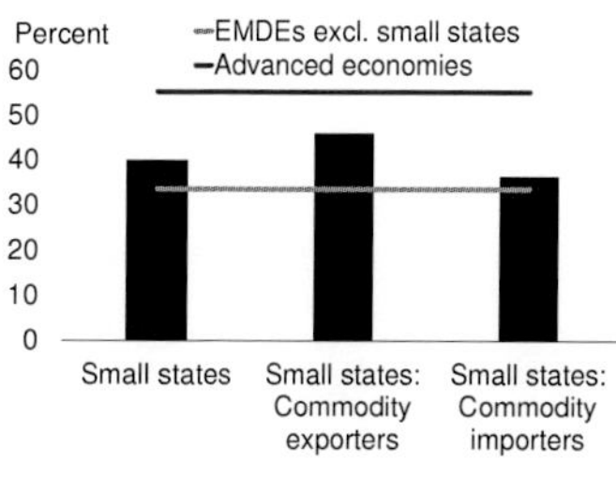

F. Quality of governance, 2000-22

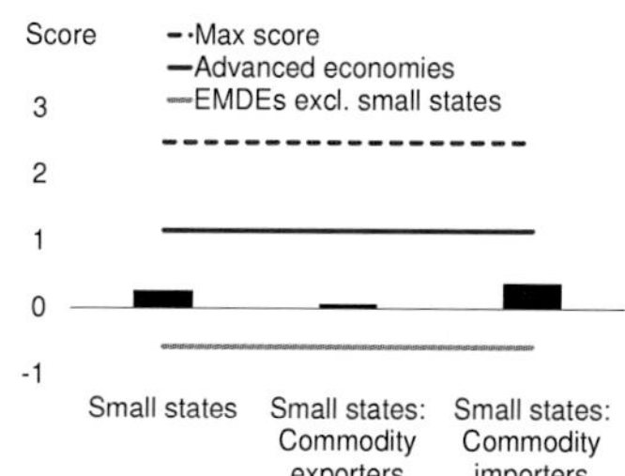

Sources: Davoodi et al. (2022a); Global SWF; International Monetary Fund; WDI (database); WEO (database); World Bank.

Note: EMDEs = emerging market and developing economies.

A. Annual growth rate of real revenue and real expenditure in 35 small states.

B. Average public debt to GDP ratio and primary balance to GDP ratio in 32 small states for the period 2020-23.

C.-E. Sample includes 35 small states, 13 small states commodity exporters, 22 small states commodity importers, 119 EMDEs excluding small states, and 38 advanced economies.

C. Percent of economies that have fiscal rules as of 2021.

D. Percent of economies that have fiscal councils as of 2021.

E. Percent of economies that have sovereign wealth funds as of 2022.

F. Average of Worldwide Governance Indicators for the period 2000-22. Sample includes 35 small states, 13 small states commodity exporters, 22 small states commodity importers, 119 EMDEs excluding small states, and 38 advanced economies. Dotted red line denotes maximum score of 2.5 for governance indicators.

2018; Mohan and Strobl 2021). Spending rigidities, associated with significant non-discretionary spending, volatile revenue, and procyclical fiscal policy all threaten fiscal sustainability (figure 4.14; Cabezon et al. 2019). Small states trail other developing countries in several areas of debt management (Prasad, Pollock, and Li 2013). Fiscal frameworks should therefore prioritize resilience to external shocks and an appropriate balance between maintaining adequate fiscal buffers and increasing investment in priority areas, notably human capital and climate-resilient infrastructure.

Rules-based fiscal frameworks. Well-designed fiscal rules, featuring clear sustainability goals and supporting countercyclical fiscal policy, within medium-term fiscal frameworks, can curb excessive fiscal deficits and support sustainable public finances (Blanco et al. 2020; Caselli et al. 2022; Eyraud et al. 2018; Heller 2022). When these rules are reinforced by strong institutions, and paired with fiscal councils and sovereign wealth funds, they can enhance resilience to external shocks, increase fiscal space for growth-enhancing policies, boost fiscal discipline, and reduce debt (IMF 2019). The reforms needed to establish such frameworks, rules, and institutions are likely to require buy-in and support from stakeholders, which are potentially more achievable in small states (Arslanalp, Eichengreen, and Henry 2024). Fiscal rules, along with well-designed macroeconomic policies, can also boost growth of GDP per capita, particularly in commodity-exporting countries, by reducing the volatility of fiscal policy (World Bank 2024b).

Among the different types of fiscal rules, primary balance rules which help build and maintain fiscal buffers could be more effective than expenditure rules, particularly for small states vulnerable to natural disasters and with high levels of public debt (IMF 2022b; Nakatani 2021). Successful fiscal rules in small states typically include targets for both debt and operational variables—for example, limits on the growth of recurrent expenditure—which provide flexibility for increases in capital spending in response to natural disasters while maintaining broader spending discipline. Robust enforceability frameworks, and a tailored approach that takes into account country-specific characteristics, notably vulnerability to natural disasters, can bolster the effectiveness of such rules (IMF 2022b).

Fiscal councils. These technical bodies, working independently of government, are integral to a rules-based fiscal framework, supporting fiscal transparency by evaluating fiscal plans and budget forecasts, and overseeing adherence to fiscal rules. Non-government actors, such as academics and private sector analysts, who can help promote prudent fiscal policy by providing public scrutiny of government decisions and demanding accountability, tend to be more limited in small states. Hence, fiscal councils can substantially strengthen fiscal frameworks, especially in commodity exporters that are susceptible to weak governance and less transparent fiscal operations. They are most effective when they operate with a high degree of independence, ample funding, and well-defined mandates aligned with fiscal rules (Davoodi et al. 2022b). Among small states, The Bahamas and Grenada have established fiscal councils to strengthen their fiscal frameworks, with the objective of monitoring and reporting on government's compliance with fiscal objectives, including fiscal rules (Mooney, Wright, and Grenade 2018). The effectiveness of fiscal frameworks in small states, encompassing both fiscal rules and fiscal councils, is exemplified by the case of Grenada. Enforceable and flexible fiscal rules were instrumental in reducing the country's public debt from 105 percent of GDP in 2013 to 60 percent of GDP in 2019 (IMF 2022b). As of 2023, Grenada's public debt stood at 62 percent of GDP.

Sovereign wealth funds and other fiscal stabilization funds. While these funds exist in several small states, their sizes vary, and in some cases, they are large relative to GDP (Gratcheva and Emery 2021). Where they do not currently exist, policy makers should consider establishing them, and using them to enhance fiscal sustainability and help manage volatility. These funds can play a particularly important role in reducing small states' vulnerability to external shocks. Sovereign wealth funds can help stabilize government consumption, and mitigate the adverse effects of revenue volatility on fiscal outcomes (Ehigiamusoe and Lean 2018; IMF 2015).

Countries with sovereign wealth funds that have a short- to medium-term stabilization objective exhibit more stable fiscal policies, with 14 percent less volatile government consumption than in countries without such funds (Al-Sadiq and Gutierrez 2023). In small commodity-exporting economies, sovereign wealth funds have been shown to reduce fiscal policy volatility (Giles, Gauto, and Khadan 2021). The benefit of these funds can be maximized by ensuring strong governance arrangements, transparency, and simple operational rules that constrain discretion. Fund balances should provide meaningful buffers against large fiscal shocks, considering the rising threat posed by climate change-related natural disasters. Sovereign wealth funds can be established using revenue windfalls from economic upturns and savings from improved spending efficiency.

Small states have considerable room to improve their fiscal frameworks. Some small states began adopting fiscal rules in the late 1990s, including, in LAC, for example, Antigua and Barbuda, Dominica, and Grenada. By 2021 about one-third (12) of small states had adopted some type of fiscal rule, compared with half of other EMDEs. All small states with a fiscal rule also have a debt rule. Eight of these countries have balanced-budget rules, four have expenditure rules, and two have revenue rules. Few small states have independent fiscal councils, as with other EMDEs. Although the proportion of small states with sovereign wealth funds is comparable to other EMDEs, both are lower than in advanced economies. Sovereign wealth funds in small states vary in design and goals. Some function as trust funds to secure long-term budget self-reliance, particularly in EAP small states (Gratcheva and Emery 2021). Others have a strong focus on investment and development objectives, with fewer emphasizing clear stabilization roles (Al-Sadiq and Gutierrez 2023). Sovereign wealth funds should aim to strike a balance between building long-term savings, including for development goals, and managing short- to medium-term fiscal risks faced by small states, such as volatility and external shocks (Ossowski 2021).

Fiscal transparency and governance. Improving fiscal transparency and broader governance, including policies to prevent money laundering and the financing of terrorism, is crucial for small states. This is particularly so given their consistently low rankings on budget transparency indexes. Enhancing accessibility to budget documentation, and increased dialogue with stakeholders and the public, can yield benefits for these countries. For example, improvements in data transparency have been associated with reductions in borrowing costs, especially for countries with strong institutional quality (Cady and Pellechio 2006; Kubota and Zeufack 2020).

In summary, taking into account the distinct challenges faced by small states, as a priority they need to establish well-designed, flexible, but enforceable rules-based fiscal frameworks with adequate buffers to withstand frequent and large external shocks. Fiscal policy in small states should be firmly anchored within credible medium-term fiscal frameworks, ensuring ample fiscal space for countercyclical policies, and reinforced by sovereign wealth funds focused on managing volatility and external shocks. These frameworks should be complemented by efforts to better harness revenues from stable tax sources and improve the efficiency of already high government spending.

International cooperation

Concerted international cooperation is needed to help small states address the deterioration in their fiscal positions in the aftermath of the pandemic. Given their substantial expenditure pressures, unique vulnerabilities—notably their particularly high exposure to climate change-related natural disasters—and limited institutional capacity and access to private finance, small states will need continued access to well-coordinated and tailored financial and technical assistance from the international community to help strengthen their fiscal positions, bolster their institutional frameworks, address reform needs, and build resilience (Fuje et al. 2023).

Flexible development finance such as concessional lending and grants—including through IDA for eligible small states—can help to provide needed resources (figure 4.15; World Bank 2023g, 2023h). So can continued international efforts to

FIGURE 4.15 Donor support for small states and other EMDEs

Reflecting their significant development challenges, small states receive substantially more official development assistance, in relation to GDP, than other EMDEs. Larger shares of small states are grant-reliant and eligible to access IDA financing than other EMDEs.

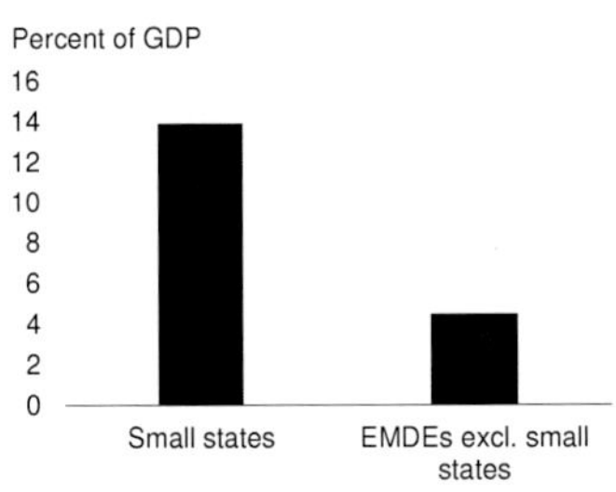

B. Shares of grant-reliant and IDA-eligible countries

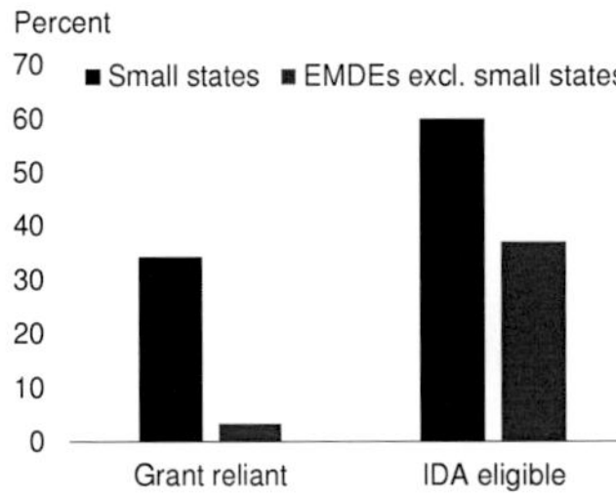

Sources: WDI (database); World Bank.

Note: EMDEs = emerging market and developing economies; IDA = International Development Association.

A. Average official development assistance as a percent of GDP. Sample includes 28 small states and 104 EMDEs excluding small states.

B. Share of countries that are grant reliant, and those that are classified as IDA eligible as of 2023, as detailed in table 4.1.

mobilize private capital. Small states face challenges in funding substantial investments in climate-change adaptation, especially because domestic revenues have been slow to recover in the wake of the pandemic. Some countries have used debt-for-climate swaps to fund climate-adaptation initiatives (Thomas and Theokritoff 2021). Belize successfully negotiated debt forgiveness in exchange for implementing a program centered on rainforest conservation and the management of protected areas (IMF 2022c). More recently, the World Bank allowed small states to prioritize disaster recovery over debt repayment during catastrophic events (World Bank 2023i).

The international community can continue to assist in building small states' resilience to natural disasters through financing and insurance solutions. Cost constraints resulting from higher exposure to natural disasters often result in inadequate insurance coverage for small states (Cebotari and Youssef 2020). For example, regional risk pooling mechanisms such as the Caribbean Catastrophe Risk Insurance Facility, the African Risk Capacity, and the Pacific Catastrophe Risk Assessment and Financing Initiative—have helped some small-states governments cushion the fiscal impact of natural disasters (World Bank 2022). These regional initiatives could be expanded to global risk pooling to boost efficiency, further diversify risks, and extending support beyond the initial response phase (Ciullo et al. 2023). Adding catastrophic bonds—which provide compensation to the issuer when predefined natural disaster risks are realized—to disaster risk financing options could further strengthen financial resilience in small states (OECD 2024).

Rising debt and borrowing costs have increased debt-servicing burdens and heightened the urgency of addressing unsustainable debt. Almost one-third of small states have defaulted or restructured debt since 2003, including two (Belize and Suriname) since the pandemic (Asonuma and Trebesch 2016; Erce, Mallucci, and Picarelli 2022). In most cases, these countries received support from international financial institutions, along with debt relief from creditors. Around one-quarter of small states benefited from IMF support for policy programs during 2011-23, including five countries since the pandemic. Debt relief and restructuring processes, including the G20 Common Framework, need to recognize the unique challenges facing small states. They should also take into account the increasingly diverse creditor landscape—particularly the crucial role of non-Paris Club members, especially China, an increasingly important lender which has been involved in debt-restructuring negotiations with several small states (Horn, Reinhart, and Trebesch 2022). The international community can also help improve debt sustainability by working to enhance debt transparency across the world, including by increasing the availability of relevant statistics and by promoting better transaction-disclosure practices (Maslen and Cigdem 2022).

Finally, the international community can continue to support small states through tailored technical assistance. Small states have limited institutional capacity. Like many EMDEs, they may lack the technical know-how required to implement in a timely manner adequate fiscal reforms—including strengthening domestic revenue mobilization, reforming SOEs, establishing a sovereign wealth fund and implementing fiscal rules

(Balasundharam and Khadan 2024; Heller 2022). Overall, small states have made good progress in some aspects of climate change adaptation planning. In other areas, however, they appear to be lagging other EMDEs (UNEP 2023). Limited economic data, such as reliable macroeconomic statistics and household surveys, often hinder evidence-based policy making in these countries. A weak civil service and complex bureaucratic processes erode government efficiency and contribute to delays in policy reforms (Lafuente and Molina 2018).

Conclusion

The unique structural characteristics of small states constrain their fiscal policy. They include high trade openness, limited economic diversification, narrow tax bases, obstacles to providing public goods and services at scale, and vulnerability to external shocks—particularly those arising from climate-change-related natural disasters and global recessions. Many small states, particularly micro states, rely heavily on external grants and non-tax sources for revenue. Meanwhile, government expenditure is skewed toward public wage bills and consumption of goods and services. As a result, small states experience higher fiscal volatility than other EMDEs, which heightens their policy challenges.

The pandemic and subsequent global shocks have compounded long-standing fiscal challenges by widening fiscal deficits and increasing public debt across small states. Government revenues in small states took a hit during the pandemic, especially in countries dependent on tourism. These revenues have been much slower to recover than in other EMDEs. Government spending also rose more in small states in the years following the pandemic than in other EMDEs. Thus, in 2020-23, around three-quarters of small states reported weaker primary balance-to-GDP ratios than their 5-year pre-pandemic average. Government debt-to GDP ratios also increased from already high levels in most small states, reflecting sustained fiscal deficits and large economic contractions followed by sluggish recoveries.

Worsening fiscal and debt positions in small states, coupled with increased vulnerability to external shocks, including from climate change, and the need to address long-standing development needs, demand action through both domestic policy measures and international support.

These obstacles are not insurmountable, however. Governments in small states retain the capacity to build fiscal resilience, with support from the international community. There is ample room to boost domestic revenues and improve spending efficiencies. Raising tax revenues requires small states to broaden tax bases; in some cases, introduce taxes that are widely used in other EMDEs; strengthen tax collection; and consider raising tax rates. Strengthening fiscal governance and financial management, and improving transparency and accountability frameworks, can significantly enhance expenditure efficiency, particularly in the large state-enterprise sectors in many of these countries. Better targeted social spending and subsidies could further increase fiscal space for governments to invest in human capital and build resilience to external shocks.

Small states should prioritize the establishment of rules-based fiscal frameworks tailored to their distinct characteristics and vulnerabilities. These frameworks should include fiscal rules that not only establish discipline but also allow countercyclical policy to manage the effects of frequent external shocks, especially those arising from natural disasters; fiscal councils to bolster fiscal discipline; and sovereign wealth funds that provide buffers against large shocks. Small states currently lacking access to adequate natural disaster insurance facilities could benefit from them to cushion the fiscal impact of natural disasters.

Small states will continue to require access to well-coordinated and tailored financial and technical assistance from the international community. These include financial support to help address debt challenges and support investment in climate change resilience, and technical assistance to help improve fiscal policy management, and the implementation of reforms.

TABLE 4.1 EMDE small states, by feature

	Tourism reliant	Commodity exporter	FCS	Micro states	Risk of overall debt distress	Grant reliant	World Bank lending category
Antigua and Barbuda	X			X			IBRD
Bahrain	X	X					
Barbados	X						
Bahamas, The	X						
Belize	X	X					IBRD
Bhutan		X			Moderate	X	IDA
Brunei Darussalam		X					
Cabo Verde	X	X			High	X	Blend
Comoros		X	X		High	X	IDA
Djibouti					High	X	IDA
Dominica	X			X	High		Blend
Eswatini							IBRD
Fiji	X	X					Blend
Grenada	X			X	In distress	X	Blend
Guyana		X			Moderate		IDA
Kiribati			X	X	High	X	IDA
Maldives	X				High		IDA
Marshall Islands	X		X	X	High	X	IDA
Mauritius	X						IBRD
Micronesia, Fed Sts.	X		X	X	High	X	IDA
Montenegro	X						IBRD
Nauru				X		X	IBRD
Palau	X			X		X	IBRD
Samoa	X				High	X	IDA
São Tomé and Príncipe		X	X		In distress	X	IDA
Seychelles	X	X		X			IBRD
Solomon Islands		X	X		Moderate	X	IDA
St. Kitts and Nevis	X			X			IBRD
St. Lucia	X			X			Blend
St. Vincent and the Grenadines	X			X	High		Blend
Suriname		X					IBRD
Timor-Leste		X	X		Moderate	X	Blend
Tonga	X			X	High	X	IDA
Tuvalu			X	X	High	X	IDA
Vanuatu	X				Moderate	X	IDA

Sources: GFS (database); UN World Tourism Organization; World Bank.

Note: Tourism-reliant countries are those with inbound tourism expenditure as a share of GDP during 2015-19 above the 3rd percentile of the share in all EMDEs, based on UN World Tourism Organization data. Commodity exporter economies are those when, on average in 2017-19, either (1) total commodities exports accounted for 30 percent or more of total exports or (2) exports of any single commodity accounted for 20 percent or more of total exports. Economies for which these thresholds were met as a result of re-exports were excluded. Micro states are those with a population of less than 200,000. Risk of overall debt distress ratings reflect the latest published ratings based on the IMF-World Bank low-income debt sustainability analysis framework. Dates of latest published results vary across countries. Grant-reliant countries are those with grants as a share of GDP during 2015-2021 above the 90th percentile of all EMDEs. FCS = fragile and conflict-affected situations; IBRD = International Bank for Reconstruction and Development; IDA = International Development Association.

ANNEX 4.1 Debt decomposition

Changes in the public debt-to-GDP ratio (denoted by d in equation 4.1.1) can be decomposed into several explanatory terms. Specifically, changes in the ratio can be decomposed into contributions from GDP growth, primary fiscal balances—which reflect the difference between revenues and non-interest expenditures—interest costs, inflation, and other factors.

Following World Bank (2023c), one equation for decomposing changes in the debt-to-GDP ratio is as follows:

$$d_t - d_{t-1} = \frac{i_t - \pi_t - g_t(1+\pi_t)}{(1+g_t)(1+\pi_t)} d_{t-1} \qquad (4.1.1)$$

$$- pb_t + other\ factors$$

In equation 4.1.1 i_t is the effective nominal interest rate; π_t inflation (measured as the GDP deflator); and g_t is real GDP growth. Debt, d_t, and the primary fiscal balance, pb_t, are scaled by nominal GDP. The term "other factors" includes factors such as exchange rate depreciation, privatization proceeds, the materialization of contingent liabilities, and other ad-hoc adjustments to debt stocks. Equation 4.1.1 can be reorganized to identify the contributions to changes in the debt-to-GDP ratio from key components in additive form as follows:

$$d_t - d_{t-1} = \frac{i_t}{1+\gamma_t} d_{t-1} - \frac{\pi_t}{1+\gamma_t} d_{t-1} \qquad (4.1.2)$$

$$- \frac{g_t}{1+g_t} d_{t-1} - pb_t + other\ factors$$

where $\gamma_t = (1+g_t)(1+\pi_t)$

Equation 4.1.2 is used as the basis for decomposing the change in the debt-to-GDP ratio into the attributable components of: (1) the primary fiscal balance; (2) interest costs; (3) inflation; and (4) real GDP growth. Due to data limitations for the countries of interest, notably on ad-hoc debt stock adjustments and the currency composition of debt, the contributions from other factors are calculated as the difference between changes in the debt-to-GDP ratio and the sum of components (1) to (4). The decomposition includes all small states with data available for all terms in equation 4.1.2, for the period 2011 to 2026, as detailed in table A4.1.1.

ANNEX 4.2 Fiscal reaction function

Fiscal reaction functions show the extent to which fiscal policy reacts to changes in the level of government debt (Bohn 1998; Mendoza and Ostry 2008). The basic equation for a government's fiscal reaction function is as follows:

$$pb_{i,t} = \tau \cdot d_{i,t-1} + \varepsilon_{i,t} \qquad (4.2.1)$$

where $pb_{i,t}$ and $d_{i,t}$ refer to country i primary fiscal balance and debt to GDP ratios at time t. The parameter τ is a measure of the responsiveness of the primary balance to changes in debt levels, and $\varepsilon_{i,t}$ is the error term. The model specification in equation 4.2.1 is extended to control for other economic, policy, and political factors as follows:

$$pb_{i,t} = \alpha + \delta pb_{i,t-1} + \tau \cdot d_{i,t-1} + \beta X_{i,t} \qquad (4.2.2)$$

$$+ \Theta_i + \gamma_t + \varepsilon_{i,t}$$

where $X_{i,t}$ includes economic growth, inflation, national elections, and the presence of a fiscal rule for country i at time t (table A4.2.1). The variables Θ_i and γ_t are dummy variables representing country fixed effects and time fixed effects. The regressions are estimated for the period 2001-2023 (table A4.2.2). As detailed in table A4.1.1 all small states for which data are available are included in the sample, except grant-dependent economies. As grants partly reflect the policy choices of donors, the presence of large grants may distort the interpretation of the results.

Endogeneity and cross-sectional correlation are key issues to address when estimating equation 4.2.2. First, the inclusion of $pb_{i,t-1}$ can cause the estimated coefficient $(\hat{\delta})$ to be biased when estimated with fixed effects estimators (Nickell 1981), although the bias diminishes when the time dimension is relatively large (Judson and Owen 1999; Nickell 1981). The bias-corrected least-squares dummy variable estimator of Bruno (2005) is used as a robustness check of the results obtained from the fixed effects estimator. However, a further methodological challenge is that inflation and growth are likely to be endogenous to the contemporaneous primary balance. As such, lagged values (first and second lags) of both variables are used as instruments in a panel fixed effects instrumental variable (FE-IV) estimator.

The sample of countries, especially for the small states group, share similar features such as high dependence on commodity and tourism exports, and susceptibility to external shocks. These characteristics may imply the presence of cross-sectional dependence. Time fixed effects are used in the FE-IV estimator to control for these common factors (see Jansen 2016). Additionally, the Prais-Winsten estimator with correlated panels corrected standard errors (PCSEs) and the Driscoll-Kraay estimators are used as robustness checks to account for the presence of cross-sectional dependence (see Prais and Winsten 1954; Driscoll and Kraay 1998).

TABLE A4.1.1 List of small states included in the debt decomposition analysis, and the fiscal reaction function analysis

Antigua and Barbuda*	Comoros*	Maldives*	St. Kitts and Nevis*
Bahamas, The*	Djibouti*	Marshall Islands	St. Lucia*
Bahrain*	Dominica*	Mauritius*	St. Vincent and the Grenadines*
Barbados*	Eswatini*	Micronesia, Fed. Sts.	Suriname*
Belize*	Fiji*	Montenegro*	Timor-Leste
Bhutan	Grenada*	São Tomé and Príncipe	Tonga
Brunei Darussalam*	Guyana*	Seychelles*	Tuvalu
Cabo Verde*	Kiribati	Solomon Islands	Vanuatu

Source: World Bank.
Note: Table lists countries included in the debt decomposition exercise described in annex 4.1. Countries with * are also included in the sample for the fiscal reaction function analysis described in annex 4.2.

TABLE A4.2.1 Variables, definitions, and data sources for fiscal reaction function analysis

Variables	Definition	Sources
Primary balance	Primary balance as a share of GDP	World Economic Outlook, IMF
Debt	General government debt as a share of GDP	World Economic Outlook, IMF
Economic growth	Real GDP growth	World Economic Outlook, IMF
Inflation	Inflation, average consumer prices	World Economic Outlook, IMF
National elections	Dummy variable equals 1 for the year of and prior to general elections in countries, and 0 otherwise	Cruz, Keefer, and Scartascini (2018)
Fiscal rule	Dummy variable equal to 1 for the period of time countries had a fiscal rule in place and 0 otherwise	Davoodi et al. (2022a)

Source: World Bank.
Note: IMF = International Monetary Fund.

TABLE A4.2.2 Small states' fiscal reaction functions: Results

	Baseline		Extended model	
	FE	Panel FE-IV	FE	Panel FE-IV
Lagged primary balance ratio	0.476***	0.461***	0.474***	0.459***
	(0.035)	(0.069)	(0.035)	(0.069)
Lagged debt ratio	0.0146**	0.0202**	0.0140**	0.0191**
	(0.005)	(0.009)	(0.006)	(0.009)
Inflation	0.0768	0.0534	0.0779	0.0553
	(0.048)	(0.049)	(0.048)	(0.049)
Real GDP growth	0.062	0.0614*	0.0624	0.0617*
	(0.042)	(0.035)	(0.042)	(0.036)
Elections			-0.439	-0.501
			(0.400)	(0.483)
Fiscal rule			0.243	0.389
			(0.657)	(0.745)
Number of observations	494	455	494	455
Number of countries	22	22	22	22

Source: World Bank.
Note: Dependent variable is primary balance as a percent of GDP. Lagged values (first and second lags) of inflation and growth are used as instruments in the panel fixed effects instrumental variable (FE-IV) estimator. Elections and fiscal rules are dummy variables. Time fixed effects are included in each regression. Robust standard errors in parentheses. *** indicates statistical significance at the 1 percent level, ** at the 5 percent level, and * at the 10 percent level. These results are robust to other approaches, including the bias-corrected least-squares dummy variable, Prais-Winsten, and Driscoll-Kraay estimators.

References

Acevedo, S., A. Cebotari, and T. Turner-Jones. 2013. "Caribbean Small States: Challenges of High Debt and Low Growth." IMF Occasional Paper, International Monetary Fund, Washington, DC.

Acosta-Ormaechea, S., S. Pienknagura, and C. Pizzinelli. 2022. "Tax Policy for Inclusive Growth in Latin America and the Caribbean." IMF Working Paper 22/8, International Monetary Fund, Washington, DC.

Afonso, A., and J. Alves. 2023. "Does Government Spending Efficiency Improve Fiscal Sustainability?" *European Journal of Political Economy*: 102403.

Al-Sadiq, A., P. Bejar, and I. Ötker Robe. 2021. "Commodity Shocks and Exchange Rate Regimes: Implications for The Caribbean Commodity Exporters." IMF Working Paper 21/104, International Monetary Fund, Washington, DC.

Al-Sadiq, A., and D. A. Gutierrez. 2023. "Do Sovereign Wealth Funds Reduce Fiscal Policy Procyclicality? New Evidence using a Non-Parametric Approach." IMF Working Paper 23/133, International Monetary Fund, Washington, DC.

Alichi, A., I. Shibata, and K. Tanyeri. 2021. "Fiscal Policy Multipliers in Small States." *Economía* 21 (2): 69 -114.

Arslanalp, S., B. Eichengreen, and P. B. Henry. 2024. "Sustained Debt Reduction: The Jamaica Exception." Brookings Papers on Economic Activity, Conference Draft, Spring 2024. Brookings Institution, Washington, DC.

Asonuma, T., and C. Trebesch. 2016. "Sovereign Debt Restructurings: Preemptive or Post-Default." *Journal of the European Economic Association* 15 (1): 175-214.

Auffret, P. 2003. "High Consumption Volatility: The Impact of Natural Disasters?" Working Paper 2962, World Bank, Washington, DC.

Bachas, P., L. Gadenne, and A. Jensen. 2023. "Informality, Consumption Taxes and Redistribution." *Review of Economic Studies*. https://doi.org/10.1093/restud/rdad095

Balasundharam, V., L. Hunter, I. Lavea, and P. Seeds. 2021. "Managing Fiscal Risks from National Airlines in Pacific Island Countries." IMF Working Paper 183, International Monetary Fund, Washington, DC.

Balasundharam, V., and J. Khadan. 2024. "Factors Supporting Sovereign Wealth Fund Adoption." *Applied Economics Letters*. doi.org/10.1080/13504851.2024.2332588

Bell, J. D., I. Senina, T. Adams, O. Aumont, B. Calmettes, S. Clark, M. Dessert, et al. 2021. "Pathways to Sustaining Tuna-Dependent Pacific Island Economies During Climate Change." *Nature Sustainability* 4: 900-10.

Black, S., A. Liu, I. Parry, and N. Vernon. 2023. "IMF Fossil Fuel Subsidies Data: 2023 Update." IMF Working Paper 169, International Monetary Fund, Washington, DC.

Blanco, F., P. Saavedra, P., F. Koehler-Geib, and E. Skrok. 2020. "Fiscal Rules and Economic Size in Latin America and The Caribbean." Latin American Development Forum, World Bank, Washington, DC.

Bohn, H. 1998. "The Behavior of U.S. Public Debt and Deficits." *The Quarterly Journal of Economics* 113 (3): 949-63.

Borg, M. 2006. "Taxation Structures in Small States with Special Reference to Revenue Implications Following Trade Liberalization." Occasional Papers on Islands and Small States 5/2006. Islands and Small States Institute, University of Malta, Malta.

Briguglio, L., and M. Vella. 2018. "Trade Openness, Volatility and Governance." In *Handbook of Small Sates: Economic, Social and Environmental Issues*, edited by L. Briguglio. New York: Routledge.

Bruno, G. S. F. 2005. "Approximating the Bias of the LSDV Estimator for Dynamic Unbalanced Panel Data Models." *Economics Letters* 87 (3): 361-66.

Cabezon, E., L. Hunter, P. Tumbarello, K. Washimi, and Y. Wu. 2019. "Enhancing Macroeconomic Resilience to Natural Disasters and Climate Change in The Small States of The Pacific." *Asian Pacific Economic Literature* 33 (1): 113-30.

Cady, J., and A. J. Pellechio. 2006. "Sovereign Borrowing Cost and the IMF's Data Standards Initiatives." IMF Working Paper 06/78, International Monetary Fund, Washington, DC.

Cantu-Bazaldua, F. 2021. "Remote but Well Connected? Neighboring but Isolated? Measuring Remoteness in the Context of SIDS." UNCTAD Research Paper 67, United Nations Conference on Trade and Development, Geneva.

Cas, M., and R. Ota. 2008. "Government Expenditure, Debt and Fiscal Adjustment in Small States." Islands and Small States Institute & The Commonwealth Secretariat, University of Malta, Malta.

Caselli, F., M. H. R. Davoodi, C. Goncalves, M. G. H. Hong, A. Lagerborg, M. P. A. Medas, A. D. Nguyen, and J. Yoo. 2022. "The Return to Fiscal Rules." IMF Staff Discussion Note 002, International Monetary Fund, Washington, DC.

Cavallo, E., S. Gómez, I. Noy, and E. Strobl. 2024. "Climate Change, Hurricanes, and Sovereign Debt in the Caribbean Basin." IDB Working Paper 1551, International Development Bank, Washington, DC.

Cebotari, A., and K. Youssef. 2020. "Natural Disaster Insurance for Sovereigns: Issues, Challenges and Optimality." IMF Working Paper 20/3, International Monetary Fund, Washington, DC.

Cevik, S., and V. Nanda. 2020. "Riding the Storm: Fiscal Sustainability in The Caribbean." *International Review of Applied Economics* 34 (3): 384-99.

Ciullo, A., E. Strobl, S. Meiler, O. Martius, and D. N. Bresch. 2023. "Increasing Countries' Financial Resilience through Global Catastrophe Risk Pooling." *Nature Communications* 14 (1): 922.

Clayton, K., and D. Rosenblatt. 2024. "Searching for a Safe Harbor: Fiscal Policy Responses in Small Island Developing States." IDB Technical Note 2918. Inter-American Development Bank, Washington, DC.

Cover-Kus, H. 2019. "Weighing Up Second Passport Power in Small States. Small States Matters." Economic Social and Sustainable Development Directorate, Commonwealth Secretariat, London.

Cruz, C., P. Keefer, and C. Scartascini. 2018. "Database of Political Institutions 2017." Inter-American Development Bank Research Department, Washington, DC.

Davoodi, H., P. Elger, A. Fotiou, D. Garcia-Macia, A. Lagerborg, R. Lam, and S. Pillai. 2022a. "Fiscal Rules Dataset: 1985-2021." International Monetary Fund, Washington, DC.

Davoodi H. R., P. Elger, A. Fotiou, D. Garcia-Macia, X. Han, A. Lagerborg, W.R. Lam, and P. Medas. 2022b. "Fiscal Rules and Fiscal Councils: Recent Trends and Performance during the Pandemic." IMF Working Paper 22/11, International Monetary Fund, Washington, DC.

Del Granado, F. J. A., D. Coady, and R. Gillingham. 2012. "The Unequal Benefits of Fuel Subsidies: A Review of Evidence for Developing Countries." *World Development* 40 (11): 2234-48.

Dornan, M., K. McGovern, C. Alejandrino-Yap, and J. Austin. 2013. *Infrastructure Maintenance in the Pacific: Challenging the Build, Neglect, Rebuild Paradigm*. Sydney: Pacific Regional Infrastructure Advisory Center.

Driscoll, J. C., and A. C. Kraay. 1998. "Consistent Covariance Matrix Estimation with Spatially Dependent Panel Data." *Review of Economics and Statistics* 80 (4): 549-60.

Ehigiamusoe, K. U., and H. H. Lean. 2018. "Sovereign Wealth Funds and Macroeconomic Stability: Before and After Their Establishment." In *Research Handbook of Investing in the Triple Bottom Line*, edited by S. Boubaker, D. Cumming, and D. K. Nguyen, 135-56. London: Edward Elgar Publishing.

Erce, A., E. Mallucci, and M. Picarelli. 2022. "A Journey in The History of Sovereign Defaults on Domestic-Law Public Debt." International Finance Discussion Paper 1338, Board of Governors of the Federal Reserve System, Washington, DC.

Eyraud, L., X. Debrun, A. Hodge, V. Duarte-Lledo, and C. A. Pattillo. 2018. "Second-Generation Fiscal Rules: Balancing Simplicity, Flexibility, and Enforceability." IMF Staff Discussion Note 004, International Monetary Fund, Washington, DC.

Favaro, E. 2008. *Small States, Smart Solutions: Improving Connectivity and Increasing the Effectiveness of Public Services*. Washington, DC: World Bank.

Fordelone, T. Y., P. Tortora, and J. Xia. 2022. "Recovering From COVID-19: How to Enhance Domestic Revenue Mobilization in Small Island Developing States." OECD Policy Responses to Coronavirus (COVID-19), Organisation for Economic Co-Operation and Development, Paris.

Fuje, H., J. Yao, S. M. Choi, and H. Mighri. 2023. "Fiscal Impacts of Climate Disasters in Emerging Markets and Developing Economies." IMF Working Paper 23/261, International Monetary Fund, Washington, DC.

Giles, L., V. Gauto, and J. Khadan. 2021. "Enhancing Fiscal Sustainability in Resource-Rich Caribbean Countries." In *Economic Institutions for a Resilient Caribbean*, edited by D. Beuermann and M. Schwartz, 297-337. Washington, DC: Inter-American Development Bank.

Gold, J., and A. Myrvoda. 2017. "Managing Economic Citizenship Program Inflows: Reducing Risk and Maximizing Benefits." In *Unleashing Growth and Strengthening Resilience in the Caribbean*, edited by T. S. C. Alleyne, I. Ötker, U. Ramakrishnan, and K. Srinivasan, 123-39. Washington, DC: International Monetary Fund.

Gratcheva, E. M., and T. Emery. 2021. "Analysis of Pacific National Funds Investment Strategies and Results: Regional Comparative Study." World Bank, Washington, DC.

Guo, W., and S. Quayyum. 2020. "Building Resilience to Natural Disaster in Vulnerable States: Savings from Ex Ante Interventions." In *Well Spent: How Strong Infrastructure Governance Can End Waste in Public Investment,* edited by G. Schwartz, M. Fouad, T. S. Hansen, and G. Verdie, 154-71. Washington, DC: International Monetary Fund.

Heinen, A., J. Khadan, and E. Strobl. 2019. "The Price Impact of Extreme Weather in Developing Countries". *The Economic Journal* 129 (619): 1327-42.

Heller, P. S. 2022. "IMF Fiscal Policy Engagement in Small Developing States." Independent Evaluation Office of the International Monetary Fund, International Monetary Fund, Washington, DC.

Herrera, S., M. Massimo, J. N. D. Francois, H. Isaka, and H. Sahibzada (database). Forthcoming. "Global Database on Spending Efficiency." World Bank, Washington, DC.

Hnatkovska, V., and F. Köhler-Geib. 2018. "Characterizing Business Cycles in Small Economies." Policy Research Working Paper 8527, World Bank, Washington, DC.

Horn, S., C. M. Reinhart, and C. Trebesch. 2021. "China's Overseas Lending." *Journal of International Economics* 133 (November): 103539.

Horn, S., C. M. Reinhart, and C. Trebesch. 2022. "Hidden Defaults." Policy Research Working Paper 9925, World Bank, Washington, DC.

Horscroft, V. 2014. "Public Sectors in The Pacific Islands: Are They 'Too Big' and Do They 'Crowd Out' the Private Sector?" Policy Research Working Paper 7102, World Bank, Washington, DC.

IMF (International Monetary Fund). 2015. *Fiscal Monitor: The Commodities Roller Coaster: A Fiscal Framework for Uncertain Times.* October. Washington, DC: International Monetary Fund.

IMF (International Monetary Fund). 2019. "Building Resilience in Developing Countries Vulnerable to Large Natural Disasters." IMF Policy Paper, International Monetary Fund, Washington, DC.

IMF (International Monetary Fund). 2022a. "Mauritius 2022 Reinstating Fiscal Rules in the Post-Pandemic Mauritius: Scenarios and Policy Options." International Monetary Fund, Washington, DC.

IMF (International Monetary Fund). 2022b. "Eastern Caribbean Currency Union 2022: Selected Issues." IMF Country Report 22/254, International Monetary Fund, Washington, DC.

IMF (International Monetary Fund). 2022c. "Belize 2022 Article IV Consultation—Press Release; and Staff Report." Country Report 2022/133, International Monetary Fund, Washington, DC.

IMF (International Monetary Fund). 2023a. "Vanuatu 2023 Article IV Consultation—Press Release; and Staff Report." International Monetary Fund, Washington, DC.

IMF (International Monetary Fund). 2023b. "Barbados 2022 First Review Under the Extended Fund Facility Arrangement and Under the Resilience and Sustainability Facility—Press Release; Staff Report." International Monetary Fund, Washington, DC.

IMF (International Monetary Fund). 2023c. "Suriname Third Review Under the Extended Arrangement Under the Extended Fund Facility-Press Release; and Staff Report." IMF Country Report 23/350, International Monetary Fund, Washington, DC.

IMF (International Monetary Fund). 2024. "The Bahamas 2023 Article IV Consultation—Press Release; and Staff Report." International Monetary Fund, Washington, DC.

Jafino, B. A., B. Walsh, J. Rozenberg, and S. Hallegatte. 2020. "Revised Estimates of the Impact of Climate Change on Extreme Poverty by 2030." Policy Research Working Paper 9417, World Bank, Washington, DC.

Jansen, S. 2016. "Time-varying Fiscal Policy Reaction Functions." University of Ghent, Ghent, Belgium.

Judson, A., and A. Owen. 1999. "Estimating Dynamic Panel Data Models: A Guide for Macroeconomists." *Economics Letters* 65 (1): 9-15.

Junquera-Varela, R. F., R. Awasthi, O. Balabushko, and A. Nurshaikhova. 2019. "Thinking Strategically About Revenue Administration Reform: The Creation of Integrated, Autonomous Revenue Bodies." Governance Discussion Paper 4, World Bank, Washington, DC.

Junquera-Varela, R. F., C. O. Lucas, I. Krsul, Y. Calderon, O. Vladimir, and R. P. Arce. 2022. Digital Transformation of Tax and Customs Administrations." Equitable Growth, Finance and Institutions Insight, World Bank, Washington, DC.

Khadan, J. 2019. "Fiscal Sustainability in the Caribbean: An Econometric Analysis." *Research in Applied Economics* 11 (2): 1-25.

Khadan, J., and A. Deonarine. 2019. "Testing the Inter -Temporal Budget Constraint for Small States." *Economics Bulletin* 39 (2): 1176-83.

Khadan, J., and R. Hosein. 2015. "Trade, Economic and Welfare Impacts of the CARICOM-Canada Free Trade Agreement." *Social and Economic Studies* 64 (3/4): 103-50.

Khadan, J., and I. Ruprah. 2022. "Taxes and Fiscal Sustainability in Caribbean Countries." In *Contemporary Issues Within Caribbean Economies,* 83-108, edited by C. Cannonier and M. G. Burke. London: Palgrave Macmillan.

Kidd, M. 2010. "Tax Administration in Small Economies." Fiscal Affairs Department, International Monetary Fund, Washington, DC.

Kose, M. A., P. Nagle, F. Ohnsorge, and N. Sugawara. 2021. "What Has Been the Impact of COVID-19 on Debt? Turning a Wave into a Tsunami." Policy Research Working Paper 9871, World Bank, Washington, DC.

Kubota, M., and A. Zeufack. 2020. "Assessing the Returns on Investment in Data Openness and Transparency." Policy Research Working Paper 9139, World Bank, Washington, DC.

Lafuente, M., and E. Molina. 2018. "Building State Capacity in the Caribbean: A Baseline Report of the Civil Service." Technical Note 1512, Inter-American Development Bank, Washington, DC.

Lee, D., H. Zhang, and C. Nguyen. 2018. "The Economic Impact Of Natural Disasters In Pacific Island Countries: Adaptation and Preparedness." IMF Working Paper 18/108, International Monetary Fund, Washington, DC.

Lis, E. M., and C. Nickel. 2009. "The Impact of Extreme Weather Events On Budget Balances." *International Tax and Public Finance* 17: 378-99.

Lum, T. 2023. "The Compacts of Free Association." CRS Report IF12194, Congressional Research Service, Washington, DC.

Martínez-Vázquez, J., E. Sanz-Arcega, and J. M. T. Martín. 2023. "Tax Revenue Management and Reform in The Digital Era in Developing and Developed Countries." In *Research Handbook on Public Financial Management*, edited by K. D. Dzigbede and W. B. Hildreth, 202-25. Camberley, UK: Edward Elgar Publishing.

Maslen, S., and A. Cigdem. 2022. "Enhancing Debt Transparency by Strengthening Public Debt Transaction Disclosure Practices." EFI Insight, World Bank, Washington, DC.

McNabb, K., M. Danquah, and A. Tagem. 2021. "Tax Effort Revisited: New Estimates from The Government Revenue Dataset." WIDER Working Paper 170, United Nations University World Institute for Development Economics Research, Helsinki.

Melecky, M., and C. Raddatz. 2011. "How Do Governments Respond After Catastrophes. Natural-Disaster Shocks and The Fiscal Stance." Policy Research Working Paper 5564, World Bank, Washington, DC.

Mendoza, E. G., and D. J. Ostry. 2008. "International Evidence on Fiscal Solvency: Is Fiscal Policy Responsible." *Journal of Monetary Economics* 55 (6): 1081-93.

Mercer-Blackman, V., and K. A. Melgarejo. 2013. "Spillovers of Global Shocks Over Caribbean Countries: So Large That There Is Little Room to Maneuver: An Impulse Response Analysis." Policy Brief 206, Inter-American Development Bank, Washington, DC.

Mitchell, M. A. W., R. James, and A. M. Wickham. 2019. " Government Wage Bill Management and Civil Service Reform in the Eastern Caribbean Currency Union." International Monetary Fund, Washington, DC.

Mohan, P., and E. Strobl. 2020. "The Impact of Tropical Storms on the Accumulation and Composition of Government Debt." *International Tax Public Finance* 28 (3): 483-96.

Mohan, P., and E. Strobl. 2021. "The Impact of Tropical Storms on Tax Revenue." *Journal of International Development* 33 (3): 472-89.

Mooney, H., A. Wright, and K. Grenade. 2018. "Fiscal Councils: Evidence, Common Features and Lessons for The Caribbean." Inter-American Development Bank, Washington, DC.

Nakatani, R. 2021. "Fiscal Rules for Natural Disaster-And Climate Change-Prone Small States." *Sustainability* 13 (6): 1-26.

Nickell, S. 1981. "Biases in Dynamic Models with Fixed Effects." *Econometrica* 49 (6): 1417-26.

Nose, M., and A. Mengistu. 2023. "Exploring the Adoption of Selected Digital Technologies in Tax Administration: A Cross-Country Perspective." IMF Note 008, International Monetary Fund, Washington, DC.

OECD (Organisation for Economic Co-operation and Development). 2024. Fostering Catastrophe Bond Markets in Asia and the Pacific, The Development Dimension, OECD Publishing, Paris.

Ohnsorge, F., and S. Yu, eds. 2022. *The Long Shadow of Informality: Challenges and Policies*. Washington, DC: World Bank.

Ossowski, R. 2021. Sovereign Wealth Funds in Resource-Rich Caribbean Countries. In *Economic Institutions for a Resilient Caribbean*, edited by D. Beuermann and M. Schwartz, 297-337. Washington, DC: Inter-American Development Bank.

Ouattara, B., and E. Strobl. 2013. "The Fiscal Implications of Hurricane Strikes in The Caribbean." *Ecological Economics* 85 (January): 105-15.

Oyebola, O., and G. Tourek. 2023. "How Can Lower-Income Countries Collect More Taxes? The Role of Technology, Tax Agents, and Politics." Policy Research Working Paper 10655, World Bank, Washington, DC.

Prais, S. J., and C. Winsten. 1954. "Trend Estimators and Serial Correlation." Cowles Commission Discussion Paper 373, Cowles Foundation for Research in Economics, Chicago.

Prasad, A., M. Pollock, and Y. Li. 2013. "Small States—Performance in Public Debt Management." Policy Research Working Paper 6356, World Bank, Washington, DC.

Reinhart, C., K. Rogoff, and M. Savastano. 2003. "Debt Intolerance." *Brookings Papers on Economic Activity* 1: 2003.

Reyes-Tagle, G., A. Musacchio, C. Pan, and Y. Park, eds. 2022. *Smoldering Embers: Do State-Owned Enterprises Threaten Fiscal Stability in The Caribbean*? Inter-American Development Bank, Washington, DC.

Reyes-Tagle. G., C. Silvani, and L. Ospina. 2022. "The Nuts and Bolts of Revenue Administration in the Caribbean." In *Economic Institutions for A Resilient Caribbean*, edited by M-J. Schwartz and D-W. Beuermann, 11-93. Washington, DC: Inter-American Development Bank.

Rustomjee, C. 2016. "Vulnerability and Debt in Small States." CIGI Policy Brief 83, Centre for International Governance Innovation, Warerloo, Ontario.

Schlotterbeck, S. 2017. "Tax Administration Reforms in the Caribbean: Challenges, Achievements, and Next Steps." IMF Working Paper 88, International Monetary Fund, Washington, DC.

Schwartz, G., M. Fouad, T. S. Hansen, and G. Verdier, eds. 2020. *Well Spent: How Strong Infrastructure Governance Can End Waste in Public Investment.* Washington, DC: International Monetary Fund.

Schwartz, M. J., and D. W. Beuermann, eds. 2021. *Economic Institutions for Resilient Caribbean*. Washington, DC: Inter-American Development Bank.

Sirimaneetham, V. 2022. "Ensuring Public Debt Sustainability in The Pacific Small Island Development States." MPFD Policy Brief 125, Macroeconomic Policy and Financing Development, Economic and Social Commission for Asia and Pacific, United Nations, Bangkok.

Sy, M., A. Beaumont, E. Das, G. Eysselein, D. Kloeden, and K. Williams. 2022. "Funding The Future: Tax Revenue Mobilization in The Pacific Island Countries." IMF Departmental Paper 015, International Monetary Fund, Washington, DC.

Talvi, E., and C. A. Vegh. 2005. "Tax Base Variability and Procyclical Fiscal Policy in Developing Countries." *Journal of Development Economics* 78 (1): 156-90.

Thomas, A., and E. Theokritoff. 2021. "Debt-For-Climate Swaps for Small Islands." *Nature Climate Change* 11 (11): 889-91.

Tiedemann, J. V. Piatkov, D. Prihardini, J.C. Benitez, and A. Zdzienicka. 2021. "Meeting the Sustainable Development Goals in Small Developing States with Climate Vulnerabilities: Cost and Financing." IMF Working Paper 62, International Monetary Fund, Washington, DC.

UNCTAD (United Nations Conference on Trade and Development). 2022. "Building Resilience in Small Island Developing States." A Compendium of Research Prepared by the UNCTAD Division for Africa, Least Developed Countries and Special Programmes, United Nations Conference on Trade and Development, Geneva.

UNCTAD (United Nations Conference on Trade and Development). 2024. "Correspondent banking relationships and trade." Policy brief 115, United Nations Conference on Trade and Development, Geneva.

UNEP (United Nations Environment Programme). 2023. "Adaptation Gap Report 2023: Underfinanced. Underprepared. Inadequate Investment and Planning on Climate Adaptation Leaves World Exposed." United Nations Environment Programme, Nairobi.

Vousdoukas, M. I., P. Athanasiou, A. Giardino, L. Mentaschi, A. Stocchino, R. E. Kopp, P. Menéndez, et al. 2023. "Small Island Developing States Under Threat by Rising Seas Even in a 1.5 °C Warming World." *Nature Sustainability* 6: 1552-64.

WMO (World Meteorological Organization). 2023. "Atlas of Mortality and Economic Losses from Weather, Climate and Water Extremes (1970–2019)." World Meteorological Organization, Geneva.

World Bank. Forthcoming. The Pacific Atoll Countries Country Climate and Development Report. CCDR Series. Washington, DC: World Bank.

World Bank. Forthcoming. Organisation of Eastern Caribbean States Countries Country Climate and Development Report. CCDR Series. Washington, DC: World Bank.

World Bank. 2022. "Risk Insurance Builds Climate and Disaster Resilience in Central America and the Caribbean." Results Brief, World Bank, Washington, DC.

World Bank. 2023a. *Global Economic Prospects*. January. Washington, DC: World Bank.

World Bank. 2023b. "Raising Pasifika - Strengthening Government Finances to Enhance Human Capital in the Pacific: A Public Expenditure Review for Nine Pacific Island Countries." World Bank, Washington, DC.

World Bank. 2023c. *Global Economic Prospects*. June. Washington, DC: World Bank.

World Bank. 2023d. "Pacific Economic Update, February." World Bank, Washington, DC.

World Bank. 2023e. "World Bank Support for Domestic Revenue Mobilization." Independent Evaluation Group, World Bank, Washington, DC.

World Bank. 2023f. "Leveraging Natural Wealth to Build Opportunities Policy: Recommendations to Boost Growth and Resilience in Sao Tome and Principe." World Bank, Washington, DC.

World Bank. 2023g. "From Crisis to Resilience: World Bank Support to Small States." World Bank, Washington, DC.

World Bank. 2023h. "Evolution of the World Bank Group—A Report to Governors." Development Committee Meeting, World Bank, Washington, DC.

World Bank. 2023i. "World Bank Extends New Lifeline for Countries Hit by Natural Disasters." World Bank, Washington, DC.

World Bank. 2024a. "Pacific Economic Update, March." World Bank, Washington, DC.

World Bank. 2024b. *Global Economic Prospects*. January. Washington, DC: World Bank.

STATISTICAL APPENDIX

Real GDP growth

	Annual estimates and forecasts [1] (Percent change)						Quarterly estimates [2] (Percent change, year-on-year)					
	2021	2022	2023e	2024f	2025f	2026f	22Q4	23Q1	23Q2	23Q3	23Q4	24Q1e
World	**6.3**	**3.0**	**2.6**	**2.6**	**2.7**	**2.7**	**1.8**	**2.5**	**2.9**	**2.6**	..	..
Advanced economies	**5.5**	**2.6**	**1.5**	**1.5**	**1.7**	**1.8**	**1.1**	**1.6**	**1.6**	**1.6**	**1.7**	..
United States	5.8	1.9	2.5	2.5	1.8	1.8	0.7	1.7	2.4	2.9	3.1	2.9
Euro area	5.9	3.4	0.5	0.7	1.4	1.3	1.9	1.3	0.6	0.2	0.2	0.4
Japan	2.6	1.0	1.9	0.7	1.0	0.9	0.7	2.5	2.3	1.6	1.3	-0.4
Emerging market and developing economies	**7.3**	**3.7**	**4.2**	**4.0**	**4.0**	**3.9**	**2.9**	**3.7**	**4.8**	**4.2**	..	..
East Asia and Pacific	**7.6**	**3.4**	**5.1**	**4.8**	**4.2**	**4.1**	**3.2**	**4.6**	**6.0**	**4.8**	**5.1**	**5.2**
Cambodia	3.0	5.2	5.4	5.8	6.1	6.4	..	..	..	..	..	..
China	8.4	3.0	5.2	4.8	4.1	4.0	2.9	4.5	6.3	4.9	5.2	5.3
Fiji	-4.9	20.0	8.0	3.5	3.3	3.3	..	..	..	..	..	..
Indonesia	3.7	5.3	5.0	5.0	5.1	5.1	5.0	5.0	5.2	4.9	5.0	5.1
Kiribati	8.5	3.9	4.2	5.6	2.0	2.1	..	..	..	..	..	..
Lao PDR	2.5	2.7	3.7	4.0	4.1	4.1	..	..	..	..	..	..
Malaysia	3.3	8.7	3.7	4.3	4.4	4.3	7.4	5.5	2.8	3.1	2.9	4.2
Marshall Islands [3]	1.0	-0.6	3.0	3.0	2.0	1.5	..	..	..	..	..	..
Micronesia, Fed. Sts. [3]	3.0	-0.9	0.8	1.1	1.7	1.1	..	..	..	..	..	..
Mongolia	1.6	5.0	7.1	4.8	6.6	6.3	11.2	7.8	4.8	8.7	7.1	7.8
Myanmar [3 4]	-12.0	4.0	1.0	1.0	..	..	..	..	..	..	..	..
Nauru [3]	7.2	2.8	0.6	1.4	1.2	1.0	..	..	..	..	..	..
Palau [3]	-13.4	-2.0	0.8	12.4	11.9	3.5	..	..	..	..	..	..
Papua New Guinea	-0.8	5.2	2.7	4.8	3.1	3.0	..	..	..	..	..	..
Philippines	5.7	7.6	5.6	5.8	5.9	5.9	7.1	6.4	4.3	6.0	5.5	5.7
Samoa [3]	-7.1	-5.3	8.0	5.5	3.5	2.7	..	..	..	..	..	..
Solomon Islands	-0.6	-4.1	1.9	2.8	3.1	3.0	..	..	..	..	..	..
Thailand	1.6	2.5	1.9	2.4	2.8	2.9	1.3	2.6	1.8	1.4	1.7	1.5
Timor-Leste	2.9	4.0	2.1	3.4	4.0	3.8	..	..	..	..	..	..
Tonga [3]	-2.7	-2.0	2.6	2.5	2.2	1.6	..	..	..	..	..	..
Tuvalu	1.8	0.7	3.9	3.5	2.4	2.2	..	..	..	..	..	..
Vanuatu	0.6	1.9	2.5	3.7	3.5	3.1	..	..	..	..	..	..
Viet Nam	2.6	8.0	5.0	5.5	6.0	6.5	6.0	3.4	4.2	5.5	6.7	5.7
Europe and Central Asia	**7.2**	**1.6**	**3.2**	**3.0**	**2.9**	**2.8**	**0.1**	**0.5**	**3.8**	**4.6**	**3.6**	..
Albania	8.9	4.9	3.3	3.3	3.4	3.5	4.4	2.8	3.3	3.8	3.8	..
Armenia	5.8	12.6	8.7	5.5	4.9	4.5	12.7	11.8	9.3	7.4	7.7	9.2
Azerbaijan	5.6	4.6	1.1	2.3	2.4	2.4	..	..	..	..	..	..
Belarus	2.4	-4.7	3.9	1.2	0.7	0.5	-4.5	-1.5	6.2	6.4	4.4	..
Bosnia and Herzegovina [5]	7.4	4.2	1.7	2.6	3.3	4.0	2.6	1.8	1.2	1.9	1.7	..
Bulgaria	7.7	3.9	1.8	2.1	3.1	2.7	3.6	2.2	1.9	1.5	1.8	1.7
Croatia	13.0	7.0	3.1	3.0	2.8	2.7	3.3	2.9	3.8	1.4	4.4	3.9
Georgia	10.6	11.0	7.5	5.2	5.0	5.0	14.5	8.2	8.1	7.0	6.9	..
Kazakhstan	4.3	3.2	5.1	3.4	4.7	3.6	4.0	5.0	5.6	4.1	5.6	..
Kosovo	10.7	4.3	3.3	3.7	3.9	3.9	..	..	..	..	..	..
Kyrgyz Republic	5.5	9.0	6.2	4.5	4.2	4.0	..	..	..	..	..	..
Moldova	13.9	-4.6	0.7	2.2	3.9	4.5	-8.3	-0.9	-0.3	3.3	0.2	..
Montenegro	13.0	6.4	6.0	3.4	2.8	3.0	3.6	6.2	6.9	6.6	4.3	..
North Macedonia	4.5	2.2	1.0	2.5	2.9	3.0	1.5	1.4	0.9	1.0	0.9	1.2
Poland	6.9	5.6	0.2	3.0	3.4	3.2	2.8	-0.4	-0.6	0.5	1.0	2.0
Romania	5.7	4.1	2.1	3.3	3.8	3.8	4.5	1.0	2.8	3.6	1.1	0.1
Russian Federation	5.9	-1.2	3.6	2.9	1.4	1.1	-1.8	-1.6	5.1	5.7	4.9	5.4
Serbia	7.7	2.5	2.5	3.5	3.8	4.0	0.8	0.9	1.6	3.6	3.8	4.7
Tajikistan	9.4	8.0	8.3	6.5	4.5	4.5	..	..	..	..	..	..
Türkiye	11.4	5.5	4.5	3.0	3.6	4.3	3.3	4.0	3.9	6.1	4.0	5.7
Ukraine	3.4	-28.8	5.3	3.2	6.5	5.1	-30.6	-10.3	19.2	9.6	4.7	..
Uzbekistan	7.4	5.7	6.0	5.3	5.5	5.7	..	..	..	..	..	..

Real GDP growth (*continued*)

	Annual estimates and forecasts[1] (Percent change)						Quarterly estimates[2] (Percent change, year-on-year)					
	2021	2022	2023e	2024f	2025f	2026f	22Q4	23Q1	23Q2	23Q3	23Q4	24Q1e
Latin America and the Caribbean	**7.2**	**3.9**	**2.2**	**1.8**	**2.7**	**2.6**	**2.7**	**3.3**	**2.1**	**1.8**	**1.6**	**..**
Argentina	10.7	5.0	-1.6	-3.5	5.0	4.5	1.5	1.4	-5.0	-0.8	-1.4	..
Bahamas, The	15.4	10.8	2.6	2.3	1.8	1.6	..	..	..	..	..	..
Barbados	-1.2	13.5	4.4	3.7	2.8	2.3	..	..	..	..	..	..
Belize	17.9	8.7	4.7	3.4	2.5	2.5	8.0	8.2	4.0	3.1	3.2	..
Bolivia	6.1	3.6	3.1	1.4	1.5	1.5	1.3	2.4	2.0	2.6	5.1	..
Brazil	4.8	3.0	2.9	2.0	2.2	2.0	2.7	4.2	3.5	2.0	2.1	2.5
Chile	11.3	2.1	0.2	2.6	2.2	2.2	-2.3	0.3	-0.4	0.6	0.4	2.3
Colombia	10.8	7.3	0.6	1.3	3.2	3.1	2.2	2.7	0.3	-0.7	0.3	0.7
Costa Rica	7.9	4.6	5.1	3.9	3.7	3.7	4.5	4.2	5.8	5.5	5.0	3.7
Dominica	6.9	5.6	4.9	4.6	4.2	3.0	..	..	..	..	..	..
Dominican Republic	12.3	4.9	2.4	5.1	5.0	5.0	3.3	1.4	1.0	2.6	4.2	..
Ecuador	9.8	6.2	2.4	0.3	1.6	2.2	2.7	4.6	5.0	0.7	-0.7	..
El Salvador	11.9	2.8	3.5	3.2	2.7	2.5	1.6	1.6	4.6	3.4	4.3	..
Grenada	4.7	7.3	4.8	4.3	3.8	3.2	..	..	..	..	..	..
Guatemala	8.0	4.1	3.5	3.0	3.5	3.5	3.4	4.0	4.1	4.0	2.0	..
Guyana	20.1	63.3	33.0	34.3	16.8	18.2	..	..	..	..	..	..
Haiti[3]	-1.8	-1.7	-1.9	-1.8	1.9	2.0	..	..	..	..	..	..
Honduras	12.5	4.0	3.6	3.4	3.3	3.4	1.8	2.7	2.9	3.3	5.2	..
Jamaica[2]	4.6	5.2	2.6	2.0	1.6	1.6	3.8	4.2	2.3	2.3	1.7	..
Mexico	6.0	3.7	3.2	2.3	2.1	2.0	4.4	3.6	3.5	3.4	2.3	1.6
Nicaragua	10.3	3.8	4.3	3.7	3.5	3.5	2.3	3.4	3.5	6.1	5.2	..
Panama	15.8	10.8	6.5	2.5	3.5	4.0	10.2	9.3	8.2	9.0	3.3	..
Paraguay	4.0	0.2	4.7	3.8	3.6	3.6	1.8	4.6	5.6	3.7	4.9	..
Peru	13.4	2.7	-0.6	2.9	2.6	2.4	1.7	-0.4	-0.5	-0.9	-0.4	1.4
St. Lucia	12.2	18.1	3.2	2.9	2.4	1.8	..	..	..	..	..	..
St. Vincent and the Grenadines	0.8	7.2	6.5	5.0	3.9	3.7	..	..	..	..	..	..
Suriname	-2.4	2.4	2.1	3.0	3.0	3.0	..	..	..	..	..	..
Uruguay	5.6	4.7	0.4	3.2	2.6	2.6	-1.0	1.9	-2.1	-0.2	2.0	..
Middle East and North Africa	**6.2**	**5.9**	**1.5**	**2.8**	**4.2**	**3.6**	**4.7**	**3.7**	**2.9**	**0.8**	**..**	**..**
Algeria	3.8	3.6	4.1	2.9	3.7	3.2	4.3	2.4	4.6	5.8	3.4	..
Bahrain	2.6	5.2	2.6	3.5	3.3	3.4	4.8	1.0	2.7	2.4	3.5	..
Djibouti	4.5	3.7	6.7	5.1	5.1	5.2	..	..	..	..	..	..
Egypt, Arab Rep.[3]	3.3	6.6	3.8	2.8	4.2	4.6	3.9	3.9	2.9	2.7	2.3	..
Iran, Islamic Rep.[3]	4.7	3.8	5.0	3.2	2.7	2.4	4.1	5.7	6.5	3.9	4.7	..
Iraq[5]	1.5	7.6	-2.9	-0.3	3.8	5.3	0.6	3.3	-7.1	-5.5	0.1	..
Jordan	3.7	2.4	2.6	2.5	2.6	2.6	2.0	2.8	2.6	2.7	2.3	..
Kuwait	1.3	7.9	-0.1	2.8	3.1	2.7	2.1	1.2	-3.2	-3.7	..	..
Lebanon[4]	-7.0	-0.6	-0.2	0.5	..	..	..	..	..	..	..	..
Libya	153.5	1.3	-1.7	4.8	5.3	5.8	..	..	..	..	..	..
Morocco	8.0	1.3	2.8	2.4	3.7	3.3	0.7	3.5	2.3	2.8	4.1	2.9
Oman	3.1	4.3	1.3	1.5	2.8	3.2	7.0	4.0	-0.2	2.2	0.3	..
Qatar	1.6	4.2	1.8	2.1	3.2	4.7	6.2	2.2	1.2	1.2	..	..
Saudi Arabia	4.3	8.7	-0.9	2.5	5.9	3.2	5.6	3.2	1.7	-3.2	-4.3	-1.8
Syrian Arab Republic[4]	1.3	-0.1	-1.2	-1.5	..	..	..	..	..	..	..	..
Tunisia	4.6	2.6	0.4	2.4	2.4	2.2	1.8	1.6	0.5	-0.3	0.0	0.2
United Arab Emirates	4.4	7.9	3.1	3.9	4.1	4.0	5.1	3.9	3.8	2.5	4.3	..
West Bank and Gaza[6]	7.0	3.9	-6.4	-6.5	5.5	4.2	2.4	3.1	2.8	2.6	-29.5	..
Yemen, Rep.[4]	-1.0	1.5	-2.0	-1.0	1.5	..	..	..	..	..	..	..

Real GDP growth (*continued*)

	Annual estimates and forecasts[1] (Percent change)						Quarterly estimates[2] (Percent change, year-on-year)					
	2021	2022	2023e	2024f	2025f	2026f	22Q4	23Q1	23Q2	23Q3	23Q4	24Q1e
South Asia	**8.6**	**5.8**	**6.6**	**6.2**	**6.2**	**6.2**	**3.9**	**4.7**	**6.7**	**7.2**	**7.3**	**..**
Afghanistan[4]	-20.7	-6.2	..	..	..	..	..	..	..	..	..	..
Bangladesh[3]	6.9	7.1	5.8	5.6	5.7	5.9	7.1	2.3	6.9	6.0	3.8	..
Bhutan[3]	-3.3	4.8	4.6	4.9	5.7	6.0	..	..	..	..	..	..
India[3]	9.7	7.0	8.2	6.6	6.7	6.8	4.3	6.2	8.2	8.1	8.6	7.8
Maldives	37.7	13.9	4.0	4.7	5.2	4.1	2.3	5.3	1.9	4.6	4.0	..
Nepal[2 3]	4.8	5.6	1.9	3.3	4.6	5.3	-0.8	2.2	4.1	3.2	4.0	..
Pakistan[2 3 5]	5.8	6.2	-0.2	1.8	2.3	2.7	2.6	-1.1	-3.7	2.7	1.8	2.1
Sri Lanka	4.2	-7.3	-2.3	2.2	2.5	3.0	-12.4	-10.7	-3.0	1.6	4.5	..
Sub-Saharan Africa	**4.4**	**3.8**	**3.0**	**3.5**	**3.9**	**4.0**	**2.8**	**2.1**	**2.7**	**2.1**	**3.0**	**..**
Angola	1.2	3.0	0.9	2.9	2.6	2.4	2.6	0.3	0.1	1.5	1.4	..
Benin	7.2	6.3	5.8	6.0	6.0	6.0	..	..	..	..	..	..
Botswana	11.8	5.8	3.3	3.5	4.3	4.0	5.6	5.3	3.3	0.5	1.9	..
Burkina Faso	6.9	1.8	3.2	3.7	3.8	4.2	..	..	..	..	..	..
Burundi	3.1	1.8	2.7	3.8	4.4	4.8	..	..	..	..	..	..
Cabo Verde	5.6	17.1	4.8	4.7	4.7	4.6	..	..	..	..	..	..
Cameroon	3.3	3.6	3.3	3.9	4.2	4.5	..	..	..	..	..	..
Central African Republic	1.0	0.5	0.9	1.3	1.7	1.9	..	..	..	..	..	..
Chad	-1.2	2.8	4.1	2.7	3.3	2.9	..	..	..	..	..	..
Comoros	2.1	2.6	3.0	3.3	4.0	4.3	..	..	..	..	..	..
Congo, Dem. Rep.	6.2	8.9	7.8	6.0	5.9	5.7	..	..	..	..	..	..
Congo, Rep.	1.0	1.5	1.9	3.5	3.7	3.2	..	..	..	..	..	..
Côte d'Ivoire	7.1	6.2	6.0	6.4	6.4	6.3	..	..	..	..	..	..
Equatorial Guinea	0.3	3.8	-5.8	-4.3	-3.3	-3.6	..	..	..	..	..	..
Eritrea	2.9	2.5	2.6	2.8	3.0	3.3	..	..	..	..	..	..
Eswatini	10.7	0.5	4.8	4.1	3.3	2.7	..	..	..	..	..	..
Ethiopia[3]	6.3	6.4	7.2	7.0	7.0	7.0	..	..	..	..	..	..
Gabon	1.5	3.0	2.3	3.0	2.3	2.8	..	..	..	..	..	..
Gambia, The	5.3	4.9	5.3	5.5	5.8	5.4	..	..	..	..	..	..
Ghana	5.1	3.8	2.9	2.9	4.4	4.9	3.8	3.1	2.5	2.2	3.8	..
Guinea	5.0	3.7	7.1	4.9	6.2	6.5	..	..	..	..	..	..
Guinea-Bissau	6.4	4.2	4.2	4.7	4.8	4.9	..	..	..	..	..	..
Kenya	7.6	4.9	5.6	5.0	5.3	5.3	4.1	5.5	5.6	6.0	5.1	..
Lesotho	1.9	1.1	2.0	2.2	2.5	2.3	-2.5	-1.2	2.3	0.8	1.7	..
Liberia	5.0	4.8	4.7	5.3	6.2	6.3	..	..	..	..	..	..
Madagascar	5.7	3.8	3.8	4.5	4.6	4.7	..	..	..	..	..	..
Malawi	2.8	0.9	1.5	2.0	3.9	4.1	..	..	..	..	..	..
Mali	3.1	3.5	3.5	3.1	3.5	4.5	..	..	..	..	..	..
Mauritania	0.7	6.4	3.4	3.8	4.5	6.3	..	..	..	..	..	..
Mauritius	3.4	8.9	6.8	5.0	4.1	3.9	..	..	..	..	..	..
Mozambique	2.3	4.2	5.0	5.0	5.0	4.4	4.1	4.2	4.7	5.9	5.4	..
Namibia	3.6	5.3	4.2	3.4	3.6	3.8	3.3	5.3	3.8	3.2	4.4	..
Niger	1.4	11.5	2.0	9.1	6.2	5.1	..	..	..	..	..	..
Nigeria	3.6	3.3	2.9	3.3	3.5	3.7	3.6	2.4	2.6	3.1	3.2	2.8
Rwanda	10.9	8.2	8.2	7.6	7.8	7.5	7.3	9.2	6.3	7.5	10.0	..
São Tomé and Príncipe	1.9	0.1	-0.5	2.5	3.1	3.6	..	..	..	..	..	..
Senegal	6.5	3.8	4.3	7.1	9.7	5.7	..	..	..	..	..	..
Seychelles	2.5	8.9	3.3	3.5	3.4	3.4	7.8	8.2	1.8	-7.1	-3.2	..
Sierra Leone	4.1	3.5	3.1	3.5	4.0	4.3	..	..	..	..	..	..

Real GDP growth (*continued*)

	Annual estimates and forecasts[1] (Percent change)						Quarterly estimates[2] (Percent change, year-on-year)					
	2021	2022	2023e	2024f	2025f	2026f	22Q4	23Q1	23Q2	23Q3	23Q4	24Q1e
Sub-Saharan Africa (*continued*)												
Somalia	3.3	2.4	3.1	3.7	3.9	4.0	..	..	..	..	..	..
South Africa	4.7	1.9	0.6	1.2	1.3	1.5	0.7	0.5	1.8	-0.9	1.4	0.5
South Sudan[3]	-5.1	-2.3	-1.3	2.0	3.8	4.0	..	..	..	..	..	..
Sudan	-1.9	-1.0	-12.0	-3.5	-0.7	1.2	..	..	..	..	..	..
Tanzania	4.3	4.6	5.2	5.4	5.8	6.2	..	..	..	..	..	..
Togo	6.0	5.8	5.4	5.1	5.4	5.6	..	..	..	..	..	..
Uganda[3]	3.4	4.7	5.2	6.0	6.2	6.6	4.5	1.8	5.4	5.3	5.5	..
Zambia	6.2	5.2	4.0	2.7	6.1	5.9	4.6	3.5	5.1	4.9	7.9	..
Zimbabwe	8.5	6.5	5.5	3.3	3.6	3.5	..	..	..	..	..	..

Sources: Haver Analytics; World Bank.

Note: e = estimate; f = forecast. Since Croatia became a member of the euro area on January 1, 2023, it has been added to the euro area aggregate and removed from the EMDE and ECA aggregate in all tables to avoid double counting.

1. Aggregate growth rates calculated using GDP weights at average 2010-19 prices and market exchange rates.

2. Quarterly estimates are on a calendar year basis and based on non-seasonally-adjusted real GDP, except for advanced economies, as well as Algeria, Ecuador, Morocco, and Tunisia. In some instances, quarterly growth paths may not align to annual growth estimates, owing to the timing of GDP releases. Quarterly data for Jamaica, Nepal, and Pakistan are gross value added. Data for Timor-Leste represent non-oil GDP.

Regional averages are calculated based on data from the following economies.

East Asia and Pacific: China, Indonesia, Malaysia, Mongolia, the Philippines, Thailand, and Viet Nam.

Europe and Central Asia: Albania, Armenia, Belarus, Bosnia and Herzegovina, Bulgaria, Georgia, Hungary, Kazakhstan, Moldova, Montenegro, North Macedonia, Poland, Romania, the Russian Federation, Serbia, Türkiye, and Ukraine.

Latin America and the Caribbean: Argentina, Belize, Bolivia, Brazil, Chile, Colombia, Costa Rica, the Dominican Republic, Ecuador, El Salvador, Guatemala, Honduras, Jamaica, Mexico, Nicaragua, Panama, Paraguay, Peru, and Uruguay.

Middle East and North Africa: Bahrain, the Arab Republic of Egypt, the Islamic Republic of Iran, Jordan, Morocco, Oman, Qatar, Saudi Arabia, Tunisia, the United Arab Emirates, and West Bank and Gaza.

South Asia: Bangladesh, India, Maldives, Nepal, Pakistan, and Sri Lanka.

Sub-Saharan Africa: Angola, Botswana, Ghana, Kenya, Lesotho, Mozambique, Namibia, Nigeria, Rwanda, the Seychelles, South Africa, Uganda, and Zambia.

3. Annual GDP is on fiscal year basis, as per reporting practice in the country. For Bangladesh, Bhutan, Egypt, Nepal, and Pakistan, the column for 2023 refers to FY2022/23—covering 2022Q3 to 2023Q2. For India and the Islamic Republic of Iran, the column for 2023 refers to FY2023/24—covering 2023Q2 to 2024Q1.

4. Data for Afghanistan (beyond 2022), Lebanon (beyond 2024), Myanmar (beyond 2024), the Syrian Arab Republic (beyond 2024), and the Republic of Yemen (beyond 2025) are excluded because of a high degree of uncertainty.

5. Data for Bosnia and Herzegovina are from the production approach. Annual GDP for Pakistan is based on factor cost, and both annual and quarterly GDP for Iraq is also reported on a factor cost basis.

6. The economic outlook of West Bank and Gaza remains highly uncertain, and the growth forecast for 2024 ranges from -6.5 percent, as shown in the table, to -9.4 percent, depending upon the outturn of different factors that affect the outlook.

Data and Forecast Conventions

The macroeconomic forecasts presented in this report are prepared by staff of the Prospects Group of the Development Economics Vice Presidency, in coordination with staff from the Macroeconomics, Trade, and Investment Global Practice of the Equitable Growth, Finance and Institutions Vice Presidency and from regional and country offices, and with input from regional Chief Economist offices. They are the result of an iterative process that incorporates data, macroeconometric models, and judgment.

Data. Data used to prepare country forecasts come from a variety of sources. National Income Accounts (NIA), Balance of Payments (BOP), and fiscal data are from Haver Analytics; the World Development Indicators by the World Bank; the *World Economic Outlook*, *Balance of Payments Statistics*, and *International Financial Statistics* by the International Monetary Fund. Population data and forecasts are from the United Nations World Population Prospects. Country- and lending-group classifications are from the World Bank. The Prospects Group's internal databases include high-frequency indicators such as industrial production, consumer price indexes, emerging markets bond index (EMBI), exchange rates, exports, imports, policy rates, and stock market indexes, based on data from Bloomberg, Haver Analytics, IMF *Balance of Payments Stati*stics, IMF *International Financial Statistics*, and J.P. Morgan.

Aggregations. Aggregate growth rates for the world and all subgroups of countries (such as regions and income groups) are weighted averages of country-specific growth rates, calculated using GDP weights at average 2010-19 prices and market exchange rates. Income groups are defined as in the World Bank's classification of country groups.

Output growth forecast process. The process starts with initial assumptions about advanced-economy growth and commodity price forecasts. These are used as conditioning assumptions for the first set of growth forecasts for EMDEs, which are produced using macroeconometric models, accounting frameworks to ensure national account identities and global consistency, estimates of spillovers from major economies, and high-frequency indicators. These forecasts are then evaluated to ensure consistency of treatment across similar EMDEs. This is followed by extensive discussions with World Bank country teams, who conduct continuous macroeconomic monitoring and dialogue with country authorities and finalize growth forecasts for EMDEs. The Prospects Group prepares advanced-economy and commodity price forecasts. Throughout the forecasting process, staff use macroeconometric models that allow the combination of judgment and consistency with model-based insights.

Global trade growth forecast process. Global trade growth is calculated as the percentage change in the average of global exports and imports of goods and nonfactor services, both measured in real U.S. dollars. Forecasts for global exports and imports are derived from a bottom-up approach, using country-level forecasts for real exports and imports produced during the forecasting process as described above.

Global Economic Prospects: Selected Topics, 2015-24

Growth and business cycles		
Economics of pandemics		
	Impact of COVID-19 on global income inequality	January 2022, chapter 4
	Regional macroeconomic implications of COVID-19	June 2020, special focus
	Lasting Scars of the COVID-19 Pandemic	June 2020, chapter 3
	Adding fuel to the fire: Cheap oil during the pandemic	June 2020, chapter 4
	How deep will the COVID-19 recession be?	June 2020, box 1.1
	Scenarios of possible global growth outcomes	June 2020, box 1.3
	How does informality aggravate the impact of COVID-19?	June 2020, box 1.4
	The impact of COVID-19 on global value chains	June 2020, box SF1
	How do deep recessions affect potential output?	June 2020, box 3.1
	How do disasters affect productivity?	June 2020, box 3.2
	Reforms after the 2014-16 oil price plunge	June 2020, box 4.1
	The macroeconomic effects of pandemics and epidemics: A literature review	June 2020, annex 3.1
Informality		
	How does informality aggravate the impact of COVID-19?	June 2020, box 1.4
	Growing in the shadow: Challenges of informality	January 2019, chapter 3
	Linkages between formal and informal sectors	January 2019, box 3.1
	Regional dimensions of informality: An overview	January 2019, box 3.2
	Casting a shadow: Productivity in formal and informal firms	January 2019, box 3.3
	Under the magnifying glass: How do policies affect informality?	January 2019, box 3.4
Inflation		
	Global stagflation	June 2022, special focus 1
	Emerging inflation pressures: Cause for alarm?	June 2021, chapter 4
	Low for how much longer? Inflation in low-income countries	January 2020, special focus 2
	Currency depreciation, inflation, and central bank independence	June 2019, special focus 1.2
	The great disinflation	January 2019, box 1.1
Growth prospects		
	Small states: Overlapping crises, multiple challenges	January 2023, chapter 4
	Global stagflation	June 2022, special focus 1
	Global growth scenarios	January 2021, box 1.4
	The macroeconomic effects of pandemics and epidemics: A literature review	June 2020, annex 3.1
	How deep will the COVID-19 recession be?	June 2020, box 1.1
	Lasting Scars of the COVID-19 Pandemic	June 2020, chapter 3
	Regional macroeconomic implications of COVID-19	June 2020, special focus
	Growth in low-income countries: Evolution, prospects, and policies	June 2019, special focus 2.1
	Long-term growth prospects: Downgraded no more?	June 2018, box 1.1
Global output gap		
	Is the global economy turning the corner?	January 2018, box 1.1
Potential growth		
	Global economy: Heading into a decade of disappointments?	January 2021, chapter 3
	How do deep recessions affect potential output in EMDEs?	June 2020, box 3.1
	Building solid foundations: How to promote potential growth	January 2018, chapter 3
	What is potential growth?	January 2018, box 3.1
	Understanding the recent productivity slowdown: Facts and explanations	January 2018, box 3.2
	Moving together? Investment and potential output	January 2018, box 3.3
	The long shadow of contractions over potential output	January 2018, box 3.4
	Productivity and investment growth during reforms	January 2018, box 3.5
Cross-border spillovers		
	Who catches a cold when emerging markets sneeze?	January 2016, chapter 3
	Sources of the growth slowdown in BRICS	January 2016, box 3.1
	Understanding cross-border growth spillovers	January 2016, box 3.2
	Within-region spillovers	January 2016, box 3.3

Global Economic Prospects: Selected Topics, 2015-24

Growth and business cycles		
Productivity		
	How do disasters affect productivity?	June 2020, box 3.2
	Fading promise: How to rekindle productivity growth	January 2020, chapter 3
	EMDE regional productivity trends and bottlenecks	January 2020, box 3.1
	Sectoral sources of productivity growth	January 2020, box 3.2
	Patterns of total factor productivity: A firm perspective	January 2020, box 3.3
	Debt, financial crises, and productivity	January 2020, box 3.4
Investment		
	Harnessing the benefits of public investment	June 2024, chapter 3
	The magic of investment accelerations	January 2024, chapter 3
	Sparking investment accelerations: Lessons from country case studies	January 2024, box 3.1
	Investment growth after the pandemic	January 2023, chapter 3
	Investment: Subdued prospects, strong needs	June 2019, special focus 1.1
	Weak investment in uncertain times: Causes, implications, and policy responses	January 2017, chapter 3
	Investment-less credit booms	January 2017, box 3.1
	Implications of rising uncertainty for investment in EMDEs	January 2017, box 3.2
	Investment slowdown in China	January 2017, box 3.3
	Interactions between public and private investment	January 2017, box 3.4
Forecast uncertainty		
	Scenarios of possible global growth outcomes	June 2020, box 1.3
	Quantifying uncertainties in global growth forecasts	June 2016, special focus 2
Fiscal space		
	Fiscal challenges in small states: Weathering storms, rebuilding resilience	June 2024, chapter 4
	Having space and using it: Fiscal policy challenges and developing economies	January 2015, chapter 3
	Fiscal policy in low-income countries	January 2015, box 3.1
	What affects the size of fiscal multipliers?	January 2015, box 3.2
	Chile's fiscal rule—an example of success	January 2015, box 3.3
	Narrow fiscal space and the risk of a debt crisis	January 2015, box 3.4
	Revenue mobilization in South Asia: Policy challenges and recommendations	January 2015, box 2.3
Other topics		
	Education demographics and global inequality	January 2018, special focus 2
	Recent developments in emerging and developing country labor markets	June 2015, box 1.3
	Linkages between China and Sub-Saharan Africa	June 2015, box 2.1
	What does weak growth mean for poverty in the future?	January 2015, box 1.1
	What does a slowdown in China mean for Latin America and the Caribbean?	January 2015, box 2.2

Monetary and exchange rate policies	
Financial spillovers of rising U.S. interest rates	June 2023, chapter 3
Asset purchases in emerging markets: Unconventional policies, unconventional times	January 2021, chapter 4
The fourth wave: Rapid debt buildup	January 2020, chapter 4
Price controls: Good intentions, bad outcomes	January 2020, special focus 1
Low for how much longer? Inflation in low-income countries	January 2020, special focus 2
Currency depreciation, inflation, and central bank independence	June 2019, special focus 1.2
The great disinflation	January 2019, box 1.1
Corporate debt: Financial stability and investment implications	June 2018, special focus 2
Recent credit surge in historical context	June 2016, special focus 1
Peg and control? The links between exchange rate regimes and capital account policies	January 2016, chapter 4
Negative interest rates in Europe: A glance at their causes and implications	June 2015, box 1.1
Hoping for the best, preparing for the worst: Risks around U.S. rate liftoff and policy options	June 2015, special focus 1
Countercyclical monetary policy in emerging markets: Review and evidence	January 2015, box 1.2

Global Economic Prospects: Selected Topics, 2015-24

Fiscal policies	
Fiscal policy in commodity exporters: An enduring challenge	January 2024, chapter 4
How does procyclical fiscal policy affect output growth?	January 2024, box 4.1
Do fiscal rules and sovereign wealth funds make a difference? Lessons from country case studies	January 2024, box 4.2
Fiscal policy challenges in low-income countries	June 2023, chapter 4
Resolving high debt after the pandemic: lessons from past episodes of debt relief	January 2022, special focus
How has the pandemic made the fourth wave of debt more dangerous?	January 2021, box 1.1
The fourth wave: Rapid debt buildup	January 2020, chapter 4
Debt: No free lunch	June 2019, box 1.1
Debt in low-income countries: Evolution, implications, and remedies	January 2019, chapter 4
Debt dynamics in emerging market and developing economies: Time to act?	June 2017, special focus 1
Having fiscal space and using it: Fiscal challenges in developing economies	January 2015, chapter 3
Revenue mobilization in South Asia: Policy challenges and recommendations	January 2015, box 2.3
Fiscal policy in low-income countries	January 2015, box 3.1
What affects the size of fiscal multipliers?	January 2015, box 3.2
Chile's fiscal rule—an example of success	January 2015, box 3.3
Narrow fiscal space and the risk of a debt crisis	January 2015, box 3.4

Commodity markets	
Russia's invasion of Ukraine: Implications for energy markets and activity	June 2022, special focus 2
Commodity price cycles: Underlying drivers and policy options	January 2022, chapter 3
Reforms after the 2014-16 oil price plunge	June 2020, box 4.1
Adding fuel to the fire: Cheap oil in the pandemic	June 2020, chapter 4
The role of major emerging markets in global commodity demand	June 2018, special focus 1
The role of the EM7 in commodity production	June 2018, SF1, box SF1.1
Commodity consumption: Implications of government policies	June 2018, SF1, box SF1.2
With the benefit of hindsight: The impact of the 2014–16 oil price collapse	January 2018, special focus 1
From commodity discovery to production: Vulnerabilities and policies in LICs	January 2016, special focus
After the commodities boom: What next for low-income countries?	June 2015, special focus 2
Low oil prices in perspective	June 2015, box 1.2
Understanding the plunge in oil prices: Sources and implications	January 2015, chapter 4
What do we know about the impact of oil prices on output and inflation? A brief survey	January 2015, box 4.1

Globalization of trade and financial flows	
High trade costs: causes and remedies	June 2021, chapter 3
The impact of COVID-19 on global value chains	June 2020, box SF1
Poverty impact of food price shocks and policies	January 2019, chapter 4
Arm's-length trade: A source of post-crisis trade weakness	June 2017, Special Focus 2
The U.S. economy and the world	January 2017, Special Focus
Potential macroeconomic implications of the Trans-Pacific Partnership Agreement	January 2016, chapter 4
Regulatory convergence in mega-regional trade agreements	January 2016, box 4.1.1
China's integration in global supply chains: Review and implications	January 2015, box 2.1
Can remittances help promote consumption stability?	January 2015, chapter 4
What lies behind the global trade slowdown?	January 2015, chapter 4

Prospects Group: Selected Other Publications on the Global Economy, 2015-24

Commodity Markets Outlook	
Potential near-term implications of the conflict in the Middle East for commodity markets: A preliminary assessment	October 2023
Forecasting industrial commodity prices	April 2023
Pandemic, war, recession: Drivers of aluminum and copper prices	October 2022
The impact of the war in Ukraine on commodity markets	April 2022
Urbanization and commodity demand	October 2021
Causes and consequences of metal price shocks	April 2021
Persistence of commodity shocks	October 2020
Food price shocks: Channels and implications	April 2019
The implications of tariffs for commodity markets	October 2018, box
The changing of the guard: Shifts in industrial commodity demand	October 2018
Oil exporters: Policies and challenges	April 2018
Investment weakness in commodity exporters	January 2017
OPEC in historical context: Commodity agreements and market fundamentals	October 2016
From energy prices to food prices: Moving in tandem?	July 2016
Resource development in an era of cheap commodities	April 2016
Weak growth in emerging market economies: What does it imply for commodity markets?	January 2016
Understanding El Niño: What does it mean for commodity markets?	October 2015
How important are China and India in global commodity consumption?	July 2015
Anatomy of the last four oil price crashes	April 2015
Putting the recent plunge in oil prices in perspective	January 2015

Inflation in Emerging and Developing Economies: Evolution, Drivers, and Policies	
Inflation: Concepts, evolution, and correlates	Chapter 1
Understanding global inflation synchronization	Chapter 2
Sources of inflation: Global and domestic drivers	Chapter 3
Inflation expectations: Review and evidence	Chapter 4
Inflation and exchange rate pass-through	Chapter 5
Inflation in low-income countries	Chapter 6
Poverty impact of food price shocks and policies	Chapter 7

A Decade After the Global Recession: Lessons and Challenges for Emerging and Developing Economies	
A decade after the global recession: Lessons and challenges	Chapter 1
What happens during global recessions?	Chapter 2
Macroeconomic developments	Chapter 3
Financial market developments	Chapter 4
Macroeconomic and financial sector policies	Chapter 5
Prospects, risks, and vulnerabilities	Chapter 6
Policy challenges	Chapter 7
The role of the World Bank Group	Chapter 8

Global Waves of Debt: Causes and Consequences	
Debt: Evolution, causes, and consequences	Chapter 1
Benefits and costs of debt: The dose makes the poison	Chapter 2
Global waves of debt: What goes up must come down?	Chapter 3
The fourth wave: Ripple or tsunami?	Chapter 4
Debt and financial crises: From euphoria to distress	Chapter 5
Policies: Turning mistakes into experience	Chapter 6

Prospects Group: Selected Other Publications on the Global Economy, 2015-24

Global Productivity: Trends, Drivers, and Policies	
Global productivity trends	Chapter 1
What explains productivity growth	Chapter 2
What happens to productivity during major adverse events?	Chapter 3
Productivity convergence: Is anyone catching up?	Chapter 4
Regional dimensions of productivity: Trends, explanations, and policies	Chapter 5
Productivity: Technology, demand, and employment trade-offs	Chapter 6
Sectoral sources of productivity growth	Chapter 7

The Long Shadow of Informality: Challenges and Policies	
Overview	Chapter 1
Understanding the informal economy: Concepts and trends	Chapter 2
Growing apart or moving together? Synchronization of informal- and formal-economy business cycles	Chapter 3
Lagging behind: informality and development	Chapter 4
Informality in emerging market and developing economies: Regional dimensions	Chapter 5
Tackling informality: Policy options	Chapter 6

Commodity Markets: Evolution, Challenges and Policies	
The evolution of commodity markets over the past century	Chapter 1
Commodity demand: Drivers, outlook, and implications	Chapter 2
The nature and drivers of commodity price cycles	Chapter 3
Causes and consequences of industrial commodity price shocks	Chapter 4

Falling Long-Term Growth Prospects	
Potential not realized: An international database of potential growth	Chapter 1
Regional dimensions of potential growth: Hopes and realities	Chapter 2
The global investment slowdown: Challenges and policies	Chapter 3
Regional dimensions of investment: Moving in the right direction?	Chapter 4
Potential growth prospects: Risks, rewards and policies	Chapter 5
Trade as an engine of growth: Sputtering but fixable	Chapter 6
Services-led growth: Better prospects after the pandemic?	Chapter 7

High-frequency monitoring
Global Monthly newsletter

ECO-AUDIT

Environmental Benefits Statement

The World Bank Group is committed to reducing its environmental footprint. In support of this commitment, we leverage electronic publishing options and print-on-demand technology, which is located in regional hubs worldwide. Together, these initiatives enable print runs to be lowered and shipping distances decreased, resulting in reduced paper consumption, chemical use, greenhouse gas emissions, and waste.

We follow the recommended standards for paper use set by the Green Press Initiative. The majority of our books are printed on Forest Stewardship Council (FSC)-certified paper, with nearly all containing 50-100 percent recycled content. The recycled fiber in our book paper is either unbleached or bleached using totally chlorine-free (TCF), processed chlorine-free (PCF), or enhanced elemental chlorine-free (EECF) processes.

More information about the Bank's environmental philosophy can be found at http://www.worldbank.org/corporateresponsibility.